THE TUDOR REVOLUTION
IN GOVERNMENT

ADMINISTRATIVE CHANGES
IN THE REIGN OF
HENRY VIII

BY

G. R. ELTON

CAMBRIDGE
AT THE UNIVERSITY PRESS
1962

PUBLISHED BY
THE SYNDICS OF THE CAMBRIDGE UNIVERSITY PRESS

Bentley House, 200 Euston Road, London, N.W. 1
American Branch: 32 East 57th Street, New York 22, N.Y.
West African Office: P.O. Box 33, Ibadan, Nigeria

First Edition 1953
Reprinted 1959
1960
1962

Printed in Great Britain at the University Press, Cambridge
(Brooke Crutchley, University Printer)

PATRI MATRIQUE

CONTENTS

CONTENTS

PREFACE

This study grew out of a thesis submitted in 1948 for the degree of Ph.D. in the University of London, and my first thanks are due to that institution which, by awarding me the Derby Postgraduate Studentship, enabled me to undertake the necessary research. Since those days, however, the book has undergone many changes: it has twice been completely rewritten, gaining (I fear) in length and (I hope) in depth. Much of this revision was done in response to the criticisms of Professor J. E. Neale under whose guidance I took my first steps in historical enquiry; my debt to him is very great. I wish also to record my profound gratitude to my parents who read both typescript and proofs and were ever ready with a comforting mixture of criticism and encouragement; to my friend, Mr E. L. C. Mullins, who likewise spared time from his own heavy commitments to read the book in an earlier guise; to Professor S. T. Bindoff whose vast knowledge is always so readily available to all who are prepared to impose on his kindness; to Mr J. Hurstfield with whom I have often discussed the court of wards; and to many others at the Institute of Historical Research, my seniors and contemporaries, who suffered so patiently the frequent intrusion of Thomas Cromwell into the conversation. As one who attended that institution in the years 1946 and 1947, I should like to mention my particular debt to Professor V. H. Galbraith. To the Secretary and Staff of the Cambridge University Press I owe thanks for their expert assistance and kindly tolerance. The faults of this book are mine; such virtues as it may have owe a great deal to these others.

CAMBRIDGE
January 1953

ABBREVIATIONS

A.P.C.	*Acts of the Privy Council*, ed. J. R. Dasent.
B.M.	British Museum.
Bull. I.H.R.	*Bulletin of the Institute of Historical Research.*
Cal. Pat.	*Calendar of Patent Rolls.*
Cal. S.P. Dom.	*Calendar of State Papers, Domestic.*
Cal. S.P. For.	*Calendar of State Papers, Foreign.*
C.J.	*Journals of the House of Commons.*
D.N.B.	*Dictionary of National Biography*, reissue of 1908–9.
E.H.R.	*English Historical Review.*
H.O.	*A Collection of Ordinances and Regulations for the Royal Household*, Society of Antiquaries, London 1790.
L.J.	*Journals of the House of Lords.*
L.P.	*Letters and Papers, Foreign and Domestic, of the Reign of Henry VIII*, ed. Brewer, Gairdner, and Brodie, London 1862–1929.
Merriman	R. B. Merriman, *Life and Letters of Thomas Cromwell*, Oxford 1902.
Span. Cal.	*Calendar of State Papers, Spanish.*
Stat. Realm	*The Statutes of the Realm*, ed. by the Record Commission, London 1810–28.
St. Pap.	*State Papers of the Reign of Henry VIII*, published by the Record Commission (1830 et seq.).
V.C.H.	*Victoria County History.*
Ven. Cal.	*Calendar of State Papers, Venetian.*

Manuscripts preserved at the Public Record Office, London, are quoted by the call number there in use, according to the following key:

C 54   Chancery, Close Rolls.

C 65   Chancery, Parliament Rolls.

C 66   Chancery, Patent Rolls.

C 82   Chancery, Warrants for the Great Seal, Series II.

C 193   Chancery, Misc. Books, Crown Office.

DL 5   Duchy of Lancaster, Entry Bks. of Orders and Decrees.

DL 12   Duchy of Lancaster, Privy Seals and Warrants.

DL 28   Duchy of Lancaster, Various Accounts.

DL 42   Duchy of Lancaster, Miscellaneous Books.

E 36   Exch., Treasury of Receipt, Miscellaneous Books.

E 101   Exch., King's Remembrancer, Various Accounts.

E 135   Exch., King's Remembrancer, Ecclesiastical Documents.

E 159   Exch., King's Remembrancer, Memoranda Rolls.

E 163   Exch., King's Remembrancer, Miscellanea of the Exch.

E 164   Exch., King's Remembrancer, Misc. Books (I).

E 315   Exch., Augmentation Office, Misc. Books.

E 323   Exch., Augmentation Office, Treasurer's Accounts of the Court of Augmentations.

E 336   Exch., First Fruits and Tenths Office, Misc. Books.

E 351   Exch., Lord Treas. Remembr., Pipe Office, Declared Accounts.

E 361   Exch., Lord Treas. Remembr., Enrolled Accounts.

E 369   Exch., Lord Treas. Remembr., Miscellaneous Books.

E 404   Exch. of Receipt, Warrants and Issues.

E 405	Exch. of Receipt, Rolls, etc., of Receipts and Issues.
E 407	Exch. of Receipt, Miscellanea.
GD 15	Gifts and Deposits, Manchester Papers.
LC 5	Lord Chamberlain's Department, Miscellanea.
LS 13	Lord Steward's Department, Miscellaneous Books.
PSO 2	Warrants for the Privy Seal, Series II.
Req 1	Court of Requests, Books of Orders and Decrees.
Req 2	Court of Requests, Proceedings.
SC 6	Special Collections, Ministers' Accounts.
SP 1	State Papers, Henry VIII.
SP 2	the same, folio volumes.
SP 3	the same, Lisle Papers.
SP 6	Theological Tracts.
SP 10	State Papers, Edward VI.
SP 11	State Papers, Philip and Mary.
SP 60	State Papers, Ireland.
Wards 9	Court of Wards, Miscellaneous Books.

Figures after references to *L.P.* and *Ven. Cal.* are to numbers of documents, that being the practice in the respective indexes; in all other cases they are to pages. Where the original of a document calendared in *L.P.* has been used, the reference to the manuscript is usually given, followed by the reference to *L.P.* In transcripts, abbreviations have been extended and modern punctuation has been adopted, with the result that capitals have occasionally been put where there are none in the original; otherwise the spelling of the manuscript has always been rendered exactly.

INTRODUCTION

English government has a special claim to be studied. It developed in comparative freedom from outside interference, producing a curious blend of decentralized and popular freedom with strong, efficient, and centralized administration. Of these two ingredients neither ought to be ignored, though the first has always struck observers as the more important. In truth, English history has been as remarkable for good government as for free and constitutional government, though the two have not always coincided. Nevertheless, either by itself will fail to explain the peculiar development of a country the whole structure of whose politics is so different from that of any other. Neither freedom nor order has ever had the field exclusively to itself. The desire for constitutional guarantees has never altogether swept away the sense that government must be strong to be worth having, nor have governments ever for long attempted to turn strength into abuse of strength. The interaction of these two principles is at the root of England's exceptional constitutional history and her exceptional stability, never seen more clearly than in times of revolution. A moment's comparison of the Puritan revolution with the great revolutions of France and Russia will show what is meant. The sanctions of that stability—the safeguards against despotism—have long been understood and often described; the other side of the matter—strong rule preventing anarchy and preserving order—requires still much exploration. Our history is still much written by whigs, the champions of political freedom; to stress the need for controlling that freedom may even today seem not only not Liberal but even illiberal.

There have been periods when the needs of 'good government' prevailed over the demands of 'free government', and of these the Tudor age was the most important. To speak of despotism and a reign of terror in sixteenth-century England was easier for a generation which had not met these things at first hand; however, it remains true that it was a time when men were ready to be governed, and when order and peace seemed more important than principles and rights. What distinguished the Tudors from their European contemporaries, who were facing similar problems, was just that they provided peace and order without despotism—certainly without the weapons of the despot. One would think, therefore, that the history of Tudor government ought to be well known. Up to a point it is: the place of the justice of the peace, the role of the privy council, even to some extent the part played by parliament, these are supposedly well established. But the methods and machinery of central government have received little attention. There is no series of monographs such as—grouped round the six monumental volumes of Tout's great work—elucidate, describe, and re-create the realities of medieval government. There are good reasons for this: for one thing, interest was bound to concentrate on the more obvious and also more important issues—religion, warfare, foreign relations, economic and social development; when matters of government attracted attention they tended to be seen in the 'constitutional' guise—the rise of parliament, the powers of the crown, the place of the council. The humbler but quite fundamental matters of financial administration, the changes in the royal household, or the altered methods of the bureaucracy, have never been properly studied, and even the council has been the subject of 'constitutional' rather than 'institutional' investigation, so that we are better informed of its theoretical significance than of its practical history. This is not to say that research has not been made into this field, with most valuable results;[1] in many ways, the most significant book on Tudor history for some time has been Professor J. E. Neale's approach to parliament from an institutional and administrative point of view in *The Elizabethan House of Commons*. But there has been no co-ordination of results. Consequently the importance of the sixteenth century in the history of public administration—on which ultimately all constitutional progress must rest—has hardly been realized.

A subtler reason for this neglect is the state of the evidence. Public records are the product of administrative processes, a truth which

---

[1] Particularly the work of A. P. Newton, the articles on the council by A. F. Pollard and W. H. Dunham Jr., and the early and self-confessedly insufficient chapters of F. M. G. Evans's *Principal Secretary of State*. Acknowledgement and full reference to all these and others is, of course, made in the proper places. Dr F. C. Dietz's work on finance is almost wholly silent on financial administration.

applies even to such less formal documents as the state papers; in the first place the records are a guide to administration and its methods.[1] In the hundred years after about 1480 they are in an unsatisfactory condition: old series run down, new ones begin towards the end of Elizabeth's reign; in the interval there is a turmoil of fragments, false starts, traces of a dying past and a germinating future, in which as often as not the administrative history of the period is to be found, while the supposedly master records give a completely false picture.[2] The administrative history of the early sixteenth century is therefore particularly difficult to study; it will be necessary, more often than can be comfortable, to deduce much from slender evidence or leave a problem unsolved because the material which would provide the answer does not exist. For the same reason, this is a particularly important period in administrative history. As is so often the case, the records reflect developments in the practice of government. The state of the evidence is so peculiar because this was a time not so much of transition as of revolution in administration. The plain fact is that Henry VII ascended the throne of a medievally governed kingdom, while Elizabeth handed to her successor a country administered on modern lines. Much had gone, much been freshly invented, much profoundly changed, in the intervening century, even though a great deal had been simply preserved. We are familiar with the notion that the sixteenth century saw the creation of the modern sovereign state: the duality of state and church was destroyed by the victory of the state, the crown triumphed over its rivals, parliamentary statute triumphed over the abstract law of Christendom, and a self-contained national unit came to be, not the tacitly accepted necessity it had been for some time, but the consciously desired goal.

In the course of this transformation there was created a revised

---

[1] Cf. V. H. Galbraith, *Studies in the Public Records* (London, 1948), 3 ff.

[2] It is well known that the financial history of the time cannot be written from the 'official' exchequer rolls; the pell of issue, e.g., was discontinued from 1480 to 1597 (with a brief revival in between), and from 1487 until 1554 the major part of government money never passed through the exchequer at all. In the chancery, the statute rolls ceased in 1468, the Scotch rolls in 1515, and the charter rolls in 1516, while other series, e.g. the dispensation rolls, started later in the century. The history of the signet office begins afresh with the keeping of docquet books in 1584. These examples could be multiplied.

machinery of government whose principle was bureaucratic organization in the place of the personal control of the king, and national management rather than management of the king's estate. The reformed state was based on the rejection of the medieval conception of the kingdom as the king's estate, his private concern, properly administered by his private organization; it conceived its task to be national, its support and scope to be nation-wide, and its administrative needs, therefore, divorced from the king's household. It is one of the paradoxes of sixteenth-century history that a dynasty, which saw the personal power of the monarchy at its height and the importance of court life greater than ever, could also transcend the purely personal view of the royal duty and treat England and the nation as the true basis of the state. The personal impetus was needed to overcome past particularism; England was not able to do without the visible embodiment of her nationhood until she had first passed through a condition where that visible embodiment was more obvious than the national foundation beneath. It will not do, however, to regard the Tudor state as a purely personal monarchy; the fact which underlay the well-known fellow-feeling of the Tudors and their people was that in reality the monarchy represented the nation —the nation called the tune. No amount of Tudor temper and bluster could disguise that fact. The most powerful dynasty ever to sit on England's throne was powerful only as long as it did not go outside the limits laid down by a nation at last fully conscious of its nationhood. The Tudor state was a national monarchy to a degree new in England, and while the apparent emphasis lay on the monarchy the real stress was already on its national character.

This is the meaning of the saying that the sixteenth century saw the making of the national state, and in that profound change administrative reform was bound to play its part. There had been bureaucratic organization on a national scale for centuries before, but the decisive and ultimate factor in medieval administration was the direct action of king and household. By the end of the sixteenth century the outlines of a purely national system had been drawn and largely filled in, and the subject of this study is the decade when the new principles were first consistently applied. It will be shown that, down to 1529, medieval government—household government in the broad sense—continued at work. The changes after 1530 in all sections of administration—finance, the secretariats, the king's council, the king's household—will then be discussed to show that new principles were indeed at work and profound reforms undertaken. This is a study of government at the centre only: local government, a vast subject in itself, needs separate treatment, though it has in any case been less neglected than have the institutions at the centre.[1]

One of the outstanding differences between the medieval and modern periods lies in their attitude to individuals; in the modern age it is usually possible to discover and ascribe personal responsibility. Individuals assert themselves where anonymity had been the rule. Whether or not this had anything to do with the humanist revival of ancient ideas on such matters and with the Renaissance worship of the individual, it is a fact which is also, once again, reflected in the records. The state papers are personal material in a way that nothing medieval is; it has been said that they 'make history possible in a fuller measure than ever before' by tearing aside 'the veil which separates us from character and personality in the Middle Ages'.[2] In the 1530's, the state papers are largely what remain of the private archives of Henry VIII's second great minister, Thomas Cromwell. There are other papers, but their bulk does not compare with the products of Cromwell's private office. There is a danger in this: it may be that Cromwell appears to dominate his age so much because his papers have survived. The accident of preservation ought not to be ignored, but it must not be overstressed. Even a casual glance shows that the scope of Cromwell's influence, the extent of his activity and power, and the attitude to him of others made him a special case: he was outstanding; and the record, though it may occasionally fail to preserve the activities and minds of others, cannot really be suspected of serious distortion when it sets the stamp of Cromwell on nearly everything done in these ten years, in the great issues of state and church as well as in the details of daily government.

[1] Cf. Conyers Read, *Bibliography of British History—Tudor Period* (Oxford, 1933), 85 ff., and compare this with the meagre list of works on the central administration in the preceding pages. The position has not altered since 1933.

[2] V. H. Galbraith, *The Public Records* (Oxford, 1934), 55.

Cromwell's name and personality, constantly appearing in the history of these reforms in government, cannot be avoided. A true understanding of the reforms depends to a large extent on a clear view of the minister, and some attempt must be made to assess the administrator behind these changes in administration. In turn, they should help to clarify the character of the man. Cromwell has been somewhat harshly dealt with by history and the historians. Seventy years ago, J. R. Green said of him that 'in the whole line of English statesmen there is no one of whom we would willingly know so much, no one of whom we really know so little',[1] and despite the publication, in the interval, of a serious and painstaking biography that state of affairs has not been much mended.[2] Even his place in English history has been far from secure, some holding that he was the leader in the great revolutionary movement of the Henrician Reformation,[3] and others making him only the subservient tool of a king whose fouler work he did with ruthless (and regrettable) efficiency.[4] A recent study of the contemporary pamphlet literature has suggested qualities of deliberate foresight, the laying of theoretical foundations for a new form of state, which indicate that Cromwell was rather more than merely the able politician of the text-books.[5] He is called by adjectives which have no meaning—sinister, machiavellian. We do not call a man sinister whom we know well, whether we like him or not, and Cromwell's contemporaries—many

---

[1] J. R. Green, *History of the English People* (1878), II. 142.

[2] R. B. Merriman's *Life and Letters of Thomas Cromwell*, published in 1902, does little but recount the political history of the time with Cromwell put in the middle of it; it is, moreover, marred by a curious but complete lack of sympathy between biographer and subject. There is no other book on Cromwell which even aspires to scholarship.

[3] Cf. Green, *op. cit.* II. 142; J. A. Froude, *History of England*, III. 339; A. Galton, *Thomas Cromwell* (1887), 158 f., 207 ff.; D. Mathew, in *The Great Tudors* (ed. Kath. Garvin), 133 ff.; A. D. Innes, *Ten Tudor Statesmen* (1906), 115 ff.

[4] Though Merriman held that Cromwell was himself a major mover in the policy of the Reformation, his deliberately cold and hostile picture has done much to undermine the common opinion of Cromwell's importance. To A. F. Pollard the king was quite capable of directing the storm alone, and Cromwell was quite a secondary figure; cf., for example, his view that in 1532–3, when the Reformation really got under way, 'it was the King, and the King alone, who kept England on the course which he had mapped out'; *Henry VIII* (1905), 306. Supporters of the divorce are described as beginning to waver—but there is no word of Cromwell. The latest authoritative statement of this view is Professor C. H. Williams's article on Cromwell in the 1950 edition of *Chambers's Encyclopædia*.

[5] W. Gordon Zeeveld, *Foundations of Tudor Policy* (Harvard, 1948).

of whom were his friends, for there was another side to his character[1] —did not think of him as sinister, as an *éminence grise* behind the scenes. The one man who did, and whose passionate denunciation has been largely responsible for the persistent label, was Reginald Pole who hardly knew him at all; by his own account, Pole met Cromwell only once, and then the young and impressionable student heard the man of the world ridicule his idealism. Cromwell did it in all good humour, but Pole, like the adolescent prig he was, was deeply shocked. Because Pole could not abide the man who thought Plato fit only for the disputations of the schools, he saw in him the 'emissary of Satan' who perverted the king and in the end destroyed Pole's family; the picture of prejudice, misunderstanding, and justifiable hatred has survived, and by it Cromwell has come to be known. Pole's revenge has had a long innings.[2]

A more realistic view of Cromwell can thus be obtained from a study of his work in government, but that is, after all, a by-product of the present purpose. Cromwell matters only in so far as one meets him at every turn in the story of administrative reform. If, as we hope to do, we can show the persistence of medieval methods down to 1529 and the subsequent modernization of government, we shall have done something to restore to the sixteenth century, and in particular to the age of the Reformation, its old character as a time of real change. More and more the Tudor century is coming to be regarded as merely an extension of the middle ages, and this is a serious error. There is, let it be admitted, much danger in too easy a use of such terms as medieval and modern, and since they will have to be used much a word of explanation is due. Naturally many very typically medieval facts and opinions persisted into very recent days, even as many facts and opinions once thought of as typically modern have been traced back into the high middle ages. Naturally, too, any rigid division of past life into chronological periods can only

---

[1] Such favourable evidence as there is on Cromwell's personality was ably collected and stated by P. Van Dyke, *Renascence Portraits* (1906), 138 ff.

[2] Cardinal Pole, 'Apologia ad Carolum Quintum Caesarem', *Epist. etc.*, ed. Quirini (Brescia, 1744), 117 ff. The meeting with Cromwell is described on pp. 133 ff.; it is worth reading but much too long for reproduction here. Pole also stuck the 'machiavellian' label on Cromwell; whether Cromwell really was a deliberate disciple of Machiavelli is still being debated, and rather fruitlessly (cf. T. M. Parker, 'Was Thomas Cromwell a Machiavellian?', *Journal of Ecclesiastical History*, I. 63 ff.).

lead to disaster. But he would be a bold man, and a bad historian, who would deny the existence of periods—even of moments in time—when things underwent changes so profound that only the word 'revolution' can adequately describe them and only a firm date can place them. Such a period, such a moment in time, came in England when Henry VIII accepted Cromwell's advice to consolidate the territory he governed under the exclusive sovereignty of the king in parliament. An attitude to the state that can only be called medieval was at that moment replaced by one that can only be called modern. It will serve little purpose to quarrel over words: let these two terms be used as convenient summaries of inescapable historical facts. When this modern state in all its self-conscious independence had taken the place of the medieval state in which king, parliament, and even the nation occupied a much less ascertained place, not everything that had gone before was destroyed— not even most of it; but lack of true sovereignty was at the heart of the earlier dispensation, and the supremacy of the king in parliament was at the heart of the new. Where it mattered most a change had occurred which entitles us to speak of a revolution from the medieval to the modern state.

Methods of government reflect the constitution of the state they serve. Medieval household methods served the medieval state; modern national methods served the modern nation state. In that sense the terms are permissible in a discussion of administrative history. No one will doubt that the government of the fourteenth century was fundamentally different from that of the seventeenth. This difference lay in the abolition of the half-formal household methods characteristic of the middle ages, and in the adoption of the bureaucratic national methods characteristic of modern times; so much is common ground. That this change, this abolition and adoption, was inaugurated in the ten years between 1530 and 1540 shall now be shown.[1]

---

[1] Since this book went to the printer, Prof. W. C. Richardson's *Tudor Chamber Administration 1485–1547* (Louisiana State Univ. Press, 1952), which is referred to below (p. 27, n. 2), has become available in this country. The book is indispensable to any student of the history of Tudor finance, and it provides much more detail, especially for the period 1485–1529, than has been thought desirable in the present study. Prof. Richardson discusses at length matters which I have been able only to sketch; there has

been, of course, a little of that duplication which I feared and for which I apologize, pleading only that this book was finished for over a year before I was able to see Prof. Richardson's work. However, I have not found it necessary to alter any of my views. On the whole, my summary agrees well enough with Prof. Richardson's thorough investigation, and where I have been more detailed—in the 1530's—there is still general agreement. Where we really differ is in the wider interpretation. Prof. Richardson seems to me to underestimate the significance of the changes made in the 1530's, with the result that he sees a unity in the period 1485–1554, whereas I hold that 1485 is a date of little significance in administrative history and 1554 only a stage in the development begun in 1534–6. In my view, Prof. Richardson does not allow sufficiently for the difference between the later financial courts and the earlier 'household' arrangements; I think he makes the term 'chamber system' cover too much when he uses it to describe all the administrative changes of the first two Tudors, and he speaks too definitely of 'offices' (audit office, office of wards) where I would prefer to speak of individuals working in a somewhat unorganized and haphazard manner, though none the less effectively for that. The consequence is, it seems to me, that Prof. Richardson's picture of financial administration under Henry VII (and perhaps even under Wolsey) is too clear-cut and definite, so that the great movement towards definition, under Cromwell and after, loses its significance.

CHAPTER I

THE LAST PHASE OF MEDIEVAL GOVERNMENT

Down to the end of Richard II's reign the history of English administration is, generally speaking, well known and fully studied; thereafter, we grope in the jungle, with few and indistinct paths blazed through it. No doubt there are gaps even in the high middle ages—questions yet unasked, doubts yet unresolved—but all is sweetness and light compared with the grim fifteenth century whose ever scantier records reflect the decay of good government at the centre. Yet if the significance of Tudor reforms is to be seen, it is necessary to arrive at least at a tentative view of what happened to England's institutions between the fall of Richard II and the fall of Thomas Wolsey. Those hundred and thirty years do, in a manner, form a unit; their discussion in this chapter is not arbitrarily determined. It is true that they comprehend a decline and revival of government; but it is the decline and revival of the same kind of government, that medieval system whose distinguishing feature, despite a growing complication of national institutions and offices, was a motive power supplied by the king's household. When the king's hand grows weak, when his household loses control of the reins, government founders and at times almost disappears; as the throne falls to strong men whose households are full of active administrators, so government revives. Exchequer, chancery, the privy seal, carry on throughout the years of anarchy of whose reality there is but slender evidence in their records, but in truth there is no one to govern because the king, his household, and his council (the administrative centre of that household) are powerless or inactive or corrupt. Without the driving force of king and household, national institutions and departments of state are ineffective.

Important though it would be to study in every detail the history of these hundred and thirty years, that is a task which cannot be undertaken on the present occasion. The history of the Tudor administrative revolution must not be burdened with the history of the declining medieval administration, or its early Tudor revival, beyond the point required for an understanding of our main theme. This chapter is not, therefore, a detailed study of one hundred and thirty years of English government, but a rapid survey based on materials in print and, especially for the fifteenth century, on the work of others. It is proposed to discuss briefly the decay of fourteenth-century administration under the Lancastrians, the revival of strong government under the Yorkists and Henry VII, and the consummation of medieval government in Wolsey's rule. The last point will receive fullest treatment, not indeed because Wolsey's methods differed greatly from those of Henry VII—they did not— but because his ministry is better documented than the relatively obscure reign of the first Tudor, and because under his guidance the changes and reforms made by Henry VII were reduced to bureaucratic forms which are more easily studied. Like the rest of this book, this chapter will deal with the categories of central government which are the same both in medieval and Tudor times, and remained essentially the same until the much greater revolution in government which began after 1830: financial administration; the seals (great seal, privy seal, and signet) with their custodians and staffs; the king's council; and the king's household.

1. *Decline*

In a peculiar way Richard II's reign was almost a Tudor period *in parvo*; this is illustrated also in the history of administration under that king.[1] Superficially at least the characteristic household features of medieval government were disappearing or had disappeared. The exchequer became for a time the sole administrative department in financial affairs; of its household rivals, the chamber did not recover from the defeat and loss of its lands inflicted in 1356 until the reign of Henry VII, and though chamber officials were the active agents of Richard II's autocracy they did not compose an administrative department.[2] Throughout the Lancastrian period chamber finance

---

[1] Cf. T. F. Tout, *Chapters in Medieval Administrative History* (Manchester, 1920–37), IV. 214: 'The regularisation and normalisation which is so outstanding a feature of Richard II's reign.'   [2] *Ibid.* ch. 13, sec. iv.

meant only the coverage, out of assignments, of internal chamber expenses—wages, and matters concerned with the king's personal interests and affairs. The wardrobe, too, now lost its character of a national administrative organ; never had it been 'so little an office of state, a wheel of the political machine'.[1] It now became simply the administrative department of the household, the 'office of household accounts'.[2] The days when most of the important financial transactions of the state were carried out by household clerks in ostensibly household departments appeared to be over.

Nevertheless, this development must not be misunderstood. Unlike the household of the later Tudors, the fifteenth-century household still did much of the work of government, and wars, in particular, continued to be administered through and by it. The treasurer of the household (ex-keeper of the wardrobe) was still an active household official; but the fact that in the French wars of the century he was also frequently treasurer of the wars has been used by Tout to prove 'how little distinction there remained between service of the court, and service of the state. The household was, then, part of the great national system of administration, in which the king was still the most powerful factor....'[3] Personal government through personal servants, the essential characteristic of medieval administration, did not cease because the elasticity which had made household departments the bureaucratic centre of government was temporarily gone. Far from making the vital distinction between service of the state and service on the king's person—the distinction which, once grasped, made possible the building-up of a truly national administrative system—the fifteenth century confused the two more than ever and virtually sank the latter in the former. In this it was merely giving expression to the prevailing notion that in fact there was no such distinction because there was none between king and state, or rather because the only conceivable form which the state could take was the person of the king. The notion was to persist in many ways for long after, and it received support from the strongly personal character of the Tudor monarchy, but in matters of machinery the Tudors were to work out the distinction to a remarkable degree.

[1] Tout, *Chapters*, IV. 187.   [2] *Ibid.* 224.   [3] *Ibid.* 225.

Finance, then, was in the hands of the exchequer, with its highly developed and ossifying organization. There is nothing to tell, in the present state of information, about its history in this century; undoubtedly it was active and points of interest could be found in a study of its workings, but it is certain enough that its machinery underwent no material changes between Stapledon's reforms in 1323 and the accession of Henry VII. Its two departments—the exchequer of receipt where the money was paid in, stored, and disbursed, and the exchequer of account with its elaborate system of audit and its enforcement machinery for the collection of debts—had reached a point of development which made changes not only unnecessary but even difficult, until the demands of a brisker age and stronger government initiated the long series of administrative reforms in the finances which began with Henry VII's revival of chamber finance and came to an end only with the restoration of exchequer supremacy in 1554. Of these reforms more will have to be said later; for the moment it is only important to remember that household finance in the true sense—the administration of national finance in household departments—was in abeyance, and that the exchequer pursued an uneventful course of routine in these years when medieval England was running down the slope to the anarchy in which it was to die.

The signs of that anarchy are, however, more obvious in the other institutions of government with which we are here concerned. Of the three seals and their staffs, the great seal and chancery had indeed settled down to as perfect a routine as that of the exchequer. Here, too, old age had produced its finished traditions, procedure, and scope. The significant history of chancery in the fifteenth century lies in its work as a court; the administrative functions of the great seal, so marked in the reign of Edward III,[1] were fifty years later reduced to the merest routine without original force, or else had been transferred to the privy seal. 'In the end', we are told, 'the administrative office of chancery became largely a thing of the past: it was only represented by the great judicial activities of the chancery.'[2] The great seal never, indeed, lost its formal position of outstanding

[1] B. Wilkinson, *The Chancery under Edward III* (Manchester, 1929), 26 ff.
[2] *Ibid.* 53.

importance; many, and some of the most important, acts of the crown have always required its authentication. The bestowal of crown patronage in lands or offices, the exercise of the royal prerogative in pardons or grants of protection, the ecclesiastical powers of the crown (not negligible even before the days of Henry VIII), these and many other things could only be done by letters patent. But even before the end of the fifteenth century the clerks of chancery had come to be no more in such matters than writers of documents copied from warrants under another seal, and the chancellor had ceased to play a truly independent or important part in administration, except inasmuch as he was also a councillor—often the leading councillor—whose influence depended only in small measure on his department. The administrative importance of chancery was never revived, though traces of it remained trailing around the office for centuries; for our purpose, the greatest and most ancient seal of the kings of England can be ignored with impunity. The future of chancery, a future which was to give it even greater importance and wider influence than its impressive past, lay in the sphere of jurisdiction; when the chancellor engrossed the bulk of petitions for redress addressed to the council and exploited the uncertainties of enfeoffment to uses, he cast his bread upon the safe waters of English litigiousness.[1]

The place of chancery as the secretarial centre of government passed in the fifteenth century to the privy seal, served by its keeper and (ordinarily) four clerks. Before Richard II lost his throne, the privy seal, which under Edward I had occupied an important place as the king's private seal kept in his wardrobe, had grown sufficiently 'formalized' to be the seal of a true office of state, and its household link was severed. Its functions as a seal of warranty to the great seal were formal and regular, though its relation with the exchequer was not yet fully resolved, and its keeper had come to be the third officer of state and an indispensable member of the council, in place of the higher civil servant of earlier days.[2] From this position the seal and office did not move in the course of the fifteenth century—they neither advanced nor declined; but the history of chancery, the

---

[1] Cf. W. S. Holdsworth, *History of English Law*, I. 400 ff.
[2] Tout, *Chapters*, v. 54 ff.

growing use of the privy seal as early as Edward III to authenticate administrative orders, and the council's increasing reliance on the privy rather than the great seal, vastly augmented the lesser seal's administrative functions. It was now that it became the clearing house of government business, receiving instructions from the king's officers at council level and redistributing them to lesser officials as well as to the king's subjects in general.[1] But no sooner had it achieved such a position of eminence than it began to be rivalled by the third royal seal, the signet, whose organization was originally undertaken by the privy seal office itself which supplied both clerks and method to its younger brother when Richard II attempted to use the signet as the weapon of his autocracy.[2] In the period of the Lancastrian decay, however, the signet still played a small part in affairs and, administratively speaking, the privy seal had it all its own way. After Richard's failure the signet became suspect and therefore at first relapsed into comparative obscurity; its keeper, the king's secretary, remained a confidential clerk with no ambitions to rival his betters who were officers of state, and its office remained rudimentary.[3] It only revived when Henry VI, somewhat incongruously following in the footsteps of his grandfather's royal victim, tried to make it the instrument of his self-assertion on attaining his majority; the signet and privy seal then became involved in a struggle for power between king and council. In order to understand how this came about, it is necessary to turn to the history of the council from the accession of Henry IV.[4]

The council of Richard II has been described as 'something of an embryonic cabinet';[5] it consisted mainly of king's servants and did the king's work. The accession of Henry IV, marking the triumph of oligarchic reaction against the attempted despotism of his predecessor, produced a new kind of council; or rather, it revived the powers of the baronage in the occasional great council and led to the

---

[1] For more detail on this point, cf. below, pp. 290 ff.

[2] Tout, *Chapters*, v. 82 f., 208 ff.

[3] For the signet in the fifteenth century, cf. J. Otway Ruthven, *The King's Secretary and the Signet Office in the Fifteenth Century* (Cambridge, 1939).

[4] This war of the seals was discovered and worked out by T. F. T. Plucknett, 'The Place of the Council in the Fifteenth Century', *Trans. R. Hist. Soc.* (1918), esp. 178 ff.

[5] Tout, *Chapters*, III. 467. Cf. *ibid.* v. 61: 'almost as much an executive body as the council of the Tudors'.

ultimate control of the continual small council by the same element.[1] If great councils ceased to meet and influence policy, either directly or through their weight in parliament, after the death of Henry IV,[2] this was largely because Henry V voluntarily surrendered to earlier demands for a smaller continual council composed largely of 'the great officers, prelates and lords'.[3] Though the work was largely done by the great officers of state or household, meeting fairly regularly, these officers were themselves magnates and only the experience of Henry IV and the popularity and warlike preoccupations of Henry V prevented the council from completely severing its interests from those of the crown. The minority of Henry VI gave the magnates their chance: when great men like Bedford, Gloucester, and Beaufort personally used the council to transact daily routine business, to deal with the major affairs of the realm at home and abroad, and to fight out their battles for power, they gave that body a novel importance by the very regularity of their attendance.[4] This was 'the time when the power and dignity of the medieval council may easily be said to have reached its height'.[5] However, the council's power led rapidly to trouble. The magnates, who had thus in some thirty years captured the king's advisory and executive board for themselves, were for the most part out only to satisfy personal ambitions and used their position in the council to control government patronage in their own interests and those of their followers. This led, in the end, to a revival of royal power when Henry VI came of age, and to the downfall of the council, defeated by the king and therefore unsuitable as an arena for faction fight. In a very real sense, the resort to war after 1450 had to come because Suffolk and Somerset could not use the council which had given way to Henry VI as freely as their predecessors had used the council of the minority.

Henry VI's victory over his council was bound up with the question of patronage, and it was won in a battle over the seals.[6] The

---

[1] This discussion is based on J. Baldwin, *The King's Council in the Middle Ages* (Oxford, 1913), 147–67, and Plucknett, *op. cit.* 157 ff.

[2] Plucknett, 167 ff. [3] Baldwin, *King's Council*, 165.

[4] *Ibid.* 187. [5] *Ibid.* 177.

[6] I here follow Prof. Plucknett (178 ff.) rather than Baldwin (187 ff.); the latter seems to hold that the council ordinances of 1440–4 marked a conciliar triumph rather than a futile gesture in the face of defeat.

council tried to control the issue of all grants through its hold over the privy seal: nothing was to pass the great seal without warrant from the privy seal and preliminary scrutiny by the council. The king, on the other hand, wished to employ the signet, which he controlled, in order to evade the privy seal and conciliar supervision by direct warrants to chancery. An outburst of energy, marked by the survival of great numbers of sign manual letters, sealed or to be sealed with the signet, followed on Henry VI's emancipation from tutelage: in those years, at least, before misfortune and hardship clouded his mind, the unfortunate last Lancastrian seems to have shown some of the stern ability of his house. A series of council ordinances between 1440 and 1444 signalled his victory. From now on all grants were to pass through the familiar routine of warrant upon warrant—signet to privy seal, and privy seal to great seal; the originating force lay with the signet, that is with the king, and the privy seal—the council's seal—already exercised in this respect a purely ornamental function. The council tried to assert a right of arresting anything it disliked at the privy seal, but this claim to make the second stage a reality never came to anything, and the crown recovered and never lost (except in times of military defeat) a secure grip on its patronage.

As far as the seals were concerned, this struggle established the place of the signet and began to undermine that of the privy seal. In the most important place—warranty to the great seal—the former was to be the real force while the latter became a mere routine interlude. Nevertheless, the privy seal continued to be the centre of administration, though the signet began to rival it even in those fields of administrative orders from which the privy seal derived its real importance. While the struggle between king and council lasted—and the victory of 1444 was reversed, in part at least, when Somerset and York attempted to revive conciliar action after Suffolk had deserted the council table in favour of force[1]—the privy seal and signet often did much the same things, the only difference being whether the council or the king stood behind the orders.[2] The privy seal was not yet defeated, but the action of Henry VI had given the

---

[1] Baldwin, *King's Council*, 189 ff.
[2] Otway Ruthven, *King's Sec.* 55 ff.

signet, condemned as unconstitutional under Richard II, a legal standing in the machinery of administration, and the lead given was not to be ignored when royal power was restored after the wars. In the course of the century the signet more and more encroached upon the privy seal, and more and more of the government's action came to be authenticated by the lesser seal. In consequence the privy seal increasingly developed its routine and showed signs of following in the footsteps of the great seal: as the seal of the council it might easily have developed into a seal of jurisdiction rather than administration, and signs of such a future were not lacking under the early Tudors. But the whole 'medieval' development, which would have ended by replacing the privy seal by the signet and the signet by yet another royal seal out of the household, was arrested by the changed emphasis and organization of the administration after 1530.

As far as the council was concerned, the 1440's proved its overthrow. Grown out of Richard II's professional executive body, captured by an oligarchy of magnates as a result of the weakness of Henry IV's position, Henry V's complaisance, and Henry VI's minority, it had reached a height of independent activity and power which reflected rather the disintegration of the monarchy, and with it of the state, than a healthy progress of government machinery. Henry VI's victory in the battle of the seals deprived the council of the only attraction it possessed for a selfish and self-seeking aristocracy; personal ambition, when it could no longer achieve its aims in council, resorted to the field of battle. After the fall in 1455 of the duke of York, who had attempted to hold up the disintegration of the council, the wars broke out in earnest, and government and administration were for a time obscured. The history of the council between 1399 and 1460 marches in step with the political and constitutional adventures of a dynasty whose weakness, whether of circumstances or personality, let loose the disintegrating forces of bastard feudalism and submerged the order of medieval government in anarchy. While government depended on the personal action of the king and his household, their surrender of the reins and their ultimate collapse destroyed government itself; by the same token, it needed strong kings and a revival of household administration to restore the order and machinery of the fourteenth century. This restoration, which not unnaturally went further than its model and produced the most powerful and complete royal government under the medieval system, was the work of Edward IV and Henry VII.

2. *Revival*

The period from the battle of Barnet (1471) to the death of Henry VII (1509) marks the recovery and renewed consolidation of medieval kingship. The so-called New Monarchy of the Tudors is, as is well known, on the point of joining other traditional categories of historical writing in the lumber-room; 1485 may soon be a date of as little significance as 1760 has been since Professor Namier's researches. More and more it is coming to be held that Henry VII did little that was not already started, or at least foreshadowed, by his Yorkist predecessors.[1] What is not perhaps sufficiently realized is that by all standards of judgement this period of reconstruction after the civil wars had considerably more affinity with the past than with the future. Because strong rule was the most obvious characteristic of the Tudor century, the foundations of that rule have been taken to be the foundations of a new system of government, but the superficial symptoms have distracted attention from the underlying realities. Not only was kingship a very different thing after the Reformation and not before, but the means and methods—and, in a way, even the objects—of government changed greatly after 1529. Especially as regards the administrative machinery, the whole period cannot be understood unless the characteristic of medieval government, namely household action, is kept in mind. Where we find administration in and through the household, there we have medieval government; where there are plentiful signs of emancipation from the household, however mingled they may be with survivals from the past, we may justly suspect the beginnings of a new attitude to government which for want of a better word

---

[1] For a discussion of administration yielding this conclusion, cf. an unprinted M.Litt. thesis in the Cambridge University Library: J. R. Lander, 'The Administration of the Yorkist Kings' (1949). Mr Lander's general argument that Edward IV practised very largely what Henry VII continued is, despite some weak points and over-large claims, convincing enough.

we call modern. By this definition, which alone gives point to any classification of fifteenth- and sixteenth-century government, Edward IV, Richard III, and Henry VII were thoroughly medieval (as the following pages will show), though none the less strong and effective rulers. Medieval government, as Edward I proved conclusively, could be quite as efficient as anything that came after it, and Henry VII in particular was to make the point again and with even greater emphasis. There is thus little purpose in attempting to disentangle the originality of Tudor from Yorkist monarch, or in allotting responsibility. The record is much fuller for Henry VII, his dynasty survived, and his work was done more thoroughly and skilfully, for which reasons his reign matters more in the history of administration; but it is more important to trace the history of the various institutions throughout these forty years than to make an artificial division at the year 1485.

Finance comes first, if only because the difference in strength between Lancaster on the one hand, and York and Tudor on the other, lay largely in their respective solvency—even as Henry VII's superiority over Edward IV may be seen in the fact that the former was rich while the latter was not bankrupt. As we have seen, the early fifteenth century witnessed a decline of household finance which left the exchequer theoretically in full control. The exchequer was an admirable instrument for bureaucratic safety and the prevention of fraud, but it was of little use to a dynamic government which needed to have quick access to the cash and a chance of telling how things stood. In fact, the exchequer suffered from three serious shortcomings. In the first place, the methods of paying in and out at the receipt were slow and burdened with bureaucratic devices of great antiquity. When money was paid in, say by the sheriff, he received from the teller, to whom he paid, a bill which he exchanged for a tally. This, however, was handed to him only after the writer of the tallies, the clerk of the pells, the cutter and striker of tallies, had all come into play, checking and double-checking the accuracy of bill and tally.[1] The tally itself did not represent the sheriff's dis-

[1] For an account of the methods in the receipt temp. Edward VI cf. B.M., Lansd. MS. 171, fo. 209; a slightly later account is in E 407/71, no. 82. These descriptions record a procedure already reformed!

charge but merely guaranteed him one when he came to his audit in the upper exchequer. The disbursement of money from the exchequer was equally cumbersome, if not more so. When the exchequer paid cash on warrant, the tellers (who paid) had to obtain the money from the chamberlains and undertreasurer in whose custody it was. However, cash transactions were rare; nearly all exchequer payments were made in assignments by tally on local receivers, customers, or other officials who actually collected money. A tally to the requisite amount and appropriated, as a rule, to a particular source of revenue, was issued to the recipient of the money who was thus compelled himself to collect what was due to him. Often the local receiver had no money in hand, and unredeemed tallies returned to the exchequer, to be exchanged for fresh ones and to lead to the most extraordinary confusion of genuine and mere book-keeping entries in the receipt and issue rolls.[1] As a treasury of money received and for payments due, the exchequer of receipt was so patently unsatisfactory that by the late fifteenth century it had become little more than a register for transactions taking place elsewhere and a machine for the issue and cancellation of tallies.

Secondly, this state of affairs meant that it was impossible for the exchequer to render any sort of survey; from the records as they stood, no 'state' could be compiled. Receipt and issue rolls gave no totals, and had they done so these sums, in great part composed of entries designed to keep the record straight and not to represent genuine incomings and outgoings, would have been meaningless. Nor did the records of completed accounts—the pipe rolls and enrolled foreign accounts of the upper exchequer—give totals; again, if they had, the way in which they were compiled and the purpose for which they were kept would have rendered such a step pointless. At the exchequer account, the accountant was confronted with a roll stating what was due from him, and he made answer—paid or yet unpaid—item by item. If unpaid items remained, the offices of the two remembrancers took note for future action; their chief function was the driving in of outstanding sums—debts not paid when the

---

[1] Cf. A. Steel, 'Receipt Roll Totals under Henry IV and Henry V', *E.H.R.* XLVII. 204 ff.; 'The Marginalia of the Treasurer's Receipt Rolls, 1349-99', *Bull. I.H.R.* VII. 67 ff., 133 ff.; 'Mutua per Talliam, 1377-1413', *ibid.* XIII. 73 ff.

account was rendered, fines assessed in the court, and the like. From this it is clear that generally speaking the rolls of the upper exchequer by this time did not represent income and expenditure for any one year, but the machinery for securing the king's revenue, a very different thing. As a result it was impossible to tell how things stood at any time—whether, in fact, the crown was solvent or not; and any doubt in that direction was assuaged by the pernicious system of payment by assignments which enabled the exchequer to drag out payment year by year until, perhaps, the unfortunate creditor decided to cut his losses and gave up the game of taking up and returning unredeemable tallies.

The third shortcoming of the exchequer was closely connected with this matter of its records. Accounts and audits at the exchequer might be safe and uncorrupt, but they took a very long time—rarely less than two years after the conclusion of the account—and in view of the documents in which they were embodied were highly artificial. Far too often the delays and peculiar entries caused the exchequer to fail in its primary purpose: it did not exact quickly and to the last penny what was due to the king. All these weaknesses had always been inherent in the exchequer machinery, but they had been less apparent while the exchequer was still flexible and supervised by energetic and professional treasurers. As this officer became more and more a great officer of state who paid little attention to departmental business, the dead hand of a highly sophisticated routine lay heavily on the exchequer.[1] Moreover, even while things were working well in the department, active kings had found it necessary to use less cumbersome methods in the financing of their government; the wardrobe as used by Edward I was the outstanding example, embodying as it did the principles of speedy action and ultimate exchequer control. As usual, medieval kings went to their household, not only in order to resist baronial control of the offices of state, but more commonly in order to help out the shortcomings of these offices.

---

[1] In the fifteenth century the treasurership became a magnate office, held for prestige reasons rather than for the purpose of doing the work, as any list of treasurers will show (e.g. F. M. Powicke, *Handbook of British Chronology*, 84 f.). Henry Bourchier, earl of Essex, treasurer in 1455, 1460, and from 1471 till his death in 1483, may have been an exception to the rule.

The position of the exchequer about the time when Yorkist rule was restoring sound government in England has been discussed at such length because an understanding of its weaknesses is essential if the history of financial administration in the sixteenth century is to be grasped. The various reforms which culminated, in 1554, in the restoration of exchequer supremacy in a new guise were all motivated by the needs of Tudor government to find a handier treasury than that provided by the receipt of the exchequer, to achieve a speedier and more effective audit, and to make possible a balance sheet of ins and outs, so as to allow of planned government. Now we must turn to what was done about these needs in the period of recovery under review; they were, of course, the same for 'medieval' and 'modern' governments, though the solutions adopted differed.

It will be best to note first what little was done to give the exchequer itself greater efficiency. In order to restore a measure of professional control which the sinecure treasurers of the age were incapable of exercising, both the Yorkists and Henry VII appointed trained administrators as undertreasurers, men like Sir John Wood (himself treasurer for a few months in 1484–5) or Sir John Cutt, who handed down a tradition of first-class service to the chancellor of the exchequer who from 1543 commonly held the undertreasurership as well by a separate patent.[1] Until the reforms of Mary's reign the undertreasurer remained the dominant official in the receipt, though after 1554 he was supplanted by the writer of the tallies whose office gave him several excellent means of supervising the tellers, on which grounds he called himself auditor of the receipt. But the most efficient and hard-working of men could not be expected to overcome drawbacks inherent in the whole structure of the department, and of organic reforms in the receipt there are few signs. A memorandum of Richard III's reign recommended that the exchequer render annual declarations of its receipts, expenditure,

[1] Sir John Baker succeeded Thomas Cromwell as chancellor of the exchequer in 1540 (*L.P.* xv. 1027, 33) and Sir Richard Weston as undertreasurer in 1543 (*L.P.* xviii. I. 802, 84). It may be noted that this combination of offices was unique; otherwise, a recommendation of 1484 that no man should hold office in both parts of the exchequer reflected ordinary practice (*Letters and Papers illustrative of the Reigns of Richard III and Henry VII*, ed. J. Gairdner, Rolls Series, 1861, I. 82).

and 'state' to specially appointed commissioners,[1] but it was not until late in his reign that Henry VII instituted several important reforms in the receipt.[2] Their effect was to turn the older officials of standing into cyphers and replace them by the tellers and undertreasurer. The tellers now took over from the treasurer and chamberlains the custody of the money paid to them and became accountable for it. At the same time the multiplicity of rolls designed to check each officer by another—a pell of receipt and one of issue for each of the three officers originally responsible for the storage of money—was reduced by the abolition of all issue rolls and two receipt rolls; the real record of the transactions carried out in the lower exchequer was now in the accounts kept separately by the four tellers. These contained genuine income and expenditure only—no book-keeping entries—and on them was based the 'Declaration of the State of the Treasury' rendered annually from at least 1508 by the undertreasurer as the officer presiding over the receipt. This system endured without change until the great exchequer reforms of the mid-century, nor was it much affected by these; in a few details procedure in the receipt might alter in the course of the years, and the restoration of the pell of issue in 1597 marked a retrograde step, but essentially the organization produced by Henry VII and built round the tellers and their accounts lasted down to the abolition of the exchequer. It made the receipt quite sound and efficient as a treasury, from the government's point of view; though even the government, not to mention debtors and creditors trying to settle their affairs, would still find the survival of tallies and the many documents required to allow money in and out of the exchequer a sad drain on time, patience, and purse.

While these reforms solved the problems of the receipt, the exchequer of audit was a much harder nut to crack. In fact, neither the Yorkists nor Henry VII ever tried to reform the upper exchequer and introduce some sensible business methods into its

---

[1] *Lett. and Pap. of Richard III and Henry VII*, I. 82.

[2] These are listed in 'A Discourse concerning the Kinges Receipt' by Sir Vincent Skinner, auditor of the receipt temp. James I (B.M., Lansd. MS. 151, fos. 104–6). Skinner speaks of the year 20 Henry VII (1504–5). It is, however, possible that the reforms started earlier: the issue rolls, e.g., cease now in 1480 and may have been abolished then (M. S. Giuseppi, *Guide to the Public Records*, I. 179).

slow and ancient accounts procedure; instead they proved themselves thoroughly 'medieval' by taking refuge in household government, to such an extent that the exchequer became for a time almost
the least important financial department. Even in the reign of
Edward IV many crown estates were removed from exchequer
control by the appointment of special 'foreign' auditors (auditors not
responsible to the exchequer), and this process of decentralization
resulted in the upper exchequer 'becoming a department to which
auditors certified that accounts had been dealt with elsewhere'.[1] The
memorandum of Richard III which has already been referred to
either codified or projected a system under which most crown lands
should be free from exchequer control, though it did not provide for
any other central authority and seemed content with individual
auditors responsible, presumably, to king and council.[2] This was
the basis of the great 'chamber system of finance' developed by
Henry VII. It was in every detail a household product; the new
treasury as well as the various methods evolved for audit and
exaction of outstanding or concealed revenue came from the household and never left it. Chamber finance was not, to be sure, anything new, but had been energetically practised by Edward II, and
by Edward III up to 1356; nevertheless, in scope and completeness
of machinery Henry VII went so much further that he can almost be
said to have turned a revival into an innovation. However, at heart
it was a revival of methods traditional in medieval government.

The fundamental fact in the restoration of royal power was the
restoration of royal wealth; in order to be the most powerful man
in the kingdom the king had to be the richest. In effect this meant,
towards the end of the fifteenth century, that he had to be the
greatest landowner. Fortescue recognized this when he advocated
that the king should keep in his hand the largest possible amount of
land,[3] and the policy was adopted by Edward IV and Henry VII

[1] Lander, 230 ff.
[2] *Lett. and Pap. of Richard III and Henry VII*, I. 81 ff. Mr Lander holds that the
whole plan here outlined was already working well under Edward IV (*op. cit.* 239 ff.).
I am not altogether convinced that he has shown more than its elements in existence
before 1484, and feel that some respect is due to the very 'futuristic' phrasing of the
document.
[3] Cf. S. B. Chrimes, *English Constitutional Ideas in the Fifteenth Century* (Cambridge,
1936), 329 f.

with huge success. Though he had other valuable sources of revenue, Henry VII built up his legendary fortune on the secure basis of the vast and ever increasing crown lands—old royal demesne, the family properties of Tudor and Lancaster, the spoils of the Wars of the Roses, the gains of repeated forfeitures and attainders. Not even Henry VIII's much advertised extravagance could seriously undermine this foundation of royal wealth, greatly augmented by the monastic confiscations of the 1530's; what really destroyed the system built up by the first Tudor was the phenomenal price rise of the sixteenth century which hit all landed proprietors hard, and therefore hardest the greatest of them—the crown. This was a disaster that no one could foresee in 1500. The policy of making the crown rich, independent, and powerful on a basis of landed wealth was sound and successful in this period of restoration.

But the policy depended for its success not only on an accumulation of estates, but also on a successful exploitation of these revenues, and it was here that the new machinery was applied. Edward IV and Richard III employed special auditors to take the accounts of estates they wished to remove from the survey of the exchequer; the memorandum of 1484 included among these the royal lands in Wales, the duchies of York and Cornwall, the earldoms of Chester, March, Warwick, and Salisbury, and forfeited estates.[1] It also excluded the duchy of Lancaster[2] which has enjoyed a remarkable history of independent self-government from 1399 when it became crown property to the present day, under all the successive houses of Lancaster, York, Tudor, Stuart, and so forth. What the Yorkists failed to provide was a central treasury to gather the revenues of these separately administered lands, as well as a central authority to supervise them. Following the example of Edward II, Henry VII directed these revenues into the chamber of the household and committed their receipt and further disposition to the treasurer of the chamber, at this time a minor household official charged largely with the payment of wages and the provision of funds for the ceremonial side of the court. The Yorkist kings had, indeed, employed the chamber as a principal spending department, but they had supplied it largely—

[1] Lander, 230 ff.; *Lett. and Pap. of Richard III and Henry VII*, 1. 82.
[2] *Ibid.* 84.

not exclusively—from exchequer assignments;[1] when he made his chamber an independent treasury administering what were in effect revenues of state, Henry VII went much further and created the machinery which dominated finance until the reforms of Thomas Cromwell.[2] In the hands of Sir Thomas Lovell and, especially, Sir John Heron, treasurer of the chamber from about 1492 to 1521, the chamber became the leading financial department, administering vast sums of money reaching to totals of over £200,000 a year, receiving the revenues of crown lands as well as money from other sources, and covering by far the greater part of the king's expenditure. From 1487 receivers of crown revenues began to pay directly to the chamber, thus cutting out the exchequer altogether. The organization of the chamber was of the simplest: the treasurer remained, throughout the reign of Henry VII, very much the king's personal servant, receiving and paying on word-of-mouth commands only which were rarely replaced or reinforced by warrants under the signet; his books were checked by the king personally and cleared by the royal signature on every page; there was no visible attempt to give to the chamber system of finance the trappings of an institution of government. Household government remained personal government.

Such informality was satisfactory enough in a mere treasury under a king who was himself a business man and administrator. It is, however, difficult to see how it could secure the revenues which fed the chamber, and this is at present rather an obscure point, at least down to 1509. It would appear that the system later codified in statutes of Henry VIII was in operation during his father's reign in a somewhat rudimentary fashion; Henry VII may have personally shared in it. The problem is not how the king knew what was his due; for that purpose machinery existed which will be discussed later. What was lacking was a permanent authority to audit receivers'

---

[1] Lander, 235 ff.

[2] For the history of the chamber at this period, cf. A. P. Newton, 'The King's Chamber under the Early Tudors', *E.H.R.* XXXII. 348 ff., an exhaustive enough account of the chamber as a treasury which makes detailed discussion here superfluous. In his forthcoming work on the Tudor chamber, Prof. W. C. Richardson of Louisiana University promises to treat the whole matter in full; I am aware that in writing before his book appears I may be duplicating points or, worse, getting them wrong, but this summarized account is necessary. (Cf. above, p. 8, n. 1.)

accounts and exact payment of outstanding debts—the work later done by the general surveyors of crown lands. The plan of 1484, following in effect the practice of Edward III,[1] suggested the appointment of one auditor and one surveyor to be in general charge of crown lands,[2] but this is one point in the memorandum of which there is little solid evidence until the reign of Henry VIII. It would appear that here again there was, under Henry VII, some personal action by the king, as well as the more permanent but still informal activity of such leading ministers as Sir Reginald Bray, Lovell, and Sir Robert Southwell.[3] There can be no doubt that beneath their general but unorganized sway the system was continued of appointing surveyors and 'foreign' auditors to take the accounts of individual receivers which Edward IV had first instituted.[4] It was not, by any standards, a very satisfactory way of administering the best part of the crown's revenue, for it not only depended on the personal action of a king who failed to train his successor in the same hard school of business which he himself had undergone, but also marked a reversion to informal household government in the midst of a highly complicated machinery of administration. We may well doubt whether it could have continued for long even under the old king; at the same time it must be admitted that it worked well and produced all the requisite results while Henry VII lived.

The chamber supplied a treasury for the king's revenues; the rudimentary organization of surveyors and auditors, directed by the king himself with the help of a few leading councillors, served to administer them. There remained the problem of discovering what sources of income existed, were insufficiently exploited, or were being deliberately concealed, a problem especially large and difficult at a time when the lost power of the crown was being painfully re-established. From 1471 onwards commissions of inquiry were issued at intervals to investigate the position in the various shires;[5] their task was to ascertain the limits of crown lands and secure the

---

[1] Tout, *Chapters*, IV. 267 ff.

[2] *Lett. and Pap. of Richard III and Henry VII*, I. 83.

[3] Newton says that the king, with the assistance of these men appointed by word of mouth, performed in effect the duties of the later general surveyors (*op. cit.* 362).

[4] There are signs of regional groupings of lands, as well as of the appointment of special commissions to administer units like the duchy of Cornwall, under Edward IV (Lander, 192 ff.). [5] Lander, 198 ff.

feudal obligations to the crown of which the right of wardship was the most important and most profitable. Henry VII revived these commissions on a vast scale, but for many years they were not provided with organized direction from above; like the administration of the crown lands themselves, the work of these commissioners was co-ordinated by the king in person and by his leading councillors—Bray and Southwell in the early part of the reign, Lovell and Empson and Dudley after 1503.[1] In December 1503 all business connected with wards was separately organized by the appointment of a master of the wards, provided with an elementary sort of staff to enable him to carry out his duties.[2] The business that remained—there was a good deal of it—was handed over in August 1508 to Sir Edward Belknap as surveyor of the king's prerogative. His office was to ascertain and exploit the king's rights on the lands of convicted felons, outlaws, widows remarried without licence, and the like; in other words, it was to make the most of the king's highly oppressive prerogative rights. He was authorized to appoint county surveyors and did so; the money obtained was paid to the chamber, and Belknap was responsible only to auditors specially appointed by the king. The office apparently ceased operations with the death of Henry VII, though Belknap was not relieved of his duties until 1513. It was a short-lived experiment, highly typical of the notorious measures for ever associated, though perhaps unfairly, with the names of Empson and Dudley. These two themselves were the mainstay in another temporary organization styled the 'king's council learned in the law at Westminster', a conciliar body under the presidency of the chancellor of the duchy of Lancaster which not only enforced legislation against riots and other offences contrary to statute, but was also responsible for collecting the revenue derived from fines on penal statutes.[3] Though in the main a judicial offshoot of the council and apparently limited to the later years of Henry VII, they were

[1] This and the following facts are derived from W. C. Richardson, 'The Surveyor of the King's Prerogative', *E.H.R.* LVI. 52 ff., q.v. for details.

[2] A document drawn up probably towards the end of Wolsey's ministry, though placed in 1540 by *L.P.* (XV. 503), described the organization of the master of the wards in Henry VII's reign (cf. below, p. 220). He had been assisted by a general receiver, an auditor, and a particular receiver in each shire, had kept full records of wardships and their disposal, and had squeezed the most out of that source of revenue.

[3] Cf. R. Somerville, 'Henry VII's "Council Learned in the Law"', *E.H.R.* LIV. 427 ff.

thus also part of the machinery of finance and seem to have survived, rather obscurely, until after Wolsey's fall.[1]

These, then, were the changes in the financial machinery worked out by the Yorkists and Henry VII in their efforts to set government on its feet again. Apart from the few procedural changes in the receipt of the exchequer, they all tended in the direction of household government. The decline of the exchequer, the creation of the chamber system of finance, the rudimentary surveillance of crown lands, the use of personal associates, councillors (members of the kind of council described below),[2] and household officers, above all the constant personal action of the king—all these leave no doubt that the years 1471–1509 saw a vast revival of the household potential in financial administration, at the expense of the national organization. Dudley's career—and he was no household official in the strict sense—has been taken to prove that 'the King's household, rather than the important offices of state, was still the real administrative centre'.[3] We are still in the middle ages.

To turn to the clerical organization: there is no sign that the routine of chancery and the great seal was in any way affected in these years. This is the formative period of the court of chancery, when the foundations were laid by such great chancellors as Cardinal Morton for the structure later erected by Wolsey, Thomas More, and lord-keeper Egerton; but on the administrative side of the department there is nothing to tell. The great seal had lost all 'original' force outside the judicial sphere long before this, and though in numbers its clerical staff continued to outweigh all the rest combined, the steady and undisturbed performance of regular bureaucratic duties provides no matter for discussion. The position of the privy seal is not very different, though a more intensive study of its keepers and clerks than is here possible might still perhaps yield some interesting

[1] A paper of 1531 refers to 'the kinges Learned Counsaile' as responsible for the profits obtained from penal statutes and from 'endes taken with his highnes or Counsaile by obligacion, Indenture, payment, or otherwise' (SP 1:67, fo. 35), but there is no trace by that date of the organized conciliar body with its regular meetings described by Mr Somerville.

[2] Pp. 32 ff.

[3] D. M. Brodie, 'Edmund Dudley: Minister of Henry VII', *Trans. R. Hist. Soc.* (1932), 149.

results. The seal continued to be the centre of the administrative machine, but its pre-eminence was much impaired by the incursions of the signet. This is what one would expect: even Henry VI, as has been seen, succeeded in having the place of the most personal of the three seals recognized in the teeth of council opposition, and it causes no surprise to find that the restoration of strong kingship was accompanied by increasing encroachments of the signet on the seal which the council had looked like making its peculiar weapon in the first half of the century. But though the Yorkists and Henry VII used the signet more freely and frequently than the Lancastrians had done, they added nothing fresh to its sphere or functions;[1] once again they revived a practice—the practice of Richard II—rather than invented new machinery. The signet continued to authenticate the king's private correspondence, directions to household officers, diplomatic correspondence, orders to the privy seal, as well as orders to the localities whose number and diversity has largely to be conjectured since the documents themselves are mostly lost.[2] The signet office developed a more bureaucratic organization, but it remained attached to the household.[3] Altogether, there was enlargement, but there was no innovation.

In one respect, however, this period is important. It saw the rise of the principal secretary who in the reign of Edward IV 'seems to take on the character of a public officer'.[4] Though the office can be traced back to the reign of Richard II, so as once more to point the 'modernity' of that reign, it is only after Edward IV's final victory in the Wars of the Roses that the secretary becomes genuinely important —and this despite the one Lancastrian secretary of renown, Thomas Beckington (1438–43), whose fame rests on his later greatness and the happy survival of his letter-book. It is important to understand the nature of this late-medieval secretaryship, for the issue has been much befogged by a failure to distinguish between even the greatest of the men who held the office between 1471 and 1534 and those that

---

[1] Otway Ruthven, *King's Sec.* 41, 59; cf. F. M. G. Evans, *The Principal Secretary of State* (Manchester, 1923), 197.

[2] Otway Ruthven, *King's Sec.* 42 ff.   [3] *Ibid.* 106 ff.

[4] *Ibid.* 74 f. Cf. *ibid.* 7: 'The history of the office of king's secretary in the fifteenth century is that of its rise from the comparative unimportance of a confidential clerkship to a position worthy of the attention of a bishop and the fitting instrument of Tudor government.'

followed after. The Yorkist secretary and his early Tudor successor based his influence on two pillars: he was keeper of the king's signet, and he was usually a trained diplomat much employed in embassies abroad. As keeper of the signet he had access to the king's person and knowledge of the king's inner councils; the man who superintended the writing of the king's correspondence and proved a useful channel of the royal patronage naturally found it easy to make a place for himself. His diplomatic activity, a direct consequence of the greatly developed tangle of international relations in Renaissance Europe, gave him a special knowledge of foreign affairs.[1] But neither function as yet elevated the secretaryship to a high place in the official hierarchy; the personal and household character of the office remained unimpaired. Absence abroad, in fact, was always likely to affect the secretary's influence where it mattered most—at court with the king. Nevertheless, this period of restored strong government, with its increased use of the signet and more forceful personal government by the sovereign, witnessed a marked expansion in the office of secretary: from the time of William Hatteclyffe (1464–80) the principal secretary was at least a man of standing, though not yet an officer of state.[2] But let it be remembered that neither the custody of the signet nor employment abroad was in the end to prove the foundation for the modern secretaryship of state.[3] Until the 1530's the leading executive ministers of the crown did not include the secretary in their number; these were rather the household officers (treasurer and controller), the lord privy seal, and most important of all the lord chancellor, while the principal secretary remained an official of the second rank much used abroad and insignificant in council. The difference cannot be stressed enough.

The small governing council of the Lancastrians collapsed in the faction strife which broke out in 1450; since the magnates had

---

[1] On this point, cf. Mrs Higham (F. M. G. Evans), 'Note on the Pre-Tudor Secretary,' *Essays...presented to T. F. Tout* (Manchester, 1925), 361 ff.

[2] Hatteclyffe's successor, Oliver King, may have continued in office even after he became a bishop; this was unprecedented (Otway Ruthven, *King's Sec.* 75). Similarly, Ruthal retained the office as bishop of Durham, 1509–16, though he was then promoted lord privy seal. Gardiner (secretary, 1528–34) became bishop of Winchester in December 1531. All this proves only the higher social standing of the office, not its real place in the machinery of government. [3] Below, pp. 300 f.

imposed their domination on the council, their wars naturally destroyed it. The great days of conciliar independence were certainly over, but the view once held that the virtual absence of formal council records from the reign of Edward IV down to 1540 reflects the fact that no organized council of any kind existed[1] is no longer tenable. The councils of this period of restoration were exactly what one would expect: groups of royal servants pledged and eager to do the king's will. Edward IV began it when he ejected the aristocracy from his council and governed with the assistance of officials carefully chosen by himself, and Henry VII continued this policy on a larger scale.[2] Of his reign, indeed, it has been said that 'the word "councillors" describes his civil service rather than his cabinet';[3] the number of councillors is supposed to have been around one hundred throughout most of the time, and such extravagances are known as the presence of forty-four 'councillors' in the star chamber to hear the Merchant Adventurers' suit against the Staplers.[4] At the same time, a council did exist, equipped with clerk and even at times president, and membership, though large, was not capricious. A councillor was a councillor, whatever the implications of that title, and 'there was clearly some continuity but a good deal of elasticity about Henry VII's council'.[5]

It will be easier to understand the position if it is clearly grasped that the council of this period was, first, a reaction against the powerful Lancastrian council, and secondly, mainly a court of jurisdiction; furthermore, it was not the predecessor of the later Tudor privy council, and only confusion is produced by reading back characteristics and developments traceable after 1540 into the period before 1509. Because Edward IV and Henry VII feared a resurrection of the baronial opposition which once before had captured a small and

---

[1] Baldwin, *King's Council*, 420 ff.

[2] Lander, 150 ff. He shows that the council was active in administrative matters as a body and formed a 'high co-ordinating and supervisory body' though 'strictly under the control of the king' (p. 167). His conclusion is that 'Henry VII's council was of the same nature as Edward's—there was no break in kind'.

[3] Pollard, 'Council under the Tudors', *E.H.R.* XXXVII. 343. Cf. K. Pickthorn, *Early Tudor Government: Henry VII* (Cambridge, 1934), 30: 'In his time councillors were the king's superior servants, diversified with a few harmless noblemen.'

[4] Cf. Pollard's review of *Cal. Pat. 1494–1509* in *E.H.R.* XXXII. 455. He there declared that 'if we can call Henry's councillors his council, it numbered over fifty'.

[5] Pollard, *E.H.R.* XXXVII. 357.

organized council, they kept their councils free from noble influence (though not bare of noblemen) and large in number, governing through a few chosen advisers (themselves, of course, described as councillors) rather than a conciliar board. In consequence such work as the council did as a body—such work, therefore, as found its way into the fragmentary records surviving—was largely part of its judicial activities and underlines the truth of the statement that the direct descendant of the medieval council was the court of star chamber.[1] This is true only because the administrative work of the council fell to individuals under the strict control of the king, so that when the council acted as a body it was bound to appear adjudicating upon petitions—it was a court. The later privy council grew out of an inner ring of more intimate, more important, councillors of whom there are a few traces under Edward IV, or in 'the Rat, the Cat, and Lovell the Dog' of Richard III, or more particularly in the Brays, Lovells, Mortons, and Foxes of Henry VII. As we shall see later, when the king did not undertake personal government, the inner ring became more evident; however, until the 1530's it remained only an informal group distinguished by the individual importance of its members and not by any kind of institutional organization. There, if we like, lies the ancestry of the privy council; the whole body of the council is of little importance in a history of administration after 1509, and of not much more before that.

This must not be taken to mean that government by members of council was not important in the years 1471–1509; above all else, Henry VII's restoration of royal power based itself on a diffusion of conciliar authority. Edward and Henry made it plain that the power of the council was only the reflected power of the crown; the councillors were the king's deputies, appointed by him and responsible to him. With a group of councillors thus disciplined the king was able to extend his influence more widely than ever before; every councillor, acting in whatever matter and whatever corner of the realm, represented the full force of royal action. Hence that ever increasing diversity of conciliar institutions, a development first marked under Henry VII though hardly begun by him. The star chamber as a court owed its organization more to Wolsey than to

[1] E.g. Baldwin, *King's Council*, 450.

Henry VII, but it represented in either period only a more efficient form of that conciliar jurisdiction which had always existed and was always producing new courts and new law.[1] Even the court of requests, once supposed to have been instituted by Henry VII in 1493, has been shown to have a history going back before 1485.[2] The council's power was reproduced in the northern and Welsh marches, and it was incorporated in temporary tribunals set up by act of parliament;[3] a lesser body of a little more permanence, the king's council learned in the law, made its appearance, sitting regularly in term time and enforcing the king's will by virtue of its conciliar derivation.[4] Good government, to Henry VII as to his successors, meant royal government through conciliar agents, but so far these agents remained in and of the household.

Of one conciliar offspring there is, as has been said, no sign. The true mainspring of governmental action must always reside in a group of ministers around the king, and acting under his real or pretended authority. The ministers existed, but the 'cabinet' was missing; there was no corporate unity for that inner ring until Thomas Cromwell turned it into the privy council. The reason may have been the king's personal activity in government which rendered an organized council superfluous, reinforced by fear and jealousy of a true council natural to men who remembered the bad days of Henry VI. But the reason is less significant than the solution adopted. While the judiciary was being reinforced on all sides by half or fully organized bodies of councillors, sitting regularly in term time and hearing cases, the administration was controlled by a few individuals among these councillors, themselves commonly members of the household, usually in close attendance on the sovereign, and deriving their authority from personal contact with the king. Once again we see that the recovery of 1471–1509 meant the restoration of efficient household government, a return to truly medieval methods which, in the case of the council especially, took government back to a more primitive stage than it had in fact reached by the end of the

---

[1] Cf. especially the development of chancery in the fifteenth century.

[2] Pollard, 'The Growth of the Court of Requests', *E.H.R.* LVI. 300 ff.

[3] E.g. the so-called Star Chamber Act of 1487 (3 Henry VII, c. 11), one of a number of acts which committed the execution of a policy to a council committee.

[4] Somerville, *E.H.R.* LIV. 427 ff.

fourteenth century. It is not important that the council was normally thought of as part of the household—that remained true as late as the reign of Charles II; but it is important that the conception does in fact represent the true condition of that inner ring of king's servants and councillors by whose assistance Henry VII governed. They might or might not be technically officers of the household, but they were all intimate associates of the king in his household.

In every way, then, the great restoration of government after the civil wars of the fifteenth century, the work of Edward IV and Henry VII, represented a restoration of medieval government at its most efficient. A financial administration based on the king's chamber and the somewhat informal means adopted for audit and control, the extended use of the signet and the rise of the secretary, and government through individual councillors rather than a council, all these marked the triumph of household methods in administration. Perhaps it is not necessary to offer a caution, but it will be safer to do so: household government of this kind was as much the king's government of his realm as any other organization since evolved. It was, however, government by a peculiar method easily distinguished from the national bureaucratic institutions which in the middle ages co-existed with household government and were destined, in the sixteenth century, to become the sole method of national administration.

3. *Wolsey's administration*

The first half of the reign of Henry VIII was a period of wars and foreign policy; in those years England attained a place in Europe which for importance and influence exceeded anything since the failure of Henry V's designs. Though the country undoubtedly put forward rather more than her proper strength, there was some real glory in all this, and it was a glory much to the taste both of the vain and eager young king and of his equally vain but much more able minister. Wolsey spent his time in these international affairs and in the judicial work which raised to new heights the court of chancery and the council in the star chamber; he also superintended the internal administration of the country in as close a fashion as

Henry VII had done, so that it is not surprising that he found no time for reforms in government. His biographer could only say that he simply continued the methods of Henry VII,[1] and though this, as we shall see, is a little oversimplified, it is true in essentials. The years when so thoroughly medieval a figure—a cardinal of the church, archbishop of York, and clerical lord chancellor—ruled England under the king were the last years of truly medieval government. After Wolsey's fall the church relinquished many official posts which till then it had usually monopolized, and the modern secretary of state replaced the medieval chancellor as the chief executive minister of the crown. What makes those twenty years from 1509 so interesting is that a new abundance of records and a genuine attempt to embody aspects of household government in more bureaucratic institutions make it possible to describe this medieval form of government much more precisely.

There is one exception to the general absence of administrative reforms in this period. Some time in 1519 or thereabouts,[2] Henry VIII, perhaps driven by one of those recurring bursts of energy to which he was subject, appears to have decided that he knew too little of what went on; he therefore had a number of reforms drafted which would enable him to exercise the government of his realm in his own person. Three papers were drawn up, all in the hand of the same clerk, of which the third—a 'Pryvie Remembraunce'—is of little interest here as it deals only with dangers to the royal person and potential risings, the navy and commerce, and the payment of annuities in the exchequer.[3] The second—matters which the king wished 'in his awne person to debate with his counsaile and to se Reformacion to be don therin'—included such general points as the 'egall & Indifferent administracion of Iustice', the reduction to order of Ireland, the best employment of 'the commodities of this his reame' and 'howe the Idle peple...may be put in occupacion', and the fortifications of the frontiers.[4] There is only one administrative matter of great interest: 'Item the kynges grace Intendith to Refourme his exchequier and to establisshe a substanciall ordre in

---

[1] A. F. Pollard, *Wolsey*, 128 ff.
[2] The date is that of *L.P.* III. 576; there is no reason to doubt it.
[3] B.M., Tit. B. i, fo. 192.   [4] *Ibid.* fo. 191.

37

the same.' The intention was laudable, and as we have seen desirable, but it remained an intention; nothing at all was done. The same is true, as far as appears, for the main body of projected reforms embodied in the first paper;[1] they are quite detailed and would have produced much centralization and much improvement in efficiency, but there is not the faintest sign that any of them were ever put into practice. From our point of view they are none the less valuable, for at least they indicate fairly fully the kind of mind and principle brought to the business of administration at this juncture.

This first paper is described as 'A Remembraunce of such thinges as the kynges grace woll haue to be doon and hath goven in Commaundment to his Cardinal to put the same in effectuell execution as hereafter Insuyth'. The words 'in the kynges awne presence' or their equivalent constantly recur; the main purpose of the direction was to provide Henry himself with the means of control. He wanted a privy purse of £10,000 a year, to be paid to him quarterly by the treasurer of the chamber; it appears that Sir William Compton was responsible for privy-purse money and accounted for it.[2] Special sums were to be set aside for the king's buildings, and the treasurer of the chamber was made responsible for paying 'Rewardes for Ambassadours and wages for postis and other necessarie expensis aswell for fortifications of the kynges frontiers and others the kynges oute warde causis', items which he had in any case been in the habit of covering. Then followed the administrative orders which may be summarized as appointing quarterly audits by the king personally on the basis of account books made up by specially commissioned auditors who were to leave one copy with the treasurer concerned and present one to the king himself. All the officials who in any way handled the king's revenues were to be treated in this fashion, and for each named commissioners were assigned: the king's plate, the great wardrobe, ordnance and artillery, ships, armoury and stable,

---

[1] B.M., Tit. B. i, fos. 188–90 v.

[2] The subject of the king's privy coffers is obscure; a reference to Compton later in the document demands accounts from him for 'aswell all such somes of money as the said sir william Compton shall Receyue as also by the kynges commaundment ley oute and pay', and it is more than probable that the privy purse was meant. Compton was one of the king's closest associates, but he held no office in which royal treasure was administered; in 1510 he received the surplus of the hanaper to the king's use—£2,787 in one full year (*L.P.* 1. 579).

Robert Amadas and Robert Gibson for the tents and toils, the treasurer of the chamber (who was to make monthly declaration of receipts and payments), Compton (for the privy purse), the general surveyors (once a year), buildings, the treasurer of England and barons of the exchequer (also once a year), and the master of the wards.[1] Similar quarterly reports were to be made by the chancellor of England and the judges of the administration of justice and the 'hole state of the reame & ordre of euery shir within the same as ferre as they haue knowlege'; the chancellor and council of the duchy were to report in like wise once a year. One paragraph declared the king's desire to put his household in 'honorable substanciall & profitable ordre with oute any further dilay', and a powerful council committee under Wolsey was appointed for the purpose; this order, indeed, took effect in the ordinance of January 1526 which, however, itself proved abortive.[2] It was once more stated that exchequer assignments to the household were to be 'goode sufficient and leviable', a pious hope never fulfilled. 'All the premissis', the order concluded, 'the kyng hath commaunded his said Cardinall to put in due execucion as that thinge which his grace hath Deliberatly advised and woll to be don effectually.'

Henry VIII might say so, but his own habits of work—or rather his reluctance to work steadily—made certain that nothing would come of such far-reaching attempts at re-establishing the king's personal control long taken over by Wolsey. While the king no doubt was responsible for the basic principle of reports rendered to himself, it may be taken that the administrative procedure to be adopted was, if not suggested by Wolsey, at least the kind of thing he himself approved and practised. There is no trace of any bureaucratic organization; individual officers, mostly occupants of household offices and including such outstanding personal crown servants of the older generation as Sir Edward Belknap and Sir Richard Jerningham, were to act as professional supervisors in those individual departments of the household which administered the king's money in affairs of state, for all the departments listed, with the

---

[1] The master of the wards was to have the assistance of Sir Edward Belknap, John Fitzjames (attorney general), and 'Roper the lerned man'.
[2] Cf. below, pp. 375 ff.

exception of the chancery, exchequer, and duchy of Lancaster, still retained their link with the household. The system envisaged was identical with that of Henry VII: it rested on direct royal control over individual officers, on household ties, and on a general absence of bureaucratically organized offices outside the household. That was still the way in which England was to be governed. The reforms came to nothing, but even if they had been carried out they would not have provided the country with a 'modern' administration; they would merely have made its 'medieval' government more efficient by making it more personal. This dependence of household government on personal action by the crown was its great weakness, especially under a king like Henry VIII; Wolsey, however, turned it to advantage by putting himself in the place left vacant by Henry's incapacity for that sort of business. Cromwell was to do the same, but he did better by deliberately creating organizations which could function independently of such personal action. It remains to see how the various sections of the government fared under Wolsey, and where they stood when Cromwell took over.

This would seem to be the proper place to say a word about the household itself. Apart from being a source of officers and institutions for national administration, the household was of course also organized for its proper function—the care of the king and his company; indeed, though the former task is in many ways the more striking, the latter ought to be mentioned first. Household officers did household work before they did national work. The great days of the wardrobe as the department dominating both household and national administration were over before the reign of Richard II; those of the shortlived chamber supremacy by 1356. From Richard II onwards dates the development which reduced the wardrobe to 'the office of household accounts',[1] till in the end it became synonymous with the 'household below stairs', and its keeper and controller adopted the titles of treasurer and controller of the household. The chamber followed a similar trend to become simply a household office concerned with the ceremonial side of court life. These

[1] Tout, *Chapters*, IV. 224.

developments were bound up with the rise to power in the two departments of the steward and chamberlain: under Richard II these lay officials outstripped their clerical colleagues in their household spheres—the keeper of the wardrobe and receiver or treasurer of the chamber respectively—and acquired a standing which rapidly turned them into 'rather ministers of state than administrators of the domestic establishment of the sovereign'.[1] That was the beginning, but it was far from being the end. The household and its departments were still there to be used as the king pleased, and Richard II's wardrobe administered his wars.[2] In Tudor times household clerks acted as treasurers at war, victuallers, and the like, but they did this work as individuals and not as officials of an organized household department.

Twice at least in the fifteenth century attempts were made to define these changes more precisely by drawing up household establishments divided into chamber and household proper, into the departments of the chamberlain and the steward; the addition of 'lord' to these titles was not common until the sixteenth century and marked the further stage in definition reached under the Tudors. In 1455 the council, acting—as they said—in the spirit of plans made by Henry VI before his madness, drew up such a list which depicts a modest but well organized household; even the counting house or administrative board of the household was already in working order, consisting as it did of steward, treasurer, controller, cofferer, two clerks of account, a clerk and an underclerk of the controlment, and a few attendants.[3] Edward IV tried to give greater reality to this organization in his 'great year of enquiry, clearance, and reform'[4]— 1478—and produced the long and very detailed description embodied in the *Liber Niger Domus Regis*.[5] This is by far the most complete account we possess of the medieval household, and it leaves no doubt about the theoretical perfection of organization attained. From the administrative point of view, the most interesting section is that concerned with the counting house; the order of Edward III that the steward and treasurer should take the daily account was amended by allowing the other officers of the board to take the head

---

[1] *Ibid.* 160, 187 ff.   [2] *Ibid.* 223.   [3] *H.O.* 15* ff.
[4] Lander, 98.   [5] *H.O.* 15 ff.

officers' places, if necessary.[1] It is in fact certain that by this time the steward was well on his way out of the household, so that the treasurer became its active head under Edward IV;[2] by the reign of Elizabeth he had followed his superior, though neither ever completely lost a tenuous link with the government of the household.[3] Henry VII does not seem to have found it necessary to deal specifically with his household,[4] but the revival by him and his predecessors of household interference in national administration helped to retard the full development of the organization set out in the *Liber Niger*. The history of the household in the fifteenth century is far from clear, and it is not safe to generalize, but it is reasonably certain that the degree of organization reflected in the ordinances bore little relation to reality. The same points recur time and again in reign after reign; the same orders are re-enacted because they are so difficult to enforce while household officials live a double life. Not until the Tudor reforms reduced the household to its proper sphere was it possible to make steward's and chamberlain's departments—the household and the chamber—conform to the plan.

On the whole it will be best to reserve the more important aspects of the history of the household during Wolsey's rule for a later chapter; both attempted reforms and the financing of the household go too closely with Cromwell's work in the 1530's to make their separate discussion here profitable.[5] Generally speaking, the household carried on much as before. It consisted by now of the two departments whose development in the fifteenth century has been outlined, and although there were other departments not under the immediate control of lord steward or lord chamberlain,[6] these two alone concern an account of the central government of England. During Wolsey's wars household officers, whether gentlemen of the privy chamber or clerks of the kitchen and the like, did good service in the national administration, and the constant employment on

---

[1] *H.O.* 65. [2] Lander, 85 ff.

[3] In the reign of Henry VIII the treasurer was certainly still in active control of the 'lord steward's department'; cf. for example, *L.P.* IV. 309, 2060. As we shall see, it was part of Cromwell's plan to restore his proper control to the lord steward.

[4] The articles of 1494 (*H.O.* 109 ff.) provided only for the many ceremonial occasions in the life of king and household.

[5] Cf. below, Ch. VI.

[6] E.g. the stable under the master of the horse, the ordnance office under its master, etc.

important government business of the king's closer attendants in the chamber, who were men of standing and political ambitions and not civil servants, caused Wolsey many a headache when Henry felt that he was not so well attended as became a king of his dignity. In 1516 the absentee lord steward, the earl of Shrewsbury, was informed of a rumour that all head officers of the household were to be ordered to attend—'here be so many things out of order';[1] a year later Wolsey had turned the rumour into reality, so that the deputy at Tournai, also a squire of the body for which office he had paid his predecessor 200 marks, had to ask permission to attend by proxy, lest the expensive office be taken from him.[2] In 1521 the king complained that he had too few men in his privy chamber and asked for the presence of Sir Henry Guildford and Francis Bryan whom Wolsey was employing on administrative and diplomatic business.[3] An attempt was made to secure at least sufficient men to attend the king at dinner by drawing up a list of names,[4] but the problem had to be tackled on a larger scale. The result was that Eltham Ordinance of 1526, foreshadowed, as we have seen, in the plans of 1519, of which a little will have to be said hereafter.[5] In March 1528 the position was temporarily reversed, and Wolsey failed to obtain the attendance of Thomas Henneage—but only because Henneage and Henry Norris were alone in looking after the king;[6] certainly, even a king less fond of his pomp and state could have justly complained at such neglect, and in this respect as in others the Eltham Ordinance seems to have achieved little.

Wolsey, as has been said, made no fundamental change in the administration of the finances but employed the methods developed since 1471. There is no sign at all that any reform within the exchequer itself was attempted. What is most marked about these aspects of government between 1509 and 1529 is the free employment

---

[1] *L.P.* II. 1959.
[2] *Ibid.* 3100.
[3] *L.P.* III. 1597.
[4] *Ibid.* 1899.
[5] Wolsey was working on the reforms in August 1525 when he wanted to see the ordinances of the household and could not because their custodian, the cofferer, had gone off home to Sussex (*L.P.* IV. 1572). The Eltham Ordinance was published in January 1526 (*H.O.* 137 ff.).
[6] *L.P.* IV. 4005.

of highly informal paymasters and *ad hoc* treasurers, often household clerks and occasionally even Wolsey's own servants. Thus, for instance, Thomas Magnus, archdeacon of the East Riding and Wolsey's receiver for the archbishopric of York, acted at various times as receiver general for wards' lands and Buckingham's lands, receiver of the money paid for conveying Queen Margaret of Scotland into England and lent out for the expenses of herself and her suite, receiver of money advanced for the war in the North, and treasurer of war in the North against Albany's invasion, for all which and other offices he received a formal discharge in 1527.[1] The abbot of St Mary's, York, acted for years as paymaster for the northern garrisons.[2] Examples of household officers in charge of government money could be cited by the dozen but a few will suffice: not only did they serve as paymasters and victuallers with the army in the field,[3] but they even assisted in the collection of dismes or tenths in the province of York.[4]

Another striking point is the wide control exercised by Wolsey personally over the various agencies of finance. The treasurer of the chamber received a letter from him ordering the payment of diets to an ambassador as early as 1512;[5] in this case the king was quoted as the source of the command, but there is no such pretence a year later in a letter authorizing the payment of wages to harbingers.[6] In 1522, Nicholas West, bishop of Ely, a commissioner for the loan, inquired of Wolsey how the money was to be collected and transported; in 1525, Archbishop Warham offered to send his clergy's share of the Amicable Grant to the treasurer of the chamber or whomsoever Wolsey would appoint.[7] A remarkable instance of his free control and authority over the various treasuries is afforded by a signed bill, filed as warrant for the great seal, which is annotated as follows:

Memorand' that where this present bill was signed by the Kinges grace to be payde in the hanaper of the Chauncery, the most Reuerend fader in god my lord Cardynall, Chauncellor of England, in the open Courte of the Chauncery the v^{the} day of Iuly the xj^{th} yere of the reigne of our

[1] *L.P.* IV. 3213(18).
[2] E.g. *ibid.* 383, 448, 1756, 1822, 2069–70, 2162, 2216, 2322, 2691, 2977, 4859, 5021.
[3] E.g. *L.P.* I. 3611–14; II. 751, 1034; III. 221, 2822.
[4] *L.P.* II. 2949.
[5] *L.P.* I. 1261.
[6] *Ibid.* 1795.
[7] *L.P.* IV. 1662, 2615.

soueraigne lord King Henry the viij^the caused the said bill to be amended and the annuytie aboue wrytten tobe payde at the Receipt of the Kinges Eschequier.

Every reference to the hanaper in the bill is corrected to receipt of exchequer.[1] Such high-handed proceedings were later laid to his charge; when his enemies hunted around for accusations they could blame him for breaking 'the order of the exchequer' by authorizing payments by his private letters and failing to render proper accounts, or—less justly—for upsetting the supposedly perfect bureaucratic order in the finances of the days before his administration.[2] This latter charge ignored the informality of Henry VII's government which Wolsey merely copied.

The lack of bureaucratic organization exemplified by the indiscriminate employment of individual officers of various kinds and by the personal activity of the minister was nothing new; nor, we must add, was it to cease altogether after Wolsey's fall. Cromwell in particular and later leading councillors like Burghley exercised such personal control even more widely and frequently than did Wolsey, and even the appointment of *ad hoc* executives could still happen, especially in war; but these were then no longer the true mainspring of financial action but merely the frills and extravagances on the edges of a bureaucratic organization. Not that Wolsey's financial government depended only on the informal: easily its most significant aspect was the development of the chamber organization into the semblance of a department of state.

As has been seen, Henry VII had greatly developed his chamber as a treasury for national purposes, and had administered its resources both in person and through officials called surveyors and auditors whom he appointed by word of mouth. This extreme informality was possible only while the king himself did so much of the work of government, and after his death other means proved necessary. In February 1511, letters patent were issued appointing Sir Robert Southwell and Sir Bartholomew Westby general surveyors of crown lands;[3] Westby was a baron of the exchequer, and from that

---

[1] C 82/478, no. 13 (*L.P.* III. 361).   [2] *L.P.* IV. 5749–50.
[3] *L.P.* I. 709(14). The commission was repeated with trifling alterations in May 1513 (*ibid.* 2137, 19).

time one at least of the general surveyors was always chosen from the barons, presumably to secure professional knowledge of finance and revenue litigation.[1] The patent specified the lands in their survey and added the accounts of Calais, the Staple, the great wardrobe, hanaper, and butlerage to their responsibilities.[2] All the revenue collected was to be paid to John Heron, treasurer of the chamber; the general surveyors were to have the use of the 'Prince's Council Chamber' in the palace of Westminster, and the nomination of a clerk and usher. As far as extant evidence goes, this was the first genuine organization provided for the officials responsible for by far the bigger part of the king's revenues. They completed it by appointing an usher, in April 1514,[3] and in July that year a clerk in the person of Thomas Tamworth who was at the same time made auditor for all accounts of subordinate officials not receivers of land revenue.[4] It may be supposed that they took over the auditors and receivers of the groups of lands under their survey from Henry VII's organization, adding to it as need arose;[5] the appointment of Tamworth suggests that the addition to their duties of the 'foreign' accounts mentioned was an innovation in 1511.

Mere prerogative action, however, whether by the king's verbal command or by letters patent, was soon found to be unsatisfactory, and in Wolsey's first parliament (1515) the first of a series of acts for the office of general surveyors was passed.[6] The preamble of this act

[1] In 1515 a commission issued to Sir Edward Belknap, Westby, and Robert Blagge (*L.P.* II. 402); in 1517 to Sir John Daunce, Blagge, and Westby (*ibid.* 3710).

[2] The lands were: the principality of Wales, duchy of Cornwall, Chester and Flint, duchy of York, earldoms of March and Richmond; lands lately of the Lady Margaret, Jasper earl of Bedford, Viscount Beaumont, the earl of Devon; the forfeited lands of Warwick, Lincoln, de la Pole, Fitzwalter, and others; lands purchased from the countess of Warwick and the earls of Kent and Nottingham; the Isle of Wight; and many smaller lots in the king's hands by reversion, or by reason of entries or alienations without licence, or of minorities, wardships, and vacations.

[3] *Stat. Realm*, III. 192, sec. xxxix.

[4] *L.P.* I. 3107(20). Tamworth had been active in the office since Michaelmas 1513. In May 1527 he surrendered the patent for one made out, in survivorship, to himself and John Mynn (*L.P.* IV. 3142, 5).

[5] E.g. Thomas Magnus became receiver general of Buckingham's lands when these came to the crown on the duke's attainder (*L.P.* IV. 3213, 18). He consequently countersigned a petition for the grant of a manor, parcel of those lands (C 82/522, no. 1).

[6] 6 Henry VIII, c. 24 (*Stat. Realm*, III. 145 ff.). The act was preceded in 1512 by one very much to the same purpose but confining itself to legalizing the work of Southwell and Westby; not until 1515 was the particular instance turned into an institution

recalled how in Henry VII's time many receivers of crown lands had accounted before auditors specially appointed by the king 'for the more spedy payment of his revenuez' and in order to clear the accounts more rapidly than would have been possible 'after the Course of his Eschequier', the money being paid into the chamber. Since these transactions were not recognized as valid by the exchequer, the men concerned might find themselves troubled, and Henry VIII, desiring the system to continue, therefore wanted this statute passed. The act outlined the powers and duties of the general surveyors much along the lines of the earlier patent, though in much greater detail, and appended a schedule of the accounts subject to them which answers largely to the list in the patent. The general surveyors were given powers to call the officers concerned to account, and the exchequer was explicitly barred from interfering. In order to enforce their will, the surveyors could order process under the privy seal and appearances in the prince's council chamber. A special discharge for all accountants down to Michaelmas 1508 disposed of the difficulties raised by Henry VII's habit of accounting by word of mouth. The surveyors' powers over individual accountants included all the details necessary to make them an effective agency in securing payment: they could examine on oath and imprison. There is much detail concerning the engrossed accounts and the legal business involved; an important point is that the lord treasurer's remembrancer of the exchequer had to take final charge of all audited accounts. The general surveyors did not preside over a court of record, and the litigation expected and judicial work to be done continued to centre on the exchequer. One section which was not, apparently, ever enforced placed the account of the receiver general of the duchy of Lancaster under the surveyors' control, an exception to the general policy of keeping the duchy quite independent. John Heron, as treasurer of the chamber, was explicitly exempted from accounting in the exchequer. The general surveyors had power to let crown lands to farm for term of twenty-one years, their bills of lease being sufficient warrant for the great seal; they were to have a clerk, messenger, and usher; and no process out of the exchequer was to lie

(cf. Pollard, *Wolsey*, 130 n.). Pollard thought that Wolsey was responsible for these changes (*ibid.* 129), and indeed this is likely.

against them. The interpretation of the act was committed to a very powerful council committee,[1] and it was to be in force until 25 March 1517.

This act was repealed and replaced in the second session of the same parliament by another statute almost identical with the first, and timed to continue until the end of the next parliament;[2] this in its turn gave way to an act of the parliament of 1523 which included a few new points of interest.[3] The surveyors were authorized to receive plaints by bill against accountants; the bill, delivered into the exchequer, was to be treated by the barons as to process and determination as though it had been a bill in the exchequer court. It was also declared that no further lands were to come under the surveyors' powers unless acquired by purchase, escheat, or attainder, or recovered for debts, or for prests (advances) delivered by the king's command for 'any his foreyn affeyres busynes and expenses'; it is difficult to see what other means of acquiring land the crown had—unless perhaps escheat was to exclude some kinds of forfeiture—and the limitation was rather pointless. This act, too, was to have force until the last day of the next parliament.

These acts, then, established the organization of the general surveyors of crown lands, freeing the greater part of the royal revenues from exchequer control and describing the manner in which these revenues were to be administered. At the same time, it is important to note that the general surveyors were far from independent; they relied on the privy seal to get their orders authenticated, and on the exchequer to store their records and deal with the legal business that might arise in connexion with their lands. The new organization merely continued, as it was declared to do, the even less formal arrangements of Henry VII, though a position resting on a statutory basis was in itself more bureaucratic than one depending on the king's word and will alone. The very limitation of the office from parliament to parliament indicates that it was not conceived as

[1] The chancellor (Warham), the archbishop of York (Wolsey interlined in the bill) if he be with the king, the lords treasurer, privy seal, steward, and chamberlain, the principal secretary, master of the rolls, and two chief justices; or four of them as a quorum (sec. xxv).

[2] 7 Henry VIII, c. 7 (*Stat. Realm*, III. 182 ff.).

[3] 14 & 15 Henry VIII, c. 15 (*ibid.* 219 ff.).

permanent—perhaps not desired to be permanent. On the other hand, these shortcomings and uncertainties of organization must not blind us to the fact that the general surveyors acted freely within the limits laid down for them and were an efficient instrument for supervising the chamber machinery of finance. The deficiencies are, however, sure signs that we are still in the realm of household government, even though it is household government getting a little more formal because its natural head, the king, is reluctant to take up the burden of business.

The manner of the surveyors' working may be briefly illustrated, to put some flesh on the dry bones of general description and show that indeed the surveyors differed little in practice from a properly constructed department of state, though the difference—however small—is important and shows in unexpected ways. Thus they were authorized by statute to send warrants for leases to the great seal and did so; these warrants might be simply drafts of the patent to be granted, signed by the surveyors alone,[1] or they might be proper 'fiats', beginning with the words 'ffiant littere domini Regis patentes in hec verba ss'' and again signed by them.[2] In neither case did anyone else's signature appear: these warrants required no royal authentication or approval, and the king retained no hold beyond the annual account over the disposal of his lands.[3] On the other hand, the limitations of the system appear from a note appended to one such warrant: 'Predictus firmarius inuenit securitatem coram Baronibus Regis';[4] once again the fact that the surveyors presided over no court, no properly organized department of state, left them linked rather inconveniently with the exchequer. They only countersigned warrants for appointments, as for auditorships of Buckingham's lands in various counties,[5] or for a market and fair to be granted to Princes Risborough;[6] such things were asked for in petitions which the king first approved by his signature. The surveyors also sat in the

---

[1] E.g. C 82/461, no. 5; 512, nos. 40, 45.

[2] E.g. ibid. 461, no. 10; 462, no. 9.

[3] In consequence there occurred occasional drives to discover the state of affairs, like the one embodied in a list of articles requiring answers from the general surveyors on such details as what lands had been acquired since the beginning of the reign, what lands had been alienated and how, what remained and where, etc. (L.P. III. 3693).

[4] C 82/462, no. 9.   [5] Ibid. 534, nos. 23, 24, 37.

[6] Ibid. 534, no. 26.

prince's council chamber and called men before them, though the extant evidence can represent only a small part of their activities.[1] They were petitioned to summon the receiver of the earldom of March and force him to pay the arrears of an annuity, and they complied, though without immediate success.[2] Such summons was made by privy seal—the famous privy seal subpoena derived from the chancery writ of the same name:

We wol and straitly charge you that almaner excuses and dilaies laide apart ye be & personally appere afore the Surveyours of our landes and other of our Counsaill at our paleis of Westminster in the Chambre called the Princes Counsaill Chambre there, in the morowe next after the fest of Ascencion of our lord god next commyng: taunswere to suche articles and causes as thenne shalbe obiected ayenst you; Not failing herof vpon payne of C li'.[3]

On this occasion the addressee 'comparuit & habet diem usque Octabas Iohannis proximas Sub pena in breve contenta', proof that in some ways the general surveyors could and did act very much like a court. Another time a man was summoned to appear to answer to charges objected against him 'on the behalf of our Welbilouede subgiett Iohn Clerk', which suggests that the general surveyors may have shown signs of rivalling other conciliar courts in matters between party and party.[4]

However, such signs are few, and in the main the general surveyors were financial officers only incidentally involved in judicial business. One of the king's debtors was told to pay to the receiver of the lordship of Brecknock or to appear before them and show 'whie ye sholdnot soo doo';[5] a local commission was to inquire whether a fishery held by the earl of Worcester was in the lordships of Usk and Caerleon, 'Et quicquid in hac parte feceritis Generalibus Supervisoribus terrarum nostrarum Apud Westm' in Camera Vocata le prince Councell Chambre in Mense Michaelis proximo futuro vnacum hijs litteris nostris Certificetis'.[6] Privy seals of 10 April

---

[1] Privy seals of summons would not normally leave any trace in the central archives. Some survive among chancery warrants; how they got there is obscure; they certainly have no business to be there.

[2] *L.P.* II. 3354.   [3] C 82/518, no. 10.

[4] *Ibid.* 527, no. 27. The penalty in this subpoena was only £40.

[5] C 82/518, no. 35.   [6] *Ibid.* 522, no. 11.

1522, addressed to gentlemen of standing, ordered the payment of the 'anticipated' loan to the treasurer of the chamber, with the usual alternative of appearing before the surveyors to show cause;[1] one of the men concerned preferred to take his chance by appearing (by attorney), and was given four weeks to pay.[2] Where issues were concerned, however, privy seals were not usually required, and the surveyors conveyed their wishes in letters signed by themselves. A letter dated 21 May 1523 from the prince's council chamber ordered the payment of an annuity to Anne countess of Derby, 'this byll Signed with our handes' being sufficient warrant and discharge 'Apon your next Accompt Afore us'.[3] Even payments out of the chamber to the messenger of the prince's council chamber were authorized in this semi-formal fashion.[4] Such were the simple means which in the chamber system of finance replaced the personal appearances, bills, entries, and tallies of the exchequer.

These details are enough to demonstrate that the general surveyors were an active department of audit, with some of the characteristics of a court, yet ultimately distinguished from their fellow-departments of the exchequer and the duchy of Lancaster by the fact that they were not really a court and had neither a seal of their own nor custody of records. They represented a rather more organized and bureaucratic form of household government, not a truly bureaucratic part of a national administration. This affected their work little while men were neither inclined nor able to question their credentials, and while zealous civil servants like Daunce and energetic ministers like Wolsey saw to their efficiency. Indeed, the elasticity which went with informality still had its uses; we find them auditing accounts of which there is no mention in their schedule, like those of an army victualler (himself a household clerk), of the household of the

[1] *Ibid.* 515, nos. 7–17.

[2] *Ibid.* no. 14, is endorsed: 'M^d quod tercio die Iunij Anno xiiij° iniunctum est Ricardo Wentworth Militi presenti &c' per Willielmum Talmage Attornatum suum quod soluat Thesaurario Camere Regis denarios infrascriptos citra octabas sancti Iohannis vel exonerat' inde medio tempore coram Supervisoribus infranominatis demonstrat' sub pena infracontenta.'

[3] SP 1:27, fo. 288 (*L.P.* III. 3042). A note on the letter says: 'Allocetur in Compoto prefati Tylldysley [the recipient of the order] determinato pro vno Anno finito ad festum pentecostes Anno xv° Regis predicti'; and there is the usual scrawled 'Allocatum' of the auditor.

[4] SP 1:21, fo. 127 (*L.P.* III. 1076).

Princess Mary, and even of the council's diets.[1] But informality and temporary statutes had their drawbacks, for efficiency depended too much on individual care and too little on the rules and routine which will carry an organized bureaucracy even through the doldrums of slackness at the top. The financial administration under Wolsey was still dominated by the household concepts which Edward IV and Henry VII had revived, and though Wolsey, putting himself virtually in the king's place, might find it satisfactory enough, the failure of Henry VIII to follow his father's painstaking example had already sealed the fate of household government.[2]

We turn to the secretarial organization. Since Wolsey headed the government as lord chancellor, one might expect some significant changes in chancery itself, but there are barely any. Wolsey greatly advanced the importance and organization of chancery as a court of equity, a matter outside the present discussion, but found it unnecessary to tamper with its administrative work. Nor did he restore to chancery its ancient pre-eminence in administration; the routine which relegated the great seal to the duty of merely acting on warrants under another seal was too firmly established for that. Indeed, the position of the three seals remained altogether unchanged: the great seal still important because it alone could authenticate grants and commissions, but of no original force in administration; the privy seal as the centre and clearing house of administrative orders; the signet as the king's special seal. There were admittedly signs that the signet may have been less used—one would expect this from Henry VIII's general apathy in the detail of government; and Wolsey seems to have foreshadowed the future in one respect at least: at times he communicated administrative orders in private letters of his own. Nevertheless he did not by any means neglect to exercise a control over the seals which fitted in well with his general position at the head of things; one of the accusations worked up against him by his enemies was that he obtained the

[1] *L.P.* IV. 281, 1577(11), 1097.
[2] For a more detailed discussion of the financial administration as it stood when Thomas Cromwell took over, cf. below, pp. 160 ff.

chancery for himself, the privy seal for his henchman Ruthal, and 'found means to order the signet' at his pleasure.[1]

The only signs of original force restored to the great seal were two commissions to Wolsey himself, one of which licensed him to grant patents of denization to 'suche personne or personnes as shall at any season sue vnto you for the same' without any further warrant,[2] while the other gave him the power of granting congés d'élire, royal assents to episcopal and abbatical elections, and patents of the restoration of temporalities, as well as the writs of *dedimus potestatem* 'to suche as ye shall think convenient to take the homagis and feaute' of such ecclesiastical dignitaries.[3] These were generous concessions which must have profited Wolsey in power and money, especially the second commission which he no doubt thought appropriate to his position in the church; but neither grant is important in a history of administration. More interesting are the difficulties created by the activities of a chancellor who was always busy on other matters and occasionally left the kingdom. During his visit to Calais in August–November 1521, Wolsey took the great seal with him; a number of warrants were delivered to him there.[4] This led to a general cessation of business at home; the term could not be kept in the absence of the great seal—a fact which underlines the vital place of that seal in judicial matters—and the king suggested that Wolsey send Tunstall (master of the rolls) back to England with the seal.[5] Wolsey does not appear to have complied, for a month after Pace communicated this instruction he wrote again to say that the earl of Devon's warrant for the grant of the reversion of Sir John Peachey's lands was being sent to Wolsey, and this warrant too was delivered at Calais.[6] On his next going abroad, in 1527, the cardinal again took the great seal but left it at Calais, in the custody of the master of the rolls, when he crossed into French territory; however, he gave strict orders that nothing was to be sealed without reference to him, except common judicial writs, and made sure by taking one of the six clerks with him to write such patents as might occur.[7]

---

[1] *L.P.* IV. 5750(ii), p. 2560.   [2] C 82/461, no. 9 (*L.P.* II. 4129); 29 April 1518.
[3] C 82/461, no. 3 (*L.P.* II. 4147); 4 May 1518.
[4] *L.P.* III. 1531, 1621 (12, 23, 24, 26, 30), etc.
[5] *St. Pap.* I. 70.   [6] *Ibid.* 83; *L.P.* III. 1773.
[7] *L.P.* IV. 3410 (Taylor, master of the rolls, to Wolsey, 11 Sept. 1527, from Calais).

Clearly he valued the control of the great seal as a means for making the royal bounty pass through his hands.[1]

He need not have insisted on this so much because his alleged control of the privy seal and signet was on the whole fairly secure. He managed to have Ruthal appointed to the privy seal in 1516, and though on the bishop's death in 1523 the office went to Sir Henry Marney, an old servant of the crown and a layman, the church recaptured it a few months later when Marney died and Tunstall succeeded.[2] Wolsey's relations with the principal secretaries were a little less close, though never so difficult as has been alleged.[3] Little fresh can be said about the lesser seals in this period, though it may be to the point to quote some examples of their use. The privy seal was still very much the centre for administrative orders. Among the extant warrants to that seal the years 1509–16 do not, indeed, show much except warrants under the signet for further warrants in the bureaucratic chain down to chancery, but the years of Wolsey's supremacy offer the traditional mixture: signet warrants, a few petitions signed by the king, fiats for privy seal summons signed by the council, the master of the wards, the general surveyors, the master of the woods, or Wolsey himself, fiats for letters of protection signed by the deputy at Calais.[4] Privy seals for summons have already been mentioned several times; they were the usual weapon of council jurisdiction and their description as 'most dread' by Lord Darcy, whose son had received one, is symptomatic of their effect.[5] At this time the star chamber, too, employed them occasionally, though it later used exclusively subpoenas under the great seal.[6] One of the outstanding uses of the privy seal in Wolsey's time was for the

[1] One other change occurred in chancery at this time: the six clerks were permitted to marry by the statute 14 & 15 Henry VIII, c. 8. This was a sign rather of the complete laicization of the secretarial offices than of a beginning, for the six clerks alleged that they were the last chancery clerks to be kept celibate. Clerks of the privy seal and signet had long ceased to be in orders.

[2] Marney was appointed in February 1523 (*L.P.* III. 2830) and received the obligatory peerage two months later (*ibid.* 2931). In July Tunstall had the salary of £1 per day (*ibid.* 3176); no patent of his appointment survives.

[3] Below, pp. 56 f.

[4] PSO 2/4, files for 1–8 Henry VIII, December 2 Henry VIII, 9–20 Henry VIII.

[5] *L.P.* IV. 541.

[6] Cf. *ibid.* 1048, a petition to Wolsey for a privy seal requiring the appearance of a person in the star chamber in an action for the recovery of purchase money for some lands.

collection of his various loans, amicable or otherwise, and the 'anticipation' of parliamentary grants of which he was fond. In 1524 Warham received a privy seal demanding payment of 1,000 marks, to be repaid out of the subsidy when it came in.[1] A lettter from Nicholas West, bishop of Ely, illustrates the importance ascribed to privy seals.[2] As commissioner for the loan of 1522, he had promised all those due to pay an individual privy seal, inducing them thereby to offer their money more readily. Then Wolsey decided that the making out of individual writs would be tedious and expensive, and offered one privy seal for each hundred with a schedule attached of those who were to pay. West complained that this would cause discontent and remissness in payments. Privy seals were the normal means of government action, and these compulsory creditors preferred to have one each as surety for repayment.

Of the signet even less can be said, unless years of research in local archives should turn up more writs sealed with it than are at present known—as indeed is likely. There are a few among warrants to the privy seal and chancery, illustrating the 'original' force of the signet but also suggesting that it was not employed very much.[3] It was, however, the ordinary seal for warrants authorizing expenditure in the household, and therefore vital in the bureaucratic chamber machinery of Wolsey's years. Payments by the treasurer of the chamber were based on verbal instructions or on signet warrants, and while the former seem to have been more common under Henry VII, the latter were bound to predominate under his son. More of this will have to be said when the later history of the chamber is discussed in another chapter. The signet was used, then, as an administrative seal of some importance, and both it and the privy seal were, of course, freely employed in the ordinary course of

[1] *Ibid.* 638. A similar privy seal, not addressed and not despatched, is among warrants to the privy seal, PSO 2/4, 9–20 Henry VIII, no. 30.

[2] *L.P.* III. 2615.

[3] Signet warrants for congé d'élire, assent, and restoration of temporalities (PSO 2/4, 1–8 Henry VIII; 2 Sept. 1515); for assent to the election of an abbot and a signed bill for a congé d'élire in reply to the usual petition (C 82/455, nos. 9, 11); for letters patent of protection (C 82/522, no. 12). These warrants in the chancery files are addressed to the keeper of the privy seal and appear to have been forwarded by the privy seal for simplicity's sake, a highly irregular procedure.

making a grant under the great seal,[1] though both of them still retained much work apart from this routine. More important than the uneventful history of the signet itself is that of its keeper, the king's principal secretary.

After Ruthal, bishop of Durham, took the privy seal in 1516, Richard Pace was appointed secretary, and it is with him and his successors William Knight and Stephen Gardiner that we are here concerned. Not one of the three had Ruthal's standing, for Gardiner became a bishop only after Wolsey's fall, and apart from Gardiner they had not his ability and influence either. Pace and Knight were skilled and hard-working civil servants, not remotely like ministers of state, though it may be doubted whether in this they fell below the standard set by Ruthal who seems to have been content to play second fiddle to Wolsey even before that minister had come to full power.[2] In fact, Pace and Knight were typical pre-Cromwellian secretaries, and for that reason alone are important; they will give us a reliable notion of what the secretaryship was like before Thomas Cromwell took it. Both were clerics, canon lawyers, and experienced ambassadors, and both spent a great part of their tenure of office abroad.[3] Both also attended regularly on the king when they were in England, to write letters to his instruction or possibly dictation, to read him his incoming mail and the drafts requiring his signature,[4] and to attend to the duties of the signet. Since king and cardinal were rarely together—a surprising fact but easily confirmed from a glance through the *Letters and Papers*—one of the secretary's most pressing tasks was to act as intermediary. All this made for a full life;

[1] Cf. a letter from Cromwell in 1528, requiring Wolsey's wishes for his colleges, then being organized; among other things he asked for 'the Bille assigned of the licence graunted to his grace by the kyng his highnes to erect the saide colledge in Gipswiche, so that the signet and pryuye Seale may be made out vpon the same' (Merriman, I. 320). This is a case where every step in the chain was to be followed, although the process was often cut short by immediate warrants (cf. below, pp. 270 ff.).

[2] Cf. Evans, *Princ. Sec.* 25.   [3] *D.N.B.*

[4] Henry hardly ever read anything himself but had letters read out to him, a sensible proceeding when he might find it necessary to cope with some of the scrawls affected by his servants (e.g. *L.P.* III. 3291; IV. 5403). On the other hand, he seems sometimes to have read Wolsey's letters; cf. Pace's answer to Wolsey's charge that he did not communicate letters in full to the king: 'I nevyr rehersydde Your Graces letters diminutely or fully, but by the Kyngis expresse commaundement; whoo redyth all your letters, wyth gret diligence...Hys Grace doith rede them all hys selffe and examine the same at laysor' (*St. Pap.* I. 79).

the office was anything but a sinecure. Naturally, therefore, one wonders what was done during the secretaries' frequent absences abroad. There was in fact no difficulty, for someone else would simply take over, write the king's letters, and keep Wolsey informed. Richard Sampson, Sir William Fitzwilliam, Brian Tuke, all stepped in when need arose, but the most important substitute was Sir Thomas More, a fact which explains his later promotion.[1] More's place was so outstanding that Wolsey even wrote to him rather than Knight on occasion, though both were at court.[2] The king needed his secretary; reluctant as he often was to do business, he yet attended to his letters with some diligence and had to have someone there to cope with the constant stream. Thus Pace was ordered to stay at court unless Wolsey had specifically asked for his services.[3]

How far was the secretary a maker of policy? Pace hotly denied that he did anything beyond embodying the king's instructions faithfully in his letters, and even went so far as to ask Wolsey to suggest to the king that nothing should leave the court unless signed by the king and sealed with the signet, 'for the suertie off all those that schall medyl wyth them';[4] but this very demand suggests that matters must at times have passed without being seen by the king. It is, however, plain enough that neither Pace nor Knight dared act independently, placed as they were between the millstones of Henry's and Wolsey's possible displeasure; as Pace pointed out, it was his duty to obey the king, 'especyally at suche tymes as he wolde, uppon goodde growndys, be obeyede, whoo so evyr spake to the contrari'.[5] Wolsey may at times have thought that the secretary, so well placed to influence the king, was getting between him and Henry, but generally speaking there is no sign that he had any reason for such fears, and the old tales of his persecuting Pace into madness have been discredited.[6] The secretaries acted simply as clerks and as mouthpieces for the king, though there cannot be any doubt that they were deep in all the secrets of policy, knew what went on as well as Henry who rarely read and even more rarely wrote a letter

---

[1] It would take too much space to quote chapter and verse for this; examples may be found throughout the correspondence of these years (*L.P.* III and IV).

[2] *L.P.* IV. 2558.

[3] *L.P.* III. 504.

[4] *St. Pap.* I. 26 f.

[5] *Ibid.* 79.

[6] *D.N.B.* (Pace).

himself, and must have had some gain in personal importance from all this.[1]

The other prop of their standing was the custody of the signet and the influence this provided over royal patronage. In the letter already quoted several times, Pace had to defend himself against the charge that he had stolen a march on Wolsey by getting places bestowed on his friends.[2] Pace himself profited on occasion.[3] There is little concrete evidence, but what we know of Tudor practice in general cannot leave any doubt that anyone so near the king and constantly occupied in getting his signature to all sorts of documents was in an excellent position for a little graft, nor would contemporaries have thought it anything but odd if he had not availed himself of his chances. A Tudor politician was known by his friends, and no friend would know him unless he served the needs and interests of friendship. The custody of the signet, too, raised difficulties when the secretary was out of the country; it seems that Wolsey kept the seal himself at such times, an irregular proceeding which gave him additional control over the administration.[4] A very interesting letter from Fitzwilliam to Wolsey, of May 1528, illustrates the incomplete organization of the signet office and the part still played by household clerks.[5] Fitzwilliam had to see to the writing out of a number of important letters missive and had therefore asked the secretary to go to court with the clerks of the signet; on arriving, he found that Knight had been before him and that the king, in ignorance of what the secretary was wanted for, had sent him back to London.

---

[1] Much play has been made with one letter from Henry to Wolsey which the king wrote with his own hand because it contained very secret matters (*St. Pap.* I. 1). Tanner printed only part of the letter and deduced that 'the Secretary took no political responsibility...Henry VIII in particular reserved all important decisions to himself' (*Tudor Constitutional Documents*, 211); Evans says that 'Henry...took care to deal himself with matters of secrecy' (*Princ. Sec.* 25). But the full letter shows why Henry deserted his usual practice: the secret was that he suspected the queen to be with child, and though he did not wish to make the matter public until it was certain he wanted Wolsey to share the good news. No question of politics was involved.

[2] *St. Pap.* I. 79.   [3] *L.P.* III. 76, concerning the archdeaconry of Colchester.

[4] SP 1:26, fo. 203 (*L.P.* III. 2719), Tunstall to Wolsey, 21 Dec. 1522: 'Plese it your grace to vndirstond that thys instant houre the Kinge...delyueryd vnto me certain warauntes and placardes sygned thys mornyng as he said by hym, which he commaundyd me forthwith to enclose and to send them to your grace, fourasmoch as the signett wherwith they must be sealyd remainyth as he saith in your graces kepinge.'

[5] *L.P.* IV. 4299.

Fitzwilliam therefore collected a mixed lot of clerks—the one signet clerk present (old Henry Conway who was already nearly past serious work), the clerks of the greencloth and the kitchen, and others—and set them to write the letters through the night. He was afraid there would be difficulty in getting the king to sign them all.

That, then, was the king's principal secretary: an official of some standing and importance, concerned with the king's correspondence, one of his household and close to him, custodian of the signet (still very much the king's private seal), and frequently abroad on important diplomatic missions. He was far from unimportant but still merely a cog in the machine, an upper civil servant and not a minister of state, though in the councils and the council of the king. In 1518 Giustinian reported that Pace had 'the third place in the secret council', whatever that may have meant.[1] Certainly the secretary was by then likely to be a member of the council, such as it was in Wolsey's time. In 1527 Knight wrote that 'My Lordes of Norfolk, Suffolk, and Rochefort, and Master Tresorere beeth preve unto thother letter that I do send unto Your Grace, at this tyme, with these; aftyr thopen redyng whereof the Kynge delyvered unto me your letter concernyng the secretes', ordering him to make answer.[2] The suggestion is that Knight was shown more than were the four councillors present. The man who read and wrote nearly all the king's letters was bound to be deeply in all secrets of state; there is no reason at all to suppose that specially secret matters were kept from him. Trust and confidence, skill and discretion, these were the elements that made the secretaryship important. The materials for the sudden rise of the office were all at hand, but no one had yet appeared to exploit them.

The position of the council during Wolsey's rule has attracted much attention, largely because of the subsequent growth of star chamber and privy council, but until recently the discussion was much hampered by the scarcity of material which led Pollard, for instance, to deprecate all precision and conclude that Henry VIII's council was as vague and protean as that of Henry VII.[3] The dis-

[1] *L.P.* III. 3885. [2] *St. Pap.* I. 261. [3] Pollard, *E.H.R.* XXXVII. 337 ff., 516 ff.

covery, among transcripts made for lord keeper Egerton, later Lord Ellesmere, in the reign of Elizabeth, of extracts from a formal 'Book of the Council', has, however, enabled an American scholar to arrive at a rather clearer picture of the council during its obscure phase.[1] Mr Dunham has demonstrated the existence of a body to be described as the 'Whole Council', a phrase used by its clerk, or by a number of other terms. This body met in term time only, sat usually in the outer chamber of the star chamber, and attended to ceremonial, judicial, and a little routine administrative business. The Elizabethan court of star chamber descended from this body, though the development into a true court could not take place until the smaller privy council was properly established and attracted to itself the exclusive title of the king's council. Wolsey's whole council, which was indeed the medieval council in its last stage as it had been reconstructed by Edward IV and Henry VII, was neither a complete star chamber nor a complete privy council. It fell short of the star chamber because it did not deal with private suits between party and party,[2] and of the privy council because its administrative work was confined to the most formal of business—the swearing in of new councillors, sheriffs, and justices of the peace, the appointment of councillors to the court of requests, the issue of proclamations on price control and similar matters. Time could not have sufficed for all the cases preserved among the star chamber proceedings of the reign: Mr Dunham has proved that it was usual at this time to delegate private suits to commissions, local or central, specially appointed for the purpose. Nevertheless, it cannot be open to doubt that the whole council, the medieval king's council, has now been shown (by Mr Dunham's clear chain of proof) to have been the immediate ancestor of the star chamber who took from it title, meeting place and time, clerk, and entry book. Once judicial and administrative functions had been more clearly separated by the

---

[1] W. H. Dunham Jr., 'The Ellesmere Extracts from the "Acta Consilii" of King Henry VIII', *E.H.R.* LVIII. 301 ff.; 'Henry VIII's Whole Council and its Parts', *Huntington Library Quarterly*, VII. 7 ff.; 'Wolsey's Rule of the King's Whole Council', *Amer. Hist. Rev.* XLIX. 644 ff.

[2] Thus Mr Dunham. I feel far from certain that no private suits at all were heard in formal council sessions at this time, even though none may have been included among the Ellesmere extracts (cf., for example, *L.P.* IV. 1048); but no doubt the majority of such cases were farmed out.

creation of the privy council, so that the whole council lost part of its work, its sole institutional character, and ultimately its very identity, the court of star chamber emerged.[1]

If by his work in the whole council where he administered 'the law of the star chamber' Wolsey can be said to have become the founder of the star chamber court, his work on the administrative side of the council was negligible. The whole council does not appear to have concerned itself with such vital matters as foreign policy, the armed defences, finance, or any domestic affairs. All these were dispatched by Wolsey himself, or by the king, or by either with the assistance of that shadowy 'council attending upon the king' from which the privy council sprang. Mr Dunham does not really become very clear about this inner ring of more important councillors, and the usual view is best summed up in Pollard's words: 'While Wolsey made the fortunes of the Tudor star chamber, the irruption of his dominant personality into the king's entourage interrupted the growth of the privy council and reduced it for the time to political and constitutional insignificance.'[2] This is true enough, but it must not be supposed that the council attendant ceased to exist altogether, and some account of it between 1509 and 1529 is necessary if the origins of the privy council are to be properly understood.

A document of 1520–1 gives a striking list of 'the kynges Counsayle' which illustrates the wide sweep of the whole council. There are listed: Wolsey, Ruthal (as privy seal), four bishops, two dukes (Norfolk and Buckingham), the marquess of Dorset, seven earls, fifteen barons, the dean of the chapel, the dean of St Paul's, the archdeacon of Richmond, the dean of Salisbury, two clerical doctors and four abbots, and 'All knyghtes and other of the kynges counsayle'; if the list is to be believed implicitly, the three secretaries (principal, French, and Latin), the clerks of the privy seal and signet, the heralds, the officers of the household, and the minstrels could also be described as of the council.[3] Indeed, the principal secretaries and the

---

[1] Mr Dunham would not date this until about 1570; I suspect that the development really came a little earlier. He also underestimates the permanent and institutional nature of the court of requests before 1540; for some account of its working see below, pp. 134 ff.

[2] Pollard, *Wolsey*, 111.

[3] B.M., Tit. B. i, fos. 128 ff. (*L.P.* III. 703).

head officers of the household were undoubtedly members of the whole council, and usually of the inner ring, too. Such a council could not govern; it could hardly ever meet in anything like completeness even for the transaction of ceremonial business or the endorsement of Wolsey's judicial decisions.[1] If the king—or Wolsey—wanted advice and assistance he resorted to the small group of intimate councillors, true ministers most of them, of whom some at least were habitually in attendance at court. Henry VII had done so; Henry VIII, even though he relied so much on one outstanding minister, did not waive his right to consult whom he pleased. Hence there grew up that inner ring of leading councillors whose work alone need concern a study of administration. It was occasionally described as the privy council, but the accuracy of this term is more than suspect; these matters must engage attention when we come to discuss the origins of the privy council.[2]

When Henry VII died, and the royal businessman was succeeded by a young man bent on enjoying himself, the hard work of government naturally devolved upon the council. Stow may have been right in his statement that Henry VIII's grandmother, the Lady Margaret Beaufort, appointed a council for him,[3] but the nine men he mentions were in fact the leading councillors of Henry VII. For the first three years of the new reign, a small group of councillors met, apparently, with some frequency and dealt with all those details of administration which later became the work of the privy council— orders for the yeomen of the guard, warrants to the exchequer or the master of the rolls, orders in council, and many other things.[4] There were always much the same men present, and it is to be noticed that the judges—especially Fyneux, chief justice of the king's bench—and the law officers still belonged to the inner circle; the largest recorded meeting is of thirteen. Wolsey first appeared in August 1510 and was

---

[1] Mr Dunham divides the meetings of the whole council into three kinds: 25–55 members for ceremonial purposes, 11–22 for normal occasions concerned with the administration of justice, and 2–11 for routine work (*Hunt. Lib. Quart.* VII. 12 f.).

[2] Below, pp. 320 ff.

[3] Quoted, Dunham, *Hunt. Lib. Quart.* VII. 36. Mr Dunham's doubts whether such a council ever met in formal sittings could have been set at rest by a study of *L.P.*

[4] *L.P.* I. 118, 168, 218 (53–8), 257 (12, 85), 313, 448 (4), 555, 596, 602 (18, 25, 26, 44), 651 (7, 13), 716, 731 (20, 52), 749 (3, 16, 24), 784 (14–16), 820, 845, 1003 (15, 17), 1123 (45), 2441, 2684 (64).

a far from regular attendant thereafter; in those early years he stuck closely to the king, while the council seems to have met mostly at Westminster. It was not, therefore, a council attendant at all, but in capacity and work done it so closely resembled the later privy council that it may be considered to have been a tentative groping towards such a narrower, more organized, governing council.

The last recorded meeting of this body took place on 14 February 1514; after that Wolsey monopolized government, the small administrative council disappeared, and the whole council in the star chamber became, under Wolsey's guidance, the centre of conciliar activity. Judicial matters recovered their primacy, while executive business lapsed. The very ease with which Wolsey relegated the governing council to the shadows indicates how ill organized this group of 1509–14 had been; it was simply the product of the king's inattention to business, of the temporary absence of one hand at the helm, and Wolsey's rise to power rendered it superfluous.

Once Wolsey had erected his power on the sure foundation of the king's implicit trust and the twin pillars of his papal legateship and the chancellor's office, he rarely attended at court and never seems to have accompanied the king on his progresses. But Henry, though no glutton for work, certainly did not ignore affairs; he was always kept abreast of everything, and he always insisted on having some councillors with him.[1] The difficulty was to assess the needs of king and cardinal suitably. In April 1518 Henry left London, taking some councillors with him; he ordered others to attend on Wolsey, but the cardinal seems to have thought himself ill served, and Pace was told to write to him that 'yff your grace schall thynke that number not to be sufficient, to aduertise hys hyghnesse theroff, schewynge your opinion therein: & hys grace wull accomplysche the same'; Pace was also ordered to 'send vnto your grace the names of hys counsylors waytynge apon hym here thys tyme'.[2] The king then had Buckingham, Suffolk, Lovell, and Marney with him, and on one occasion at least he summoned them to a formal meeting though he kept some points from their knowledge.[3] In November 1521 he had four other councillors debate the question of a new deputy in

---

[1] E.g. *L.P.* II. 4288, 4326; III. 5, 14, 2317; IV. 3278.
[2] SP 1:6, fos. 214–15 (*L.P.* II. 4060).   [3] *L.P.* II. 4124.

Ireland; they were reluctant to express an opinion until the other judges could be consulted and the king consequently summoned these.[1] At times the king felt himself ill attended by council; in August 1520 Ruthal excused himself for not awaiting Wolsey's arrival by saying he had been summoned to the king as there were then few councillors with him, and in June 1522 Henry expressed a desire for other councillors to be at court besides Thomas More, so that strangers arriving should not 'find him so bare without some noble and wise sage personages about him'.[2] When Wolsey asked for the presence of Suffolk the king refused to spare him, though this is a special case: Suffolk was of more use as a boon-companion than as a councillor.[3]

The council attendant, however attenuated at times, did, then, continue to exist during Wolsey's ministry, but it was very definitely a group of individuals and not an organized body. When the king was with his cardinal, the conciliar splinters naturally reunited, and officially the council was always being consulted on such occasions, though the decisions arrived at can be seen to have been little influenced by the council.[4] The councillors of the inner ring who occasionally attended Wolsey must have had a thin time of it, for their opinion was not asked, debate was cut short, and the cardinal demanded nothing but ready endorsement of what he put before them.[5] Now and again he mentioned their views, as when he sent the king a letter for signature which expressed condolence with the widow of the judicially murdered duke of Buckingham and quoted Sir William Kingston and Sir Henry Wyat as concurring with him in the need for such a gesture;[6] as the chief assailant of Buckingham he may well have had scruples about so hypocritical an act. More commonly he held the view of the council which he intimated to Charles V: the emperor was much astonished on one occasion at

---

[1] *St. Pap.* I. 92. The four were all legal counsel—Sir Thomas Neville, Sir Thomas More and his father the judge, and baron Broke.

[2] *L.P.* III. 957, 2317.

[3] *L.P.* II. 4355. Suffolk seems to have done his best to avoid working with Wolsey, though whether he objected to Wolsey or to work may be left open. On one occasion he accounted for his failure to appear by his wife's being sick: twice she had asked for him to be with her just as he was about to journey to London (*L.P.* III. 684).

[4] E.g. *L.P.* III. 1169; IV. 469, 582, 605, 1902.

[5] *Ibid.* 6075, points 9, 10, 15.   [6] *L.P.* III. 1292.

being upbraided for neglecting to fulfil an undertaking which Wolsey had represented as a mere form to satisfy the council.[1] As late as January 1529 the council were kept ignorant of so important a matter as the instructions with which Gardiner left on his mission to Rome,[2] and it was not until September that year that the imminent collapse of Wolsey's power brought other councillors to the fore and gave the council as a body more influence.[3]

So much for the council attendant under Wolsey, a group of leading councillors who gave the king the benefit of their advice but were generally kept from true organization and real influence by Wolsey's jealousy, and by the fact that until the last year of the cardinal's ascendancy the king put an almost unquestioning trust in his opinions. The 'whole council', the scene of Wolsey's glory and the ancestor of the star chamber court, was meeting regularly—in term time only—and doing much work, under Wolsey's guidance, in the sound administration of the law; that circle of more important councillors who assisted Henry VII in the work of government and enjoyed a short spell of premature independence before Wolsey rose to power, was reduced to practical impotence while Wolsey ruled. In the council, too, medieval government was once more re-established, for the whole council was only the council of the fifteenth century, with its meetings at Westminster and in term time, though much altered in size and composition since the defeat of the baronage and the reforms of Edward IV and Henry VII who filled it with their own nominees. The modern council, on the other hand, the privy council, was not only not developed but positively retarded by Wolsey's administration. The one attempt to reform the council, made as part of the household ordinances of 1526, led to nothing; its meaning and history are best reserved for the full discussion of the privy council.[4] In the council, as in every other field, Wolsey's government was truly medieval.

---

[1] *Ibid.* 2881.
[3] *Ibid.* 5911, 5953, 5982.
[2] *L.P.* IV. 5209.
[4] Below, p. 321.

CHAPTER II

THE BUREAUCRAT MINISTER

1. *Henry VIII and his ministers*

Before the administrative revolution can be studied, it is desirable to penetrate, as far as possible, into the mind and method of the man who presided over its beginnings, and before that can be done we must try to decide who that man was. In the first place, it will help if we collect here such evidence as there is on the relative importance in these matters of the king and his servants. As has been pointed out several times already, the fact that Henry VIII was not a business-like king who would attend personally to the dull routine of government greatly assisted the rise of Wolsey, but it is not uncommonly assumed that after Wolsey's fall the king turned over a new leaf and became his own prime minister. That is a large guess which there is little to support. Not even Wolsey could, or tried to, govern in defiance of the king or without consulting his wishes, a point which might be illustrated at length from such major issues as the cases of Richard Hunne and Friar Standish down to little details like Henry's displeasure at the meagre communication between Wolsey and ambassadors abroad,[1] or his annoyed surprise at the inclusion of Sir Thomas Lovell in an enquiry where he would not, in the king's opinion, be impartial.[2] Very wisely, and in a manner which contradicts the idea that until 1529 Henry was a child in affairs, he wished younger men to take over and be properly instructed as the tried councillors grew old.[3] Henry VIII was never totally aloof from the business of government. He had all the remarkable mental powers hereditary in his family, and neither Wolsey nor anyone else ever held him in the hollow of their hands. It is possible, indeed it is likely, that he spent a greater part of the day on matters of government after the cardinal's fall, but he was never out of things at any

---

[1] *L.P.* II. 4673. Wolsey seems to have succeeded in shifting the blame on to wind and weather (*ibid.* 4680).

[2] *L.P.* III. 1437.   [3] *Ibid.*

time during his reign. What Henry VIII did lack was the power of logical and creative thought; he was a slave to his passions and snatched at expedients to serve them. But rarely have expedients been used so consummately; rarely has an opportunist of the highest intelligence found so many brilliant servants to supply him with ideas.

The reign of Henry VIII falls naturally into three major and two minor divisions: Wolsey's supremacy, Cromwell's rule, and the last seven years on the one hand, with the first three years and the interlude between Wolsey and Cromwell on the other. Every one of these periods has a character of its own; there is remarkably little uniformity about this thirty-eight years' reign of one king. Lack of colour and precise outline are typical of the two short periods, more obviously so of the second (1529–32) when great problems agitated the state and very manifestly were brought no nearer solution. Power abroad, the search for glory, energetic but uninspired administration at home, and financial weakness mark Wolsey's rule; revolutionary stresses, the grim execution of a detailed plan, efficient government, and financial skill stand out in Cromwell's time; vacillation, lack of direction, uncertainty in conception and action make Henry's last years a period of frequent failure and few achievements. To some extent, of course, these differences were due to altering circumstances, but the undisputable fact that such problems as arose were tackled in a strikingly different fashion at different times cannot be so explained. Each section of the reign differed from the rest in a manner which can only rationally derive from changes in the men who directed affairs. The king was always there, and though no doubt his character and even his abilities changed with advancing age, there is no development along any lines, however complicated, which would make it possible to see in these periods no more than the history of one man's life. The differences lay in the men he employed. This fact in itself goes a long way to substantiate the view that Henry was not, despite his overpowering personality and his ultimate control, the maker of his own policy; of course he alone could turn it into his own, but he did not invent it and relied on others for the mind that must inform action.

If this is true, it puts Henry in a very different light from that now

5-2

normally shed upon him—from the lantern of Pollard's great book; but the point cannot be argued here at length and is only stated at all because it is necessary to arrive at some definite view of the part played by this very puzzling king. If he was not the moving spirit in matters of high policy, it is likely that he was even less active in matters of ordinary administration, and indeed this can be shown to have been so. In the day to day business of governing England Henry VIII was not so much incapable as uninterested and feckless. He complained that writing was to him 'somewhat tedious and paynefull',[1] and one glance at his square, involved, and cramped handwriting shows why. He wrote more than a little, but he never wrote like a practised writer. Long letters had to be written by a secretary, lengthy matters were committed to the memory of a messenger, while secrets—like the queen's suspected pregnancy or suspicions of the loyalty of leading noblemen—were laboriously put down by a reluctant king.[2] In 1521 Wolsey begged him to write in his own hand to his sister Margaret of Scotland, 'though it shall be to your pain', adding that 'women must be pleased';[3] the depth of Henry's devotion to Anne Boleyn may fairly be assessed from the many extant love letters he wrote to her. To make life easier for him, Wolsey would edit letters from abroad by summarizing them in his own,[4] and while this has never been unusual between sovereigns and their ministers it also limited the measure of control which Henry really enjoyed. The king would on occasion revise a letter going under his name, as when he told Pace to bring a draft 'to hys Pryveye Chiambre, wyth penne and inke, and there he wolde declare unto me what I schulde wryte',[5] but usually, one is given to understand, he was satisfied with the version prepared for him by others.

From the point of view of good government, Henry was even more liable to create havoc by his addiction to sports and pastimes, and his easy surrender to a passing indisposition: he seems to have had a great deal of the true and appalling hypochondria with which only really selfish men are gifted. A headache would make him refuse to write letters for two consecutive days,[6] and a headache and cold

---

[1] *L.P.* III. I.
[2] *St. Pap.* I. I; *L.P.* III. I.
[3] *Ibid.* 1424.
[4] *St. Pap.* I. 165.
[5] *Ibid.* 79.
[6] *L.P.* IV. 4538, 4546.

combined incapacitated him completely.[1] But the king's worst habit
was to put off work for whatever else came along, as when Pace could
not get him to write one day 'for the seyynge of hys matens in
honorem Divae Virginis; and thys daye hartes and howndys let Hys
Grace to do the same'.[2] So odd a pair of excuses evokes a picture of
this large, jovial, energetic, and still young man, grasping any excuse
to save himself from the laborious task of writing a letter. Sir
Thomas More once described the difficulties encountered by those
who tried to keep the royal nose to the grindstone. He had, by
Wolsey's wish, read some letters to the king and also remarked that
Wolsey would like the business in hand to be settled with speed, only
to be met with the laughing rejoinder, 'Nay, by my so[ul], that will
not be; for this is my removing day sone at New[hall], I will rede the
remenaunt at night'. More tried again, after dinner at six o'clock,
and the king signed two letters, putting the remainder off till the
morning.[3] It may be thought that this at least proves him to have
read all he signed, an admirable trait, but his overworked secretaries,
hounded on by Wolsey to obtain the royal signature, had cause to
wonder how often they would have to disturb the king to get the
least thing done. When Bishop Clerk came with urgent business from
Wolsey, the king was out hunting and did not return till nine at
night; though he made a start at getting some of the business done
at once, he cut it short in the end—and not unnaturally—by first
demanding his supper. Clerk added that he could doubtless have had
word with him after supper, 'but we thought that the matter shold
be to displeasant for His Highnes to here to bedwardys'.[4] Such were
the troubles of ministers dealing with an active and autocratic king
whose first interest was in his harts and hounds.

Nor did these habits change much as the king grew older and less
fond of outdoor exercise; he found other amusements to occupy his
time, and affairs—more particularly their details—were still tedious.
He lamented Gardiner's absence in 1532 which overwhelmed him
with business that there was no one to do for him;[5] he drove Ralph
Sadler to distraction by refusing to read important instructions to an

[1] *L.P.* III. 1399.   [2] *St. Pap.* I. 51.
[3] *Ibid.* 110 f.   [4] *Ibid.* 163 ff.
[5] Merriman, I. 344.

ambassador because he did not feel like signing, and Sadler spoke of this sort of thing as something only too common;[1] throughout the 'thirties many letters and warrants were signed with a stamp and almost certainly never seen by the king at all. Henry occasionally corrected a draft in his own hand, and this is then adduced as proof of intensive and detailed attention to business.[2] It is true that he now and again studied and corrected papers concerned with church matters in which he had a species of intellectual interest, and that he had his ministers' letters read to himself and kept his control over everything that was being done in matters of policy. But there are almost no traces of him in administration—no such traces as are to be found of Henry VII in his much less well documented reign. Henry VIII rarely signed account books, scrawled no marginalia on papers concerned with the daily business of government, and wrote with his own hand only under protest and rarely. Such a king could well reign and rule, but he could not administer, and he was quite prepared to admit and accept the fact. For that sort of work he had his ministers, his Wolseys and Cromwells. But what he may not have realized, and what is too little realized even today, is that such a delegation of power reduced his effectiveness a great deal; when the work was done by others, the administrative organization of the country was naturally directed and developed in the way which seemed desirable to the minister, and the king's hand cannot be assumed in these matters unless it appears. The minister's can and must.

This is important. The government of England was at one time in the hands of Wolsey, lord cardinal and last medieval chancellor, at another in that of the 'new man' Thomas Cromwell, layman and principal secretary, at a third in that of an immature and faction-ridden board. If we wish to understand the history of administration at this time we must understand something of the men who administered. Wolsey, eager to sit in state as a judge and to manipulate the strings of European diplomacy, contented himself with administering the country as he found it. Household finance, the traditional seals,

---

[1] *L.P.* x. 76 (1536).
[2] Cf., for example, W. S. Holdsworth, *Hist. Eng. Law*, xi. 368, n. 1, and my comment in *E.H.R.* LXIV. 196, n. 3.

a household itself insufficiently organized for its departmental duties, a council on the verge of turning into a court but unable to act as a board of government and hamper the minister, these were the weapons that he employed. Cromwell, on the other hand, was to show himself less easily satisfied, and he attacked the 'medievalism' of English administrative institutions—the household core—in every particular, not of course sweeping the board and creating an entirely fresh set, but yet changing everything profoundly. Wolsey had looked after the administration because he wanted control and freedom to put his ideas into practice in the courts and in foreign policy; Cromwell, engaged on refashioning the very basis of the state, found it necessary to remodel its government. It therefore becomes advisable to see what kind of mind and attitude he brought to the business of government. With Thomas Cromwell, a modern type of English statesman took up the reins of power: the lay businessman and bureaucrat of genius whose sober dress has neither the flash of steel nor the cardinal's scarlet. Government had always been a professional business for the rank and file; now the man at the top was to be a professional and specialist too.

2. *Thomas Cromwell's rise to power*

Like so much else in his life, Cromwell's way to the king's confidence and to power in the state is far from clear. When Wolsey fell, in October 1529, his servant seemed to be on the point of falling with him; by the beginning of 1533, he was—in the words of the imperial ambassador—the man who had most influence with the king.[1] So much is certain: in the space of three years he had built himself a position which in importance at least, though not in outward glory, differed little from that once occupied by the cardinal. However, while the achievement is not in doubt, there is doubt whether Chapuys was not rather slow to see the truth; a story soon grew up that some little time after Wolsey's fall Cromwell had presented the king with a plan for his divorce and the break with Rome, so that he immediately became the power behind the throne. The tale has found its believers and disbelievers, the former on the whole predomina-

---

[1] *Span. Cal.* 1531–3, 644.

ting;[1] what is surprising is that it survives in at least two, and possibly three, apparently independent versions, for which reason it certainly deserves attention. It is vouched for by Chapuys, ambassador of Charles V and the Greek chorus of the English Reformation, Cardinal Pole, and John Foxe, the martyrologist, who all make it appear that Cromwell entered the royal service and achieved immediate pre-eminence as the result of one interview with the king at which he submitted the plan for solving Henry's difficulties which was subsequently adopted. Foxe may have borrowed from the others, but it is difficult to see how Pole and Chapuys could have owed anything to each other; if there was a common ancestor in some unrecorded story going round the 'informed circles' of the time, each reporter seems to have picked some different elements from it and perhaps added embroideries of his own. The fact is that none of the three stories are convincing or consistent; but they must first be disposed of if the way is to be clear to a correct understanding of Cromwell's rise to power.

In a dispatch of November 1535, Chapuys related how soon after Wolsey's death (November 1530) Cromwell was involved in a quarrel with Sir John Wallop and therefore sought the king's protection.[2] 'He asked and obtained an audience from king Henry whom he addressed in such flattering terms and eloquent language— promising to make him the richest king in the world[3]—that the king at once took him into his service and made him counsellor, though his appointment was kept secret for four months.' As we shall see, it is quite true that Cromwell became a councillor some time soon

---

[1] Merriman saw proof of the 'sinister genius of Cromwell' behind the scenes, in the methods employed to carry through the Reformation and in the contrast between the policy of Wolsey and that pursued after 1529 (I. 89 ff.). This view has generally found favour with the text-books (H. A. L. Fisher, *Pol. Hist.* v. 296; H. Maynard-Smith, *Henry VIII and the Reformation*, 45 f.; K. Pickthorn, *Early Tudor Govt.: Henry VIII*, 137). On the other hand, Gairdner (in his article on Cromwell in the *D.N.B.*) and Pollard (*Encycl. Brit.*, 11th ed., VII. 500a) were more cautious, Gairdner because it was his nature and Pollard because he believed in Henry's prime responsibility: he held Cromwell to be not the author of the Reformation policy but its most efficient instrument. At least Pollard had no difficulty in disposing of Merriman's extraordinary argument that Henry was keeping his minister in the background and taking the responsibility himself, in order to protect these 'measures universally unpopular'.

[2] *Span. Cal.* 1534–5, 568 f.

[3] Thus *Span. Cal.* The original French says more reasonably that Cromwell promised Henry 'de le faire le plus riche que oncques fut en angleterre' (Merriman, I. 17).

after Wolsey's death, but we shall also see that he had entered the king's service before this time and moreover had had several interviews with Henry already. Further, men were sworn of the council: they took an oath before their fellows which made their appointment manifest.[1] Besides, if Cromwell was appointed towards the end of 1530 and the secret was kept for four months, surprise must be expressed at the deep knowledge of an obscure priest of York who addressed him on 10 January 1531 as 'one of the kinges most graces Counsaill'.[2] Chapuys wrote his report at a time when Cromwell was undoubtedly the king's leading minister; he was looking for information and had to rely on people claiming to be in the know. Only Cromwell or the king could have told him what happened at the supposed interview, and, apart from the unlikelihood of either telling him about it at all, they would certainly not have told him this particular story. Chapuys, as often, was reporting a current tale, a rumour, and he was not even successful in making his rumour coherent.

Even less credence can be placed in Cardinal Pole's account, written—some nine years after the events it purports to describe—in 1538.[3] He tells of Cromwell, the 'messenger of Satan', persuading the king to choose the evil way in an interview at which he submitted the whole policy pursued in the years 1529–36. Easily convinced, Henry 'sine mora dedit ut inter intimos et primarios consiliarios cognosceretur ille'.[4] This story still tends to be believed—on the basis of Pole's personal reputation as much as anything—despite the fact that its reliability was torn to shreds nearly fifty years ago.[5] When Pole wrote about these critical years he was not unnaturally influenced by his wisdom after the event and oppressed by his knowledge of what had happened in England since he left it in 1531, especially by the recent onslaught on his own family. It is not surprising that he ascribed both to himself and to Cromwell such views and insight at

---

[1] Holdsworth, *Hist. Eng. Law*, IV. 64; Baldwin, *King's Council*, 71, 346, 354. Fortescue thought the oath an essential feature of the council (*ibid.* 207), and the swearing-in of councillors was noted in the *liber intracionum* of the reign of Henry VII (*ibid.* 347; cf. *E.H.R.* XXXVII. 356 f.).

[2] SP 1:65, fo. 60 (*L.P.* V. 38).   [3] Pole, 'Apologia', 66 ff.

[4] *Ibid.* 125.

[5] Paul Van Dyke, 'Reginald Pole and Thomas Cromwell', *Renascence Portraits*, 377 ff.

so early a date as 1529–30 as ought in truth to have been spread over the whole intervening period.[1] Nor does he claim strict historical accuracy for his account: in defending himself against the obvious charge that he had invented Cromwell's speech because he thought it suitable to what he knew of the man, he admitted that—since he was not present at the interview—he could not guarantee that this particular speech was made, but, he asserted, he had included nothing of moment 'quod non vel ab eodem nuncio [Cromwell] eo narrante intellexi vel ab illis qui eius consilii fuerunt participes'. He had, he continued, simply collected sayings heard at various times and composed the speech from them.[2] A sound enough defence, perhaps, against the self-professed charge of inventing Cromwell's sentiments 'ut verisimilia', but no proof at all that the whole story of the interview was true; to question this seems never to have occurred to Pole, though anyone critical enough to query the words put in Cromwell's mouth might be expected also to doubt Pole's warrant for the setting he had provided. The chances are that Pole had heard the same tale as Chapuys, had accepted it as dramatically impressive, and had set about clothing its bare bones from his personal knowledge of Cromwell's views.

The third witness to produce the story of an early and decisive interview, Foxe, was for long considered unimpeachable but is now perhaps too little regarded. However, his story of Cromwell's entry into the royal service is an example of Foxe at his most inaccurate and unreliable.[3] It contains the well-known statement that Cromwell was brought to the interview by Russell (described as earl of Bedford though he was but plain knight in 1529) whom he is supposed to have served at Bologna in 1525, a year when Cromwell was certainly not in Italy.[4] Cromwell, Foxe goes on, went to the king armed with the bishops' oath to the pope in order to prove his allegations against the clergy—this is a clear borrowing from Hall's remarks about the importance of the oath when 'revealed' to the

[1] Van Dyke, op. cit. 387 f., 397 f.
[2] Pole, 'Apologia', 123 f. Merriman (I. 92 n.) does not appear to realize that Pole's words prove nothing for the story of the interview, whatever light they may throw on Cromwell's political opinions.
[3] John Foxe, Acts and Monuments (ed. Pratt), v. 366 ff.
[4] D.N.B. XVII. 445 b.

commons in 1532;[1] he left with the king's signet ring to go down to convocation and scare the bishops out of their wits. This, a pretty enough tale, is quite sufficiently contradicted by the silence of other sources and the impossibility of dating it to any particular session of convocation. Foxe's reliability is not increased when he continues by stating that Cromwell was knighted and made master of the jewels 'the next year' (1531), and then admitted to the council: Cromwell was not knighted until 1536, on the occasion of his elevation to the peerage,[2] and was officially styled 'armiger' in September 1532;[3] he became master of the jewels in April 1532,[4] and—as we shall see— was of the council well before he attained the office.

The stories of Cromwell's one decisive interview with the king which made him chief adviser on the spot are thus extremely doubtful. That kind of story is of the popular sort that gains credence by appealing to the imagination;[5] the explanation already given that it originated in court gossip seems likely enough, and it may have been based on the fact that Cromwell took every opportunity of seeing the king and acquiring his confidence. The one contemporary who saw a good deal of Cromwell at this time of his struggle for survival and left an account was Cavendish, Wolsey's gentleman usher and first biographer. He spoke of Cromwell's rise as a gradual increase of power and confidence, and mentioned a number of interviews without ascribing to them such startling and immediate consequences. More soberly he remarked that Cromwell, having the 'ordering and disposition of the lands' of Wolsey's colleges, 'grew continually into the king's favour'. 'The conference', as he put it, 'that he had there-in with the king, caused the king to repute him to be a very wise man, and a mete instrument to serve his grace.'[6] As his point about the

---

[1] Edward Hall, *Chronicle* (ed. of 1548 reprinted 1809), 788.

[2] W. A. Shaw, *Knights of England*, II. 50.

[3] Thomas Rymer, *Foedera* (1712), XIV. 439.

[4] *L.P.* v. 978 (13).

[5] An appeal which still continues; cf. P. Wilding's 'reconstruction', *Thomas Cromwell* (1937), 42.

[6] George Cavendish, *Life of Wolsey* (ed. 1852), 199. Although Cavendish wrote some twenty-five years after the events described, and although his memory might easily have been at fault, the general precision and fullness of detail which he supplies prove that he kept voluminous notes. Pollard rather arbitrarily rejected him on a point for which there is no other evidence—Cromwell's defence of Wolsey in 1529 (Pollard, *Wolsey*, 262)— but accepted him on the whole.

lands shows, Cavendish's 'conference' did not mean one particular interview; rather he was thinking of the several meetings at which Henry and Cromwell discussed the disposal of these lands.

At any rate, the stories which make Cromwell spring fully armed from the head of Henry's credulity have been shown to be unreliable in detail and in general. If the truth can be discovered, it must be sought in the record of his day-to-day activities which the extant Cromwell correspondence provides. There is no reason to suppose the collection of in-letters seriously deficient in any part, though it is a pity that the business methods of the time had not advanced as far as a regular record of out-letters. Henry and Cromwell, it has been said, in these years 'made every effort to conceal their traces; scarcely any information can be gleaned from their correspondence'.[1] It is truer to say that hardly any correspondence between them survives for this time; there are three letters from Cromwell to Henry belonging to the last months of 1532 when Cromwell had gone far in his rise to power,[2] and the one or two examples of Henry's letters to Cromwell are formal warrants or written records of what had obviously first been said by word of mouth.[3] But there is no concealment: Cromwell reports in detail on various administrative activities in which he was engaged, while Henry frankly enough instructs him on the work he was to perform. In these early years Cromwell knew that his influence and future depended on proximity to the king, so that naturally there was rarely any correspondence between them. But other letters survive: from Cromwell's papers and other evidence it is possible to discover what he was doing at any given time, though it may not always be possible to say with certainty what he was not doing.

In October 1529 it must have seemed that the cardinal's fall would involve his servant, too; Cromwell himself appeared for a moment to have given way to despair, though the mood was soon replaced by a more characteristic spirit of purpose and energy.[4] If Pole can be believed, people were clamouring for his head, and the rumour went

---

[1] Merriman, I. 89.
[2] *L.P.* v. 1055, 1092, 1298.
[3] E.g. *L.P.* v. 394, 829.
[4] Cavendish, *Wolsey*, 169 ff.

round London that he had been sent to the Tower and was to be executed.[1] Stephen Vaughan, merchant adventurer and Cromwell's friend, wrote in great perturbation from Flanders: 'I...am greatly in doubt how youe ar intreated in this sadyn ouerthrow of my lorde your master. I neuer longed so sore to here from youe as now'; he advised him to 'praye to god to lende you a constant and pacient mynde, not doubtyng that ye shall...escape without any daungier'.[2] This was on 30 October 1529; three months later he could reply to a letter from Cromwell in terms which show that something more active had sustained his friend than a constant and patient mind: 'I...was thereby asserteyned all thinges to haue succeded euyn as I desired; you now saile in a sure havyn.'[3]

Cromwell had succeeded in saving himself from the wreck. On 1 November 1529 he left Esher, determined—in his favourite phrase —to make or mar, and promising Cavendish that he would shortly hear from him again. Two or three days later he returned 'with a pleasaunt countenance' and told Cavendish that he had 'once adventured to put in his feete, where he would be better regarded, or ever the parliament was finished'.[4] He had entered parliament, and it is in the manner of his so doing that the cause of his self-confidence will be found. According to Cavendish he had at the last moment changed places with an elected member, the son of his friend Thomas Rush, and Cavendish told the story with some circumstantial detail, claiming that he saw Cromwell ride off from Esher in the evening of 1 November with Ralph Sadler, his clerk;[5] yet he was mistaken. At four o'clock on that same day Sadler wrote a letter from London which, though now without address, cannot have been meant for anyone but Cromwell, and which reveals how Cromwell entered parliament.[6]

Sadler had been to court and spoken with Sir John Gage, the vice-chamberlain, 'and according to your commaundement moved him to speke vnto my lorde of Norffolk for the burgeses Rowme of

---

[1] Pole, 'Apologia', 121.   [2] SP 1:55, fo. 246 (*L.P.* IV. 6063).

[3] SP 1:56, fo. 252 (*L.P.* IV. 6196).   [4] Cavendish, *Wolsey*, 177, 180.

[5] *Ibid.* 177. There is a known case of such an exchange being effected (A. F. Pollard, 'A Changeling M.P.', *Bull. I.H.R.* x. 20 ff.), so that the story is not in itself incredible.

[6] B.M., Cleop. E. iv, fo. 178 (*L.P.* IV, App. 238). The letter was printed in full by Merriman (I. 67 f.), with one small but important mistake (see next note).

the parlyament on your behalf.... Wherevppon my saide lorde of Norffolk answered... that he had spoken with the king his highnes and that his highnes was veray well contented ye should be a Burges, So that ye wolde order yourself in the saide Rowme according to suche instructions as the saide Duke of Norffolk shall gyue you from the king.' Cromwell was to come to London to discuss matters with the duke, and possibly with the king himself; Sadler's language is not quite clear on that point. 'As touching Master Russhe... I will speke with him this night, god willing, and know whether ye shalbe Burges of Orforde[1] or not. And if you be not elect there I will then, according to your further commaundement, repayre vnto Master paulet and requier him to name you to be one of the Burgeses of one of my lordes townes of his busshopriche of Wynchester.'

Sadler's letter makes it plain that, while the king's approval was sought for Cromwell's entry into parliament, neither the king nor Norfolk had anything to do with the provision of a seat. There was no question of official patronage.[2] The men who were to get Cromwell into parliament were both old friends: Rush had been associated with him in the establishment of Wolsey's college at Ipswich,[3] while Paulet had been Wolsey's servant before he became the king's as master of the wards and was still active on Wolsey's behalf in June 1530.[4] Orford, a Suffolk borough, might be regarded as within the duke of Norfolk's sphere of influence, were it not for the fact that no connexion between duke and borough can be established until 1532 when Norfolk was granted some property there;[5] on the other hand, Rush was styled a burgess of Orford in 1521 and his family owned land there in 1538,[6] so that the chance of that seat obviously depended on his personal influence. Again, as regards the alternative of a borough belonging to the see of Winchester, it might be thought that royal influence was supreme there at the time, since Wolsey had

---

[1] This is the correct reading, as the original proves beyond doubt (cf. also Pollard in *Bull. I.H.R.* x. 24). Both *L.P.* and Merriman misread 'Oxford'.

[2] Merriman thought that 'from this letter it seems probable that Cromwell obtained his seat... through the influence of the Duke of Norfolk' (I. 68). It seems to me that the letter proves the exact opposite.

[3] *L.P.* IV. 1024 (vi), 4598; cf. also *ibid.* 6110.

[4] *Ibid.* 6436, 6438.

[5] *L.P.* v. 1207 (37); *Hist. MSS. Comm., Var. Coll.,* IV. 279; *V.C.H., Suffolk,* II. 79.

[6] *Hist. MSS. Comm., Var. Coll.,* IV. 274, 259.

surrendered all his possessions to the crown,[1] but an inquisition held after 14 July 1530 declared Wolsey still seised of certain manors,[2] even though the bishopric was not restored to him and he only drew a pension from it in 1530. The Winchester hope thus depended on Cromwell's connexion with the cardinal and his interests. There is a clear distinction made in the wording of the two possibilities: Sadler will find out if there is a chance at Orford or not, failing which he will secure a nomination from Paulet about which, it is plain, there is no such doubt as about the first alternative. It may be surmised that Cromwell hoped to enter parliament without using the now doubtful advantage of his connexion with Wolsey, and that Sadler was therefore instructed to try the less certain way first. Another point which emerges from the letter is that Sadler had received his instructions before the king's approval had been obtained: Cromwell expected no help from Henry in the finding of a seat and appears to have determined to enter parliament whether or not the king proved gracious.

In the end he sat for Taunton,[3] which was one of the oldest and most valuable possessions of the see of Winchester, producing as late as the seventeenth century one-third of its enormous income.[4] The bishops, as lords of the manor, appointed the bailiff of the borough who was also the returning officer,[5] so that Winchester influence was supreme at Taunton and Cromwell actually sat for the pick of the Winchester boroughs. Though Rush could do nothing for him, Paulet responded nobly. Nor need it surprise us that Cromwell could be slipped in at so late a stage, on the day before parliament met. It was not unusual for a return to be made after the opening of the session, and Taunton itself was not in time for the sheriff's return in 1543.[6] One may suppose a similar vacancy in 1529, the

[1] *L.P.* IV. 6017.   [2] *Ibid.* 6516 (13).

[3] *Official Returns of Members of Parliament*, Parl. Pap. 1878, LXII, i. 370. Pollard thought at one time that this proved both approaches to have failed (*Henry VIII*, 254; *Factors in Modern History*, 120), then seemed to think that the seat was obtained by royal influence, likely to be stronger in a borough than a county (*Evolution of Parliament*, 321), but later appears to have realized the true significance of Taunton, though he never worked the matter out (*Bull. I.H.R.* x. 24).

[4] R. G. Hedworth Whitty, 'The History of Taunton under the Tudors and Stuarts', unpub. thesis (London, 1939), pp. 182, 187.

[5] J. Toulmin, *History of Taunton in the County of Somerset* (ed. Savage, 1822), 307 f.

[6] Cf. Pollard in *Bull. I.H.R.* x. 24.

borough possibly having granted the appointment of one of its members to Paulet who appears to have had a personal connexion with it.[1]

While Cromwell, then, did not rely on the king or Norfolk to find a seat for him, he sought their approval for his membership, or rather, he sought the king's and used Norfolk to obtain it. There is no question of his going straight over to Wolsey's 'bitterest enemy':[2] he was after a higher and more important favour than the duke of Norfolk had to bestow, and there is no reason at any time to suppose that he wished to work for Norfolk. His main ambition in entering parliament was to prove to Henry how useful he could be and to win his approbation. No doubt there were other reasons why he might wish to take part in the important business with which it was generally supposed the new parliament would concern itself; we may well believe that he already had his plans. He had sat in 1523 and may have acquired some liking for the work of parliament in which he was soon to show himself so proficient.[3] But his chief hope was surely that in parliament he would be able to live down the associations of the past and would have a chance of building a new career; as he told Cavendish, he wished to be 'better regarded'. Entering parliament was something in itself; entering it with the king's approval was everything.

Thus Cromwell's entry into parliament appears as the first definite step in his rise to power. It was the point at which the new allegiance became possible, though the old was not therefore discarded. He had seemed set on the road to fortune as Wolsey's trusted servant, but the cardinal's fall had made this start a false one, and Cromwell now began again. For the future of Cromwell himself, for the future of parliamentary institutions in England, and as a sign of what he was going to do, the fact that he determined to base his career on membership of the house of commons was of the utmost importance. Few traces survive of his activities in the first session.

[1] *L.P.* IV. 5407.
[2] Merriman, I. 68 f.
[3] The peculiar argument that his jesting letter of 1523 (Merriman, I. 313) proves Cromwell to have despised parliaments (e.g. Maynard Smith, *Henry VIII and the Reformation*, 49) is disproved not only by Cromwell's later career but also by a less earnest study of that letter.

He defended Wolsey and procured the dropping of his attainder.[1] He headed a committee appointed to consider the problem of 'protections', a matter on which Cromwell, a lawyer and merchant, may have been an authority; the committee included also Paul Withepoll, a leading London merchant, and the lawyer and chronicler Hall.[2] As a lawyer he is not unlikely to have sat on one of the committees appointed to reduce the commons' grievances against the church to legislation; Hall, at any rate, suggests that all the lawyers in the house were thus employed.[3] Most important of all, it was in this session that he took charge of the commons' complaints against the spiritual courts and began the drafting of the document which two years later, as the 'Supplication against the Ordinaries', secured the submission of the clergy to the royal will.[4] Not yet in the king's service, he was active in parliament on his own account, proving his ability and—we may suspect—gaining the ascendancy over the house to which his abilities called him and which in later years was so complete.

Entry into the king's service, not achieved but foreshadowed by the king's approval of his membership of parliament, was the next step. It cannot be stressed too strongly that the title of king's servant implied a definite recognized status.[5] The relationship between master and servant governed the social and political life of the country; it was bad for a man to be masterless.[6] Though retainers no longer composed those large bodies of armed men who had fought their lords' private wars in the fifteenth century, every nobleman and most gentlemen still had their servants who, despite the statute, often wore livery, and were sworn to the service of their master, even if that service

---

[1] This well-known story rests wholly on Cavendish's testimony (*Wolsey*, 180), and Pollard doubted its truth (*Wolsey*, 261 f.). But there is not really any reason for thinking it false: the case was decided in the King's Bench (Pickthorn, *Henry VIII*, 143), and the attainder was pressed by Wolsey's special enemies of whom Henry was not one. Cromwell's defence of his master, so much in accord with the rest of his activities on Wolsey's behalf until the cardinal's death, would not therefore have gone counter to the king's desires.

[2] *L.P. Add.* 663.   [3] Hall, *Chronicle*, 766.

[4] Cf. my paper on 'The Commons' Supplication of 1532', *E.H.R.* LXVI. 507 ff.

[5] In answer to Dr Pickthorn (*Henry VIII*, 130) it must be said that 'king's servants' ought to have meant something more definite than either 'capitalists' hirelings' or 'Mr Baldwin's followers', and that probably it did.

[6] Cf. *LP.* v. 588 where Sir John Gage discusses the case of a man whom he had dismissed from his service and not yet provided with a new master.

now consisted more commonly in keeping his accounts or collecting his rents, or in improving his social standing by increasing his household, than in dispatching his enemies; men entered service either to make a career or as a finishing school, not for the sake of brawling and loot.[1] In the political sphere a man's servants composed his secretariat. Wolsey, as is well known, had virtually built up a civil service within his household, and even before his fall some of his servants had entered the king's service, so that training and knowledge acquired in the cardinal's affairs were put at the disposal of the state. Henry fully recognized the usefulness of such a body of experienced men, and as early as 1 November 1529 Cromwell was informed that 'dyuers of my lorde his seruauntes...been elect and sworne the king his seruauntes'.[2] The phrase demonstrates the formal, quasi-feudal, nature of the transaction.[3]

The king's servants were not necessarily about the court or engaged on the king's immediate business. Among the men thus described were, for instance, the mayor and an ex-mayor of Oxford who benefited from the status to the tune of fourpence a day.[4] While their case illustrates one advantage to be derived from being in the king's service, a different aspect is shown in a letter from Sir Thomas Percy, brother to the earl of Northumberland, who explained his desire to become the king's servant by the fact that his brother did not treat him fairly;[5] by entering the royal service he hoped to gain the royal protection. Cromwell, in 1530, had a similar reason for the same desire. If he wanted to get on he had to attach himself to some person of importance, and, as his manoeuvres of November 1529 show, he had from the first decided to go as high as possible in his search for a master. He was certainly sworn of the king's service by January 1533, a grant of that date describing him as king's servant and

---

[1] Household servants apart, retainers of the old type hardly existed any longer. Charged at his fall with keeping them, Cromwell replied that he had not offended because—though compelled by friends to increase his household by many rising young men—their families had 'found them', i.e. paid for their keep (*L.P.* xv. 776). When a young man, son of a knight, wished to enter Cromwell's service, his father promised to 'furnish him to do you service like an honest man' (*L.P.* x. 206).

[2] B.M., Cleop. E. iv, fo. 211 (*L.P.* iv, App. 238).

[3] It is true, however, that one man claimed to be Cromwell's servant by the simple fact of being receiver of certain lands which Cromwell had acquired (*L.P.* xiv. II. 298).

[4] *L.P.* xiii. I. 1342.   [5] *L.P.* viii. 1143 (4).

councillor,[1] but there can be no doubt that he achieved the status long before that.

It is, however, difficult to establish the precise date of that step. One of his correspondents, Reynold Lytylprow of Norwich, wrote to him in a letter dated 6 February that 'I here that yow be the Kynges sarvand & In hys heye favor'.[2] This letter the editors of the Calendar placed in 1531, presumably on the basis of the only other sentence of importance it contains: 'I do here saye that my Lorde Cardenall ys ded wyche I thynke ys not trewe'. If this referred to a true report of Wolsey's death, which took place in November 1530, Lytylprow's doubts suggest a quite incredible slowness of news; two months after such an event it would have been known for certain at Norwich. However, the story may have been earlier and false, and Lytylprow's doubts may have been justified; it is quite possible that Wolsey's death was rumoured freely after his disgrace, and it is a fact that he was very ill in January 1530.[3] The letter is therefore likely to have been written on 6 February 1530. It makes quite certain that Cromwell had not entered the king's service when parliament was prorogued on 17 December 1529,[4] for Lytylprow, member for Norwich,[5] would have known all about it and would not have written as though it were news.

This letter is supported by one of Stephen Vaughan's who wrote, on 3 February 1530, that he had heard Cromwell was to be included in Rocheford's embassy to France,[6] a mistaken report which could hardly, however, have been made about a man not in the king's service. Hall who by implication puts Cromwell's entry into the royal service at about April 1530, does not really stand in the way of a slightly earlier date: his statement is too vague to be pressed very close.[7] It may be said, therefore, that Cromwell became the king's

---

[1] *L.P.* VI. 105 (13).　　　　　　　[2] SP 1:65, fo. 132 (*L.P.* V. 86).

[3] *L.P.* IV. 6151.

[4] Parliament was prorogued several times from 17 December 1529 to 16 January 1531 (cf., for example, DL 28/7, no. 1, fo. 16); this despite Pickthorn's statement, quoting Busch, that it was prorogued from 5 December (*Henry VIII*, 132; cf. *Span. Cal.* 1529–30, 353, Chapuys to Charles V, for the source of the error).

[5] *Official Return of M.P.s*, I. 370.　　　　　[6] *L.P.* IV. 6196.

[7] Hall, *Chronicle*, 769. He states that Cromwell changed masters while Wolsey was preparing for his journey northwards; that journey was undertaken in April, but Hall's own description suggests that the period of preparation was somewhat prolonged.

servant after 17 December 1529 and before April 1530, and that the step was most probably taken late in January 1530. Perhaps we shall not go far wrong if we suggest that it was the fruit of Cromwell's activities in parliament which he had entered with the king's approval and pledged to support the royal cause.

Throughout 1530, then, Cromwell was the king's servant, and it becomes necessary to inquire whether that fact is reflected in his work—whether, in fact, his service made him also, as has been suggested, the man behind the royal policy. The one positive fact which emerges from his correspondence is that from Wolsey's fall to Wolsey's death his main business was with and for Wolsey. Though intent on power, he spent the greater part of his time on the affairs of a fallen man; while it is true that he used Wolsey's business to advance himself, the fact also emphasizes his essential loyalty. He used the improvement in his position which Henry's approval of his membership of parliament meant to see the king himself about Wolsey's licence to go to York as early as November 1529,[1] and all through the year we find those numerous appeals from the fallen master to the rising servant which have earned so much moral censure.[2] For the next few months Cromwell was Wolsey's only hope.[3] He was to see to Wolsey's pardon, to achieve the restoration of Winchester, to intercede with the new powers—Norfolk and the Boleyns.[4] If his visits to Esher lacked the regularity which seemed desirable to the cardinal's sick and worried mind, he was assailed with abject and pressing entreaties.[5] He still drafted Wolsey's letters to the king.[6] His attitude to Wolsey must be said to have compared favourably with that of Gardiner who, as the king's secretary, might have been thought better able to assist, and whom he tried to persuade into action.[7] In small things as in great Cromwell was Wolsey's stand-by this year: he obtained medical aid, looked after a horse-deal and after cash, settled Wolsey's bills and handled his library, drafted a privy seal to ensure Wolsey hospitality on his way north, looked into some trouble among the tenants of Wolsey's house

[1] *L.P. Add.* 665.   [2] E.g. Merriman, I. 73.
[3] *L.P.* IV. 6076, 6098, 6114, 6181.
[4] *Ibid.* 6222, 6181, 6226, 6076, 6098, 6114, 6226, 6262, 6554.
[5] *Ibid.* 6114, 6203, 6263.   [6] *Ibid.* 6467.
[7] *Ibid.* 6112, 6202.

at Battersea, and was deeply involved in the complicated story of
Thomas Strangways' suit for £700 against Wolsey.[1] In short, he was
still, as for years he had been, Wolsey's solicitor.

On the other hand, there was profit to be derived from handling
Wolsey's affairs. The cardinal made some grants of land to influential
men at court, and the negotiations were in Cromwell's hands. It is
not improbable that he persuaded Wolsey to make these grants; at
any rate, as Cavendish realized, he used them to make himself better
known.[2] The advantages of this business, which continued to occupy
Cromwell into September 1530,[3] are well illustrated in a letter which
John Russell wrote to him on 1 June 1530.[4] The king wished Lord
Sandes, the lord chamberlain, to have the keepership of Farnham
Castle, an office in Wolsey's gift, and he had told Russell to ask
Cromwell 'that yt wold please you' to draft the necessary patent.
Further, he wished Cromwell to draft a letter 'how the kyng shuld
wryte to my Lord Cardenall for his Consent of the same & for his
signe and seale. . . . And also that you wold sende hym worde whether
my Lorde Cardenall haue the seale of Wynchester or ellis the
Chauncellor of Wynchester.' Russell enclosed a letter of his own to
be forwarded to Wolsey, and continued: 'After your departure from
the Kyng his grace hadd very good Comvnycacion of you, whiche
I shall aduertise you at owr next metyng.' Cromwell thus acted as
the link between court and cardinal, and some of the glory stuck to
his hands. The polite and friendly tone of the letter, conveying a
royal request rather than a command, may be ascribed more to
Russell than to Henry, but it shows that Cromwell had become a man
whom a courtier would be well advised and ready to address with
special courtesy. The last sentence, however, proves that while
Cromwell had such freedom of access to the king that it caused no
surprise to see them together,[5] he was still much in need of being
recommended to Henry; he was still trying to prove his worth. The
advantages of his mediatorship emerge clearly enough from the

---

[1] *Ibid.* 6151, 6249, 6108, 6436, 6186 (ii), 6390, 6294, 6494, 6582-8.
[2] Cavendish, *Wolsey*, 198 f.; Merriman, I. 71 f.
[3] *L.P. Add.* 693-4, 697.
[4] SP 1:57, fo. 145 (*L.P.* IV. 6420).
[5] Cf. Wolsey's words in August: '...and hauyng suche [means of access] to the
Kynges presens...' (*St. Pap.* I. 371).

letter of thanks which Sandes, a beneficiary worth putting under an obligation, wrote to him.[1]

Apart from doing Wolsey's business and arranging the judicious bribing of his enemies, Cromwell had other important work to do as part of the Wolsey legacy. He had superintended the dissolution of the monasteries carried out by the cardinal and the founding on their lands of the colleges at Oxford and Ipswich,[2] and his close connexion with both these institutions continued. When the dean of the Ipswich college did not know to whom to turn as the real master of his fate—Wolsey or the king—he appealed as a matter of course to Cromwell, and Cromwell continued to do the college's legal business.[3] At Oxford he still supervised the collection of rents, and his servant William Brabazon made the rounds at two Buckinghamshire monasteries belonging to the college.[4] Cromwell assisted in the sale of goods belonging to the colleges.[5] But he did all this not as a member of the government, a servant of the king's: when a royal commission went to Ipswich to take an inventory and depart with a portion of what was found, Cromwell, who had acted midwife to the college, was not on it and does not even seem to have known of its activities until he was told.[6] Nor did he play any part in the negotiations which followed the king's decision, in the middle of 1530, to dissolve both colleges, even though he was appealed to for help by the distracted Wolsey.[7] The representatives of neither college mentioned his name in their reports to Wolsey, despite the fact that his connexion with their charges had been and still was of the closest.[8] The men they approached—Norfolk, Gardiner, More, Fitzwilliam—all held official and influential positions; king's servant or not, Cromwell was far from being their equal as yet,

[1] *L.P.* IV. 6435, 6460.

[2] *Ibid.* 989, 1137 (2–20), 3360, 3461, 3536, 4117, 4229 (9), 4230, 4441, 5186.

[3] *Ibid.* 6055, 6230.

[4] *Ibid.* 6033, 6217. The monasteries were Tickford and Ravenston; for their being granted to Cardinal's College cf. *V.C.H., Bucks.,* II. 113, 363 f. Brabazon was also surveying Daventry lands at this time (Feb. 1530), which suggests that Cromwell continued to look after some of Wolsey's own property; Daventry was still in Wolsey's possession in March 1530 (*L.P.* IV. 6263).

[5] *Ibid.* 6222.   [6] *Ibid.* 6061.

[7] *Ibid.* 6524. Wolsey also appealed to Gardiner, the chief justice of the king's bench, the attorney general, and Henry himself (*ibid.* 6529, 6574–8).

[8] *Ibid.* 6377, 6579, 6666; 6510, 6523.

and the work he had done for the colleges was not work done for the king.

What time was left him by these matters arising from Wolsey's eclipse he appears to have spent mostly on his private business which occupies a good deal of space in the correspondence of 1530. His legal practice continued to flourish, arbitration between parties being the commonest form it took;[1] but he also advised a parson threatened with *praemunire*, represented in a suit for debt, and drafted petitions to the council.[2] He traded on his own behalf, especially in the spermaceti he asked Vaughan to sell for him in Flanders,[3] and some light is thrown on his business methods by Vaughan's remark that the stuff was 'very subtly packed', being nothing like as good on the inside as on the outside.[4] Like every man of his standing he received a good many appeals for help and begging letters; it is significant that in 1530 such letters never requested official patronage but were addressed either to Wolsey's right-hand man or to the private individual.[5] Cromwell did not yet occupy a position of sufficient consequence to justify any speculation about his influence behind the scenes.

Nevertheless, he was, as has been said, the king's servant from early in 1530, and some evidence might be expected to survive of work in that capacity. Some evidence does survive, but it is so little as once more to give the measure of Cromwell's standing in the state. The draft of a council letter of May 1530, requesting Ripon to deliver up two criminals who had taken refuge in its liberty, is ascribed to Cromwell by the Calendar; as it is not in his hand or in that of any known clerk of his, the identification seems rash.[6] In any case, the letter was written on behalf of 'vs of the counsell'; at the most we could see Cromwell as some sort of government draftsman. That impression is certainly given by the one piece of work he is known for certain to have done in the royal service in this year: he drafted two receipts to be signed by messengers of the king's receipt, a very minor job indeed.[7] Any other work he may have done for the crown

[1] *Ibid.* 5948, 6005, 6102, 6126, 6133, 6137.
[2] *Ibid.* 6058; *L.P. Add.* 676, 666, 705.
[3] *L.P.* IV. 6744, and in many other letters from Vaughan.
[4] *L.P.* V. 808.　　　　　　　[5] *L.P.* IV. 6116–18, 6139, 6682, 6783; *Add.* 691.
[6] SP 1:236, fo. 307 (*L.P. Add.* 687).　　　　　　　[7] *L.P.* IV. 6958.

was not important enough to have found its way into his papers. In the first year of his rise to power he was busy on Wolsey's behalf and on his own, but did little for the king, and that little was of no consequence. Not yet a member of the government, not yet in a position to influence policy, he had none the less saved himself from the dangers of October 1529, had entered the king's service, and was bringing his business ability to the notice of king and court.

Wolsey died on 29 November 1530, and it is almost as if Cromwell had been waiting for this happy release before throwing himself heart and soul into the king's service, though no doubt any change in his position is more likely to have been at Henry's promotion than his own will. But the dates coincide. On 27 November a friend, who had been grieved by the knowledge that Cromwell was 'in grete troble for my Lorde cardynall causes and matters', now rejoiced at the 'comfortable tydynges that you be in fauour hilie with the Kynges grace, lordes, and comunyaltie aswell spirituall as temporall'.[1] Hall describes Cromwell as 'newly come to the fauor of the kyng' in January 1531,[2] and, as we shall see, his correspondence from that time testifies to a very different employment from that of the previous year. In fact, Cromwell took another step forward towards the end of 1530, when he was sworn of the council. The first letter addressing him as a councillor was dated 10 January 1531,[3] and the address became common thereafter. What the council was like at the time of Wolsey's fall has already been discussed;[4] Cromwell's position in that amorphous and fluctuating body can only be determined, once again, from an examination of his correspondence.

Wolsey being dead, work on his behalf ceased, and though the colleges continued to trouble Cromwell a little they occupied a very small portion of his time.[5] Private affairs still played a much larger

---

[1] SP 1:68, fo. 65 (*L.P.* v. 551): the letter is dated 1531 in *L.P.* with a note that it may be 1530. As Cromwell's troubles on Wolsey's account were over by more than a year in 1531 a reference to them would have been pointless. I hesitate to see any special significance in the parliamentary nature of Cromwell's good repute in this letter which may have been a mere rhetorical flourish; perhaps it was more.

[2] Hall, *Chronicle*, 775.   [3] *L.P.* v. 38.   [4] Above, pp. 59 ff.

[5] *L.P.* v. 196, 228, 334, 341, 899, 1623, 1647. Though it was only in 1532 that he was appointed receiver general and supervisor of the lands lately belonging to the colleges

part than they were to do in years of real power. Cromwell bought
and rented lands and houses in 1531–2, and began his building
activities in London;[1] he did not allow his private legal practice to
drop altogether,[2] and his business enterprises were not yet at an end.[3]
But while those building activities increased steadily in the years
1531 and 1532, betokening an ever growing wealth and importance,
activities in his private concerns declined rapidly as his time became
less and less his own. An occasional letter of appeal might still not
suggest any official powers in the man appealed to, but the large
majority—and they are a very large number—requested things which
only a man in favour and power at court could procure.[4] People who
sought his favours now included men of consequence like the earl of
Huntingdon, Sir Nicholas Carew (master of the horse), Sir John
Gage (vice-chamberlain of the household), Sir Christopher Hales
(attorney general), the earl of Essex, the duke of Suffolk.[5] Cromwell's
fortunes were mending marvellously.

The bulk of Cromwell's work now concerned royal and official
business, and especially matters which always continued amongst his
major preoccupations: the legal and financial affairs of the crown.
Salisbury appealed for a jail delivery long overdue;[6] advance notice
was sent of legal suitors coming to appeal;[7] Cromwell was joined with
the law officers in executing the king's legal business;[8] alone or with
others he heard and adjudged appeals;[9] prisoners and felons were
brought to his notice and disposed of at his pleasure.[10] Frequently he
received grants of lands to the king's use;[11] he was, for instance,
Henry's agent in the exchange of lands which secured the manor of
Pishow for Anne Boleyn;[12] on one occasion he personally took seven

---

(ibid. 701), he looked after the collection of their rents all through 1531 (ibid. 83, 174–5,
273, 842). He was also a trustee at the refounding of the Oxford College (Rymer,
Foedera, XIV. 443).
  [1] L.P. IV. 671, 679, 963, 1028, 1065 (33), 1562; 1192, 1339, 1435, 1442, 1454, 1464,
1573, 1723.
  [2] Ibid. 142, 172, 386, 440–2, 499, 451, 620, 672, 1161.   [3] Ibid. 311, 808.
  [4] Such letters occur constantly from 1531 onwards; there are something like 200 in
L.P. V (1531–2) alone.
  [5] L.P. V. 323, 429, 588, 620, 945, 1403.   [6] Ibid. 182.   [7] Ibid. 23, 298, 360.
  [8] Ibid. 627 (18).   [9] Ibid. 507, 668–70, 759, 793, 1057, 1298.
  [10] Ibid. 830, 1092, 1139 (18), 1120; Add. 771.
  [11] L.P. V. 285, 409, 814, 1136, 1309, 1445, 1470, 1537, 1571, 1580–1, 1607, 1611, 1684.
  [12] Ibid. 915–16, 1015, 1445. Cf. statute 25 Henry VIII, c. 31.

indentures concerning land exchanges to have the great seal affixed.[1] He supervised the king's works at Westminster and the Tower of London.[2] When Russell wanted repairs done at the manor of the More, Henry would do nothing before he had seen Cromwell.[3] On 31 December 1530 there appears in the king's accounts the first trace of Cromwell in charge of royal money—he received a sum for the building of the king's tomb;[4] in 1531 he was supervising the collection of the revenues of the vacant see of Coventry and Lichfield and of the clerical subsidy.[5] This was a councillor's work inasmuch as a councillor of Henry VIII might be no more than an administrator—a member not of a policy-making cabinet, but of the outer ring of royal servants who attended to the hard routine of government. Cromwell worked his way up through such administrative hack-work for which he manifestly had a taste, for he never gave it up altogether. The evidence quoted shows that in the two years between his joining the council and appearing to the world as Henry's chief minister, the bulk and scope of this kind of work were constantly growing; he seems to have been gathering more work to himself all the time—to have been increasing his influence and the king's confidence in his ability.

As early as the second half of 1531, however, there are signs that he was raising himself out of the common ruck of councillors and had secured promotion to the inner ring of ministers. In the autumn of 1531 he received 'Instructions yoven by the Kinges Highnes unto his trusty Counsailor Thomas Crumwell, to be declared on his behalf to his Lerned Counsaill and indelayedlie to be put in execucyon' in the following Michaelmas Term,[6] instructions which show that he already stood above the higher civil servants among whom his normal work indicates that his lot was still cast. He was instructed to supervise details of legal business, the drafting of parliamentary legislation, and similar matters, and though such supervision was, of course, still the field of an executive minister of the second rank, it distinguished him from the men whose work he was to organize. In parliament, in particular, he was already a recognized leader and

---

[1] C 82/646, no. 10.
[2] *L.P.* v. 260, 1086, 1467, 1487, 1719, 1781. [3] *Ibid.* 967.
[4] Sir Harris Nicholas, *Privy Purse Expenses of King Henry VIII* (1827), p. 101.
[5] *L.P.* v. 277, 332, 848-9, 1475. [6] *St. Pap.* I. 380.

promoter of government policy; in June 1531, soon after the second session ended, the rumour that 'one master Cromwell penned certain matters in the Parliament house which no man gainsaid' had reached the remoter countryside.[1] But his councillorship had not made him the leader of the council, as Chapuys, Pole, and Foxe, would make out; it had made him a leading civil servant and administrator and then—no other term will so well describe his position—a junior minister; by November of the same year he was sufficiently advanced to be mentioned in the report of the retiring Venetian ambassador as the seventh of eight leading councillors.[2] Two years after Wolsey's fall he had entered the inner ring of the king's advisers, so that at last it becomes reasonable to seek his hand in the political developments of the time.

One business in which he was engaged in 1531 deserves a little closer attention: the attempt made through his friend Stephen Vaughan to enlist Tyndale's pen in the king's cause. Merriman held that Cromwell, needing an 'intelligent and consistent ally to help him carry out his schemes of "political Protestantism"', hoped to find one in Tyndale on the strength of the views on Church and State expressed in the *Obedience of a Christian Man*.[3] It is true that Henry had a few months earlier, on 25 May 1530, expressly denounced Tyndale as a pernicious heretic;[4] if Cromwell was indeed able to persuade Henry to try to use Tyndale, Merriman would seem to have been right in rating his influence high as early as the last months of 1530, and the evidence of Cromwell's correspondence would go for nought.

The story of the negotiations is simple. On 26 January 1531 Vaughan wrote from Flanders that in accordance with instructions (perhaps received before he left England at the end of November)[5] he was trying to get in touch with Tyndale. On 25 March he had a copy of Tyndale's *Answer* to More whose printing he hoped to hold up, and on 18 April and 20 May he reported conversations with his quarry which seemed to indicate that the reformer might at last begin to trust Henry's promises.[6] However, in May Cromwell wrote his

---

[1] *L.P.* v. 628.   [2] Gardiner being the last: *Ven. Cal.* IV. 694.
[3] Merriman, I. 99 ff.   [4] Hall, *Chronicle*, 771.
[5] J. F. Mozley, *William Tyndale* (S.P.C.K. 1937), 187.
[6] *L.P.* v. 65, 153, 201, 246.

friend a violent letter in which he described Henry's anger at Tyndale's latest book and ordered an immediate end to the negotiations.[1] Nevertheless Vaughan once more recurred to the business,[2] but all chances of bringing Tyndale to England were obviously gone.

The king himself directed the negotiations. Vaughan was commissioned to obtain 'the knowlage of such thinges as your magestie commaunded me to lerne and practise in these parties, and therof taduertise youe',[3] he received his instructions 'from my Maister, maister Crumwell, at the comaundement of your magestie',[4] and though Cromwell was his usual channel to the king he was not the only one.[5]   Furthermore, there were no schemes of 'political Protestantism' behind the business: no one wanted Tyndale's help because he was a reformer. The argument which Cromwell put forward in the king's name shows clearly that Tyndale would have to recant before Henry would condescend to make use of him,[6] and Tyndale's steadfast refusal was based on an accurate knowledge of the persecution of heretics then going on in England.[7] When Vaughan was told to turn his attention to Frith it was made equally clear that an abjuration of Lutheran views was the first condition of the king's mercy.[8] Whoever backed the plan had no new policy in view; all that was hoped for was another recruit in the growing group of able men who supported Henry's 'great matter' with word and pen, another propagandist. Such ideas were as old as the beginning of the divorce itself, and they were moreover highly congenial to Henry, as the readiness shows with which he embraced the obscure Cranmer's suggestion that the universities of Europe might be asked for their opinions. However, it soon became clear that no help for the divorce could be expected from Tyndale who had just condemned it in his *Practice of Prelates*;[9] the book against More clinched the matter: this was no possible meek advocate of the royal views.[10]

---

[1] *L.P.* v. 248.   [2] *Ibid.* 303.
[3] B.M., Galba B. x, fo. 46 (*L.P.* v. 65).   [4] SP 1:65, fo. 271 (*L.P.* v. 246).
[5] B.M., Galba B. x, fo. 47: 'Wheras I lately apperceyued by certeyn letteres directed to me from Maister ffitzwilliam, tre[sourer] of your householde...'.
[6] *L.P.* v. 246.   [7] *Ibid.* 65, 201.
[8] Merriman, I. 338.
[9] This book probably did not reach Henry until after Vaughan had received his instructions, though it was published earlier (Mozley, *Tyndale*, 163 ff.; R. Demaus, *William Tyndale*, 282 f.).   [10] Merriman, I. 336.

Henry, then, controlled the negotiations and decreed their end, and Cromwell was, as might have been expected, only an agent in the matter; nor can we discover any new policy ascribable to the new adviser. At the same time, it is quite true that Vaughan was Cromwell's servant and not the king's; he resided in Flanders on his own account, and everything points to Cromwell having put forward his name as that of a useful man happily on the spot. Cromwell may also have suggested the recruitment of Tyndale. He was newly come to the council; why should not such a suggestion be made by him and accepted by Henry who had listened to Cranmer of whom he knew nothing? This does not prove any influence on the shaping of policy; though the whole affair shows Cromwell as an executive agent of the royal will in a somewhat larger matter than any yet noticed, he was still no more than that. The very hysteria with which he told Vaughan to drop the business indicates how precarious the position was which he feared might be ruined by such a false step.[1]

Thus, having slowly and painfully worked his way up, Cromwell at last became a leading councillor towards the end of 1531. A leading councillor, though not yet the leader of the council and the king's chief minister. Events in parliament are the surest indication of that. For it must be said that the accepted interpretation of the history of the Reformation Parliament is very much open to question. The common view is that everything that happened between 1529 and 1536 was part of one plan. From the first session pressure was being put on the pope, and measure after measure was designed to reduce his powers; the work 'began with the outworks of the papal fortress; as soon as one was dismantled, Henry cried "Halt", to see if the citadel would surrender.... First one, then another of the Church's privileges and the Pope's prerogatives disappeared, till there remained not one stone upon another of the imposing edifice...'.[2] Some might see Henry's mind behind the plan while others supposed Cromwell's,[3] but essentially the view is the same, and the work of those years has been regarded as a steadily developing attack, the

---

[1] The letter is printed by Merriman, I. 335 ff.
[2] Pollard, *Henry VIII*, 276 f.   [3] Merriman, I. 89 f.

whole planned beforehand and deliberately. A different view may, however, be advanced.[1] If the years 1529–36 are studied without prejudice, it becomes apparent that the real attack both on the papal position in England and the liberty of the English church did not begin until the session of 1532. In 1529 abuses were corrected; in 1531 a title was forced upon convocation which might mean anything or nothing, was freely explained away at the time, and in any case did not represent a new point of view. As far as the pope was concerned, vague threats had been uttered in the hope of getting an answer to the prayers they accompanied, but no material attack had been made. Throughout those years Henry was in hopes of obtaining what he wanted from the pope; he was eager to reduce the church to greater dependence on himself, as Francis I of France had succeeded in doing in 1516; but there is no indication in anything actually done that he yet contemplated the destruction of papal authority in England. The keynote of those two and a half years is indecision: trust was put in the power of persuasion, the efficacy of the voice of the universities, the success of vague and violent threats—in anything but action. There is no sign that anyone in charge of affairs had any real plan for breaking the deadlock should these feeble weapons fail, as fail they clearly must while Clement remained the emperor's virtual prisoner.

In 1532, however, an entirely new note appeared in the work of parliament. The pope was attacked through his revenues in the first act of annates, though the old hesitation survived in the clause postponing its coming into effect; and the church was reduced to complete impotence, not by the imposition of a sounding title but by the very practical and humdrum destruction of its legislative and jurisdictional independence. The government appear at last to have found a way in which to make their intentions felt; action has replaced indecisive procrastination; a plan of detailed measures has emerged where before there was nothing but the hope that anti-clerical feeling and propaganda might cause a change of heart at Rome. This new spirit alone might suggest the arrival of a new mind on the scene, and

---

[1] Cf. also A. Ogle, *The Tragedy of the Lollard Tower* (1949), 204 *et al.* Mr Ogle's book appeared after I had formulated my own theories on this point; while I largely agree with his conclusions I cannot but feel that his argument is marred by extravagance.

it would be a suggestion corroborated by the opinion of contemporaries that Cromwell produced the plan which gave Henry what he wanted; what is more, the measures of this session which heralded the new policy are the first to provide proof of Cromwell's hand at work in the higher realms of government. He was engaged in the drafting of the act of annates,[1] and it was he who supplied the idea of using the Commons' Supplication for the coercion of the church, as well as a new version based on the 1529 drafts of which he had taken charge.[2] In the session of 1532 his ideas at last gained the king's ear; weary of the hopeless battering at the gates of Rome with voices and papers, Henry turned to the man who intended to throw out the pope with the cast-off wife, to carry through the divorce in England, and to create the 'empire' of England where no foreign potentate's writ should run.[3]

The session of 1532, then, saw Cromwell for the first time engaged in the making of policy; he had a hand in the act of annates, more than a hand in the Supplication, and took part in the drafting of the abortive treason bill of that year.[4] This is sufficient proof that the period of apprenticeship was coming to a close, and that Cromwell was by the end of 1531 a member of the inner ring of the king's council. Even so he had not yet achieved complete mastery over his rivals, and in January 1532 he still found it convenient to deprecate his own importance in a letter to Gardiner, then ambassador to France but also principal secretary, whose absence Henry apparently bewailed as 'the lacke of my right hand, for I am now so moche pestred with busynes and haue nobodie to rydde ne depeche the same'.[5] However, he could hardly even have had such first-hand

---

[1] Cf. my 'Note on the first Act of Annates', *Bull. I.H.R.* XXIII. 203 f.

[2] Cf. above, p. 81, n. 4.

[3] Cf. the preamble of the act of appeals (24 Henry VIII, c. 12).

[4] Cf. I. D. Thornley, 'The Treason Legislation of Henry VIII', *Trans. R. Hist. Soc.* (1917), 87 ff. Miss Thornley placed Cromwell's influence as early as the session of 1531, claiming that the corrections on all five extant drafts of the Treason Act are in Cromwell's hand. I have carefully studied the script again, and I must say that I have no doubt that the calendar was right in ascribing only corrections on two drafts to Cromwell: the remainder are by Thomas Audeley whose handwriting, superficially similar to Cromwell's, can be distinguished by several orthographical peculiarities and distinctive letter formations. It follows that the only drafts Cromwell corrected were those called by Miss Thornley A2 and A3, i.e. those prepared for 1532 in accordance with the instructions given in *L.P.* v. 394.

[5] Merriman, I. 344.

information about the king's laments if he had not been replacing the absent secretary in Henry's confidence, and though Cromwell preferred a pretence which might smooth his relations with the ministers he was superseding, Gardiner had no doubt about the real position. In August 1532 he sent Cromwell some documents—a treaty with France and a commission signed and ready for the seal—'to the doing wherof ye must necessaryly helpe or it shal I feare me be vndoon'.[1] These negotiations with France also offer proof that at last Cromwell was beginning to take a hand in foreign affairs, and in September 1532 a draft letter on the king's divorce was sent to him for correction with a view to leaving out things too secret for communication to France.[2]

Thus in 1532, in contrast to 1531, Cromwell entered the circle of advisers on policy surrounding the king; the success of his policy in the session of January to May that year, the absence of Gardiner, and the promotion of his associate Audeley to the keepership of the great seal in May, all indicate that he was becoming supreme in that circle. When the king went to the Boulogne meeting with Francis I, Cromwell accompanied him, remaining close to the royal person where alone power could be firmly established and maintained; his work in connexion with that expedition, however, was mainly to grapple with those administrative details of finance and preparation which had been his chief employment in the previous two years.[3] A friend thought it worthy of remark that Cromwell had earned golden opinions with both kings; apparently his position, though by now well entrenched, was new enough for comment still to be made on it.[4]

The year 1532 also brought him the first of those many offices which were to be a source of both income and power. In April he became master of the king's jewels, and in July clerk of the hanaper of chancery.[5] The long struggle for the king's favour and the power in the state which it alone could give was nearing its end. After saving himself from Wolsey's fall and entering parliament with the

---

[1] SP 1:70, fos. 230–1 (*L.P.* v. 1245). [2] *L.P.* v. 1307.
[3] *Ibid.* 1237, 1239, 1297, 1298–9, 1392, 1600.
[4] SP 1:72, fos. 11–12 (*L.P.* v. 1509): 'Also I am veray glad to here the good Reaporte howe the Kynges grace hath you in so great favour, and the ffrenche King also.'
[5] *L.P.* v. 978 (13), 1297 (36).

king's approval, Cromwell had been steadily but gradually rising to the top. It was not the sudden inspiration of a great and detailed plan (though he was in time to produce that), nor yet the hidden machinations of Satan, that gave Henry the second great minister of his reign. Cromwell had to prove himself by hard work and administrative efficiency, by showing himself to be a skilful and swift agent of the royal will to whom gradually more and more work came to be entrusted. He succeeded in being sworn of the king's service early in 1530, and of the council towards the end of that year; some six or eight months later he had become one of the small inner circle of councillors who under the king governed England. By the beginning of 1532 his influence over the king was gaining the ascendancy over that of all other advisers, and in the course of that year he acquired office and trust, establishing a voice in policy on the singular administrative ability which was to make him virtually indispensable.

After his return with Henry from the Boulogne meeting Cromwell seems to have taken the last steps in his rise, so that soon the outside world was seeing in him a rival to Norfolk,[1] hitherto supposed to be supreme.[2] The fact that Cromwell was employed only in domestic affairs until the beginning of 1533 naturally obscured his growing importance to foreign observers who were more likely to come into contact with Norfolk or Wiltshire, Gardiner or Fitzwilliam. The Venetian ambassador deserves the more credit for realizing the truth as early as November 1531. As we have already seen, in April 1533 even Chapuys had come to the conclusion that Cromwell was 'ruling everything'. Cromwell had reached his goal: beyond any possibility of doubt he was now the king's chief minister. He had been very nearly that for about a year but not much longer, and he was to dig himself in still more deeply as offices and honours fell thick upon him; nevertheless he was never to be more than he was then—the most powerful man in England after the king. He had achieved this position by sheer hard work and detailed ability; he had achieved it after two years of dogged persistence; and he had raised it on a foundation of executive and administrative work before ever he had

---

[1] *Span. Cal. 1531–3*, 601, 618.
[2] *Ibid.* 292, 416, 460; *Ven. Cal.* IV. 694.

a chance of putting into practice his own views in the field of policy, a choice of ground, or an imposed necessity, which indicates where his special abilities lay.

3. Cromwell's offices

Though Cromwell made his way to power by dint of his exceptional ability in administration and business, he did not set the seal on his achievement by obtaining office until after the parliamentary session of 1532 had shown that he had made the king listen to his political schemes. In March 1532 the Commons' Supplication against the Ordinaries was presented to the king, a document with whose origin, purpose, and ultimate use Cromwell was most intimately associated; early in April he became master of the jewels. None of his early offices were important; none gave him an outstanding place in court or council; yet he was already beyond doubt one of the king's foremost councillors and soon appeared head and shoulders above the rest. Eminence in the royal councils did not depend on office which might be added by way of reward: the mastership of the jewels was very probably granted in acknowledgment of Cromwell's parliamentary services early in 1532. Administrative control, on the other hand, was a different matter. Though personality still meant more than position, the central government was already sufficiently organized to compel a man to seek specific offices if he wished to exercise minute and precise influence on its working. The kind of process by which Hubert Walter, for instance, in the late twelfth century, on being forced to relinquish the office of justiciar, took that of chancellor and made it in turn supreme in the administration, was not yet entirely dead; where Wolsey had ruled as chancellor, Cromwell was to display equal power as secretary and later as lord privy seal. At the top the man mattered more than the office. But in the ranks of the civil service proper, office meant more than the man; a household official had no voice in the exchequer, a chancery official like the master of the rolls could not control the clerks of the signet or privy seal, and the detailed working of any department could only be supervised effectively from inside it. For that reason Cromwell's offices are important: they describe the character and extent of his administration.

He was a lay pluralist; as Wolsey gathered ecclesiastical prefer-ments, so he collected offices under the crown. It was unusual for one of the king's ministers to occupy so many different positions at the same time, though it was not unknown: Sir John Heron, treasurer of the chamber, had in addition been made clerk of the jewel house, chamberlain of the exchequer, supervisor of customs in London, and clerk of the hanaper, a collection which gave him a share in a good many different branches of the finances.[1] However, Heron was after all only a senior civil servant; Cromwell, the king's chief minister, was much more than that, and his engrossing of lay preferments sounded a new note. His purpose may have been Wolsey's—enrichment—or it may have more nearly resembled Heron's—influence; only detailed discussion can discover what lay behind Cromwell's astonishing ubiquity. It is not proposed to deal with all the offices he held; his ecclesiastical appointments (vicar general and vicegerent in spirituals) played no part in the government of the state, the mastership of the wards, wrongly ascribed to him, will not appear,[2] and several minor posts need not be considered. There remain his six major secular offices, acquired in this order: master of the king's jewels (14 April 1532),[3] keeper or clerk of the hanaper of chancery (16 July 1532),[4] chancellor of the exchequer (12 April 1533),[5] principal or chief secretary (about April 1534), master of the rolls (8 October 1534),[6] lord privy seal (2 July 1536).[7] When in addition he was made great chamberlain of England in April 1540,[8] he acquired a high dignity but not an office of importance in the administration.

Cromwell's first three offices had several points in common. They were all concerned with financial matters: the master of the jewels occupied a minor but not unimportant place in the household as the official responsible for the custody of jewellery and plate in which the age generally laid up its reserves; the clerk of the hanaper adminis-

---

[1] A. P. Newton, in *E.H.R.* XXXII, 357.
[2] See App. I.
[3] *L.P.* v. 978 (13).
[4] *Ibid.* 1207 (36).
[5] *L.P.* VI. 417 (22).
[6] *L.P.* VII. 1352 (3).
[7] *L.P.* IX. 202 (3).
[8] *L.P.* XV. 540.

tered the treasury of chancery; and the chancellor of the exchequer kept the exchequer seal. The salaries appertaining to the offices were not large. Most significant of all, not one of the three offices could be described as really important; it must cause some surprise that a man of such power in the state as Cromwell was from 1532 onwards should have troubled himself with these minor posts. He retained all three until his fall, though he shared the mastership of the jewels from some date late in 1535 or early in 1536 with John Williams, hitherto clerk of the jewels,[1] and the hanaper from 24 April 1535 with another of his servants and followers, Ralph Sadler, who was to be connected with the office for some fifty years.[2]

The salaries may first be considered. The master of the jewels, a chamber official but paid by the exchequer,[3] received £50 a year, paid in equal portions at Michaelmas and Lady Day,[4] and Cromwell's private accounts show that he received this sum and no more.[5] It is not quite clear what happened after the appointment of the two joint holders. One would suppose that the fee was divided, and indeed it

---

[1] The patent is dated by the regnal year only—27 Henry VIII, the year ending on 21 April 1536 (*L.P.* x. 776, 1). The first year in which Cromwell and Williams shared the fee of the office was 1536-7 (E 405/203), but the exchequer was commonly rather behindhand in these matters: in 1532 the fee was recorded as going to Robert Amadas, dead for six months, and in 1540 to Cromwell, despite his fall in June, as well as Williams (B.M., Add. MS. 33376; E 405/205). Cromwell had a copy of the 'patent of the jewel house' sent to himself by one of his servants in September 1535 (*L.P.* IX. 359, 372); presumably he was then beginning to think of sharing the office. The fact that the exchequer recorded the payment of the fee to him alone in 1536 (E 164/69) also suggests that the joint patent was granted rather late in 27 Henry VIII. Williams does not appear in the office until the beginning of 1538 (*L.P.* XIII. I. 384, 98; B.M., Arundel MS. 97, fo. 55—the lord privy seal is mentioned separately on fo. 54 v.), but after that references to him are frequent. He succeeded as sole master on Cromwell's death (*D.N.B.*), no new patent being required since the old one was granted in survivorship.

[2] Cromwell's and Sadler's joint patent does not appear to have been enrolled but survives in a copy in a precedent book (C 193/2, fos. 61 v–64). The hanaper accounts name them together from Michaelmas 1535 onwards (E 101/222/8).

[3] Newton in *E.H.R.* XXXII. 349.   [4] C 66/659, m. 36.

[5] *L.P.* VI. 841: half year's fee of the jewel-house—£25; *L.P.* IX. 478: £75 for the period Michaelmas 1533 to 1535 (that is, £25 each at Lady Day 1534 and 1535 and at Michaelmas 1534, so that the exchequer must have been backward in its payments). *L.P.* XI. 135 gives Cromwell's accounts for Michaelmas 1535 to 21 July 1536, and records £25 as the half year's fee of the jewel-house, so that the £25 due at Michaelmas 1535 seems to have slipped through. The tellers' accounts for that year are missing. Whatever the answer, it is plain that Cromwell drew at most his official salary.

was paid in equal parts, and separately, to Cromwell and Williams in
1537.[1] For the remaining three years it was all paid into Williams'
hands though supposedly meant for both of them,[2] and one cannot
be sure whether Williams kept the total or made over £25 to Cromwell. It may be conjectured that the latter happened, for there could
hardly be any reason for Cromwell to continue holding such a minor
office except the money which it brought him.

The fees and emoluments of the hanaper were also described in
the patent of appointment.[3] There was the traditional salary, 'vadia
feoda robas & regardia quecumque eidem officio aliquo modo ab
antiquo debita & consueta'. These had for centuries consisted of
sixpence a day, or £9. 2s. 6d. a year, in fees[4] and of winter and summer robes for which the keeper received the sum of £2. 6s. 8d. in
cash.[5] The keeper further had an annuity of £40 chargeable on the
revenues of the hanaper and, lastly, the sum of 1s. 6d. for every day
spent 'attendendo & equitando cum cancellario nostro Anglie'.
Though it has been stated that as early as 1516 this had become
stereotyped at 1s. 6d. for every day of the year,[6] the first year for
which a fee for 365 days—£27. 7s. 6d.—was paid was the first year
of Edward VI (1547);[7] there are no variations after that date. While
Cromwell held the office, the accounts show that at least a pretence
was kept up of paying only for days actually spent on duty.[8] The
clerk of the hanaper could, therefore, expect to draw £51. 9s. 2d. plus
an average of about 200 days at 1s. 6d. each, a rough total of £65
a year altogether.

In addition to this there would be the profits from suitors to the
seal, but there is no knowing what they amounted to. A chancery
order of 1622 stated that 'one of the cheifest proffitts belonginge
formerly unto the said office of clerke of the hanaper was the receipt
of fynes for all licences and pardons of alienacion writts of covenant

[1] E 405/203.　　　　　　　[2] Ibid. 204–5.
[3] C 66/660, m. 33.
[4] H. Maxwell Lyte, Historical Notes on the Use of the Great Seal (1926), 284.
[5] Cf. expense accounts of the hanaper, e.g. E 101/222/11.
[6] Lyte, loc. cit.
[7] E 101/224/7. In 1544, only 278 days were charged against the hanaper revenues
(ibid. 224/2), and no accounts survive for the two years following.
[8] The figures are 192, 194, and 213 days for the years ending Michaelmas 1535, 1536,
and 1540 (E 101/222/7, 11; 223/6).

and writts for entry of recoveries', no doubt a considerable sum, for it was the granting away of these profits ('which were auncyently payd into the hanaper') under Elizabeth which led to the order appointing very large fees for the clerk.[1] However, these fines were entered in the hanaper accounts, and the complaint in 1622 was that owing to their cessation the office no longer paid its way; in the early sixteenth century they were certainly not part of the clerk's per-quisites. It is possible that even in Cromwell's time the keeper was entitled to the two shillings for the sealing of every 'perpetuity' which he received later[2] and which did not go into the official account, but nothing is known for certain. At any rate, the office provided a good income for a minor official.

The question of how much Cromwell received from the hanaper is complicated by the fact that the official accounts tell a different story from that revealed by his private accounts. If we believe the 'petitions for allowances' presented by the clerk,[3] all the fees listed above were paid out year by year, allowance being claimed regularly for the keeper's salary, robes, and annuity, and for a specified number of days of the special allowance. However, the date of an account is small guarantee for the date on which it was actually made up, nor were salaries normally paid in the sixteenth century on the day on which they were due. More accurate knowledge about Cromwell's income from the hanaper is obtained from his own accounts. During the period from January to July 1533 he received £66. 17s. 4d.,[4] which seems reasonable enough: something over £30 would have been due in fees in that half year, and the balance was made up of those unofficial profits on which it is generally supposed officials of the time lived. But what may be made of the fact that for the two years ending at Michaelmas 1535 he had only £58 from the hanaper?[5] At the very least, even leaving out the troublesome eighteenpence a day, something like £100 ought to have been expected. For the half year which followed this account Cromwell got £29. 6s. 4.,[6]

---

[1] G. W. Sanders, *Orders of the High Court of Chancery* (1845), 136.
[2] Lyte, *Great Seal*, 336.
[3] Those surviving for the period of Cromwell's keepership are E 101/222/7, 11; 223/2, 6, for the years ending at Michaelmas 1535, 1536, 1539, and 1540.
[4] *L.P.* VI. 841.   [5] *L.P.* IX. 478.
[6] SP 1 : 105, fo. 97 v (*L.P.* XI. 135).

broken down in the account into items: his half year's annuity (£20), fee at sixpence a day (£4. 11s. 3d.), winter livery (£1. 6s. 8d.), and a fee for his clerk at 4½d. a day which is not mentioned at all in the official hanaper accounts. If this clerk was Cromwell's deputy, the underclerk of the hanaper, the accounts provide no trace of such a sum being paid to him either. The money and its recipient must remain an unsolved mystery.[1]

At any rate, after the first half year there is no sign that Cromwell was receiving large sums in customary but unofficial fees. In fact, he barely got the minimum due to him, and it can be said with some assurance that he did not draw the 1s. 6d. a day for special expenses to which his patent entitled him. What became of these sums, which appear year by year in the hanaper accounts, can only be surmised; perhaps they went to his deputy who did most of the work but ostensibly received only one mark for his winter robe from the hanaper.[2] The accounts use a curious phrase, describing the money as spent 'pro expensis equorum circa attendentium cum Cancellario', a wording which offers no clue to the real destiny of the fee.[3] It is more than likely, too, that the underclerk, as the active official, also received the customary profits due on certain instruments under the great seal. At any rate, Cromwell did not get these, and he did not use the clerkship of the hanaper for the purpose of enriching himself; at most, he received his basic fees, amounting apparently to anything between £30 and £60 a year, and probably shared with Sadler from 1535.

The chancellorship of the exchequer presents a much easier

---

[1] A further difficulty is introduced by the fact that this full half year's fee was received at a time when Cromwell was sharing the office with Sadler who surely did not go without a share in the profits. Would he perhaps receive the fees for the second half year?

[2] E 101/222/11.

[3] Down to the keepership of Thomas Hall the phrase ran 'in expensis dicti Custodis & deputati sui equitantium cum domino Cancellario' (E 101/220/7). Perhaps because the fiction of a travelling chancery could no longer be maintained, it was then changed to 'pro expensis equorum' (ibid. 221/10; used for the last time in 1544, ibid. 224/2). The change to a fixed payment for 365 days coincided with yet another change in the wording. The money was thereafter spent 'pro omnibus custubus & expensis dicti Custodis in seruiciendo domino Cancellario' (ibid. 227/8): the pretence that especially arduous duties were to be covered by it had been given up. It may not be fanciful to connect the last change with the appointment of John Hales as Sadler's partner in October 1545 (C 66/785, m. 34), and perhaps with lord chancellor Wriothesley's orders of May 1545, part of which is lost (Sanders, Orders of Chancery, 8 f.).

problem; the annual fee of the office was £23. 13s. 4d.,[1] and Cromwell's accounts show that he normally received this and no more. For each of the half years ending in March 1533 and 1536 he had £13. 6s. 8d.[2] For the two years ending at Michaelmas 1535, however, he got £65. 10s., or some £12 more than his salary would account for;[3] if this £12 constituted special pickings for a period of two years they cannot be said to have amounted to much, and altogether the emoluments of the office were not considerable. In fact, the emoluments of all three offices were not particularly striking—some £140 a year unshared, or £85 after 1535. Cromwell, who had a heavy expenditure in these years in buying land and building houses as well as the ordinary cost of an ever increasing household, may well have welcomed the possession of even such a comparatively small addition to his revenues, but it is likely that there was more behind his accumulation of lesser offices. It becomes necessary to inquire in detail what real standing and precise functions these three officials had.

The mastership of the jewels, as has already been indicated, was a household office, closely connected with the chamber; in the time of Richard II the receiver of the chamber had also been keeper of certain jewels there.[4] Although jewels were kept in various places, a special keepership evolved from this office, and when the office of the jewel-house became established in the fifteenth century its head might be called either the keeper of the king's jewels or the treasurer of the chamber, so close was the link between the two.[5] The posts were still combined under Edward IV and Richard II,[6] and as late as 1533 a royal official—Sir William Skeffyngton, master of the ordnance—could make the mistake of addressing Cromwell as treasurer of the chamber.[7] The keeper of the jewels was responsible

---

[1] 'Declarations of the State of the Treasury' (E 405: cf. Giuseppi, *Guide*, I. 192), *passim*. It may be taken as one of the first signs of greater importance attaching to the chancellorship that these Declarations always put the chancellor before the barons who received a higher fee, though the assessment of an office by its salary is a more reliable guide.

[2] *L.P.* VI. 841; XI. 135.   [3] *L.P.* IX. 478.

[4] Tout, *Chapters*, IV. 197, 204. However, another keeper of the jewels of the same period appears to have had no connexion with the chamber (*ibid.* 334–5).

[5] *Ibid.* 336–7.   [6] Newton, *E.H.R.* XXXII, 350–1.

[7] *L.P.* VI. 1290.

for looking after the king's bullion reserve in plate and jewels which was kept in the chamber, and until Henry VII promoted the treasurer of the chamber to a high position in the national financial administration the treasurer was on the whole more important for that part of his duties which made him keeper of the jewels. However, the reforms of Henry VII separated the two offices, and by advancing the treasurer of the chamber rendered the keeper of the jewels of secondary importance.[1] Cromwell's predecessor in office, Robert Amadas, was a goldsmith and citizen of London,[2] who appears to have been in charge of Wolsey's jewels before he took over the keepership of the king's.[3] He was concerned exclusively with jewels and plate, and the accounts of the treasurer of the chamber note him only as receiving and paying money for such matters, usually for plate given to ambassadors.[4] As master of the king's jewels he did the work which a strict interpretation of the title allowed, and the appointment of a goldsmith was both obvious and significant. Cromwell's first office was therefore one which by a fairly recent tradition had become no more than the custodianship of the king's plate and jewels but which had at one time come near to being the leading financial appointment in the chamber; even so it was never more than a minor office. The chamber no sooner entered upon its career as a major department of state than the master of the jewels dropped back into obscurity. However, it was a household office, and like most household offices up to this time it was capable of being exploited in new and unexpected directions.

The clerk of the hanaper, on the other hand, occupied a fixed place in the administration; his was not an office which could be modified by an energetic man, but it was in itself rather more important than the mastership of the jewels and had achieved its

---

[1] A complication is introduced by Sir Henry Wyat, treasurer of the chamber from 1524 to 1528, who was also drawing £20 a year as master of the jewels, at a time when others, called treasurers of the jewels, were paid their £50 ('Declarations, etc.', *passim*). This is the only case where a distinction was made between a master and a treasurer, and it was obviously merely one of convenience to exchequer officials. Wyat drew his money without doing any work connected with jewels, all of which was in the hands of Cromwell and his predecessor Amadas.

[2] *Lists of Early Chancery Proceedings*, VI. 2, 4.

[3] *L.P.* IV. 1662, 6748 (5). His patent was dated 20 April 1526 (*ibid.* 2114), but he was active in the office as early as October 1524 (*ibid.* 695).

[4] *L.P.* V. 311, 315, 316, 319, 321, 323, 325.

position in the administration by the reign of Richard II.[1] Its duties are defined easily enough: the clerk administered the profits of the great seal; he was the treasurer of chancery.[2] An order in chancery of 1622 declared that the office had always been one of great trust and involving considerable business for the clerk who had to be in continual attendance on the great seal, either in person or by deputy; 'the clerkes of the Hanaper heretofore were men of great account, as the Lord Cromwell Earle of Essex'.[3] Cromwell's joint keeper and successor, Sir Ralph Sadler, was to be principal secretary and keeper of the great wardrobe while he held the office. Though, therefore, the clerkship of the hanaper was not in itself very important, it could well be held by men aspiring to importance; as the department which dealt with the financial side of chancery business, with the collection of its profits and the payment of its running costs, the hanaper had a place of some note in the administration. Its accounts record a considerable and steady income from a number of sources:[4] the fees for the sealing of all documents issued by the chancery, as well as fines payable on certain types of grants—these made up the income of the chancery proper; the fees payable for writs sued out of the courts of justice, collected there but delivered into the hanaper where they were accounted for term by term; and lastly, some odds and ends—fines payable on the restitution of the temporalities of ecclesiastical benefices, or fines on the bonds known as statutes staple. It is difficult to arrive at accurate totals, for where a check is possible the figures invariably disagree,[5] but it can be said that income in the hanaper fluctuated between about £2,000 and £3,000 a year. The significant figures are those of surplus after the expenses had been paid, and these averaged something like £1,200 a year, though here again there were considerable fluctuations. Of this the better

---

[1] Tout, *Chapters*, III. 444.

[2] *Ibid.* I. 286: 'The keeper of the hanaper received the fees of the seal, paid the expenses of the chancery organisation, and presented the accounts of his administration for review.'   [3] Sanders, *Orders of Chancery*, 135.

[4] The hanaper accounts for this period are preserved among the Various Accounts of the exchequer, E 101.

[5] The detailed account for the year 1533–4 adds up to a total of £2,069 (E 101/222/4), while the abstracted statement of account gives £2,889 (*L.P.* VII, 1204). A similar discrepancy exists for 1538–9, the figures being £2,279 and £2,486 (E 101/223/1; *L.P.* XIV. I. 252).

part went to the chamber which could expect between £800 and £1,000 from this source, while the balance remained in the hanaper. The chancery thus supplied a not inconsiderable sum every year to the royal revenue, the chief merit of which must have been its regularity and reliability; Tuke, treasurer of the chamber, once spoke of 'the hamper money whiche was wont to be to me a good shote-anker'.[1] The clerk of the hanaper controlled an independent financial department whose reliable profits any minister was bound to find useful in the government of England.

The place of the chancellor of the exchequer is less easily discovered. One thing is certain: when Cromwell obtained the office it did not yet occupy an important position in the financial administration. The chancellor of the exchequer was descended from the chancellor of England's clerk at the exchequer table, and his duties were confined to the upper exchequer.[2] While he was, by the reign of Elizabeth, the second officer of the exchequer, having 'in Court the proper place of the Bench above the Lord Treasurer',[3] his position was much less exalted in early Tudor times. Then the lord treasurer rarely attended the exchequer court, leaving his work there to be carried out by the barons, the chancellor, and the under-treasurer,[4] of whom the chancellor was the lowest paid and therefore the least important. In the court the barons officiated under the presidency of the chief baron; in the lower exchequer the under-treasurer supplied the place of his master, the lord treasurer; there was no place for the chancellor whose duties at this time are obscure enough. It appears from a writ sent to the exchequer on Cromwell's appointment that the chancellor kept the exchequer seal and exercised a certain control over its records.[5] A sixteenth-century disquisition on the exchequer[6] admits that there is no trace in the records of its chancellor giving judgement in law or equity, either alone or with the treasurer and barons, of his dealing with any debts, taking accounts for

---

[1] SP 1:153, fo. 9 (*L.P.* xiv. II. 13).
[2] R. L. Poole, *Exchequer in the Twelfth Century* (1912), 189; Newton, *E.H.R.* xxxii. 353.
[3] Sir Thomas Fanshawe, *The Practice of the Exchequer Court* (1658), 19 f.
[4] *Ibid.* 13.
[5] E 159/312, Communia, Easter Term, Recorda, m. 3.
[6] Preserved in a precedent book, E 369/118, fos. 13–15. There is a copy at the B.M. (Tit. B. iv, fo. 55 v.).

the king, or being put in authority by any of the king's writs or statutes 'to doe any of these things, which have & bee not only magna but maxima in Scaccario'; they had always been done by the treasurer and barons. The writer then describes what he conceives to be the chancellor's proper sphere: he appoints the controller of the pipe and the clerk of the common pleas, keeps the seal, and is usually learned in the law so as to be of counsel. He was an adviser and assessor, retaining as the lord chancellor's representative some control over the chancellor's or counter-roll of the pipe. His oath indicates that he was mainly employed in the sealing of writs;[1] this Cromwell might no doubt carry out by deputy, while the exercise of patronage would be no difficulty, and he could lay claim to sufficient learning in the law. The treatise mentioned winds up by referring to the changes made in the office 'recently', as a consequence of the exchequer reforms of Mary's reign, changes which were embodied in a writ of 10 July 1559, describing the new work to be done by the chancellor and assigning him new fees.[2] But this was long after Cromwell's day.

Until, therefore, the middle of the sixteenth century the chancellor of the exchequer was a minor official. He must not be confused with the undertreasurer;[3] although the two offices came to be held by the same man they were definitely separate.[4] Cromwell's successor, Sir John Baker, was the first man to combine them; in Cromwell's time, Sir Richard Weston was undertreasurer, having succeeded Sir Thomas More in 1528. Thus the chancellor had not, by virtue of his office, any dealings with the lower exchequer where receipts and issues were administered, and his place—an inferior place at that— was in the exchequer of audit, as a kind of superior clerk. But there were possibilities in an office which entitled its holder to a seat in the exchequer court and put no great specific duties upon him. It might be turned into a sinecure, as it was by Cromwell's predecessor, Lord

---

[1] B.M., Lansd. MS. 168, fo. 280. [2] *Ibid.* fo. 274 (a copy).

[3] Even Dr Dietz asserted that the 'Declarations of the State of the Treasury' were made by the chancellor (*English Government Finance 1485-1558*, 234), whereas the documents themselves state explicitly that they were submitted by the undertreasurer.

[4] Even in the nineteenth century the same man would still hold the two offices by different patents (F. S. Thomas, *Notes on Materials for the History of Public Departments*, 11 f., 15).

Berners;[1] but for that very reason it could be made into a post of importance, as its subsequent development was to show. It was one of those offices with an ill-defined scope which left much to the energy and will of the individual holder.

Each of these three offices gave Cromwell a definite place in the administration of a financial department. In 1533 it must have seemed that he was making for an accumulation of financial offices in one hand similar to that which Heron had had before him: he had acquired a standing in the chamber machinery of finance, in the treasury of the chancery, and in the exchequer. Such a collection made the detailed control of finance easier. The sixteenth century knew no one office which could be described as a ministry of finance; the lord treasurer, ostensibly best fitted to fill it, had charge of the exchequer only, and until the tenure of office of the marquess of Winchester (1550–72) even that charge was little more than nominal. The lord treasurer of Cromwell's day, the duke of Norfolk, was a great officer of state and a leading king's councillor, but his connexion with the exchequer was confined to occasional attendance and the occasional signing of a warrant. Moreover, at this time the chamber and not the exchequer was the chief financial department; if any man could be called minister of finance, Heron, treasurer of the chamber, deserved the name. Since his death in 1524 this important but officially not recognized position had remained unfilled. Now it appeared that the king had found another man ready to take upon himself the detailed work which was required. The office of treasurer of the chamber was occupied by Sir Brian Tuke, but the almost parallel office of the jewels fell vacant at a convenient moment; and the same was true of the chancellorship of the exchequer which had to do duty for Heron's chamberlaincy of that department, though it failed to provide a place in the lower exchequer where the actual money dealings took place. The hanaper had also been one of Heron's offices. Though less complete and widespread,

---

[1] Berners was appointed chancellor of the exchequer in May 1516 (*L.P.* II. 1946) and held the office until his death in 1533. During most of that time he was also deputy at Calais (cf. *D.N.B.* and additions in *Bull. I.H.R.* VIII. 107). During 1532, e.g., he spent all his time in Calais (*L.P.* v. 787, 857, 1041, 1219, 1543), and there is only one mention of him as chancellor of the exchequer: in that capacity he was owed money by the wardrobe (*ibid.* 1710).

Cromwell's collection of financial offices was impressive enough. In these early years, when his power over the government was still new and incomplete, it gave him a chance of establishing himself, virtually, as a minister of finance; and in any case, the offices of the jewel-house, the hanaper, and the chancellorship of the exchequer secured to their holder a more direct and more detailed influence over their affairs than the mere general supervision of a great minister, however powerful, could have given.

Admittedly, this requires proof. It must be shown that Cromwell, in actual fact, used these lesser offices in just that detailed and personal way which would make holding them a point of interest even to the all-powerful minister who directed the king's policy. That he personally looked after the king's plate and jewels in 1533 is proved by notes about such matters in his remembrances: he was responsible for the refashioning of the king's plate and the storage of the surplus created by the degradation of Katharine and Mary.[1] The king's goldsmith delivered plate to him in 1534, and although the transaction was recorded as having been made with Master Secretary, it was rather as treasurer of the king's jewels that Cromwell was concerned in it.[2] He took charge of the plate received on New Year's Day 1534,[3] and in all probability also of the plate coming to the king when Bishop Fisher was imprisoned.[4] In February 1535, a survey of jewels delivered to the goldsmith for alterations was carried out by his personal servants, Sadler and Vaughan, and in November that year he personally conveyed some gold plate into the jewel-house.[5] After that, of course, he left the work to Williams. Though the daily routine of the jewel-house was in the hands of its yeoman and groom, the master took a personal and active part in it. But Cromwell did not content himself with these elementary tasks: he exploited this household treasurership in a way not very different from the exploitation of the treasurership of the chamber by Henry VII. This use, depending in part on the office but in greater part on Cromwell's personal action and power, must be fully understood if the character

---

[1] *L.P.* VI. 1194, 1382. Cromwell's remembrances—notes of things done, to be done, or to be discussed with the king—are the readiest guide to an appreciation of his all-pervading activity. The word is commonly put between inverted commas, but I see no reason for that coy device, even though the term has gone out of use.

[2] *L.P.* VII. 1688.   [3] *Ibid.* 91.   [4] *L.P.* VIII. 888.   [5] *Ibid.* 206; IX. 909.

of his administration is to become clear, and it will receive full treatment in the last section of this chapter. In Cromwell's hands the mastership of the jewels became one of the leading financial ministries of state through which Cromwell rivalled, and in a measure superseded, the treasurer of the chamber as the head of a spending department which financed wars and garrisons and paid the better part of the day-to-day expenditure on embassies, rewards, buildings, naval affairs, and a dozen other purposes, from an income mainly supplied from the reserves in the king's coffers. Such a development naturally depended on the man. The master of the jewels usurped considerable functions because Cromwell held the office; but it is equally true that Cromwell was able to usurp these functions because of the office he held. He created no organized department, transacting this additional business with the assistance of his household servants, and the office dropped back into relative unimportance when he relinquished it, though it remained one of the royal treasuries and continued to be drawn on for incidental expenditure. As the repository of the normal reserves of the age, the jewel-house would naturally and without Cromwell's career have held a place of its own among royal treasuries, and the significance of Cromwell's tenure of office lay rather in the fact that he made it into a major spending department.

As far as the hanaper is concerned, it is reasonably certain that Cromwell took almost no part in the routine work of the office. The post may have been useful, early in his career, in giving him a standing; thus, when he was present at the handing over of the great seal to lord chancellor Audeley in January 1533, together with such chancery officials as Pexsall, clerk of the crown in chancery, Croke, first of the six clerks and controller of the hanaper, and Judde, under-clerk of the hanaper, as well as some officers of state and household (Norfolk, Cranmer, Wiltshire, Gardiner, Fitzwilliam, Paulet), it is very likely that he, too, attended because of his office—because he also was an officer of the chancery.[1] In July 1533 he appears to have personally paid to the chancellor the money due for his wax.[2] But these meagre signs disappeared quickly and entirely as Cromwell grew more powerful; what evidence there is indicates that the under-

[1] *L.P.* VI. 73.　　　　　　[2] *Ibid.* 861.

clerk—first John Judde, and from 1538 Richard Snowe[1]—did the actual work. Judde had been deputy to Cromwell's predecessor, Thomas Hall, and was left in charge when Hall died; on Cromwell's appointment he handed over the surplus remaining after Hall's discharge, a sum of £300.[2] It was he who received from Cromwell the fee for the sealing of his patent as master of the rolls, he who paid him the profits due to that office from the hanaper and the keeper's own emoluments.[3] Even after Cromwell had co-opted Sadler to the office, the underclerk continued to do all the work. A file of receipts for money paid from the hanaper to the chamber, which happens to survive, proves that Snowe did the paying, though Cromwell and Sadler, as keepers, were of course responsible to the auditor; the formula employed ran 'De Thoma domino Crvmwell Custode Privati Sigilli domini Regis et Radolfo Sadler clericis Hanaperij Cancellarie dicti domini Regis per manus Ricardi Snowe'.[4] The hanaper was an old-established office, well set in its routine; it did not need the detailed attention of its keeper, and it did not receive it. The fact was assumed by the clerks who addressed warrants to 'our trusty and welbiloued Counsaillour Thomas Crumwell keper and Clerc of our Hanaper of our chauncery, and in his absence to his deputie'.[5] In practice the keeper would normally be 'absent' and the deputy attended to the work.

Nevertheless, Cromwell kept an eye even on the hanaper, and an irregularity brought him into personal action. In August 1532, Judde informed his master that 'my lorde of the greate seale hath sealed the patent of Armys, at the sealyng of which patent I was at Ippiswich'.[6] Apparently the presence of neither the clerk nor the

---

[1] *L.P.* XIII. I. 1490.

[2] *L.P.* V. 1730; VI. 228 (1). Hanaper surpluses usually went to the treasurer of the chamber (*L.P.* XIV. II. 13), but in this case Cromwell seems to have used them for his own financial ministry (cf. below, p. 145). [3] *L.P.* IX. 478; XI. 66 (1), 135.

[4] E 101/222/15, nos. 1–6.

[5] E 163/10/19, a warrant ordering the delivery to Anne Boleyn of the patent creating her marquess of Pembroke 'without taking any fine or fee for vs or to our vse for the seales'. This is the sole surviving example of an undoubtedly large group of documents; many items in the hanaper accounts are marked 'pardonatur' or 'excusatur per warrantum regis' or 'per cartam', or with some such phrase.

[6] SP 1:70, fo. 207 (*L.P.* V. 1214). The 'angnus' referred to later in the letter was the strip of parchment which was doubled through a slit in the document for the attachment of the seal.

underclerk was considered essential at the sealing, though the provision of eighteenpence a day for every day spent in attending the
chancellor implied a theory that it was. In Judde's absence things
had gone wrong: 'for, and I had ben at thensealyng of it, it shuld
haue ben sealed with grene wax and lacis of sylke, which cannot nowe
conuenyently be don by cause of the cutte that the angnus is in'.
He went on to elaborate some details of procedure for the benefit of
his new superior:

For it is a perpetuyte graunted to hym and to his heyres, whiche must
pay for the seale to the kynges highnes viij li' ix s', oneles your Mastership
do atteyne a warraunt for the discharge of thesame. For, and if the kynges
hightnes gave but lycence to any man to Inparke any grounde, or to
Inbatell his house, for hym and his heyres, it is a perpetuyte and shall pay
viij li' ix s'.

Cromwell probably needed this instruction; he had not been trained
in the chancery and its rules were no doubt strange to him, a sufficient reason for leaving the routine work to an experienced underclerk. But there was nothing of the sinecurist about Thomas
Cromwell; Judde had always to reckon with him, concluding this
letter with a promise to come to know Cromwell's 'ferther pleaser'
as soon as he returned to London.

It is not easy to discover to what extent Cromwell exercised the
functions, ill-defined as they were, of the chancellor of the exchequer.
He used his powers of patronage, appointing to the office of clerk of
the pleas two men, one of whom, William Brabazon, had been his
own servant and must have been an absentee official as he was undertreasurer in Ireland at the time.[1] Apparently, Cromwell attended the
court occasionally. It was noted in the reign of Elizabeth that

only this is remembered by some auncient of the Court yet living that
Tho: Cronwell being Chauncellor & the Kᵍ Secretary & after Lᵈ privy
seale did take place vppon the first bench ex dextra domini Thesaurarij:
but Sir John Baker being the next Chauncellor & after vndertreasorer also
did alwayes sit vppon the second Bench where the vndertreasorer now
doth. And Sir Walter Mildmay next Chauncellor after him did take place

---

[1] The office was conferred by Cromwell's deed of 27 April 1538 and confirmed by
patent in the January following (*L.P.* XIV. I. 191, 31).

& sitt where the L: Crumwell did, but by what authority or reason the Chauncellor hath sitten in these severall places it appeareth not in writing found.[1]

Perhaps the reason can be guessed: Cromwell quite probably usurped the seat on the first bench, and Mildmay followed his precedent though Baker was too prudent or personally unimportant to do so. Cromwell must have invested the chancellorship of the exchequer with some of his own importance; a chancellor who in other capacities governed as the king's chief minister could not be expected to take an inferior place in the exchequer.

It is this question of his various capacities, and of the importance which attached to his person rather than his office, which makes it difficult to be certain how far he acted as chancellor of the exchequer. When he appears in the exchequer records as present in the court he is nearly always designated by that title, though sometimes some other office, secretary or lord privy seal, is also mentioned. He used his position in the exchequer to appear as the king's mouthpiece. The record of an action against one William Evan, merchant stranger, for transgressing a statute of Henry VII concerning the import of Gascon wine, breaks off with the note, 'Non fiat hic vlterius execucio per mandatum domini Regis nunciante Thoma Cromwell Armigero Cancellario huius Scaccarij, quosque &c.'[2] In 1540 he acted together with the barons when another merchant stranger, John Tolarge, was before the court; apparently Cromwell had given the chancellor sufficient standing to make him part of the judicial machinery of the exchequer. In fact, the wording of the record suggests that he had reduced the barons to mere assistants in a court presided over by himself,[3] but if this was so the office certainly did not justify or maintain so exalted a position, and Cromwell was here using his personal authority. In another case, concerning a country rector fined for non-residence, he acted together with the lord treasurer.[4] There cannot, then, be any doubt that on occasions he sat in the

---

[1] E 369/118, fos. 12 v–13.

[2] 2 May 1533; E 159/312, Communia, Easter Term, Recorda, mm. 28 r–d.

[3] *Ibid.* 315, Communia, Easter Term, Recorda, m. 1. Part of the case is annotated 'Parcatur per mandatum Domini Cromwell & Baronibus presentibus hic xxviij° Ianuarij A° xxxi°'.

[4] *Ibid.* 317, Communia, Trinity Term, Recorda, m. 15: 'Parcatur per mandatum Thesaurarij Anglie & Domini Cromwell ad instanciam Gosneld'.'

exchequer court and that he did not confine himself there to his supposed duties of sealing writs. A petition of 1533, addressed to him as chancellor, for the restoration of a horse which his servant Swyfte was alleged to have detained, opens up some further speculations. The petitioner lost the animal at Hackney, afterwards recognized it and claimed it as his own in Smithfield market, and then brought an action in the Guildhall. Swyfte succeeded in getting the suit removed into the exchequer, before the chief baron and Cromwell.[1] It is possible that Cromwell sat as a judge in the exchequer with some regularity, at least in these early years; perhaps the memoranda rolls conceal the true constitution of the court by the use of a formula which implies that all cases were heard by the barons only. But the evidence permits no certainty beyond the fact that Cromwell used his place in the exchequer in order occasionally to put in an appearance—perhaps for business which concerned him or his clients. In any case, he could hardly be often in the court, for he had other calls upon his time.

He found the time, however, to attend when new officials were being admitted. He was there, on 27 April 1534, when Thomas Walsh was made fourth baron, and the day after when Humphrey Bowland appeared to fill the now vacant post of king's remembrancer; though he was on neither occasion the sole councillor present, he alone is mentioned by name.[2] He was alone, however, on 4 May 1535 when his servant Richard Pollard was admitted to Bowland's office, vacated by its holder's death.[3] On 2 December 1539, John and Clement Smyth were admitted to the office of lord treasurer's remembrancer, 'per Barones'; but they swore their oath before Norfolk, as lord treasurer, and Cromwell, as lord privy seal and chancellor of the exchequer,[4] and the same procedure was observed with Nicholas Luke, the new third baron, on 14 April 1540, except that others of the council were also present to hear the oath.[5] The

---

[1] L.P. VI. 1668.
[2] E 159/313, Communia, Easter Term, Recorda, m. 26: 'In presencia Egregij viri Thome Cromewell Armigeri Secretarij dicti domini Regis Ac Cancellarij huius Scaccarij & aliorum de Consilio dicti domini Regis hic adtunc existencium.'
[3] Ibid. 314, Communia, Easter Term, Recorda, m. 4.
[4] Ibid. 318, Communia, Michaelmas Term, Recorda, m. 60.
[5] Ibid. Communia, Easter Term, Recorda, m. 4.

same interest in the staff of the exchequer also explains his negotiations with William Elys who was fourth baron at the time of his rise to power. Elys was a very old man, over eighty, with long service to his credit and desirous, as he told Cromwell, to die in harness. Despite his rather pathetic assertions to the contrary Elys was obviously too old and ill to attend to his duties; but when Cromwell asked him to surrender his patent of office, he was met by a counter-request from Elys that he might be allowed to carry on a year or two. Cromwell retorted by sending his servant John Gostwick to collect the desired resignation, but all he got from Elys was another letter about his age, service, and continued suitability.[1] In the end Elys solved the problem by dying, and Thomas Walsh was appointed in his place.[2] Although Cromwell dealt with Elys as the king's minister rather than as chancellor of the exchequer, his concern was to secure an efficiently working exchequer; the man who succeeded Elys was an exchequer clerk himself, and there was no question of Cromwell trying to find places for friends.

These were administrative matters rather than judicial, and Cromwell's correspondence offers further examples of the importance which this aspect of the office had for him. In 1533, Edward Lee, archbishop of York, was in trouble with the exchequer about some money due before his appointment to the see which he refused to pay. He appealed to Cromwell who, Lee alleged, ordered the barons not to issue process; nevertheless the sheriff attempted to secure payment, claiming that Cromwell had ordered the money to be levied.[3] Lee pointed out that Cromwell now had a place of authority in the exchequer and could well see to it that such unjust claims were not pressed; he at any rate ascribed a standing to the chancellorship as exercised by Cromwell which would enable him to enforce orders on the barons which he had unsuccessfully issued before his appointment. The sheriff of Cornwall, addressing his letter to Cromwell as chancellor of the exchequer, begged to be excused from attending the court and promised to send the money of his sheriffwick by his attorney there.[4] Another letter, employing the same address, in-

---

[1] *L.P.* VI. 1308, 1458; VII. 34 (but cf. *ibid.* 35, where Elys admits that illness prevents his doing his exchequer duty).
[2] *Ibid.* 589 (10).   [3] *L.P.* VI. 1158, 1219.   [4] *Ibid.* 1309.

formed him of frauds committed in connexion with a wardship, though this was hardly an exchequer matter; a man against whom a *scire facias* was out for collection of a debt asked for the judgement to be deferred until he should have recovered his health sufficiently to come to Westminster and arrange matters with Cromwell and the undertreasurer; the mayor of Southampton thanked him for his reassurance in respect of an exchequer fine hanging over the borough, but had to add that Cromwell's orders did not seem to have prevented attachments issuing against some ex-sheriffs.[1] The general impression is that in his early years at least Cromwell relied on the chancellorship to impose his will on the exchequer from the inside, and that he backed up his influence by such attention to the details of exchequer administration as his other duties allowed. Nor was this inconsiderable. Clearly he exploited the office for rather more than it was worth; refusing to be tied by the traditions of a minor office, he extended its scope to fit his ambitions and designs.

Cromwell's first three offices, then, were minor ones. He obtained from them a useful though not remarkable income, and a position in three separate treasuries which enabled him to act to some extent as a minister of finance. He held these offices at a time when he was already well to the fore among the king's councillors, and he continued to hold them to the end of his career; but while they were of practical importance at the beginning, there can be little doubt that they were retained later mainly for financial reasons. This is less true of the chancellorship of the exchequer than of the two offices which were shared in 1535; as has been seen, as late as 1540 Cromwell could still find a use for his one exchequer office when he wished to exercise influence over a case in that court. Otherwise the evidence of his activities has supported the reasonable supposition that these earliest offices grew less important as time went on. The hanaper was probably the least administratively important of the three; little scope was given to its clerk, and Cromwell appears to have done no more than keep an occasional eye on things. It is to the point to note that the hanaper was also the most profitable of the three offices. The

---

[1] *L.P.* VI. 1680; VII. 113; VIII. 964.

mastership of the jewels, on the other hand, proved to be the solid foundation of Cromwell's control of government expenditure, until he found other means demanding less direct personal activity for achieving the same end.[1] The chancellorship of the exchequer offered a way of influencing the exchequer, especially in seeing to its staffing and efficient working, which a mere councillor without office could not command. Office was far from being everything in Cromwell's control of the administration, but the specific offices which he held did make that control peculiarly precise and all-embracing.

Cromwell had little immediate effect on any of these lesser offices. The mastership of the jewels may have gained a trifle in standing: Cromwell's successor, Sir John Williams, later first baron Thame and treasurer of the court of augmentations, was a more important man than his predecessor, Robert Amadas, citizen and goldsmith of London, and by that measure the importance of the office had increased as a consequence of his mastership. In the financial administration of England, however, it did not keep the place which Cromwell gave it. At the hanaper, too, Cromwell's successors—such men as Sadler or John Hales of Coventry—were bigger men than his obscure predecessor Hall; but Heron had held the office, and nothing of weight was added by Cromwell's tenure. Nor did he, properly speaking, create the modern office of chancellor of the exchequer, though his use of the post forecast future development. He took advantage of its vague duties and ill-defined scope to exercise ministerial control over the permanent officials in the exchequer, and it was for these very reasons that the office ultimately became supreme in national finance. Its fee rose to £113. 6s. 8d. by the time of Elizabeth, making the chancellor the third highest paid officer in the court, after the lord treasurer and undertreasurer whose salaries remained practically unchanged.[2] This enormous increase was in the main due to the exchequer reforms of Mary's reign which had thrown much additional business on the chancellor; he was picked to do the new work because his office was of small described scope but had large inherent possibilities of expansion—for the reasons, that is, which had made it useful to Cromwell. Though Baker did not follow Cromwell's example in visibly asserting the chancellor's

[1] Cf. below, p. 157.   [2] B.M., Harl. MS. 5174, fo. 80.

authority in the court, Mildmay, who remembered it, succeeded in his long tenure of office in establishing it as one of the important posts in the exchequer. It was reserved to the chancellors of James I to complete the work started by Cromwell and to make the chancellor of the exchequer a leading officer of state. All this is not to say that Cromwell deliberately set out to add stature to the office as an office. He was interested in it only inasmuch as it gave him access to the exchequer, but in the manner of his exploiting it he showed a sure sense of the administrative possibilities which ultimately produced the modern chancellorship of the exchequer.

Before we discuss Cromwell's major offices, it will be useful to consider the question whether he was a free agent in the acquisition of any post he held. Did he choose, or did the king appoint? It is not incorrect, though also not very helpful, to reply that he chose and that the king also appointed. Not only must it be remembered that the king took no active part in the administration, leaving Cromwell full powers and discretion, though this in itself makes it likely that Cromwell could decide what offices he wished to hold. The method of appointment must also be considered: though the king signed the warrant, it was Cromwell who had to submit the petition on the strength of which the place was granted. In general, then, it may well be supposed that the initiative had to come from the minister.

There is an obvious difference between the first three and the last three: the jewel-house, hanaper, and chancellorship of the exchequer were held by patent and for life, and Cromwell succeeded in each case on the death of the previous holder, while his predecessors in the other offices survived the loss of their places. To deal with the former first: Cromwell may well have asked for the succession but he could hardly plan it. The most that can be said is that in 1532 and 1533 Cromwell snapped up every financial office of some standing that happened to fall vacant. The accident of death and his dependence on it explain also why he did not base his financial ministry on more, or more obviously useful, offices—why he did not, like Heron, become a chamberlain of the exchequer, and why he was content with the jewels rather than the chamber; he had to be satisfied with pressing for what was available and with making the most of that. As it was, his luck in fatalities was good enough. Whether the king appointed him or he asked to be appointed is not a question to which a definite answer can be given; as has been said, the chances are that the initiative came from him. As far as the chancellorship of the exchequer is concerned, there are faint traces of a deliberate interest. It seems that even before October 1531 he had acquired various documents connected with that court—a paper declaring the exchequer to be the highest court of record and a number of exchequer accounts and declarations by customers, tellers, and an under-treasurer.[1] Later he added documents which prove a growing concern with the chancellorship itself: a copy of the chancellor's oath, a copy of Lovell's patent of the office, an abstract from the Red Book of the exchequer.[2] Berners, the chancellor, was a very old man as old age then went (he was born in 1467), and his death or resignation could at least be considered probable. It may therefore be that Cromwell was laying plans for obtaining the office which was very necessary if indeed he contemplated—as we have maintained he did —to emulate Sir John Heron's methods of controlling the finances. But despite all this it remains true that in obtaining his first three offices he depended on accidents outside his control, though he was quick to take advantage of them when they occurred.

His other three offices—those of principal secretary, master of the rolls, and lord privy seal—present a very different picture. The secretary and lord privy seal held office during pleasure, and Cromwell succeeded both Gardiner and the earl of Wiltshire by a deliberate act of dismissal and appointment. In both cases, a struggle of some sort preceded the appointment. We shall see later how his triumph over Gardiner in the battle for the control of the king's counsels was completed by the transfer of the secretaryship, and it was the collapse and fall of the Boleyns after Queen Anne's disgrace which enabled him to secure the privy seal. There is no doubt at all that he wanted to be secretary, for he acted in the office while Gardiner was abroad;[3] there is a little less certainty about the other office, but Cromwell

---

[1] *L.P.* VII. 923 (xii, xviii). The Hasilwood there mentioned was one of the tellers of the receipt, while Sir John Cutt preceded More as undertreasurer.
[2] *Ibid.* 923 (xix, xxv, xxxiv).   [3] Below, p. 124.

played a major part in the political upheaval of 1536, and if he had not had his eye on the privy seal all along, he certainly stepped at once into Wiltshire's shoes at the very moment when his own growing greatness rendered the secretaryship rather insufficient and required some further mark of the royal favour. Though as secretary he had had all the power he could want, that post was not yet one to be held by a peer,[1] and apparently it was thought that the time had come for the king's chief councillor to be rewarded with a title of nobility. The dates of Cromwell's promotion to the privy seal (2 July or 24 June 1536)[2] and of his creation as baron (8 July)[3] are so close together as to make it probable that both steps were decided on together and taken conjointly. If Cromwell was to be promoted, the office of lord privy seal was the obvious next step. Not only was it the only high office of state occupied by a councillor fallen from grace and therefore readily removed,[4] but it was also the traditional promotion for the secretary.[5] It alone offered possibilities similar to those which Cromwell had exploited in the secretaryship. The chancellor was overwhelmed with legal business and had lost his place at the head of the administrative machinery. The lord treasurer's departmental duties were to supervise the exchequer, but the exchequer was the least important financial department of the time, so that the treasurer did not regain great practical and administrative influence, in addition to his traditional high standing, until the reforms of Mary's reign restored exchequer supremacy in the financial field. As for the president of the council, his position was so obscure and purely titular that his very existence might be doubted if he were not mentioned in two acts of parliament.[6] The office of

---

[1] The first secretary of state who was also a peer was Dorchester, appointed in 1628 (Evans, *Princ. Sec.* 350). Burghley, unlike Cromwell, relinquished the secretaryship soon after he was ennobled.

[2] The patent was dated 2 July 1536 (*L.P.* XI. 202, 3), but the exchequer was ordered to pay his salary from 24 June (E 159/314, m. 39 d).

[3] *L.P.* XI. 46, 202 (14).

[4] The lord chancellor, Audeley, was not the man to oppose either Cromwell or Henry. The offices of lord treasurer and president of the council were held by the two dukes, Norfolk and Suffolk, who were firmly enough in favour and whom Cromwell could not afford to antagonize seriously.

[5] In the fifteenth century, six secretaries had become keepers of the privy seal (Otway Ruthven, *King's Sec.* 87, n. 2).

[6] 21 Henry VIII, c. 20, and 31 Henry VIII, c. 10. Cf. Pollard in *E.H.R.* XXXVII. 353 f.

privy seal, on the other hand, provided all the opportunities for a premiership which were also inherent in the secretaryship. Its holders during the reign—Ruthal, Marney, Tunstall, Wiltshire— had all been great men in the state and leading councillors, though the use which Cromwell was to make of the office was peculiar to himself. But nothing else would have done so well, and it is, to say the least, very probable that Cromwell definitely desired the office and asked for it.

The manner in which he obtained the mastership of the rolls and the way in which he avoided the office of lord chancellor confirm the impression that from 1534 Cromwell decided himself what offices he wished to hold. The master of the rolls held office for life, but in May 1534 the occupant of the post, Dr John Taylor, was reported to be on the point of resigning, and Dr John Tregonwell, one of the leading chancery officials and civilians of the day, a man clearly in the running for the succession, thought that Cromwell had talked about appointing him;[1] he was wrong, for on Taylor's resignation Cromwell took the office himself.[2] Tregonwell's appeal to Cromwell underlines the fact that opinion at the time saw in him the man who held control of public offices—the dispenser of patronage; a good enough reason for supposing that he picked his own. Officially, of course, all patronage was the king's, but what that really meant is aptly illustrated by a perplexed letter from the council in the north to Cromwell, written in January 1540. Cromwell had told them that the king's pleasure was for a certain property to go to a man he named, but they had had instructions from Sir Richard Riche, chancellor of the court of augmentations, that it was the king's pleasure that the property should go to another man. They had therefore committed the house to a third party, till the king's pleasure be known![3] Everything was ostensibly by the king's pleasure, but in reality Henry's ministers had considerably latitude and discretion, provided they pretended to be authorized by his will. It is difficult to escape the conclusion that the disposal of the rolls was entirely

---

[1] *L.P.* VII. 743.

[2] Cromwell's patent declared that the office was vacant 'per sursum reddicionem literarum nostrarum patencium per nos dilecto nobis Iohani Tayler Clerico...' (C 82/689, no. 2).   [3] *L.P.* XV. 36.

in Cromwell's hands, though the king's formal approval would of course have to be obtained.

As for the office of lord chancellor, Cromwell did not take over when More resigned, for reasons which will be elicited later, but the new chancellor, Audeley, coupled his name with that of the king when he later complained that he had been induced to take the office to the detriment of his finances.[1] There appears to have been an idea about that Cromwell had put Audeley in to keep the place warm for himself, and as late as November 1535 Chapuys reported that, though Cromwell would not hitherto accept the chancellorship, it was thought he would soon allow himself to be persuaded.[2] He never did, but the very supposition shows what contemporaries took to be the true position.

It may therefore be said with some confidence that Cromwell obtained his last three offices because he wanted them, while he had had his first three because they fell vacant and happened to be the kind of thing he was looking for. In every case there is a certain amount, more or less, of deliberation on his part; Henry's share in the business was confined to allowing the minister to accumulate his collection of offices. The first three had given Cromwell control of the finances; the last three were not only more important—in accordance with his greater power—but also had a common denominator. They gave control over the three government secretariats: the secretary ruled the signet clerks, the lord privy seal those of his seal, and the master of the rolls those of chancery. If Cromwell had an object in seizing upon these particular offices, the fact that they enabled him to exercise the same kind of detailed and precise control over the bureaucracy which, to a lesser degree, his minor first offices had given him over the machinery of finance, may well have been at the root of his planning. Though the first condition of power under Henry VIII was the possession of the king's ear, a personal standing at court, anyone who wished to rule through a close control of the machinery of government would have to make himself master of those who provided the means of government, and of those who transmitted the orders of the executive. He would have to be master of the financial machine and the bureaucracy. Dogmatism is out of

[1] *L.P.* VI. 927.   [2] *L.P.* IX. 862.

place, but it looks very much as though Cromwell was trying to do precisely that. We must now turn to his three major and secretarial offices.

Exactly when Cromwell entered upon the office of secretary is not certain because it was not bestowed by patent; the king's verbal order and the handing over of the signet made a secretary. In consequence there is no evidence of the actual date on which Cromwell was appointed though it can be put within fairly narrow limits. Gardiner, the first secretary regularly to countersign signet warrants,[1] signed his last extant warrant on 3 February 1534,[2] while the first warrant signed by Cromwell is dated 15 April 1534.[3] The office therefore changed hands some time between these two dates. The traditional month of April 1534 is most probably correct; on the 15th of that month it was reported that Gardiner had lost the secretaryship.[4] Nevertheless, Cromwell acted as secretary in the last months of 1533. On 30 September, Thomas Derby, one of the clerks of the signet, dispatched a warrant to be sealed with the signet to Cromwell or his servants Richard Cromwell and Ralph Sadler.[5] In December of the same year, Cromwell delivered to Lord Lisle's agent a bill signed by the king, a duty usually performed by the secretary.[6] The agent had asked Cromwell to let the licence in question pass without fees paid, 'but suche comandement he said lay not in hym; notwithstonding, bicause the signett is in his keping, now in the absens of the secretary, Raufe Sadeler wold take nothing for the signett'.[7] The absent secretary was Gardiner, away from England from 3 September until the end of the year,[8] and it appears

---

[1] The warrants preserved for his secretaryship are so signed (PSO 2/4, files for 22 & 23 Henry VIII).

[2] C 82/679, no. 4.   [3] *Ibid.* 681, no. 26.

[4] *L.P.* VII. 483. In view of all this evidence no importance can be attached to the fact that warrants to Cromwell do not address him as secretary until later. A warrant of 27 May 1534 calls him master of the jewels only (E 101/421/6, no. 37). It appears that for a short time at least some attempt may have been made to differentiate between the purposes of his various offices.

[5] SP 1:79, fo. 114 (*L.P.* VI. 1177).   [6] SP 3:7, art. 120 (*L.P. Add.* 886).

[7] By putting another comma after 'Sadler', *L. P. Add.* 886 makes nonsense of the letter. Sadler was not, of course, to be described as (principal) secretary in 1533.

[8] *D.N.B.* VII. 860b.

that in his absence the signet was entrusted to Cromwell who had given it into the temporary custody of Sadler who was his private clerk. Cromwell thus acted as Gardiner's deputy, taking advantage of the bishop's absence to insinuate himself into an office which gave him proximity to the king and almost unlimited powers of government. He occupied the place held by Thomas More in the 'twenties during Pace's and Knight's embassies on the continent, but then Wolsey had kept the signet while now Cromwell was secretary in all but name before he could wrest the office itself from Gardiner's grip. On his return, early in 1534, Gardiner opposed the act of supremacy; the result was his temporary disgrace and banishment from court in April,[1] the very month in which he had to relinquish the secretaryship. Cromwell occupied the post while his rival was out of the country and then took advantage of his ascendancy in the king's counsels to rob Gardiner of office: he had determined on obtaining the secretaryship, and his quarrel with the bishop of Winchester took at this time the form of a contest over an office.

The importance of that office certainly did not lie in its financial advantages. Admittedly, it is difficult to know what its emoluments amounted to—no patent gives details, and there is no mention of a fee in any of the accounts of exchequer, chamber, or household—but it can be shown that they were not large. Cromwell's immediate successors had £100 each, paid to them by the treasurer of the court of augmentations;[2] but the augmentations account preceding Cromwell's surrender of the office lists no payment to the principal secretary.[3] The fee was clearly an innovation made on the appointment of Wriothesley and Sadler in 1540; the silence of the household accounts is quite trustworthy—Cromwell had no fee. The only piece of evidence for his income from the office is an item in one of his private accounts which gives the profits of the signet as £94.[4] This account covers the period from Michaelmas 1533 to Michaelmas 1535, or about a year and a half of Cromwell's secretaryship. The

---

[1] *L.P.* VII. 441.

[2] E 315/249, fo. 35. This account covered the whole year ending at Michaelmas 1540, but the secretaries got only a half year's fee since they were appointed in April 1540. Cf. also E 323/2B, m. 50 (augmentations account, 31–35 Henry VIII) which gives the full annual fee of a principal secretary as £100.

[3] *L.P.* XIV. II. 236. [4] *L.P.* IX. 478.

accountant noted that he had received the money from another of Cromwell's servants, so that it must be doubtful whether the £94 constituted the whole income from the signet for that period. The secretary took a proportion of the fees paid into the signet office; he shared in the sealing but not in the writing fees of the signet, for whereas he had custody of the seal he did not write the documents.[1] Surprising though it is, it is thus quite certain that as secretary Cromwell drew no money except his share of the signet fees, a share which may have amounted to a rough average of £60 a year, though the evidence for this figure is very slender and quite insufficient. The only other material benefit he had was comprised in his position in the royal household; he was entitled to lodging in court, with 'bouge of court' amounting by the terms of the Eltham Ordinances (1526) to £22. 7s. 11d.[2]

While then the office was neither unduly lucrative, nor as a matter of fact one of great social distinction, it yet offered an immense scope. No patent circumscribed the secretary's duties; he was hardly even bound to feel restricted to a customary sphere of action. The vast expansion of the secretaryship, which is a commonplace of the administrative history of the sixteenth and seventeenth centuries, goes back no farther than Thomas Cromwell; it was he who, by the force of his personality, 'brought the office of King's secretary into a position of eminence entirely new to it'.[3] But the history of the secretaryship during Cromwell's tenure belongs less to the personal story of the minister than to the general story of administration. It is an outstanding part of the administrative revolution of the century, comprising as it does a far-reaching alteration in the bureaucratic organization and the whole attitude to government. The part which Cromwell played in this development must therefore be allowed to stand over till we come to discuss the clerical departments themselves; here it will suffice to note that through the secretaryship

[1] Evans, *Princ. Sec.* 206–7.

[2] *H.O.* 162–3. This was increased some time after 1540 to £33. 19s. 1d. (*ibid.* 210). In addition there appears a great sum for diets: two messes, each worth £406 p.a., were to be served to the secretaries, a term which included the French and Latin as well as the principal secretaries, and probably also their staffs (*ibid.* 192). This entry must be dated after 1540 as the lord great master is mentioned.

[3] Mrs Higham (F. M. G. Evans), 'Note on the Pre-Tudor Secretary', *Essays... presented to T. F. Tout*, 361.

Cromwell made himself the all-powerful minister, with his hand over and in every event and detail of the government. That was something new in itself; the office had never been used in that way before. As we have seen, it had not emerged from the second rank when Wolsey fell; after Cromwell's tenure it never again was anything less than 'the binding force of the state, holding together all the various units of the administration'.[1]

Cromwell was never more powerful, more ubiquitous in the administration, more completely in control of the day-to-day government of the country, than he was through the office of principal secretary. Nevertheless he found in the mastership of the rolls and the keepership of the privy seal further means of that direct and immediate influence on sections of the civil service which all his offices provided in greater or less degree. Also, he acquired with these last two offices much more considerable salaries than he had had from the first four; in the circumstances it is interesting to note that he surrendered the rolls on obtaining the privy seal.[2] The mastership of the rolls was a very profitable office. In the first year of his tenure (1534–5), Cromwell received from it £291. 4s. 10d.,[3] and the period from Michaelmas 1535 to 12 July 1536, when he ceased to hold the office, yielded him £317. 13s. 10d.[4] As Cromwell's accounts show, this income was chiefly derived from the fees due to the master of the rolls for every patent written, being paid to him by the clerks of the petty bag and the six clerks. He was also entitled to 2s. for every patent sealed,[5] and entries under that head are duly noted as received from the underclerk of the hanaper. He further got 'casualties' from the cursitors, that is occasional fines on documents prepared by them. He had £8 out of the hanaper for his summer and winter robes, £4 from the chief butler of England for a tun of wine traditionally his due, a small Christmas gift from the

---

[1] Evans, *Princ. Sec.* 41.

[2] He became lord privy seal on 2 July 1536 (*L.P.* IX. 292, 3), and Sir Christopher Hales succeeded to the rolls on the 10th (*ibid.* 17).

[3] SP 1:105, fos. 24–5 (*L.P.* XI. 66, i). The same period yielded £284. 1s. 6d. by another account (*L.P.* IX. 478). The difference is probably due to several items in the later account not having come in in time for the earlier.

[4] SP 1:105, fos. 26–8 (*L.P.* XI. 66, ii), or £310. 17s. by another account (*L.P.* XI. 135).

[5] Lyte, *Great Seal*, 333.

prior of the knights of St John, the rent of the London assize court, and—very much a survival from earlier times—ten marks from the abbot of Thame for a horse to carry the king's records. As keeper of the house of converts, an office combined with the mastership of the rolls since 1377 at the latest,[1] he was paid a regular annual allowance of £29. 10s. 2d. out of the hanaper, of which £13. 6s. 8d. was for himself, while the rest went to the other officials and the inmates of the house.[2] The income which Cromwell derived from the mastership of the rolls therefore averaged the considerable sum of £300–330 a year, though it was as nothing compared with what the master might expect to draw seventy years later.[3] The great exploitation of crown offices for private gain had not yet begun.

The office provided one other material benefit: the master was entitled to an official residence, the Rolls House in Chancery Lane, on the site of the present Public Record Office. Very soon after Cromwell became master, his letters begin to be dated from 'the Rolls'.[4] The residence went normally with the office, but Cromwell's letters prove that he continued in possession long after he had ceased to be master;[5] he had some clothes there as late as 1537.[6] In view of this it is hardly surprising to hear that his successor 'Sir Christopher Hales being Master of the Rowles dined after at the Kinges Head taverne. He is reported during his time at the Rowles to have kept verye small house or none at all.'[7] The unfortunate man was being kept out of his official residence by the lord privy seal who treated the house as his private property and throughout these years was busy building around it.

Though Cromwell surrendered the rolls and the profits attached (except the house) soon after becoming lord privy seal, he did not

---

[1] Lyte, *Great Seal*, 11.

[2] This sum appears also in the hanaper accounts (e.g. E 101/222/11) and, as it was charged on tallies, in the exchequer's 'Declarations'. In 1536 the money was entered as allowed to Thomas Cromwell, keeper of the hanaper, for payment to Thomas Cromwell, master of the rolls (E 164/69).

[3] Cf. Lyte, *Great Seal*, App. B, pp. 409 ff. In 1614, Sir Julius Caesar was told to expect a yearly income of £2,380 from the rolls, but he found that it decreased year by year from £2,200 to £1,600, though even that was still vastly more than the amount of Cromwell's profits. Of course, the value of money had decreased.

[4] Merriman, II. 279. The first surviving letter so dated is of 17 October 1534.

[5] *Ibid.* 281. The last surviving letter so dated is of 19 January 1538.

[6] *L.P.* XII. I. 669.   [7] Sanders, *Orders of Chancery*, 17.

suffer thereby; the new office provided not only a high place in the official hierarchy but also a handsome income of £365 a year, specified in the patent of appointment as derived from the customs collected at various ports.[1] This fee had originally been intended for the maintenance of the keeper of the privy seal and his staff when absent from the royal household, but it had long since become the lord privy seal's private salary.[2] There survive no private accounts of Cromwell's with details of official salaries for later than the beginning of 1536, so that it is not known whether he received more from the office than the basic salary. It is likely, however, that he shared in the profits of the seal.[3]

In obtaining the keepership of the rolls, Cromwell overthrew a long-standing tradition, for these officials had always been clerks and chancery trained. His successors were laymen, too, and usually common lawyers at that. The development is of significance in the history of the court of chancery but cannot concern a discussion of administrative problems; in this respect the duties and scope of the office were basically the custody of the chancery records and of the house of converts. The master of the rolls was still personally responsible for the records; there survive orders to Cromwell's predecessor and to his successor to cancel recognisances or make alterations in documents among the records in their keeping,[4] and while no such orders to Cromwell are extant it may be concluded that he, too, exercised at least a theoretical supervision. The keeper of the records in the Tower was appointed by the master of the rolls, as were the clerks of the Rolls Chapel;[5] if the master did not himself deal with the records, he was in charge of the officers who did. As for the house of converts, this contained during Cromwell's tenure of office one chaplain, two clerks, and three (female) converts;[6] with one official to every inmate, the administrative duties falling to the

---

[1] £90 from the port of Poole, £56. 13s. 4d. from Bristol, £200 from the petty customs of London, and £18. 6s. 8d. from Plymouth and Fowey.

[2] Tout, *Chapters*, v. 83 f.

[3] In 1634 the keeper of the privy seal was one of the officials authorized to profit from the process by which tobacco licences were granted (Lyte, *Great Seal*, 355).

[4] C 82/631/1, 635/10, 650/5, 664/23, 768/35, 767/12.

[5] J. S. Wilson, 'Lord Chancellor in the early 17th Century', unpub. thesis (London, 1927), p. 5.

[6] Cf. the accounts of the keeper, e.g. E 101/254/5.

master's share must have been negligible. At any rate, there is no evidence that Cromwell ever had to attend in person to either of these aspects of his office.

The master of the rolls, as the chief of the twelve masters of chancery,[1] was one of the officials entitled to 'write to the seal', that is to write documents to which the great seal was to be affixed. Ever since the reign of Edward I it had been chancery practice to write the name of the officer primarily responsible for a document in the lower right-hand margin;[2] though originally the clerk who wrote the writ may also have signed, this was clearly not the case in Cromwell's time. His name appears under a multitude of documents issuing from the chancery, as is testified by original letters patent as well as by copies on the memoranda rolls or in precedent books.[3] But the originals show that the name was appended by the writing clerk; there are no autograph signatures, and Cromwell's name on a document does not prove that Cromwell had anything to do with the drafting, writing, or checking. The reason why his name, or for that matter the names of other masters of the rolls, appeared with such frequency, is supplied by the evidence of John Croke who in 1554 described the organization of the chancery.[4] Of those entitled to write to the seal, he says that the six clerks, the clerks of the petty bag, and the two examiners wrote 'in the Master of the Rolls his name': all documents written by them would bear the name of the master of the rolls, and the master would technically be responsible for them. Thus the master of the rolls supervised the greater part of the clerical side of chancery, the only officials outside his immediate control being the clerk of the crown, the other masters, and the cursitors. The clerk of the crown, according to Croke, was responsible for 'all commissions and proces of the Crowne, and generally all processes that towcheth eyther life or member'. The other masters were theoretically able to write the same kind of writs as the master of the rolls, without exercising his supervision of other clerks, and some of their names occasionally occur under a document. They were, however, usually such leading civil lawyers as, for instance,

---

[1] He was named as such by an order of the time of Henry V (Sanders, *Orders of Chancery*, 7b).   [2] Lyte, *Great Seal*, 266.
[3] E.g. C 193/2.   [4] Sanders, *Orders of Chancery*, 10 ff.

Doctors Tregonwell and Oliver who were widely employed in various capacities by the government and cannot have attended much to their chancery duties; though it should be noticed that according to Croke they alone could make writs of *supersedeas*. One of their number, the prothonotary, was responsible for treaties and the like, as far as they were written in chancery. The cursitors could only write writs of course, or standardized judicial writs whose issue required no special authority. That left all patents of grants and appointments and many writs to the six clerks and the petty bag,[1] the clerks who composed the special department of the master of the rolls. He had the appointment of both groups in his gift.[2]

Cromwell was, therefore, directly in charge of those parts of the chancery machinery which kept its records and issued, among other things, the less stereotyped kinds of documents. As the chief of the masters and second-in-command of the whole of chancery, he could exercise a general control over the whole of its clerical organization. In this respect, the office was one of considerable importance in the administration, for though the chancery was no longer the sole, or even perhaps the most important, secretariat of the crown, it was still far and away the biggest. It handled much the greater part of the routine clerical work which enabled the government to be carried on. Even if Cromwell did not personally write, check, or 'ply' chancery documents,[3] he was, as master of the rolls, responsible for a great many of them and was altogether in charge of the whole writing side of chancery. On the available evidence it is impossible to say whether he ever carried out the duties of the office, but perhaps it may be considered significant that he seems never to have appointed the deputy whom his patent permitted, and that he relinquished this profitable office as soon as he became lord privy seal. This was a time when his star was definitely in the ascendant, so that the reason for his resignation must not be sought in opposition from king and

---

[1] Croke gave a long list of writs affecting the judicial side of the chancery 'where the Master of the Rolles has a ffee' and reserved to the petty bag.

[2] Statute 14 & 15 Henry VIII, c. 8; *L.P.* XII. II. 638.

[3] In May 1545, Lord Chancellor Wriothesley ordered 'that no ordinarye processe do passe to the seale...but the same be first perused and plyed [folded] by some one of the Maisters of Chauncery' (Sanders, *Orders of Chancery*, 8). Wriothesley learned his business under Cromwell.

court. Nor would fear of pluralism explain it: one more office would hardly have made much difference. The mastership of the rolls cannot have been considered too lowly for a man who continued to hold the much inferior offices of the jewels, the hanaper, and the chancellorship of the exchequer until his fall. It seems more likely that the duties of the new office, involving the supervision of yet another secretariat, and the mounting pressure of business which fell to the share of the king's first minister, forced him to surrender an office which, in that case, can have been no sinecure.

Today we think of the master of the rolls as first and foremost a judge; did Cromwell act as one? The answer is complicated by the fact that he was a councillor, and therefore endowed with quasi-judicial functions; the many appeals to him, his frequent arbitration between contending parties, and particularly his concern with political cases, are really to be ascribed to that side of his official life.[1] Without investigating all the yet unsorted chancery proceedings for the relevant two years, a task quite beyond the scope of the present study, it cannot be asserted with complete assurance that he never sat as a judge in chancery, either as the lord chancellor's deputy at Westminster or hearing cases in the Rolls Chapel, as did the master of the rolls in the early seventeenth century;[2] but the possibility is very remote. Wolsey had begun to delegate part of the chancellor's judicial duties to the master of the rolls,[3] but while commissions are known to Cromwell's predecessor and one of his successors to hear cases because the chancellor was too busy in other affairs,[4] there survives no such commission for Cromwell. During his rule the chancellor, Audeley, confined himself to his judicial duties and needed no help, nor is it easy to see how Cromwell could have spared the time to give him any. The weight of probability is, therefore, against the supposition that Cromwell ever acted as a

---

[1] In March 1535, e.g., a number of men were cited to appear before Cromwell, sitting either by himself or with others in the star chamber, or with the chancellor; the very mention of the star chamber indicates that conciliar jurisdiction was referred to, and the fact that most of the cases concerned treasonable utterances strengthens the interpretation (*L.P.* VIII. 457).　　[2] Wilson, 'Lord Chanc. in early 17th Cent.', 6.

[3] Holdsworth, *Hist. Eng. Law*, I. 419.

[4] *L.P.* IV. 5666, commission to John Taylor, master of the rolls, and others, to relieve Wolsey; *L.P.* XIX. II. 527 (24), the same to Sir Robert Southwell and three masters in chancery, to relieve Wriothesley.

judge in chancery, and so far, at least, there is no evidence to the contrary.[1]

Though Cromwell was not commissioned to hear cases, there was some special business he had to transact as master of the rolls. Perhaps nothing particularly appertaining to the office was implied by his acting in land purchases for the crown—such action had been common before he became master; but when he is found associated with the chancellor, attorney general, and solicitor general, his tenure of a near-legal office may have played its part.[2] Of more interest is a commission to him, as master of the rolls and jointly with the chancellor, which gave him power to grant denizations;[3] the patent rolls show that he used the powers thus conferred only a little.[4] As master of the rolls he was also commissioned to take compositions for first-fruits under the act of 1534; the details of this are discussed below.[5] It is arguable that he took the office, after first planning to put Tregonwell in, mainly because it offered a means of controlling the new revenue, but the point cannot be proved.

The mastership of the rolls thus did three things for Cromwell. It greatly increased his income and gave him a house; it gave him control over the clerical—that is, the administrative—side of chancery; and it gave him an office of antiquity and standing. He seems to have attended to the administrative duties of the office rather than to its legal and judicial possibilities. There is nothing to show that he altered its scope or functions in any way, or gave it an increased importance in the official hierarchy.

If the chief importance of the rolls lay in the salary, the privy seal added to this attraction the further advantage of a very high standing. When Cromwell succeeded the earl of Wiltshire, he became the fourth great officer of state, after the chancellor, treasurer, and president of the council, and for the rest of his life he governed the

---

[1] It appears to be agreed that the real rise of the master of the rolls as a judge dates from the early seventeenth century (Holdsworth, *Hist. Eng. Law*, I. 420; Wilson, *op. cit.* 5 f.).

[2] *L.P.* VIII. 362. He is described there as chief secretary and master of the rolls.

[3] *Ibid.* 291 (17).

[4] E.g. C 66/665 (25 Henry VIII, pt. 2), where of 105 denizations entered on the last three membranes 11 are marked 'per T Crumwell'.

[5] Pp. 194 f.

country, and controlled the administration, in that capacity. Even after he obtained the greater but empty dignity of lord great chamberlain of England, he was still habitually addressed as lord privy seal, for by virtue of that office he headed the government. Like the secretary, the keeper of the privy seal had few fixed duties but great opportunities, if he were ready to take them. However, in all the centuries of the office Cromwell was the only lord privy seal who as such was also chief minister of the crown; he did not establish this office as he did that of secretary. There is no need to recite the spheres of government with which he concerned himself; they were the same as those of his secretaryship, which means that they were all-embracing. Cromwell's work continued unchanged after he took on his new dignity, and the significance of his promotion was social and personal rather than political. As for his specific duties, the lord privy seal was very definitely the head of the privy seal office, but this and Cromwell's dealings with it will be discussed in another place.[1]

It is, thus, unnecessary to study in detail his work in the office of lord privy seal, but one aspect of it, which falls rather outside the administrative limits of this investigation, must be considered. The lord privy seal was regarded as the *ex officio* president of the court of requests. Although this association was never established by anything more definite than custom, or at the most prescription, and although the normal practice of the sixteenth century contradicted it, it was taken for granted by legal writers like Coke.[2] It is true that Bishop Foxe, as lord privy seal, presided over the early years of the court;[3] that a letter of 1608, addressed to the lord privy seal, enumerated its shortcomings and suggested that these might be remedied if 'it pleased your lordship to grace and honour the Court sometymes with your presence' and if the acting judge daily reported to the lord privy seal on what had taken place;[4] and that in the reign

---

[1] Below, pp. 268 f., 286 ff.

[2] Coke, *Fourth Institute*, 97: 'wherein the Lord Privie Seal at his pleasure, and the Masters of Requests do assemble and sit.'

[3] Pollard, *Wolsey*, 83. Pollard suggested that it was Foxe's long association with the budding court that established the connexion.

[4] Printed by I. S. Leadam, *Select Cases in the Court of Requests 1497–1569* (Selden Soc. 1898), pp. xcvi ff.

of Charles I a reforming lord privy seal at last revived Foxe's activities in the court.[1] But this theoretical connexion between the lord privy seal and the court of requests was rarely noticeable in practice. Though, in Cromwell's time, the court always described itself simply as the king's council, it was referred to as a court[2] and had a fixed personnel: the phrase 'court of requests' occurs for the first time in its order books at the beginning of the Hilary Term, 20 Henry VIII (1529) where a list is given of 'suche Counsaillours as be appoynted for the Heryng of Power mennes causes in the Kynges Courte of Requestes'.[3] There is no mention in this list of the lord privy seal; the fifteen names are headed by the bishops of Lincoln and St Asaph and the dean of the chapel. Nor is there any evidence that any keeper of the privy seal took an active part in the affairs of the court under Elizabeth.[4] Cromwell was no exception to this determined divorce between theory and practice. He did nothing to advance the growth of the court which, though it might continue to call itself the king's council in general terms, was a clearly defined branch of that body by 1529, with its residence fixed in the White Hall of the palace of Westminster and some councillors delegated to do its work.[5] It does not appear that the work of the court either increased or decreased noticeably during the 1530's. The real question, however, is whether Cromwell ever sat in the court—whether, that is, he exercised one of the more precise functions theoretically belonging to the office of the privy seal. The books of orders and decrees do not mention his name, but their entries are after a pattern and never specify any of the members of the court.[6] We are, therefore, forced to rely on the proceedings of which the 172 cases which have so far been dated to the years of Cromwell's

[1] The earl of Manchester: *ibid.* p. xlvii.

[2] Thus a defendant would declare himself ready to abide by the decision of 'thys honorable Court' (Req 2/1/18, no. 3).

[3] Req 1/5, fo. 86. The list is not later than the date given because the Sir John Huse (Hussey) mentioned in it was created a peer in the 1529 session of parliament (*D.N.B.*).

[4] W. B. J. Allsebrook, 'The Court of Requests in the Reign of Elizabeth', unpub. thesis (London, 1936), p. 5.

[5] Leadam, *Select Cases...Requests*, pp. xii–xv. By 1531, the order books at times use the phrase 'court of requests' (Req 1/5, fo. 254 *et al.*), though later they revert to an exclusive use of 'king's council'.

[6] Req 1/5–7.

supremacy have been examined; though there are probably more, the number is large enough to permit some generalizations.[1]

Many of the documents in the files bear notes and endorsements in the hand of the clerk of the court[2] and signed by a number of councillors. In the period concerned there are eight such names: Nicholas Hare, Edward Carne, Thomas Thirlby, Richard Sampson, John Tregonwell, William Sulyard, Richard Wolman, and Edmund Bonner.[3] Of these, Sampson, Sulyard, and Wolman were in the 1529 list quoted above. The signatures appear singly or in pairs; once Hare, Tregonwell, and Thirlby are associated,[4] and twice we find four names.[5] These, then, were the men who did the actual work of the court. It might be argued that bigger men, more important councillors, might have been present, and that the smaller fry were deputed to see to the issue of privy seals for appearances, or to the committal of cases for local inquiry, but the same men also signed the decrees of the court.[6] Interrogatories and letters concerning cases were addressed to Hare and Thirlby;[7] a petition was endorsed to the effect that 'yt is ordred by Sʳ Nycholas Hare Knyght, on[e] of the kinges honerable Councell';[8] a defendant was ordered to appear 'per mandatum magistri Hare'.[9] Hare himself wrote to a defendant in terms which show him to have been in charge.[10] These councillors, who did the work, already deserve the name of masters of requests, though they did not bear it and though their number indicates that the ultimate system of two masters-in-ordinary had not yet evolved.[11]

[1] All the cases have been gone into which are dated into 27–31 Henry VIII (1535–40) in Hunt's MS. Calendar at the P.R.O. It may be supposed that among those he left undated there are at least some belonging to that period, but there could be no thought of going through them to date them.

[2] Richard Turnour, the senior clerk of the privy seal (cf. W. Lambarde, *Archeion*, 1635, p. 230).

[3] A ninth, Robert Southwell, occurs on a document marked in a modern hand as later than March 1539 (Req 2/9/134), but Southwell was not appointed till March 1540 when he succeeded Hare (*L.P.* xv. 436, 56).

[4] Req 2/3/147.

[5] Req 2/3/112—Sampson, Hare, Carne, Thirlby; and 12/184—Hare, Thirlby, Bonner, Carne.

[6] Req 1/5, fos. 379, 453 (Wolman and Sulyard); Req 2/3/31, 147, 187 (Hare and Tregonwell).   [7] Req 2/4/104 and 6/172.

[8] *Ibid.* 2/78.   [9] *Ibid.* 6/175.

[10] *Ibid.* 6/107: 'otherways I shall be drevyn of Iustice at the request of the said partye to send for you by proces.'

[11] In this connexion it is of interest to notice that the two most frequent signatories,

A number of councillors were specially detached to the work of the court of requests, and the lord privy seal was not one of them. There is nothing to show that Cromwell ever took an active part in this work.

There are, however, two cases among the 172 investigated in which Cromwell appears. The first is that of *Henry Reed (alias Sagon)* v. *Sir Thomas Tyrell*, and is to be dated roughly into the second half of 1538.[1] It is not obviously different from any other case, except that plaintiff addressed his petition to the 'right honorable the lord pryvyseale', in defiance of the custom that bills in the court of requests were addressed to the king, or to king and council. This same petition bears endorsements signed by Hare and Carne which prove that the case went through the usual stages in the court. So does the whole of the file which contains plaintiff's petition, defendant's answer, commission under the privy seal—all parts of the regular procedure. The reason for the petition's address would seem to lie in its contents. Reed's quarrel with Tyrell was of long standing; he had appealed four times to the duke of Norfolk and once before to Cromwell, and had secured a temporary end to the nuisance. Now Tyrell was causing trouble again, and Reed repeated his personal appeal to Cromwell; the fact that the case was investigated by the court of requests suggests either that Cromwell grew tired of so persistent a petitioner, or more probably that he was doubtful of achieving the desired result against a man who had already disobeyed his instructions. Perhaps he did not wish to antagonize a man who was one of the leading gentlemen in his shire and had been of some use to the government during the northern rebellion.[2] For some such reason, at any rate, he preferred to leave the matter in the hands of the established court into whose jurisdiction this 'poor man's cause' belonged; he passed a petition meant for himself personally to the court whose officers handled it in

and the only two common lawyers in our list (the others were all well-known civilians), Hare and Sulyard, do not appear ever to have acted together. Hare first appears on 22 November 1537 (Req 2/3/162), and Sulyard last on the 27th of that month (*ibid.* 8/284). He was appointed to the council in the marches of Wales towards the end of 1537; was Hare his successor as representative of the common law? If so, he was in his turn succeeded by Robert Southwell (above, p. 136, n. 3).

[1] Req 2/1/18. The privy seal included in the file is dated 1 July and orders an answer by 14 October; an endorsement bears date of 29 June 1538.

[2] *L.P.* XI. 615, 642.

the usual manner. Ordinarily Cromwell dealt with such petitions directly, as he had done with Reed's earlier appeal; since this case was an exception, it is clear that he normally had nothing to do with the court.

The other case to be considered does not at first sight fit so well into the picture here presented; it is that of *Simon Stretton* v. *William Butler*.[1] Here we have none of the procedure usual in the court of requests. The file consists of five documents: an order to defendant signed by five Warwickshire J.P.s, a petition (or rather a reminder) from plaintiff to Cromwell, a personal letter from Cromwell to three magistrates in Warwickshire, their reply, and witnesses' depositions taken by them. The only sign that the papers belong to the court is an endorsement on the last-named document, 'det' est ut inf[ra]'. This is written in a different hand from the one which wrote 'conserning streton' above it; the latter hand is one which occurs frequently on the back of Cromwell's papers and must therefore belong to one of his private clerks. The documents suggest the procedure of the court in a rudimentary way. Plaintiff's petition was apparently replaced by a personal interview and a written reminder that Cromwell had promised assistance. There is no defendant's answer, but Cromwell's letter shows that one local gentleman had written on his behalf. Instead of a commission under the privy seal there is an informal letter signed by Cromwell which is, however, described by the recipients as a 'lettre commyssyve'. Their answer is not a formal certificate rendered to the council, but again an informal letter, this time to Cromwell. The documents make it plain that Cromwell dealt with the case personally and on his own. There is no mention of court or council, no name or signature of one of the regular judges, everything is on paper instead of parchment. We have here, in fact, an example of the way in which Cromwell handled petitions addressed to himself: he used the method common in the council and conciliar courts of getting the facts established by the local magistrates before deciding on the merits of a case. Nothing in all this shows him acting as a member of the court of requests.[2]

[1] Req 2/4/203.
[2] For the probable explanation of the fact that the file is found in the records of the court, cf. my note in *Bull. I.H.R.* XXII. 37.

Cromwell's last two offices thus contained judicial elements; the master of the rolls, as the chancellor's deputy, and the lord privy seal, as president of the minor conciliar court of requests, could both act as judges. Cromwell, however, refused to let either office involve him in those particular routine duties; he ignored the chances offered of devoting to the law courts such minute and direct interest as he applied to the administration. The working of the courts, whether common law, chancery, or conciliar, was not a reason for which he acquired any of his offices; that detail is conspicuously absent from the overwhelmingly large record of his work. As master of the rolls and as lord privy seal he occupied a notable place and earned a considerable salary; moreover, he controlled two administrative secretariats through these offices. As lord privy seal, also, he superintended the government of England. More even than the secretaryship, the greater title and office enabled him to stand forth as the king's chief minister.

4. *Cromwell as a treasurer*

One of Cromwell's offices, so far only briefly touched upon, must now be discussed in more detail; its significance lies more in the light it throws on his methods than in the ephemeral part it played in national administration. It has already been remarked that as master of the jewels Cromwell himself acted as a treasurer for the king's money. This is altogether a different thing from his constant activity about the king's revenues; it will be shown that he not only occupied himself largely with the finances of the state, supervising other officials who in actual fact handled the money whose use he directed, but that he was personally in charge of considerable sums for which he was as responsible as, for example, the treasurer of the chamber was for his share of the revenues. When Cromwell was still very new to the king's service he was entrusted with such tasks as the receipt of a small sum for the king's tomb,[1] or the payment of money on the king's account to an Italian sculptor;[2] as late as April 1536 a paper recording payments was endorsed as 'A declaracon of money paid by Master Secretary to the kinges vse'.[3] This is the last sign

---

[1] Nicolas, *Privy Purse Expenses*, 101 (31 Dec. 1530).
[2] *L.P.* v. 32 (7 Jan. 1531).   [3] SP 1:103, fos. 58–9 (*L.P.* x. 598).

extant of a personal treasurership; of course, Cromwell continued to authorize and order payments by other treasurers, but as far as is known he ceased about that date to perform such tasks in person and through his private office. For the first five years of his ministry, however, Cromwell was himself part of the machinery of the financial administration, receiving and paying the king's money either in person or through his private servants, such as Williamson, Cavendish, and Body who held his 'letter of attorney...to receive all sums of money due to the King's highness' in his name.[1] He was accountable for the money; he was as much the king's treasurer as were the officers of the exchequer, the treasurer of the chamber, or any other official responsible for part of the royal revenues. It is important to remember that he did not relinquish these tasks until 1536; though undoubtedly his treasurership in its beginnings was part of his apprenticeship in the business of government, he was, from early in 1533 at the very latest, the king's chief minister who made and directed policy and generally occupied himself with every aspect of administration. For three years, therefore, after he had reached the summit of power under the crown, he continued in personal charge of money for the king.

The reasons underlying all this cannot become clear without a detailed investigation of the sums involved, the sources of the money, and the purposes on which it was spent. Though his treasurership extended from January 1531 to April 1536, figures and details are available only for the period April 1532 to April 1535; but from them all the necessary deductions may legitimately be made. Four of his accounts survive for money received and spent on the king's behalf, proving that he had to answer for his office, though there is no sign of an audit. Possibly he was sufficiently powerful to discharge himself or to do without a formal discharge; the accounts were found among his private papers—some are drafts only—and may represent rather his private servants' answers to himself than his to the king.[2] The first (hereafter called A) ostensibly covered the time from

---

[1] *L.P.* IX. 234 (1535).

[2] The only trace of these affairs in the exchequer are his warrants (cf. below, p. 142, n. 2), preserved among the Various Accounts (E 101), which suggests that they were handed in as 'particulars of account' at the time of audit. But who audited Cromwell's accounts or when this was done, if at all, cannot be discovered.

29 September 1532 to 17 December 1532.[1] There had been a previous account, made up at Michaelmas,[2] but it is clear from the body of the document that this did not take matters further than 2 April 1532, twelve days before Cromwell's appointment as master of the jewels took effect, and that A started on that date.[3] Quite possibly he was regularly receiving and disbursing money to the king's use from the beginning of 1531, though at that time he perhaps had only the handling of the revenues from the lands of Wolsey's colleges.[4] The existence of an earlier account, closed on 2 April, suggests that he may have taken over the business of the master of the jewels on that day, having drawn a line under the account of the money he had so far dealt with and started a new one to include the new business. The date of his patent, being the date of its delivery into chancery, is not, of course, a sure guide to the actual date of appointment. But whatever may be surmised for the first year of Cromwell's treasurership, there is no difficulty from April 1532 onwards: the second account (B) covered the period from 22 November 1532 to 11 March 1533,[5] the third (C) that from 29 September 1532 to 28 June 1533,[6] and the fourth (D) that from 2 April 1533 to 2 April 1534.[7]

There is thus considerable overlapping, nor are all these accounts of one kind. A and D are 'views' or short abstracts made from the detailed accounts, stating simply totals of receipts, payments, and surplus or deficit, though A contains other detail not strictly proper to a view of account. B and C, on the other hand, are detailed. They analyse both receipts and payments into individual sources and destinations, and for that reason will be of great use in determining whence Cromwell derived the money and to whom he paid it. For assessing the amount of money that passed under his hand they are naturally less reliable. A and D are taken from finished accounts; B and C are drafts, C being in Cromwell's own hand and B

---

[1] SP 1:72, fos. 156–7 (*L.P.* V. 1639); given below, App. II, A, p. 431.

[2] *Ibid.*: '...chargid for the Arrerages of the last accompt...endid at the said ffeast of saint Michell tharchangell Anno xxiiij^{to} Regis Henrici viij^{ui}.'

[3] *Ibid.*: 'sence the Determinacion of the saide Accompte, which was the Secunde day of Aprill...'.

[4] Cf. *L.P.* V. 341, 774.   [5] SP 2:N, fos. 114–17 (*L.P.* VI. 228).

[6] SP 2:O, fos. 190–5 (*L.P.* VI. 717).

[7] SP 1:83, fos. 61–2 (*L.P.* VII. 430). The recurrence of the date of 2 April suggests some significance which, however, I have been unable to discover.

containing additions in his writing. The results which they provide
may be tabulated thus:[1]

	Receipts	Payments
A (2 April 1532–17 Dec. 1532)	£25,655	£24,606
B (22 Nov. 1532–11 March 1533)	£20,567	£21,240
C (29 Sept. 1532–28 June 1533)	£12,496	£12,332
D (2 April 1533–2 April 1534)	£38,504	£37,232

The three and a half months of B (the only account in which payments exceed receipts) are included in the nine months of C, but the
former accounts for £8,000 more than the latter, though both mention much the same sources of revenue. They cannot both be right,
and unless one is prepared to suspect deliberate misstatements, a
suspicion for which there is neither reasonable ground nor reasonable
explanation, C will have to be discarded as less complete. It may be
supposed to be a first and unfinished draft of an account, and the
fact that Cromwell himself wrote it supports the supposition.
Incompleteness is also suggested by a comparison with D which,
accounting for only three months more than C, gives figures three
times as large, the general reliability of D being corroborated by the
other full account, A, which for its seven and a half months accounts
for a sum roughly equal in proportion to that given in D.

Cromwell's income and expenditure can be calculated from these
accounts with some accuracy. If A and B are added they will account
for about twelve consecutive months, in which time, therefore,
£46,222 would have been received and £45,846 spent, rather larger
sums than those given in D for the full year ending on 2 April 1534.
A check is provided by the warrants for expenditure from which it is
possible to arrive at a minimum figure for the year ending in April
1535.[2] Twenty-four of them cover the year after the last surviving
account, the earliest being dated 4 April 1534 and the last 2 May

---

[1] All sums of money will normally be given in pounds only.

[2] The warrants to Cromwell are preserved in three bundles: E 101/421/5 (calendared
in *L.P.* v. 825, 1052, 1237, 1314, 1346, 1392, 1590, 1646, 1668, 1671); *ibid.* 421/6
(33 items not calendared in *L.P.*); and *ibid.* 421/9 (*L.P.* vi. 6, 130, 131, 149, 170, 220,
229, 283, 326). There are also a number of loose ones: E 101/421/1 (*L.P.* v. 341); B.M.,
Tit. B. i, fos. 449–50 (*L.P.* ix. 217); and some bound with the state papers at the P.R.O.
(*L.P.* v. 1119, 1215, 1370, 1645; vi. 1057, 1367, 1508; vii. 137, 1557, 1564; viii. 653;
x. 598; *Add.* 1013).

1535.[1] They prove that during this year Cromwell paid at least £32,407 for purposes of state. There is, of course, no way of discovering what proportion of these warrants has been preserved, and the actual sums involved may have been much larger. Twenty-four warrants for one year, even though many of them authorized the payments of a large number of items,[2] and even though they add up to the total quoted, is not a great number, and it is as well to remember that they can but provide the lowest possible figure for the year. A mere fourteen warrants survive for the year covered by account D, and they record payments to the sum of only £10,310.[3] Cromwell, then, received sums averaging about £40,000 a year and spent them nearly all. The slight gradual decline year by year is probably due to the natural fluctuations of expenditure in an office concerned (as will be seen later) with irregular and unrecurring business, or to the incompleteness of the evidence; it proves nothing else.[4] One thing the facts put beyond doubt: a treasurer who spent practically the whole of his income was less a collector of revenue than a paymaster. The point is important, especially in view of the sources from which Cromwell received his money.

Dr Dietz has noted that in 1532 Cromwell 'began to act as a special treasurer for new revenues',[5] a remark which prompted one reviewer to demand a more detailed discussion of the administrative significance of this phenomenon, especially as he thought that Cromwell must have been encroaching on the chamber.[6] Both were right to some extent, though Dr Dietz was wrong in laying so much stress on the novelty of the revenues administered by Cromwell. Account B gives these sources of income: suppressed lands, restitu-

[1] E 101/421/6, nos. (in chronological order) 22, 52, 37, 34, 38, 36, 39, 35, 40, 41, 47, 42, 43, 45, 50, 46, 44, 49, 48, 51, 32, 33; and *L.P.* VII. 1557; VIII. 653.

[2] E 101/421/6, no. 50 contains 14 items, no. 45 twelve, nos. 38 and 49 eleven, nos. 51 and 52 ten, etc.

[3] *L.P.* VI. 326, 1057, 1058, 1367, 1508; VII. 137. E 101/421/6, nos. 23, 25, 24, 26, 27, 29, 30, 28.

[4] Though the figures have already been given, here is a table for convenience' sake:

	Receipts	Payments
April 1532—April 1533 (A+B)	£46,222	£45,846
April 1533—April 1534 (D)	£38,504	£37,232
April 1534—April 1535 (warrants)	—	£32,407

[5] F. C. Dietz, *English Government Finance 1485–1558*, 103.

[6] Prof. J. E. Neale in *E.H.R.* XXXVIII. 280.

tion of temporalities, money due by obligation, chains molten, money due without specialties or bonds (from the jewel-house), vacation of bishoprics and abbeys, the 'mount'[1] of the late arch-bishop of Canterbury (Warham), 'performes and fee ffermes', first fifth of the money granted by the spiritualty at the last convocation (1531), from the hanaper, from the king's coffers, money lately prested (lent out) by the king, and forfeited lands and goods. Account C repeats some of these and adds fines for the appropriation of houses to the item headed restitution of temporalities, £100 for conduct money given to the king by the merchant adventurers for 'wafters',[2] fines for the knights, and money for 'certain provisions' for the king—probably the prest money mentioned in B.

Some of this was new revenue which the crown had not hitherto received, and some of it was diverted from the chamber. As receiver general of the lands of the suppressed monasteries used to found Wolsey's colleges (suppressed lands),[3] and as the man in charge of the lands of Rice ap Griffiths (attainted lands),[4] Cromwell drew money from land revenues which ought by rights to have gone to the treasurer of the chamber, under the terms of the act which directed the revenues of all forfeited lands, old and new, into that depart-ment.[5] Receivers for vacant sees and of fines for the restitution of temporalities accounted before the general surveyors,[6] but the act did not say whether the money itself was to be paid into the chamber, though it has to be assumed that such extraordinary revenues were almost certainly handled by the chamber before Cromwell appeared on the scene.[7] Then he took them, for he is found controlling the revenues of the vacant sees of York and Chester.[8] Part of his income came to him as master of the jewels ('chains molten' represent not so much revenue as a capital expenditure); he cut in further on chamber preserves by taking some of the repaid debts due to the king

---

[1] I.e. mounter=heriot?

[2] 'Wafter—an armed vessel employed as a convoy', *N.E.D.* (1928), vol. x, pt. ii, 8c.

[3] *L.P.* v. 701.

[4] *Ibid.* 724. Para. 7 is in Cromwell's hand, and the commissioners mentioned in para. 9 include his confidential servant William Brabazon.

[5] 14 & 15 Henry VIII, c. 15 (*Stat. Realm*, III. 229).   [6] *L.P.* v. 397.

[7] Newton, *E.H.R.* xxxii. 363 f. Tuke, treasurer of the chamber, indicated that he got something from vacancies (*L.P.* xiv. II. 13).

[8] *L.P.* v. 95, 237, 277.

(obligations and prests);[1] a number of small and incidental sources of income need not detain us; the hanaper money Cromwell might claim the right to expend as clerk of the hanaper, even though it had hitherto swollen the resources of the treasurer of the chamber and was to continue to do so;[2] more important, there was the money granted by the spiritualty.

This point needs some discussion. The money in question must have been part of the *praemunire* fine imposed on convocation in 1531, but as that amounted to £118,000 for both provinces the £242 accounted for in B cannot have been more than a small proportion of the 'first fifth'. Dr Dietz maintained that the whole of the fine was paid to Cromwell.[3] However, the original grant stated that the money was to go to the treasurer of the chamber,[4] the exchequer was informed likewise,[5] and the treasurer, Tuke, proved that this condition was carried out when he deplored the remission of the last payments in exchange for the new revenue from first-fruits and tenths.[6]

The kinges highnes remytteth to the clergie of the province of Canterbury xl M li' of the ij last payments besides a some to the province of yorke, And of these ij last payments on[e] was due at mychelmas last; for levye wherof commyssions be oute, collectours appointed, and the money euery day nowe payable to the particular collectours; and to the general collectours after cristenmas; and to the treasorer of the chambre by our lady day in lent next...I have vsed sone after cristenmas to receyue som parte, and so contynually as it can be had.

It seems most unlikely that Cromwell ever got much of this fine, and the £242 he received was possibly the part of the fine resting on clergy with whom he had a special connexion—those of vacant sees, for instance.

Further, Cromwell revived Henry VII's expedient of enforcing distraint of knighthood. This source yielded £390 in account C;

---

[1] Cromwell never handled all the royal debts, and Tuke continued to concern himself with a good many.

[2] As the hanaper accounts show, the surplus continued to go to the treasurer of the chamber. The £300 of hanaper money mentioned in B are clearly the 'profit of the office in Thomas Hall's time' which Cromwell had received from the underclerk (*L.P.* v. 1730), and represent a unique case of hanaper money coming to Cromwell.

[3] Dietz, *Eng. Gov. Fin.* 227.   [4] E 135/8/37.

[5] E 159/310, Communia, Trinity Term, Recorda, m. 22.

[6] B.M., Tit. B. i, fo. 286 (*L.P.* VII. 1490).

a schedule annexed to A, reciting sums of money due but not yet collected, includes unpaid fines for knighthood, and the considerable figure of £2,180 is mentioned.[1] Cromwell's correspondence contains a good deal on this subject in 1533 and 1534. People asked to be excused, claiming that they had been assessed too high or pleading similar excuses on the behalf of friends and servants;[2] even the Princess Mary joined in the chorus.[3] Among the papers which apparently came into Cromwell's custody before October 1531 there was one described as a copy of 'the King's letter to write to knights', and among the remembrances of 1533 occurs the note 'to make a search through the Book of Knights for the names of them who shall be enclosed in the King's letters':[4] the machinery for enforcing fines for knighthood seems to have been well developed. The necessary orders appear to have been embodied in royal warrants authorizing Cromwell to compound for knighthood and assess fines of which some are listed among his papers.[5] As late as March 1535, the sheriff of Oxfordshire was told to have persons mentioned in an enclosed list appear before Cromwell ('principal secretary') to compound for their knighthood or send up their fines.[6] The numbers involved were large: in 1533, 1,010 were returned as suitable to be made knights, and 425 had already made out obligations for payments to discharge them of the honour.[7] This method of extorting money was certainly not new—it had helped to bring about the fall of Empson and Dudley; it had always been most unpopular, and was likely to be so now. Its revival by Cromwell is significant as a sign that in one respect at least his accession to power was involving the government in a partial return to the policy of Henry VII. Once more money was needed, for Wolsey had done nothing to keep the coffers filled,[8] and for the time being the new minister, in his capacity

---

[1] SP 1:72, fo. 157. The other items are fines made with 'sondry persons spirituall and temporall to the kinges vse whiche be vnpaide', specialties forfeit for conveying corn (out of the kingdom), and money lent by the king's orders—a total of £18,031 outstanding. Some such factor may be behind the discrepancy between B and C.

[2] *L.P.* vi. 425, 468, 514, 516, 521, 575, 607, 1160, 1178, 1260, 1360, 1390, 1659; vii. 80, 123, 833, 1305, 1662. Cf. also Hall, *Chronicle*, 795, to the effect that Cromwell improved the occasion of Anne's wedding at Easter 1533 by raising large sums on 'that sessyng of fines' for knighthood.

[3] *L.P.* vi. 550.

[4] *L.P.* vii. 923 (vii); vi. 1056 (i).

[5] *L.P.* vii. 923 (xli).

[6] *L.P. Add.* 988.

[7] *Ibid.* 877.

[8] Dietz, *Eng. Gov. Fin.* 102.

as treasurer, was trying to use the old and proven methods. The sums obtained, however, were hardly large enough to justify the risk of alienating the gentry and middle classes at a time when their support in parliament became essential.

However, all the sources of revenue so far discussed, some of which were new and more of which should have gone to the chamber, add up to less than half the money which Cromwell actually received. By far the biggest item in his accounts is money derived from the royal coffers, that is, from reserves built up in the Tower and possibly in other royal palaces. Such money accounts for £11,034 of the total receipts recorded in B (£20,567), and for no less than £10,991 in C (total: £12,469). The subject of how 'the king's coffers' were filled and administered is a dark one; it is likely that surpluses in such departments as the treasury of the chamber were not kept there but were deposited in special and quite informal treasuries, called by that name. For the present purpose it is enough to say that such depositories existed, and that even at this time they must have contained quite considerable reserves. Cromwell's expenditure was, therefore, largely of capital, and the true significance of his treasurership must not be sought in the collection or increase of revenue. It is of interest and some importance that he was actually receiving money which would otherwise have gone into the chamber, though, taking it all in all, his personal treasurership had little effect on the income of the treasurer of the chamber. He showed a distinct tendency to acquire any revenue, repetitive or occurring only once, which had no traditional channel by which to reach the government, but as he so largely relied on capital reserves this cannot have been his chief interest in his personal treasurership. It must be concluded that what mattered to him was the need of having sufficient money to meet the expenditure which fell to his share, and to that expenditure we must now turn.

Account B lists ten groups of payments, with an eleventh un-provided with a marginal heading, of which these account for the larger sums: buildings at the Tower, costs and rewards to ambassadors and others, loans, and in particular £12,584 sent north for employment against the Scots. It includes such sums as 8*d.* for carriage and 14*s.* 4*d.* for paper and ink, but these are the only expenses which can be called, in the language of the time, 'necessary' or current office expenditure. £1,100 paid into the king's coffers would be of greater interest if it did not appear that it was received in bulk, being revenues of the vacant see of Canterbury and the late archbishop's 'mount'; this is not a case of surplus being deposited in the coffers. However, another £1,000 was paid into the coffers after the first part of the account had been made up.[1] There is the usual item for the king's tomb which runs through the whole of Cromwell's association with the royal finances, and £55 was spent on silks and velvet. Account C adds some interesting points: buildings at Westminster, the king's ships, £300 to Cornelys Hayes, the goldsmith, and £3,591 to creditors of the great wardrobe. Twenty-four shillings was paid for paper, parchment, ink, and wax. Cromwell did not control a large regular office; no wages were paid to clerks and internal expenses were confined to money spent on writing materials. The treasurer of the jewels naturally had dealings with the king's goldsmith, and other items resulted from his connexion with the royal household, but these were but a small part of the total payments. Most of the money went in paying for such purposes as the diets of the king's ambassadors or rewards given to foreign ambassadors, or for exceptional outlays—the consequence of acts of high policy. Thus Cromwell supplied Sir George Lawson, who as treasurer of Berwick administered the money sent north for the defence of the border. By the end of 1532, Lawson had received £4,534 from Cromwell,[2] and throughout 1533 he was always writing to him for money.[3] Lawson's accounts show that between 14 September 1532 and 17 June 1533 he received £23,368 of which £20,033 was supplied by Cromwell,[4] large figures but not so large as the somewhat exaggerated sum of £30,000 which Cromwell was supposed

---

[1] There are a few other examples of Cromwell paying sums into the king's coffers (*L.P.* v. 577, 825, 1040, 1052, 1119), but they are all of an early date, before Cromwell rose to real importance. None of these warrants and receipts call him master of the jewels, all but two being of a date earlier than his appointment. After he became a treasurer in the full sense he rarely paid money into the coffers.

[2] *L.P.* v. 1670 (2); the warrants are *ibid.* 1590, 1571. He was also getting large sums through the abbot of St Mary's, York, by the king's warrant (*L.P.* VI. 86), but the abbot was controlled by Cromwell (*ibid.* 1162, 217).

[3] *L.P.* VI. 25, 29, 51, 107, 124, 185, 269, 343, 553, 1162.

[4] SP 2:O, fo. 185 (*L.P.* VI. 664).

to have sent north by 11 January 1533.[1] Similarly, Cromwell was responsible for financing the war in Ireland after Fitzgerald's revolt in 1534, and warrants show that between July 1534 and August 1535 he paid out £21,522 for this purpose, not counting rewards given to Irish officials whose loyalty was thought open to purchase. Nearly all this money went to William Brabazon, vice-treasurer of Ireland and treasurer at war there, and once one of Cromwell's own household servants.[2]

Altogether, the warrants are important evidence for the purposes on which the money was spent which passed through Cromwell's hands, and they serve to confirm and augment the testimony of the accounts. There is not one 'dormant' warrant among them; that is to say, Cromwell was not made responsible for regularly recurring payments. The purposes for which he paid were numerous, from such small items as £35 for South Wales iron mines or ten marks for alms,[3] to the thousands of pounds spent on military affairs in Ireland and the Scottish marches. Diets and post money to ambassadors are one large group of payments, and it is possibly of some significance that the ambassadors paid by the master of the jewels were particularly those who went to Germany and the Lutheran princes, that is those engaged in what was more specifically Cromwell's own policy.[4] Rewards given by the king both to foreign representatives and his own servants account for another considerable number of entries.[5] Frequent payments were made to William Gonson,

[1] *Ven. Cal.* IV. 842.

[2] E 101/421/6, nos. 33, 35, 36, 39, 41, 43; *L.P.* VIII. 654; IX. 217. In May 1535, Brabazon's accounts showed a receipt of £34,628 from England (*L.P.* VIII. 788). He may not have had all this from Cromwell: another of his accounts (*L.P.* XI. 935, October 1536), which probably covers only the year ending Michaelmas 1536, shows that Cromwell was responsible for £13,718 out of a total of £35,692; the largest single contributor was the treasurer of first-fruits who, however, did not exist during the period of the first account.

[3] *L.P.* V. 1215, 1346.

[4] E.g. Thomas Legh (*L.P.* V. 1646; VII. 137; E 101/421/6, no. 38); Heath and Paget (*L.P.* VII. 137); Christopher Mount (*L.P.* IX. 217; E 101/421/6, no. 27); Cavendish (*ibid.* no. 49); Foxe, bishop of Hereford (*L.P.* IX. 217). However, Cromwell also paid other ambassadors, especially later when he was in complete control of the government: Hackett (with the emperor), Rocheford and Gardiner in France, and Lord William Howard in Scotland (E 101/421/6, nos. 27, 32, 38; *L.P.* IX. 217).

[5] A few examples will show their catholic range: John de Lenope, senator of Lübeck (*L.P.* VII. 1557), one 'that brought bowstaves' from the king of France (*L.P.* VIII. 653), Robert, groom of the chamber to the duke of Norfolk (E 101/421/6, no. 24), John

surveyor of the king's ships, for the navy; from October 1533 to December 1534, Gonson gave twenty receipts for a total of £4,195.[1] Cromwell also supplied the household of Katharine of Aragon,[2] advanced large sums to the cofferer of the household,[3] paid the creditors of the great wardrobe,[4] and paid the salaries of the king's legal officers, the judges and king's serjeants.[5]

In order that the significance of Cromwell's expenditure may be seen in its true light, it is necessary to discuss briefly of what government expenditure in the sixteenth century consisted.[6] In an age which was only beginning to emancipate itself from the idea that national expenditure was equivalent to the king's personal outlay, the government had a much more restricted field of payments than it is easy to realize. The basic division, made by contemporary officials, was into ordinary and extraordinary. The ordinary expenses were those that recurred regularly and could be allowed for in advance, as wages, salaries, pensions, grants on patents, annuities. These were charged on specified paymasters, each treasurer being responsible for some indiscriminately allotted to him in addition to those naturally falling to his share; the treasurer of the chamber, for instance, paid most chamber and household wages, but also various annuities that had nothing to do with either. Not technically 'ordinary' expenditure but rather in a class of its own was the up-keep of the royal household and wardrobe whose cofferer and keeper were supposed to keep the king and his court supplied, fed, clothed, and generally looked after, out of fixed allocations; this item was also foreseeable, at least within narrow limits, and the household was in fact the first department to begin proper budgeting.[7] The extra-ordinary payments, which covered everything else—everything that

---

Alleyn, master of the rolls in Ireland (no. 27), Thomas Orgall, for 'writings concerning our causes' (no. 30), the orator of the count palatine (no. 28), for bringing pirates from Grimsby to the Tower (no. 22), the ambassadors from Hamburg and Lübeck with their 'families' (no. 47), Thomas Derby and Thomas Wriothesley, clerks of the signet (no. 42).

[1] *L.P.* VII. 1564.
[2] E 101/421/6, nos. 37, 48, 49; *L.P.* VII. 1557; IX. 217.
[3] E 101/421/6, no. 26.   [4] *Ibid.* nos. 25, 50.
[5] *Ibid.* 34, 48; *L.P.* VII. 1557; X. 598.
[6] This account is based on a general study of the accounts of all contemporary treasuries (exchequer, chamber, duchy of Lancaster, augmentations, first-fruits); detailed evidence to support the statements made can be found in them all.
[7] Below, pp. 398 f.

had to be paid for in the day to day conduct of an ever more complicated government—were thus, from a statesman's point of view, the most important aspect of the national expenditure. Most of the items which loom largest in a modern budget were accounted extraordinary, despite the fact that they had long ceased to come but occasionally: purchases of land and building activities, the army, the navy, sea and coastal defences, the upkeep of overseas stations as well as border outposts like Berwick and Carlisle, war, diplomacy and foreign affairs. The payment to ambassadors, whether resident or special, of their diets (daily allowances) and post money—naturally a considerable sum—fell under this head. Very important were the many rewards ordered to be paid to all whose services or good opinion was useful, whether they were local men who had acquired merit by some service in their locality, or royal servants of every degree whose meagre salaries had to be helped out by bonuses if the civil service was to be kept in a sound working condition, or foreign ambassadors arriving or leaving. The haphazard nature of these transactions must not disguise the fact that without them the government could not have been carried on; if the ordinary expenditure provided for the basic needs of king and crown, it was the extraordinary expenditure, often much bigger than the regular part, by which the demands of high policy and detailed administration were satisfied.

Cromwell's place in the administration of the finances can only be properly appreciated if both the size and the character of his payments are compared with those made by the other two national treasuries, the exchequer and chamber.[1] The growth of the chamber had been largely due to the great increase in 'extraordinary' expenditure after Henry VII's accession and the unsuitability of the exchequer for the rapid transaction of such business. Cromwell's turnover of about £40,000 compared well with both departments; if anything, it was a little larger than that of the exchequer which averaged about £37,500 a year, and rather less than that of the chamber which varied roughly from £55,000 to £35,000.[2] But the

---

[1] The duchy of Lancaster made very few payments of national importance; it was chiefly an organization for the collection of revenue.

[2] Exchequer expenditure in the years ending Michaelmas 1532, 1533, and 1534 was £38,935, £37,789, £37,106 respectively (Dietz, *Eng. Gov. Fin.* 216). For the chamber, cf. below, pp. 170 f.

exchequer's disbursements included assignments of £19,394 to the royal household and £1,175 to the great wardrobe, so that some £20,000 went to other spending departments. The remainder was largely made up of such regular payments as the salaries of exchequer officials and other officers of the crown, or annuities granted by patent. The only items which varied at all were the assignments on exchequer revenue made by the king as rewards to collectors of customs or minor servants and officials about the court.[1] Like the exchequer, the treasurer of the chamber had a great deal of ordinary expenditure in weekly, monthly, quarterly, and half-yearly wages, and in pensions and annuities; in May 1537 it was estimated to amount to £40,000 a year.[2] Though this was probably too generous an estimate, it is clear that the extraordinary payments in that department could not compare with Cromwell's. While the exchequer paid almost none of the charges which arise daily in the business of government, and while the chamber expended only less than half its money on such purposes, Cromwell, who concerned himself with almost nothing else, must have been chiefly responsible for keeping the wheels turning. His payments were, practically without exception, of the 'extraordinary' kind, though for some reason he paid the salaries due to the king's legal counsel. Others saw to the regular items of expenditure, big and small; the money which he administered went towards those expenses without which policy could not be transformed into reality and the country could not be governed. Though he never monopolized this important side of financial business, he took most of it and paid for very little else.

It may be thought that a busy minister like Cromwell cannot also have attended to the routine duties of a treasurer. However, it will not do to think of him as no more than largely supervising the work of others: that was—though the supervision was close—his relationship with other treasurers of the king's money; but it was not his relationship with those personal servants of his who collected and disbursed

---

[1] These facts and figures are derived from the annual 'Declaration of the State of Treasury', complete for the years 1530–40, except for the year ending at Michaelmas 1535. The documents in question are, in chronological order: E 405/199, 200; B.M., Add. MS. 33376; E 405/201, 202; E 164/69; E 405/203–5.

[2] SP 60:4, fo. 78 (*L.P.* XII. I. 1297): 'and myn ordinary paymentes besides casual warrantes be almost xl M li'...'.

the cash, and kept the accounts, of the money involved in his personal treasurership.[1] As has already been seen, he personally drafted and corrected the accounts before they were completed. Some significance may also be seen in the fact that he was constantly appealed to for money, by such men as the overseer of the works on Dover harbour,[2] the chamberlain of the princesses' household,[3] the treasurer of Calais,[4] or the overseer at the Tower[5]—to mention only appeals for expenditure which he is known to have covered personally. Most important of all, there is the testimony of Cromwell's remembrances in which one may read notes 'to Remembre the Iudgges for the payment of thayre wagys' or 'to remember Morettes reward at his departing';[6] or a long list of matters to be reported to the king which prove the closest personal attention to every detail involved in the office of a treasurer:[7]

ffirst that I haue depeched the money into Ireland.
Item that I haue delyuered to Will' Gonson CCCli.
Item that I am redy to send on Mli' for the buyldinges at Calais.
Item that I haue also made redy Mli' to be imployed vppon the making of the haven at Dover.
Item that will' Gonson hath conuented with Cavendish[8] for the provision of Ropes and Cables to be provyded in Esteland, wherein will' Gonson sayeth wilbe saved the costes of the rigging of the Mynyon now into those partes, the which charges for one Moneth will amount to xxxvli' xis' viijd'; and it requireth at the lest provision of the same charges for iij Monethes, which amountith to Cvjli' xvs'.

Or, for detail alone will help to prove the case, another list of things yet to be done:[9]

To disspace Holcroft and Barlow[10] with their wages for iij monethes apece.
To dispace my Lorde of Wynchester[11] with his dietes.

[1] The most important of these seems to have been William Body who rendered accounts A and D and was probably in direct charge of the money until at least April 1534.
[2] *L.P.* x. 1, 214, 295, 347, 537, 985; xi. 99; xii. I. 1049; II. 1129 (i.e. from January 1536 to November 1537).   [3] *L.P.* XI. 312.
[4] *L.P.* VII. 887; XI. 1311.   [5] *L.P.* VII. 1011.
[6] B.M., Tit. B. i, fos. 463 (*L.P.* VII. 108: January 1534), 475 (*L.P.* VIII. 892: June 1535).   [7] *Ibid.* fo. 433 (*L.P.* VIII. 527: April 1535).
[8] A member of Cromwell's private staff employed in business connected with the king's money (cf. above, p. 140).
[9] B.M., Tit. B. i, fo. 431 (*L.P.* IX. 218: August 1535).
[10] Envoys to Scotland.   [11] Gardiner, on embassy to France.

To disspace my Lorde of Hertheford[1] with his dietes.
To disspace master heth[1] with his dietes.
To disspace William Shyrlande[2] with his dietes.
Tow hundreth poundes to be sent to the skottis quene.
Thre hundreth and syxtene poundes to be paide to my lorde leonarde.[3]
To be paid to John Alen xx li'.

This was written by a clerk, but on the back are notes in Cromwell's hand, for £298. 13s. 4d. 'to my lord of Wynchester', the same 'to my lord of Herefforde', £316 'to my lorde leonard greye', 112 crowns 'to William Shyrlande', £74. 13s. 4d. 'to maister heth', and 'more to be payd: To barlow—l li'; To Holcroft—xl li'; ffor the quene of Skottes—CC li'; CCC crownes ffor Melancton; Thomas Wrythese-ley—xx li'; Thomas Solyman—x li'.' That Cromwell paid the sums mentioned in the last paper himself and not through some other treasurer emerges from a 'Docket of certain money paid by my master', drawn up a little later.[4] The man who worked out these details was being personally most active as a treasurer and paymaster.

One last point arises out of all this activity. Cromwell, it has been shown, attended personally to the routine of a subordinate office even after he had achieved pre-eminence amongst the king's ministers. There is thus a possibility that well into 1536 he continued to discharge very minor administrative duties under someone else's control. His payments were normally authorized or covered by a warrant under the signet and sign manual, after the manner usual with household treasurers. There may have been occasions when Cromwell paid money either by the king's verbal instructions or completely on his own authority, but in the nature of things such transactions have left no trace. On the whole, Cromwell is unlikely to have acted in this fashion; it could be dangerous if things went wrong, and it was unnecessary, for—as we shall see—he could always obtain the requisite warrants. These documents are completely formal; their phrasing is no guide to the importance of the person addressed, and if one accepted them at their face value one would have to think of Cromwell doing no more than pay when ordered.

---

[1] Edward Foxe and Nicholas Heath, on embassy to the German princes.
[2] A servant of Cromwell's employed in the royal service; it is not known where he was sent.
[3] Lord Leonard Grey, about to depart as deputy to Ireland.   [4] *L.P. Add.* 1013.

However, things were far otherwise. That Cromwell, as often as not, paid money on his own initiative and for purposes of which he alone was the judge, is proved by the evidence that he frequently obtained warrants for payments already made. 'Item, to cause Warrantes to be Drawen for suche money as is newly laid owt by me for the king', runs a typical note in his memoranda,[1] and there are many similar jottings between February 1533 and April 1534.[2] Perhaps the most revealing entry reads: 'To know what things that I do lack warrant for, and to cause a warrant to be made thereof to sign.'[3] Independence of action disguised as obedience to orders could hardly go further. Sometimes he would draft his own warrants,[4] though no doubt that part of the work was more usually left to a clerk. Since, then, it is certain that Cromwell paid many sums for which he obtained a warrant later, he was clearly more than simply a subordinate paymaster, even if at times he may have paid on warrants in hand. On the whole, it is reasonable to suppose that he pursued the less independent course more often at the beginning of his career, before he fully established his supremacy in the government; the first surviving warrant strongly suggests that the recipients of the money came to him with the warrants in their hands.[5] The sort of thing that must normally have happened can be reconstructed in one particular case—the payments listed in the last of the notes quoted above. In the first place, Cromwell had a list made out of things to be done which involved outlay of money; probably he dictated it. On its back he then jotted down some of the sums involved.[6] Then he had warrants drawn up 'to be Signed by the kinges highnes', which embodied these items amongst others.[7] Everything

[1] B.M., Tit. B. i, fo. 427v (*L.P.* VII. 48, i).
[2] *L.P.* VI. 150, 284, 1370; VII. 48, 257, 583.
[3] *L.P.* VI. 1056.   [4] SP 1:78, fos. 243-4 (*L.P.* VI. 1057).
[5] E 101/421/1 (*L.P.* V. 341); cf. App. II, C. This warrant of 18 July 1532 is addressed to Cromwell simply as 'our trusty and welbiloued seruaunt', though he had been master of the jewels for three months. It may be significant that the money in question had nothing to do with the master of the jewels, but as there is no reason to think that Cromwell normally kept apart the money which came to him in his various capacities, nothing can be made of this administratively.
[6] *L.P.* XI. 218-19.
[7] *Ibid.* 217. The sequence in *L.P.* is, of course, wrong. Some of the figures were reduced from Cromwell's first estimate; the fact that these warrants were drafted in Cromwell's office (as the handwriting proves) and before the king can have seen the details, indicates that Cromwell himself made the reduction.

so far—what needed doing, how much was to be paid, the drafting of the warrants—had been decided and done by Cromwell with the assistance of his private office. The king came in touch with the business only when the warrants were submitted for signature, which is not to say that he was ignorant of the political measures involved, as the sending of ambassadors; no doubt he knew. The point is that the administrative details were attended to by Cromwell; the decisions as to the precise expenditure were taken by him. The warrants themselves do not survive in this case, which is a pity; they may well have been signed with a stamp, like so many of those extant, which would prove that even at this stage the king took no active interest in the whole affair. A formal warrant was, of course, necessary. It was obtained, and a little later a note was made that the items authorized had been paid by Cromwell.[1] Clearly he was no mere subordinate agent in his treasurership; he protected himself with warrants, but it was he, as often as not, who decided how much money should be spent and on what.

For what reason, then, did Cromwell undertake these heavy routine tasks, even continuing to attend to them long after he had become the most powerful man after the king, with enough important work on his hands to satisfy half a dozen men? The answer, as has already been indicated, must lie in the nature of the payments made. He did not interest himself in personally collecting revenue; as long as he had enough money to pay the better part of the extraordinary expenditure of the crown, he was satisfied. The purpose behind his treasurership was, it seems, a desire to be independent of all other agencies in the covering of that expenditure. He wished to be free to employ ambassadors, to build the king's palaces, to fortify the realm and supply the navy, and to fulfil all the other tasks of government to which he attended, without having to go to others for the necessary money. Until this time the treasurer of the chamber had provided most of this money, but the chamber was essentially the most intimate part of the royal household, and its peculiar position in the administration of the realm was compatible only with a degree of personal government by the king to which Henry VIII did not rise. Its treasurer was too much the king's officer, too little a tool of

[1] *L.P. Add.* 1013.

Cromwell's making or for Cromwell's use. For five years Cromwell therefore personally administered considerable sums and kept the government going. He not only governed and made policy; he also made himself responsible for the routine of administration.

If that was his purpose, it must cause surprise that he should have given up an office and employment which, however troublesome, were essential to his unfettered government. However, it can be shown that, though he ceased personally to administer the money which he needed about the time that he shared the mastership of the jewels,[1] he continued his treasurership by delegation in the hands of a personal servant, John Gostwick, whom he appointed to be treasurer of first-fruits and tenths.[2] Throughout his years of power, Cromwell's administration rested on his immediate control over sums of money large enough to pay for most of the pressing expenditure caused by the demands of the government and its policy. Quite apart from the general control which he exercised over every section of the financial machinery, he thereby gave himself a particularly wide freedom in government; without the knowledge of this foundation of virtual financial independence, Cromwell's place in the state and the true character of his administration cannot be fully appreciated.

This discussion of Cromwell the administrator should have made plain the peculiar nature of his administration. Fundamentally, no doubt, his power in government depended on his remarkable capacity for business, his untiring devotion to work and precise grasp of detail, as well as on his standing with the king. But this only made him an administrator of power and influence; it did not make him

[1] Cf. above, p. 100, and authorities cited there. Cromwell's treasurership is linked with the office of master of the jewels mainly by the fact that the office was the only 'household' post he held, and that it had inherent possibilities as a treasurership. Warrants for payments were normally addressed to him by that title, though the secretaryship is also mentioned occasionally. The connexion was therefore superficial and not essential, but it was marked enough for the coincidence between the dates when Cromwell ceased to act as a treasurer and when he gave up the sole mastership of the jewels to be significant.

[2] Below, pp. 191 ff. Cf. also *L.P.* XI. 1411 (ii), a declaration of money paid to the king's use from the revenues of the suppressed monastery of Calwich. The items carry on from three paid to Cromwell (27 October and 26 November 1533, 15 May 1534) to one paid to Gostwick (28 November 1535).

the special kind of administrator he was. What distinguished him was his personal and direct control of every aspect of the day-to-day government of the country, based on the tenure of a number of offices in the bureaucratic hierarchy whose work he either did in person, or even created for himself, or at least supervised with a closeness and constancy unusual in a man busy with the higher spheres of government action and outstanding in its wide sweep even in a century which contained a Wolsey and a Burghley. Three offices which gave powers of control over the important parts of the financial machinery, three offices which subordinated to his charge the three royal secretariats (even though he let chancery, the least important of them, go)—these were the foundations on which he erected his administration. At the same time he enlarged the scope of the secretaryship, and later the office of lord privy seal, until no part of the secular government of England was outside his purview; that he also held offices which made him an autocrat (by delegation) over the church is a staggering fact which can here only be mentioned in an aside. When the reforms of various organs of the government are studied in the following pages, it will be essential always to remember the true nature of Cromwell's rule—intensely personal, intensely detailed, but also, since it rested on office, intensely bureaucratic—if the part he played in these changes is to be understood. Often it will be difficult to bring indisputable proof of his participation; but where these offices and their significance in government are concerned, Thomas Cromwell's hand may safely be deduced in the shadows when it fails to come out into the light.

The discussion of the offices has done one other thing: it has clarified to some extent the kind of administrative machine that Cromwell was part and head of. These were all bureaucratic offices: they had their allotted place in the hierarchy of administration, and they had specific tasks and functions to fulfil in a reasonably well ordered civil service. Cromwell often pressed them further than they had been pressed before; his use of the jewel-office, the chancellorship of the exchequer, and the secretaryship could hardly be justified from precedent. The administration was in the hands of a bureaucracy, but it was as yet an unsettled bureaucracy, not hardened in its ways, and capable of being twisted and moulded by a great personal administrator. There was a great deal of organization, but it was mixed with flexibility and lack of final definition, the more so because the period of recovery with its revival of the household potential in administration had broken down some of the fixity of later medieval administration. Such a machine of government gave a special chance to a minister whose bent was towards organization as well as personal influence and rule—towards the establishment of safety in bureaucratic institutions and efficiency in personal ascendancy. Cromwell was such a minister. One may point the contrast between him and Wolsey. Both were the king's chief ministers, exercising a greater power under the crown than any one man had ever held before during the reign of a strong king; but while Wolsey concentrated on his work as a judge and a foreign minister, seeking power in the star chamber and the councils of Europe, Cromwell turned to the work of detailed supervision and reform of the administrative machine for which his abilities so peculiarly fitted him. The nature of his work, less obviously brilliant, was by the same token also more enduring.

CHAPTER III

THE REFORM OF
THE AGENCIES OF FINANCE

1. *The financial administration in about 1530*

We have already traced the history of the financial machinery from
Richard II to Wolsey, from the decay of household finance in the
late fourteenth century to its revival in the late fifteenth and its
apogee in the statutory general surveyors of the 1520's. It will, however, be advisable to preface the account of the reforms begun by
Cromwell and continued by his successors with a summary description of the financial administration as it stood about the time of
Wolsey's fall. We are fortunate in possessing a document which
makes such a description easy. The paper is headed 'A Memoriall
for the Kinges Highnes, declaring the kynde of thingis Wherin
Risith yerelye aswell his Certein Reuenue as his Casuall Reuenues,
and who be officers to his highnes in that behalf'.[1] Some additional
notes on it in Cromwell's hand, and the fact that one of the last two
paragraphs was first drafted by Cromwell himself, suggest strongly
that he was responsible for having it drawn up; the state of affairs it
describes (without the new revenues taken from the church) dates it
into the early part of his ministry. It is probable that when he first
took charge of affairs he found it necessary to acquaint himself in
detail with the financial administration and had the statement prepared both for his master and for himself. It gives a detailed and
clear account of the sources of the royal revenue, though it does not
arrange them by administrative departments. The revenues themselves are divided into two parts—certain and casual, terms which
had a perfectly precise meaning in the technical language of the day.
Certain revenues were the fixed items of income whose yield never
varied, such as rents and the like; while casual revenues, though
possibly as regular, varied in yield from year to year. The customs

---

[1] SP 1:67, ff. 32–7 (*L.P.* v. 397); *L.P.* date it towards the end of 1531. The paper is
given in full in App. II, B.

therefore came into the second group.[1] Each financial department received its income in both certain and casual sums, but the distinction is not one which will clarify the structure of the finances, and it will be more useful from the administrative point of view if we divide matters into true revenue on the one hand, and the yield derived from debts and bonds (delayed revenue) on the other.

Among the items of true revenue there were first those that might be called the ancient revenue of the crown, which were accounted for in the exchequer. These included the money collected by the sheriffs (farms of the counties and fee farms of cities and boroughs), the escheators (the yield of outlawries and other escheated lands), and the customers (customs and subsidies), as well as the profits of royal justice in fines, amercements, and forfeited recognizances imposed by the central courts (chancery, star chamber,[2] king's bench, and common pleas) and by local commissions (justices of assize, sewers, the peace, quorum, and oyer and terminer). An interesting omission here was parliamentary revenue (tenths and fifteenths, and subsidies); it was, of course, occasional and exceptional, whereas even the 'casual' revenue came in every year. The exchequer continued to administer the collection of these taxes, but they were usually handed to the chamber to spend.[3] The revenues accruing from the lands of the duchy of Lancaster and the profits of its court were the sole province of its chancellor and council. Most of the remaining sources of income were controlled by the general surveyors of crown lands who audited the accounts of many individual treasurers and receivers. The list is a mixed one, including as it does revenue administered by the general surveyors themselves—the lands as signed in the schedules of the statutes of 1515 and 1523, the surplus of the hanaper, the yields of vacant temporalities—and accounts for money handled by separate treasurers and merely audited in the

---

[1] Cf., for example, the classification of the revenue made in 1552, B.M., Harl. MS. 7383.

[2] In passing it may be noted that as early as this a fiscal document could refer in brief to the 'Sterred Chambre' as one of the 'kingis Courtes': we cannot doubt that in popular estimation the council in the star chamber was a plain court long before it was fully divorced from other conciliar bodies—and long before modern scholars would allow it to have been (cf., for example, J. R. Tanner, *Tudor Constitutional Documents*, 253).

[3] Cf. below, p. 171.

prince's council chamber—those of the master of the wards, the surveyor of liveries, the chief butler of England, the surveyor of the king's woods, and the treasurer of Calais. There remain two minor sources of income, the profit of the mint, which was to acquire temporarily great importance in the days of the debasement after 1543, and the income derived from penal statutes in fines or by obligations and settlements. These last were supposed to be administered by the king's learned council which had indeed at one time been an active section of the council but does not seem to have continued its work after the fall of Empson and Dudley.[1] Both these last were added to the memorandum as an afterthought and need not concern this discussion, the mint because its profits were ordinarily so negligible as to make it less a revenue department than a coin manufactory, and the learned council because it is doubtful whether it existed at all by this time except on paper.

The other kind of income, hardly to be described as revenue in the modern sense, comprised sums derived from recognizances entered upon and forfeited before the various officials mentioned, sometimes by way of security and sometimes as an obligation binding the party to a definite course of action (such as the bonds taken by customers 'for Imployment of merchaundise'). These were usually a fair sum, since many of the transactions of the time tended to be made in a peculiarly roundabout fashion under the guise of a legal penalty. Instead of taking profits directly, the king's officers would often extort them by means of a bond which fell due later, though from the first it was understood that the obligation entered into would be broken and the bond forfeit. It was one of the normal overheads of sixteenth-century business. There were further the debts of subordinate officials owing to their superior departments, as a rule a collector's surplus on his previous year's account which he might either pay in cash or hold against the deficit which would arise sooner or later.

Though there was, therefore, a large number of officials concerned in the securing of the king's revenue, a clear structure can be discerned behind the apparent confusion. It is outlined in the marginal

---

[1] Above, pp. 29 f. The memorial wanted them to declare their revenues in an annual statement so that the government might know what was coming in.

notes of the memorandum which is our guide in this business—notes, which indicate the department of audit ultimately responsible for the revenue with whose collection it did not necessarily concern itself. These departments were the exchequer, the duchy of Lancaster council, and the general surveyors of crown lands. The exchequer handled 'ancient' revenue, or rather the revenues collected by officials who had always been responsible to it. The division in the medieval exchequer is most easily made not by types of revenue, nor even by officials, but by enrolments. By the end of the Middle Ages a classification of the chief records can be made into pipe rolls (sheriffs' accounts), escheators' enrolled accounts, customs accounts, and foreign accounts.[1] The reforms of Edward IV, Henry VII, and Wolsey, which are usually described as the creation of the chamber machinery, consisted essentially in removing the foreign accounts from the exchequer and transferring them to the land revenue department of the general surveyors for speedier audit.[2] This is, of course, a somewhat simplified statement of a very complex problem, but in general it holds good. With the removal of the foreign accounts, the exchequer was left with the three sets of officials (sheriffs, escheators, and customers) whom the memorial lists, as well as the fines and amercements which were separately enrolled.[3] The many different kinds of revenue officers who had year by year accounted for the affairs of their offices without paying in their receipts—who had, that is, used the exchequer only as a board of audit—now ceased all connexion with the old department. The exchequer was left with an almost fixed annual income.[4]

For these reasons, the exchequer could quietly pursue its old methods, without interfering too much with the general efficiency of the financial administration. In the lower exchequer, indeed, as has been seen, certain reforms procured a speedier paying in and out of revenue,[5] but in the upper exchequer no reforms were undertaken until the great revision of 1554 which terminated the period of

---

[1] This rather sketchy description, which is confined to essentials, is based on Giuseppi, *Guide*, I. 71 ff.

[2] The rolls of foreign accounts come virtually to an end with the reign of Richard III, though a few items were carried on until Charles II (*ibid*. I. 124).

[3] *Ibid*. I. 81.   [4] Cf. Dietz, *Eng. Gov. Fin.* 216.

[5] Above, pp. 23 f.

change and experiment and re-established exchequer supremacy in the management of finance. There is only one sign of an attempted reform in the exchequer during Cromwell's ministry, a draft bill corrected by Cromwell and foreshadowed in his memoranda,[1] which shows that he tried to abolish the delay common in the delivery of collected revenue, a delay designed to give the collector time to speculate on his own account with government money. The draft—which only Cromwell's corrections made refer to the exchequer as well as the chamber machinery—appointed 1 May and 1 November as settling days on which the receipts for the half years ending on 25 March and 29 September were to be paid in. The bill does not appear to have been introduced into parliament, and it certainly did not result in a statute. The reform, though probably unenforceable in the sixteenth century, would have been beneficial; the evil grew worse, and by the end of the century revenue officers sometimes died hopelessly in debt to the crown, having lost the royal revenues in their private speculations.[2] Apart from this small straw in the wind, however, there is no sign that the exchequer was thought in need or worthy of attention until the troubles of the 1540's re-opened the whole question of the financial administration. The sources of revenue which it still administered were not those which the government hoped to enlarge, for until the second half of the century land revenue rather than the customs was the basis of Tudor finance. The fact that the customs were left to the ancient and creaking machinery of the exchequer, when all that really mattered was removed from it, goes far to explain why Elizabethan governments found it necessary to increase the customs revenue through the doubtful expedient of farming it.[3]

The second audit department, the council of the duchy of Lancaster, was a much simpler organization. It concerned itself

---

[1] B.M., Harl. MS. 1878, fos. 22–5 (*L.P.* x. 246, 18); *L.P.* x. 254. The date of this projected reform, not to be discovered from the draft, would therefore appear to have been 1536.

[2] Cf. *S.P. Domestic, 1566–79*, 46, for the case of a customer who did not employ his charge in this way, though he did not fare any the better for his honesty. The letter makes it plain what the usual practice was.

[3] This point has been missed in the discussion of the customs farms: A. P. Newton, 'The Establishment of the Great Farm of the English Customs', *Trans. R. Hist. Soc.* (1918), 129 ff.; F. C. Dietz, 'Elizabethan Customs Administration', *E.H.R.* XLV. 35 ff.

solely with the revenue of the duchy lands and the profits of justice derived from litigation over these lands. It cannot be stressed too often that medieval administration tended to be done in the guise of judicial administration—by courts, and with the weapons of courts of law—and that the separation of judicial from ordinary administration, which characterizes modern government, was only beginning in the sixteenth century. If we ignore the question of the law and its application, we are making a legitimate but none the less quite arbitrary distinction which would not have appeared obvious to sixteenth-century officials; even though the two forms of administration clearly existed separately and side by side, they were very often the province of one and the same institution of government. Thus the court of duchy chamber, a law court concerned with cases arising from duchy lands, was also the council of the duchy and as such part of the financial administration of England.[1] In effect, it was a department of land revenue, kept separate through nothing but the conservatism of official arrangements; it audited the accounts of individual receivers of duchy property, and of the receiver general who administered the receipts and expenses of the organization. The duchy was a true revenue department, with few expenses except on the internal affairs of the department;[2] it recorded a steady annual surplus which went entirely 'to the king's use' in his two great spending departments of the household and the chamber.[3] Sitting at the Savoy in London, the council looked after a vast landed property distributed all over England, and employed for the purpose up-to-date methods of account and audit. In distinction from exchequer practice with its rolls, accounts in the duchy were kept in a simple manner with detailed marginal headings, making possible

[1] For the court of duchy chamber, cf. R. Somerville, 'The Duchy of Lancaster Council and Court of Duchy Chamber', *Trans. R. Hist. Soc.* (1941), 159 ff.

[2] Running expenses, fees of duchy officials, and a number of fixed annuities. Annuities charged on duchy revenues had as a rule some slight connexion with duchy affairs: e.g. Lord Darcy's £100 was granted to him as constable of Pontefract (DL 28/7/5, fo. 11), and when Audeley received £200 as the speaker's reward in 1531 (*ibid.* vol. 1), he was also attorney general of the duchy.

[3] Out of a total expenditure of £9,080 in 1529–30, contributions to the household amounted to £4,303, while the chamber received £3,748 (DL 28/7/1). After 1531, the duchy assignments to the household were £5,486 (by the act of 22 Henry VIII, c. 18); the rest of the surplus, which in total varied between £8,052 and £8,825, in 1531–40, went to the chamber (*ibid.* vols. 2–7).

both a clear view of what had come in, gone out, and was yet out-standing, and a quick summing up of totals. The accounts were audited by the duchy's auditors and then declared by them before the council—so far the methods used differed little from those of the exchequer; but there followed no complicated process of enrolment, the engrossed account in the auditor's hands remaining as sole authority for the collection of outstanding debts. Though lacking the exchequer's careful security, the system was quick and worked well. Under the early Tudors, the duchy rendered 'states' of its revenue, as did the receipt of the exchequer.[1] So far from requiring the attention of a reforming minister, it was to serve as a model in the reforms of the decade, and of its uneventful history nothing need be said here.

The most recent department of audit were the general surveyors of crown lands. We have already had occasion to discuss them: it has been pointed out that they were not a court of record, but merely an aspect of household government given some of the trappings of a court. In this they differed profoundly from the exchequer and the duchy. Since their existence and tasks had been established by acts of parliament, it would not be right to describe them simply as agents of the prerogative; yet that is what in effect they were. It remains to define the place occupied by this household organization in national finance. As has been said, they were responsible for two things: the land revenue upon which the financial stability of the crown rested, and the foreign accounts removed from the exchequer. The first they administered directly, controlling the subordinate collectors and receivers and seeing to it that these revenues passed into the hands of the treasurer of the chamber, their departmental treasurer whose accounts they also audited. The groups of lands given in the memorial were those of Warwick, Spencer, and Buckingham, the duchy of Cornwall, those administered by the chamberlains of Chester, North Wales, and South Wales, and the principality of Wales. The receivers of each of these groups returned an annual account, declared by the auditors before the general surveyors in the manner practised in the duchy court. Although the lands of Warwick or Spencer, or the duchy of Cornwall, for instance, were scattered through many counties, no attempt was made to break them up; as in the duchy of

[1] Giuseppi, *Guide*, I. 327.

Lancaster itself, these smaller but still considerable masses of property were kept in the honorial structure in which they had come into the hands of the crown.[1] As we shall see, in this the practice of the general surveyors was old-fashioned and was not to be copied by the next land revenue department to be set up, the court of augmentations.[2]

The other officers listed in the memorial as accountable to the general surveyors were all more independent than the receivers of land revenue, though as far as can be seen many of them handed the yield of their office to the treasurer of the chamber. The master of the wards and the surveyor of liveries in effect had charge of what remained of the feudal revenue of the crown: of the profits of lands in the king's hands because of the tenant's minority, of the sales of such wardships and the right of marriage to interested parties, and of the fines exacted on livery of seisin when the heir attained his majority. Though so closely connected in the scope of their work, they were at this time separate, Sir William Paulet and Sir Thomas Englefield being masters of wards,[3] while Sir Thomas Neville, whose signature appears on many warrants for livery, held the other office in which Sir Richard Riche was joined with him in 1535.[4] The office of chief butler had little importance in the revenues since that officer took the import duty on wines known as prisage or butlerage mostly in kind.[5] Special surveyors of vacant temporalities and for the restitution of these to new incumbents (against a fine comparable to the fine on livery of seisin) did not exist as part of the permanent machinery; they were appointed locally for each see or abbey as vacancies occurred and delivered the profits to the chamber, except during Cromwell's treasurership when he himself seems to have engrossed this source of revenue.[6] The surveyor or master of the

---

[1] Cf. the description of the minister's accounts in *Lists and Indexes*, vol. xxxiv. For the inviolability of honours and the various reasons underlying the practice, cf. Pollock and Maitland, *Hist. Eng. Law*, i. 260 f.; F. M. Stenton, *First Century of English Feudalism*, 55.

[2] Below, pp. 206 f.   [3] Cf. App. i, on the tenure of this office.

[4] *L.P.* viii. 632 (34).   [5] Cf. Giles Jacob, *Law Dictionary* (1744), s.v. 'botiler'.

[6] Cf. above, p. 144. Such surveyors or receivers were William Strangways who administered the temporalities of York after Wolsey's death (*L.P.* v. 822) or Richard Street who did the same at Coventry and Lichfield before Rowland Lee succeeded there (*ibid.* 277).

woods was an official of some importance since a considerable revenue could be got from wood sales; he was not, however, associated with the ancient and profitable jurisdiction of the royal forests, being indeed a very much less influential man than the various stewards and justices of the forests.[1] The office of clerk of the hanaper has already been discussed at sufficient length.

All this indicates that the general surveyors, for a time the veritable rag-bag and maid of all work of the finances, occupied a place in the administration which was both central and peculiar. It was central because they controlled the greater part of the finances—everything in fact that was neither ancient exchequer revenue nor duchy lands; it was peculiar because they were a distinctly underdeveloped department. With all their vast scope they had none of the organization of exchequer or duchy—no seal, no separate staff of subordinate officials, not even strictly speaking a treasurer all their own; they kept no records and had to use the exchequer for all things that could only be done by a court of record. The most important part of the royal revenues—the greatest part, the most flexible, and the most useful—rested with apparent ease in the hands of a thinly disguised offshoot of the royal household. That is what is meant by saying that until 1529 the administration of the finances was dominated by the household, was chamber finance—despite the existence of two proper departments by the side of the general surveyors whose departmental organization was so incomplete. It was they who administered most things that mattered and everything fresh.

This, then, was the organization of the finances as it stood when

---

[1] This office did not seem important enough to receive special mention in Ch. II, though Cromwell held it jointly with Sir William Paulet by the beginning of 1533. There are frequent references to their activities in the records (*L.P.* VI. 210, 231, 406; *Add.* 839). No patent survives, though one existed among Cromwell's papers (*L.P.* VII. 923, xxxv). Cromwell and Paulet were also appointed joint surveyors of the woods of the duchy of Lancaster (*L.P.* VI. 1623), a parallel and conjunctive office, as it were; from the endorsement on this patent it may well be the one mentioned in Cromwell's catalogue. Their activities concerned mainly sales of wood from the royal forests; warrants authorizing these were signed by both (*L.P.* VI. 1575–6). Keepers of the king's woods rendered accounts to them (*L.P.* VII. 46). After the beginning of 1534 Cromwell's connexion with the office is shadowy; he may have given it up, and he certainly ceased doing its work. There is no record of any fees being paid to the surveyors, though on the whole it is probable there were some; an office under the crown without some kind of profit to the holder would have been most unusual.

Wolsey died, when Cromwell took over, when the period of reform was about to begin. The exchequer with its old revenues but without the great 'foreign' accounts, the duchy with its lands, the general surveyors and chamber organization based on the new land revenues of Henry VII and Wolsey but taking in also the foreign accounts and anything else in the way of financial offices that required supervision. Household finance dominated the scene. The history of financial administration in the 1530's is the history of the transformation of that household finance and of the creation of new departments. There is nothing to tell of the old courts: neither the exchequer nor the duchy of Lancaster attracted for the time being the attention of the reformer. Being already bureaucratic offices of state, they did not come within the scope of changes designed to create such departments by their side.

2. *The decline of the chamber*

The revival of household government by Edward IV and Henry VII had, as we have seen, made the treasurer of the chamber, under the general surveyors, the leading financial officer of the day, occupying a special and favoured position commensurate with his heavy obligations. That was the case down to 1529. Thereafter the story of the chamber took a sharp turn for the worse, and with that development we must now concern ourselves. From April 1528 to his death in October 1545, the office was held by Sir Brian Tuke, a leading civil servant of the time, who combined its duties with those of the French secretary and, until 1539, of the clerk of parliament.[1] The material in which his administration can be studied is in some respects less satisfactory than that for his predecessors, though it is rather more lively. We possess no complete accounts of his receipts and only two of his book of payments, one for October 1528 to May 1531 and the other for February 1538 to June 1541,[2] as well as some scattered partial accounts, acquittances, and warrants; there is

---

[1] The salient points of Tuke's career are given by A. F. Pollard in the *D.N.B.* He describes him mistakenly as treasurer of the household instead of the chamber. For the fact that despite the patent roll (*L.P.* xvi. 65) he ceased to be clerk of parliament in 1539 and not in 1540, cf. E 101/223/6.

[2] E 101/420/11, and B.M., Arundel MS. 97. Both are fully calendared in *L.P.*

further a considerable number of letters written by him from which information about the working of the office and about its finances can be obtained.

The first thing to engage attention is that Tuke's payments decreased considerably in the ten years between 1529 and 1539. While he spent £55,270 in the full year ending at Michaelmas 1530, the corresponding figures are about £33,000 in 1539 and £40,000 a year later.[1] A decline of business by from thirty to forty per cent in ten years implies a serious decline in the importance of the office, the more so as the general expenditure of the government had greatly increased.[2] Later still, in the three months of July to September 1541, Tuke received £6,838 and spent £6,716;[3] if these sums may be taken as representative of an ordinary quarter, totals in the neighbourhood of only £25,000 are arrived at, a far cry indeed from the six-figure totals of the days of Sir John Heron and Sir Henry Wyat. Things grew even worse under Tuke's successors, so that in December 1548 Sir William Cavendish had to inform the commissioners appointed to investigate the office of the treasurer of the chamber that his yearly income covered only about one-sixth of his normal expenditure.[4] There was thus a marked and persistent decline in the scope and competence of the office, a decline which set in with Cromwell's ministry. Too much stress must not be put on the treasurers' complaints: financial departments in the sixteenth century were rarely in a good way by modern standards because so little reliance could be placed on a regular income. Times were good if the money came in at length—so that debts incurred to other departments or the reserves in the 'king's coffers' could be paid off,

[1] The first figure is given in *L.P.* v, p. 321. For the later years the accounts are missing for September (monthly) and Michaelmas (quarterly and half-yearly) totals, but the figures for the three-quarters of a year ending on 30 June are £24,450 and £30,406 respectively. When proportionately upgraded they give the totals in the text. That such upgrading is permissible is shown by the fact that the expenditure for the three-quarters of a year ending on 30 June 1530 was £42,163, near enough three-quarters of the sum spent in the whole year.

[2] Dietz, *Eng. Gov. Fin.* 140 ff.   [3] B.M., Royal MS. 7. F. xiv, fo. 77.

[4] *Trevelyan Papers* (Camden Soc.), II. 11 f. He added that the office was in debt to the tune of £14,000, but that £28,991 was owing to it. There was an improvement in the following year, but expenditure still exceeded income (*ibid.* 13, 34).

the treasurers who had defrayed expenses from their own pockets recouped, or creditors, by long experience inured to such delays, satisfied. Times were bad if no more money could be expected and much remained to be paid. However, the decline of Tuke's expenditure in the years of Cromwell's administration is a sign that must not be ignored, and in the light of this odd retrenchment his frequent letters to the minister assume an added importance.

He was always appealing for funds. 'Sir', he wrote on 19 December 1534,[1] 'I assure you as I wol answer at my peril that towardes iij M li' that I nedes must pay this cristenmas for wages and for rewardes for newyeres giftes, besides all other ordynary paymentes nowe due, amounting to asmoche, I haue not in my handes l li'.... As I haue don more than ons, I must endanger my self for my furniture...I thought to haue besought you to lende me M li' til marche, And yet I must have made shyft for M li' or ij besides.' And again, on 28 March 1537:[2] 'I shal not have of money assigned to my receipt xx M li' by yere, and myn ordinary paymentes besides casual warrantes be almost xl M li' by yere.'[3] On 18 July 1537:[4] 'My Lorde, I shal not nede to aduertise your Lordship howe sklenderly I at this tyme am and of long season am like to be furnished of the kinges money.' In letter after letter he appealed for the Fifteenth and Tenth granted in 1534, which had always 'come from the tellers of the receipt to the treasorer of the chambre'.[5]

In short, he was not getting his accustomed revenues, and in August 1539 he compiled a long list of complaints and difficulties to acquaint Cromwell with the true position.[6] He had received nothing

---

[1] SP 1:87, fo. 133 (*L.P.* VII. 1556).   [2] SP 60:4, fo. 78 (*L.P.* XII. I. 1297).

[3] £40,000 was an overestimate; as we have seen, his total expenditure by this time hardly reached that figure. Tuke was given to budgeting too carefully. In August 1539 he wrote: 'August wages almost iiij C li', and then in the nek mychelmas wages litel lak of xxiiij C li'. This, my lorde, is besides al other warantes...' (*L.P.* XIV. II. 13). In fact, he paid £311 in wages that August (B.M., Arundel MS. 97, fos. 86–87 v). At Michaelmas he paid £808 in quarter wages (*ibid.* fos. 91 v–93 v); the half-year's wages are lost but may be estimated from the items preserved for March and September 1538 and March 1539 at about £360–370.

[4] SP 1:123, fo. 10 (*L.P.* XII. II. 276).

[5] *Ibid.* Cf. also SP 1:128, fo. 54 (*L.P.* XIII. I. 47): 'There nedeth no grete disputacion whither this xv^th shulde be paid to myn office, seing that first it is the veray ordre and course It shulde so be, And secondely, It is necessary.' Cf. further, *L.P.* XIII. I. 309, 1288.

[6] SP 1:153, fos. 9–10 (*L.P.* XIV. II. 13).

from the exchequer for a year, and assignments before that time had always been ear-marked by Cromwell for some specific purpose; his income from the hanaper—'whiche was wont to be to me a good shoteanker in suche vacacion tymes'—had suffered the same fate; he had large extra expenditure on fortifications and the like; and he had lost a number of good sources of income—the assignments to the household ('chaunged from desperate paymentes to the best that I had') now went directly from the exchequer to the cofferer of the household,[1] 'al the eschequer money cometh nowe to other handes', purchased lands contributed to the court of augmentations, forfeited lands to the treasurer of first-fruits and tenths, and money from vacant sees and abbeys was no longer coming to the chamber (it too, we may note, went to the treasurer of first-fruits). A good deal of money had at one time been obtained from debts owing to the king, but there was not much more to be had from that source;[2] he had explained in an earlier letter that

the grete dettes that be leviable be for the most parte either paid or stalled to smal yerely paymentes, and the new dettes, sens I was officer, be but vpon wardes and lyuereys, payable by smal somes. The grete dettes arose vpon lones of money and licences wherof fewe or none have passed sens I was officer. And I have cut them short that wer afore, ffor I have answerd and levyed this x yer that I have ben the kinges officer ferre above x M marc' by yere of his graces dettes, whiche is C M marc'; and I am sure, to the emperour, to the frenche king, to the frenche quene deceaced and my lorde of Suffolk, to the staple, to my lorde of Northumberlande, the lorde Audelay, & other, there is ferre above C M li' of dettes discharged in my tyme by warant, for the whiche the kinges highnes is otherwise recompenced or agrede with. And many revenues that I was wont to receyue be gon, som in other courtes, som otherwise by gift or exchange of Landes.[3]

[1] Cf. statute 22 Henry VIII, c. 18.

[2] Between 17 December 1536 and 10 November 1537 Tuke received a minimum of £1,036 from 'stalled' debts, as a file of receipts shows (E 101/422/6); for the year ending Michaelmas 1542 his income from debts was £2,348 (*ibid.* 423/5). To stall a debt was to commute it for payment in instalments. The difficulties of collection are well illustrated by some letters Tuke wrote to Lord Lisle. In January 1539 he asked for payment of a debt sixteen years old, adding that he had been told to forbear but not so long; in February he apologized for putting the pressure on; in May he declared that there must be an end some time—he had respited nothing so long. There was another reminder in November (*L.P.* XIV. I. 66, 221, 965; II. 460).

[3] SP1:133, fo. 245 (*L.P.* XIII. I. 1288).

That was his main grievance: there was not enough money coming in to defray the payments charged against his office, though he would not have minded if his expenses had been cut down along with his income;[1] and this had come about because much of his revenue had disappeared, either because it could not be repeated (like the debts he had recovered), or because it had been squandered (like the lands which the king had given away), or because it had gone to other treasurers. This last is the most interesting and the most important reason, for more plainly than anything else it shows the fate of the treasurership of the chamber and what caused its decline. Between 1485 and 1529 that office had acquired ever larger sources of revenue, gathering in both new and old, but in the period of Cromwell's ministry it was deprived of many of these in the course of a number of administrative reforms which are associated with the setting up of new financial departments, and which were the immediate consequence of the extension of the king's income carried out by Cromwell at the expense of the church.[2] The treasurer of the chamber emerged from these reforms shorn of many of his extraordinary revenues and deprived of his commanding position in the financial system.

At the same time, it may be noticed that the general surveyors also lost in standing. They had been very important and very active officials indeed under Wolsey; in the 1530's they are much less in evidence. They continued to administer the crown lands, but there are signs that their control over the treasurer of the chamber was weakened by the interpolation of Cromwell who assumed control of the treasurer's payments. No warrant to Tuke survives from the general surveyors, and there are no traces of that activity in the prince's council chamber that was noted earlier.[3] The overwhelming personality of Cromwell pushed the older officials into

---

[1] SP 1:128, fo. 54 (*L.P.* XIII. I. 47): 'Being I alwais best contented with lest receiptes, So my paymentes be cut of accordingly', and SP 1: 129, fo. 28 (*L.P.* XIII. I. 249): 'I am in no doubt but that your Lordship in your grete wisedome wol take ordre, So as I be charged as I shal receyue'.

[2] Newton thought that the period 1497–1553 was 'divided naturally into two portions by the great financial measures of Henry VIII in 1529' (*E.H.R.* XXXII. 350). I am at a loss to understand what measures he was thinking of. There certainly was a departure from earlier policy resulting in far-reaching administrative changes, but that did not come until the new revenues were assigned to the crown in 1535–6 and was the work of Cromwell rather than Henry himself.

[3] Above, pp. 49 ff.

the background; as we shall see more than once, his personal activity temporarily obscured developments which his own reforms were initiating.

Though chamber expenditure declined, it continued to be largely on the business of government; for the time being, its scope remained unchanged. It had always been the habit of the government to use any available treasury for the purpose of paying expenses. The duchy of Lancaster paid pensions to the marquess of Dorset and the king's master cook, or was commanded to pay £200 reward to the speaker of the parliament, in addition to payments which would naturally fall to its share, as the fees of its officers and annuities to the stewards of duchy lands.[1] Similarly, the treasurer of the chamber paid annuities to the earl of Angus[2] and to Thomas Paston of the privy chamber,[3] to give two widely differing examples, while the exchequer paid another group of annuities and pensions.[4] The money in all the royal treasuries was available for any assignment on it, and choice was presumably governed by immediate convenience. When Lord Lisle was granted an annuity his agent was in great doubt where it ought to be paid:

> I wold know wher and in what plasse it were most ffor your proffytt to be payde. They saythe that the treseror of the chamber is often without mony, and the Joyell howsse, augmentacions, and fyrst frywttes is as ill, and the checcker warsse; and to be payde at Calays by the treseror or the resceyuor is warst of all.[5]

Though as master of the jewels Cromwell paid many items previously in the charge of the treasurer of the chamber, later accounts show the chamber still engaged on the same sort of business, while being rivalled in importance by the treasurer of first-fruits and tenths; Cromwell's personal treasurership did not withdraw all extraordinary government expenditure from the chamber.

But while Tuke continued to pay many of the government's expenses, he did so as a mere treasurer: he was no minister like

---

[1] Cf. the surviving accounts for the years 1529–39, DL 28/7/1–7.
[2] B.M., Arundel MS. 97, fos. 2v, 6v, 34, 62, 88, 102v, 116v, 121.
[3] *Ibid.* fos. 120, 133.
[4] E.g. E 405/199, where the tellers' payments are given in detail.
[5] SP 3:4, fo. 94 (*L.P.* XIII. II. 434). In the end Lisle was paid by augmentations (*L.P.* XIII. II. 1069, 1112).

Heron, and his actions were directed from above—not by his departmental heads, the general surveyors, but by Cromwell himself. As early as April 1533, the ambassador with the emperor applied to Cromwell when he thought that Tuke was being dilatory in paying his diets.[1] Bonner, in 1539, wrote to the king for the speedy issue of a warrant as Tuke would not pay without one, and a few days later Cromwell ordered Tuke to make out letters of bank to Bonner's servant;[2] once again it may be noted that in Cromwell's years of power the king rarely interfered in administrative matters and that Cromwell, not Henry, was really the government. Even a leading councillor like Sir William Fitzwilliam, treasurer of the household and lord admiral, approached Cromwell for a warrant to Tuke when he was about to leave for Calais on a commission of investigation.[3] Cromwell's remembrances and correspondence contain quite a few references to warrants to be made out to Tuke, or orders to him for payment,[4] indicating that Cromwell used the treasurer of the chamber as a paymaster under his own control. Complaints to Cromwell that the treasurer did his duty rather too slowly were frequent: Bishop Rowland Lee, for instance, wrote that he had difficulties in getting the money due to the council in the marches of Wales and that, moreover, Tuke's demands for warrants and writs cost him anything up to £20 a year.[5] Tuke was aware of these complaints but had his answer ready; there were, he said

a grete many moo of the kinges dettours beyonde the see and at home whiche when your lordship appointeth them money at my handes, doubting that I wol stop their dettes, do, as I vnderstonde, sue to your lordship to be paid elleswhere, saying they be delayed at my handes. And yet, as god helpe me, I neuer retarded any in that cace on[e] pater noster tyme.[6]

---

[1] *L.P.* VI. 372.   [2] *L.P.* XIV. I. 620, 709.

[3] *L.P.* IX. 4, where he asks for Cromwell's letters to Tuke. The actual warrant issued, however, appears to have been a regular royal warrant: '...haue receyved the kinges Letteris and therwith his graces warraunt to Sir Bryan Tuke addressed, for the Dyettes of me and part of my Colleges in this our Iourney to Calays...' (SP 1:95, fo. 52; *L.P.* IX. 50).

[4] E.g. *L.P.* VI. 995, 1056 (ii), 1194; IX. 232, 498 (3); X. 376, 1124; XI. 398; XII. I. 73; XIII. II. 221.

[5] *L.P.* XII. II. 1094; XV. 398, 562 (2). He alleged that Tuke got £5 and his clerk 26s. 8d., and that the servant collecting the money had to wait for six or eight weeks for the business to go through.   [6] SP 1:126, fo. 110v (*L.P.* XII. II. 1048, i).

Whatever the rights of the matter may have been, the fact of Cromwell's central and controlling position stands out clearly.[1]

The clearest evidence for Cromwell's relations with the chamber is provided by Tuke's accounts for 1538–41.[2] These accounts always quoted the authority for payments made; nearly all were authorized either by royal warrant or by Cromwell. Those stated to be authorized by the king are almost all regularly recurring payments—payments for the king's buildings, the annuity of the earl of Angus,[3] wages and victuals for the king's ships, household deficits, the garrison at Berwick, the council in the marches of Wales, regular wages and annuities in the household, diets to certain ambassadors. Frequently the warrant for such payments is described as dormant, that is to say, it was made out for a series of recurrent disbursements. Other payments are given, up to June 1539, as 'by the king's commandment, certified by my lord privy seal's letters', and after that date almost invariably as by Cromwell's letters only. In a document which generally gives the impression of careful accuracy, such a clear-cut change is likely to represent an actual change of practice, and it is permissible to conclude that about June 1539 Cromwell ceased to employ a formula which pretended that he was merely communicating the king's orders. However that may be, all these payments were certainly made and authorized on his initiative. Analysis shows that they were by far the larger number, and that they were concerned with a variety of purposes. Most of them were made only once; in contrast to those authorized by ordinary royal warrant they were not regular or recurring, which means that they covered the unpredictable and varied affairs of government rather than its routine. And let it be noted that in the last year of his supremacy Cromwell issued personal orders to the treasurer of the chamber which were treated with the respect normally reserved for royal warrants under the signet and sign manual. Despite its household

---

[1] Occasionally, his new administration made recourse to Tuke unnecessary, as when—asked for a warrant to Tuke to hand over the 'cesses' which were to pay for the draining of Lesnes marsh—he directed the warrant to himself (*L.P.* VI. 843, 1057).

[2] B.M., Arundel MS. 97.

[3] In May 1534 Tuke wrote that he had so far paid this annuity by special warrants issued separately for every payment. He wanted to know what was to happen about it (*L.P.* VII. 713). It seems that Cromwell ordered the issue of a 'dormant' warrant.

origin, the chamber had become, in effect, a treasury at the minister's disposal. But this was a temporary phenomenon which vanished together with Cromwell; it is time to turn to the more permanent developments of these years.

The chamber declined because it ceased to be the outstanding department, the sole office for the day-to-day payments of the government, and because it became more strictly limited in its sources of revenue. These matters, however, were really only important aspects of a more deep-seated change: the chamber became bureaucratized. It has already been shown that Henry VIII's reluctance to work at the business of government, and the substitution of cardinal for king, produced a measure of bureaucratic organization based on acts of parliament. At the same time, we have had occasion to point out that the treasurer of the chamber remained essentially a household officer entrusted with extraordinary duties and supervised by officials (the general surveyors) to whom the characteristics of household government continued to cling. Bureaucratization had begun, but it had not gone far, before Wolsey fell from power. It was afterwards that really fundamental changes took place. Cromwell seems to have turned his attention to the chamber fairly soon after he had come to full power, for in February 1534 Tuke drafted a minute to him which he headed 'Remembrance to Mr Cromwel', and in which he dealt with two aspects of his internal organization, his audit and warrants.[1] The minute begins as follows:

SIR, the effect of my humble peticion and desire of the kinges highnes is this. Ye knowe that al the kinges officers and mynystres, intromedeling with any receiptes or paymentes for his highnes, haue an ordinary way and meane to be charged and discharged at the lest ons in the yere, except the treasorer of the kinges chambre who by acte of parliament is specially and only exempt that he shal not accompte in the kinges eschequer ne bifore any other person but bifore the kinges hignes or such as his grace shal appoynt.

This accompte bifore the kinges highnes hathe bothe in sir Thomas Lovelles tyme, sir Iohn Herons tyme, and other, ben made by bookes of

---

[1] B.M., Tit. B. iv, fos. 117–18 (*L.P.* VII. 254, there dated February 1534).

their receiptes and paymentes dailly enterd and made, and somtyme wekely somtyme quarterly or euery moneth signed with the kinges hande withoute any other accompt or rekonyng; til nowe of late that sir Henry wyat, leving that office, sued a commyssion to sir Iohn Dauncy to prove and cast his bokes, whiche was perfourmed and remayn or debet thervpon conveyed, whiche was a visage or president of seconde accompte, rekenyng, or declaracion, besides the said bokes signed. And [it] may be demaunded of me or my successours occupying that office hereafter, specia[lly] seing that the wordes of the said acte do not expresse whither the said bokes shal[be] taken for a sufficient accompte bifore the kinges highnes, or whither by the same acte his grace besides those bokes may appointe other to take a further accompte of that office.

fforwhiche cause my most humble poursute and desire is to knowe herin the kinges most gracious pleasure, So that if his highnes be mynded to haue a further declaracion than by the said bokes bifore his maieste onely, It may stonde with his high pleasure to geue commyssion vnto suche a person as can do and may attende to the same, to peruse examyn viewe and cast vp my bokes....

Tuke went on to point out that to leave such a second account standing over for many years would lead to trouble as evidence may so easily disappear—'When thinges be oute of memory; strowes billes and remembrances broken perished or gon; the parties ded; or the treasorer percase hym self, or his clerkes that coude bifore haue answerd to it, ded or gon.' He had his idea how this was to be prevented:

And for the tyme to come, my most humble poursute is that the said person so auctorised by commyssion may monethly peruse examyn and viewe my said bokes, and therupon set his name to the same for a more manyfest declaracion when I shal present my bokes to be signed by the kinges highnes.

Tuke's first demand, then, was for a more regular audit of his accounts, and he took the opportunity of the precedent set by Sir Henry Wyat to press for specially commissioned auditors to check the books every month. His words show that he still envisaged the king signing them, presumably once a year; as a matter of fact, the surviving account books are nowhere signed by Henry, and the treasurer may merely have been keeping up pretences. He had recently tried to get the king's signature, but without success; the king had then demanded a preliminary audit, but nothing had been done.[1] The routine work of administration continued to bore Henry VIII.

A regular audit would cover, as Tuke put it, 'the tyme to come', but even a monthly check did not seem quite safe enough to this careful civil servant. He went on: 'The thinges be so grete in receiptes and payments as ferre excede any meane mans charge to supporte or beare, if he shulde haue no discharge til the vewing or signature of his bokes', which may be attended with delays, and therefore he asked that 'for thinges ordinary I may haue for paymentes an ordinary warrant, And that for thinges extraordinary I may alwais haue special warantes' or some other valid discharge,

ffor if I shulde make paymentes by commaundment and afterwarde sue my self for perticuler warant, I myzt be vndone in a day, lakking any warant when I sue for it. And there shulde be no day but I shulde molest the kinges highnes to signe my warantes;[2] And I shulde entre into a common sute for euery mannes money, bring my self into mystrust whiche of all men shulde not make or sue myn own warantes, nor neuer man did in that office or any other. And besides that, it myzt be said that my warant wer no warant when I make it and spede it my self; for It myzt be said, though I made a false warant, the kinges highnes, trusting me, did signe it withoute further examinacion, which if his grace wolde do I were as good haue neither warant nor boke signed when al is put to myn own reaporte. And then shulde my warantes nede asmoche comptrolment as my boke.

Tuke's caution and reasoning are alike unimpeachable, though we may imagine Cromwell smiling at that 'nor neuer man did in that office or any other'. However, even though he himself commonly obtained warrants after he had made the payments so authorized, he probably approved such bureaucratic zeal on the part of a subordinate. Tuke's insistence on special warrants before he would make extraordinary (other than regularly recurring) payments made things difficult at times for the recipients of the money, a fact which shows that Cromwell had good reason for being less particular about his own warrants; bureaucracy has ever been the friend of safety,

---

[1] B.M., Tit. B. iv, fo. 118: 'my bokes whiche I had redy at cristenmas to be signed and was put of by reason that the kinges highnes appointed them first to be seen, whiche is not yet done.'

[2] Here again we may justifiably wonder if Henry VII would have considered such carefulness to be molestation.

care, and certainty, but the enemy of speed and adaptability. As Tuke told Lord Lisle:

I pay no thing to ambassadours or their seruauntes for diettes, postage, or other thing, but as I have from tyme to tyme special warant...if that wer not requisite, neither the kinges grace nor his honourable counsail wolde take the payn at so sodeyn and hasty depeches as they be to make and signe warantes to me, being somtyme xl myle of or more or les.[1]

In Tuke's refusal to pay by 'commaundment' only we see the alteration in the position of the treasurer of the chamber: bureaucratic organization was coming in fast, and the old flexibility, the main reason for employing the chamber at all, was going.

There are other indications that Tuke was himself to a great extent responsible for this fuller organization of what had apparently been a somewhat free and easy office. He assured Cromwell that he had tightened matters up within the office:

Your lordship shal have herd what ordres I do vse, whiche never treasorers of the chamber dyd, bitwene my clerkes and me. Your lordship shal fynde that it is not veray easy either for me or them to deceyue the kinges highnes, or for them to deceyue me.[2]

He was introducing new methods of procedure. On the one hand, even warrants did not satisfy him and he began asking for receipts on payment, but this innovation met with opposition and 'many gentilmen aboute the kinges highnes...bringing me their warantes vtterly refuse to subscribe or geve acquitance, Affermyng that the possession of the warant is my discharge'.[3] One can sympathize the more readily with these members of the royal household in their objection to excessive red tape because warrants were commonly sufficient for the auditor; Tuke's demand seems motivated by nothing except bureaucratic zeal. On the other hand, he was more clearly in the right when he asked payees of annuities on patents to obtain a dormant writ of *liberate* from the chancery. He admitted that this was a new demand, but then, he added, it was a new thing for patents to be made payable by the treasurer of the chamber, and he had

---

[1] B.M., Tit. B. i, fo. 169v (*L.P.* x. 136).
[2] SP 1:127, fo. 117 (*L.P.* xii. II. 1250).
[3] *Ibid.*

to have some means of covering himself after payment had been made.[1]

All this proves clearly enough that the office of the treasurer of the chamber was being organized on the lines of a civil service department. It had originally been a kind of money-spending right hand of the government, directly accountable to the king alone, but the increase of business, the king's reluctance to attend to administrative matters, and the definition of its duties by act of parliament, had begun to develop it into a separate department. Tuke's tenure of office saw its internal development; his innovations in procedure and insistence on bureaucratic caution further deprived it of its unique position within the financial administration and helped to take away much of its special usefulness by limiting its flexibility.

Tuke's minute was followed, on 25 April 1534, by royal letters patent fully discharging him of all his payments in the past, as he had asked to be.[2] The patent was taken from a signed bill, filed as a warrant to the great seal, which is in Tuke's own hand.[3] It may be surmised that after receiving the 'remembrance' Cromwell asked Tuke to submit a formal petition in terms suitable to himself, and that a patent was made out accordingly. While Tuke must therefore be held responsible for the wording of the grant, the king's minister, to whom he had appealed, agreed with it and approved it as a matter of policy. The patent provided both for past payments and for future lack of warrants. A lengthy introduction elaborated Tuke's difficulties along the lines of his memorandum, and it was then stated that 'the said bokes of paymentes signid with our hand...shalbe sufficient warraunt and discharge for al and singuler somes and pay-

---

[1] SP 1:137, fos. 65-6 (*L.P.* XIII. II. 499): 'It was sufficient to the treasorer of the chambre to knowe the kinges pleasure by mowthe, or in his absence by lettre, warant, message, or token. And al this endured but at the kinges most gracious pleasure, and at the same pleasure wer revocable. Nowe they be for the most parte during life And many by patent.... If I shal pay by vertue of lettres patentes I must have som thing to shewe for my self. The lettres patentes the partie dothe kepe for his suretie, and I may no more pay by the sight of his lettres patentes than I may by the onely sight of his warant. Wherfor, rather than I wolde drive the partie to sue the kinges warant, I am contented only with a liberate whiche he may have for ij s' vj d', or dormant for vj s' viij d' if it be during life.'

[2] *L.P.* VII. 589 (4).

[3] C 82/683, no. 9. Tuke, who had been a signet clerk, cannot have found it difficult to draft a patent.

mentes mencionid in the same to haue bene by him paid...and so to be alowid and takyn at al tymes hereafter'. The difficulty of payments made without warrant before the books were signed ('before the ende of the monethe or of the tyme that we shall eftsones signe the said bokes') was dealt with by allowing the entry of such payments in the books as a valid discharge if they were entered before the audit of the period to which they belonged. Nothing, however, was said about the specially commissioned auditors for whom Tuke had asked; in fact, the general surveyors should have seen to that part of his request.

This discharge, given under pressure from the treasurer himself, cleared the ground, and in the next year, 1535, the government took direct action to deal with the office. The chamber machinery had to come up for review in the Reformation Parliament, for the act of 1523 provided only for the existence of the general surveyors until the end of the next parliament. But the statute of 27 Henry VIII, c. 62, went beyond precedent when it made the office of the general surveyors of crown lands permanent. This was another step in the organization of the treasurership of the chamber, another and in a way the decisive step towards making the whole chamber machinery one of a number of bureaucratic departments dealing with the finances. The fact is underlined by the section in the act by which purchased and exchanged lands were exempted from its terms, a stop thus being put to the acquisition of fresh sources of revenue by the chamber. These lands were assigned in the same session to the new court of augmentations,[1] a fact of which Tuke complained when he recited his losses in 1539.[2] As this court, so closely linked with Cromwell's financial measures, was assuredly established by him, it is only reasonable to suppose that he was also responsible for thus permanently limiting the revenues of the chamber.

The supposition can be strengthened. It had apparently been intended to renew the act for the general surveyors in 1531, at a time when Cromwell was not yet head of the government; the draft which survives differs in only a few particulars from the statute passed in 1535/6.[3] The existence of the general surveyors was to be continued

---

[1] 27 Henry VIII, c. 27, sec. vi.   [2] *L.P.* XIV. II. 13.
[3] SP 2:L, fos. 112–14 (*L.P.* V. 721, 9).

until the end of the next parliament (as had been the custom in the earlier statutes), 'And after the laste daye of the said next parliament duryng his gracys pleasure'; and the proviso about purchased lands was absent. This draft was used in drawing up the enacted statute, for the phrase concerning the prolongation of the office is underlined in the way which was commonly employed by Tudor draftsmen wishing to cancel a passage. There is any amount of evidence for the fact that Cromwell was, of all servants of the king, the one most active in the preparation of legislation, and that he was the man most interested in financial matters; by 1535 he was so fully in control of the government that no important act of parliament concerning the administration could possibly have been drafted without reference to him. The changes from 1531 were the two significant points which have been discovered in the statute: the office was made permanent, and it was deprived of the possibility of further revenues. In other words, these—the only important—points of the act were added after Cromwell had taken over the control of the administration. It would therefore appear that he sponsored the measure which further circumscribed, defined, established, and limited the chamber as a national treasury.

The act of 1536 indicates what plans Cromwell had for the chamber. It was to be part of a national administration of the finances, a bureaucratic department responsible for one particular section of the king's revenues. The general surveyors with the treasurer of the chamber were to look after the old crown lands— those, that is, that Henry VIII had inherited from his father's and Wolsey's acquiring—and after no other. New lands, however come by, were to be administered by the court of augmentations. The peculiar position of the chamber machinery had rested on its incomplete separation from the household. But a household treasurer active in national administration was an anachronism by the standards of the new principles in government that Cromwell was introducing, and it appears that the treasurer of the chamber was being groomed for a purely national part. There was a chance, absurd though it may sound, of the chamber 'going out of court'. Cromwell never completed the process, but in making the chamber machinery permanent and allotting to it a well-defined and inelastic revenue he deprived it of the characteristics which had made it something special and outside the ordinary processes of the administration. It ceased to depend for its very continuance on 'the king's pleasure', as the draft of 1531 had so aptly put it, and it was no longer available for any and every bit of income that happened to fall to the crown. It was in effect already a bureaucratic department of state. Towards the end of his ministry, Cromwell took another step designed to weaken the tie which bound the treasurer of this department to his household origin; he transferred the payment of some of the household wages paid in the chamber to the cofferer of the household.[1] Here again the process was not completed, but the intention was plain. The department of the general surveyors was to confine itself to collecting the land revenue and paying such items of government expenditure as were assigned to it. At the same time, it must not be forgotten that the general surveyors continued to audit the various 'foreign' accounts transferred to them by the statutes, but these were always something of a sideline in a department largely concerned with revenue from lands, though the machinery for distinguishing one kind of account from the other was not evolved until 1547.[2]

The reforms initiated by Cromwell achieved their natural consummation after his fall in the act of 1542 which established the court of general surveyors.[3] In effect, this act removed the limitations which still clung to the department as a legacy of its household origin and somewhat haphazard creation. The surveyors had not been able to keep records, issue process, or deal directly with the litigation arising from the lands in their charge. In other words, they had not been a court.[4] All that was now remedied. The court set up was to be a court of record whose clerk was to keep a book of proceedings and enrol leases, equipped with a privy seal of its own under which alone process was to issue for matters pursued in the court. The exchequer was expressly forbidden to interfere, while hitherto it had acted in all cases where their incomplete organization prevented the surveyors from acting directly. The new department was built on the

---

[1] Cf. below, pp. 403 f.   [2] Below, pp. 227 f.
[3] 33 Henry VIII, c. 39 (*Stat. Realm*, III. 879 ff.).
[4] Cf. above, pp. 48 ff.

new model of which the court of augmentations was the first example, and which in turn copied the organization of the duchy of Lancaster.[1] It consisted of two general surveyors, a treasurer (the treasurer of the chamber being *ex officio* treasurer of the court), an attorney, the master of the woods (who controlled the woods on crown lands), auditors, receivers, a clerk, usher, and messenger. Its competence covered the lands in the old schedule only. The petty bag of chancery was to notify inquisitions as into the exchequer. In every way this court was a fully organized department capable of doing all its work under its own power, with the sole exception of the granting of leases for which the great seal continued to be necessary: the court was to move chancery by bills signed by the general surveyors, either as immediate warrants to the great seal for lands worth less than ten marks a year, or as a warrant to the signet for the full course of warranty in all other cases. By this act of 1542 the general surveyors, with the treasurer of the chamber, were at last organized simply as another financial department of state, a development forecast by Cromwell's reform but not worked out till after his fall, probably because under his close personal administration complete bureaucratization was less essential.

By 1542 the chamber machinery had thus become part of the national administration of the finances to a much higher degree than Henry VII's household arrangement, Wolsey's statutory informality, or even Cromwell's permanent department had been. But the act perpetuated rather than solved the great inconsistency—under the new dispensation—embodied in the chamber. It was also still a department of the household, and its treasurer continued to be an important household official. There had been nothing unusual in this while household government dominated the administrative scene, but with the change to national bureaucratic institutions the problem became serious. Cromwell, as we have seen, gave signs of wishing to take the treasurer of the chamber out of the household and attach him exclusively to a national department under the general surveyors, and the 1542 statute gave form to this aim. However, it did not sever the treasurer's connexion with the household. Further reforms became necessary, in part at least because of this

[1] Below, pp. 203 ff.

unresolved confusion, and in their course Cromwell's intention was reversed and the treasurer of the chamber once again became nothing but a household officer. As a result of the reforms begun under Cromwell, the chamber machinery of finance declined into simply one of a number of parallel bureaucratic departments; it is necessary now to show how the chamber passed completely out of the national government.

As has already been briefly indicated, the chamber really fell on evil days soon after Cromwell's fall. Like the rest of the administration, it was being worked to a standstill: little revenue came in, while the king's expenditure grew constantly. From 31 March to the end of September 1547, Cavendish received a few sums in arrears— a total of a mere £6,000; even in that time his expenses were £7,166.[1] By this time, however, a step had been taken which altered the whole position. A patent of 1 January 1547 amalgamated the courts of general surveyors and of augmentations.[2] Though the general surveyors themselves were incorporated in the new organization, so as to preserve the knowledge and experience requisite for dealing with the old land revenue, the amalgamated department needed only one treasurer, and the treasurer of the chamber was left out of the scheme. He ceased to occupy two posts and live a dual existence, but only at the expense of altogether dropping out of the national financial administration. The land revenue machinery which Cromwell and his successors had embodied in a bureaucratic department of state was finally divorced from the household when it lost the link with the chamber for which there was now no need; though Cromwell had apparently hoped to free the treasurer of the chamber from his household duties, the amalgamation of 1547 rendered so difficult and revolutionary a step superfluous.

For the time being, the treasurer of the chamber continued to be employed in the payment of various items of government expenditure, though their number and variety had much decreased from the great days of Sir John Heron, or even the lesser days of Sir Brian

---

[1] E 101/426/5.
[2] *L.P.* XXI. II. 771 (1); cf. below, pp. 224 ff.

Tuke;[1] what was completely taken away was the direct chamber revenue. The patent of January 1547 ordered that the chamber, deprived of the lands which had supplied its resources, should receive such revenues of the duchy of Lancaster and the court of wards as were not already assigned to the household; the remainder was to come from the new court of augmentations.[2] At the same time the treasurer of the chamber continued to be responsible to the general surveyors; his accounts were to be treated in the same way as the accounts of the treasurer of the new court. The chamber was now to pay its share of expenditure—mostly payments in court expenses and wages—from an income supplied by true revenue departments. In the first year of the new arrangement Cavendish received £16,000 in this fashion —from the court of wards and the duchy without further warrant (the words of the patent being sufficient authority), from exchequer and augmentations by warrant from the council.[3] With this, the part played by chamber finance in Tudor administration was practically at an end, though the final steps in returning the chamber to purely household duties were not taken until ten years later.

It would appear that the chamber continued at the uneasy half-way stage reached in 1547 as long as Sir William Cavendish was in office: it was charged with certain payments in the household, was occasionally called upon to pay on extraordinary warrants, and received its income from wards and the duchy, helped out by large drafts on augmentations, exchequer, and the mint.[4] A commission appointed in 1552 to investigate the state of the revenue reported that the treasurer of the chamber had only payments and no receipts to record; he was only a paymaster who disbursed the money collected

---

[1] Expenditure in 1547–8 totalled only £18,489 (E 101/426/5). Cavendish's claim, in December 1548, that his ordinary payments without extraordinary warrants amounted to £25,000 a year (*Trevelyan Papers*, II. 13) may have been exaggerated; at any rate, it confirms the general impression that the treasurer's extraordinary payments were few by this time.

[2] C 66/790, m. 22.

[3] E 101/426/5, fos. 6v–10. The details are as follows: Exchequer—£2,000 (Nov. 1547), £2,000 (April 1548); augmentations—£2,400 (Nov.), £600 (Dec.), £1,000 (July); duchy—£2,000 (May); wards—£1,000 (Nov.), £1,000 (Dec.), £3,000 (Feb.). It is stated that the chamber continued to receive the net revenues of the duchy of Cornwall and the hanaper of chancery until 1595 (Dietz, *English Public Finance 1558–1641*, 408), but there is no sign of this in the years 1547–58.

[4] Cf. E 101/426/6, Cavendish's account for 1548–9. The records of his tenure are scanty.

by others.[1] They also stated that since 1547 the treasurer's income had been very uncertain: before that time he had used to receive all the surplus in the court of wards and £4,000 from the duchy, but since then he had had to rely on money paid by occasional warrant and usually from unreliable sources like the mint or the land sales.[2] It seems, therefore, that the provisions made by the patent of January 1547 never worked too well, though the commissioners undoubtedly only echoed the stereotyped complaints of an office which seems to have quickly forgotten the uncertainty prevailing even before 1547. No particular recommendations were made, beyond a few suggested economies and the need for more frequent audits.

In 1557 Cavendish died, and for the time being no successor was appointed. A minor official, Edmund Felton, a member of an exchequer family, was deputed to stand in, under the supervision of Sir Henry Fernegan, the vice-chamberlain, and Sir Thomas Cornwallis, controller of the household; a privy seal of 14 December 1557 ordered the payment of £3,000 out of the exchequer to cover his charge which was outlined in full to him in a letter from the temporary supervisors, dated 21 March 1558. His account for the year ending Michaelmas 1558, from the introduction to which all these details are derived, was the first of the declared accounts of the chamber enrolled at the exchequer.[3] It therefore appears that after Cavendish's death a general survey of the office was made, with a caretaker under the eye of two leading household officials to hold the place open until the ground was cleared, and that the chief reform was a more stringent control from the exchequer, itself recently reformed. At the same time, the treasurer of the chamber was reduced to the mere payment of household wages, and though other court and household matters were later again put to his charge, he never again paid national expenses; the career of the chamber— the part played by the household in national finance—was at an end. The appointment, on 31 October 1558, of Sir John Mason[4] to fill the vacant treasurership marked the beginning of a new period in the

---

[1] B.M., Harl. MS. 7383, fos. 29 seqq.

[2] Ibid. fo. 56. The report added that the treasurer's diets (£120) were larger than they used to be, and commented on some other sources of extravagance and lack of supervision.

[3] E 351/541, mm. 1 ff.

[4] Mason's appointment, with a new fee of £200, plus £40 for two clerks and 1s. a day

history of the chamber; it once again became the chief financial department of the household, and nothing more.

That concludes the story of a peculiar interlude. The revival of chamber finance by the Yorkists and Henry VII was of a piece with their general policy of restoring medieval government to its pristine power, though it went exceptionally far in that direction. Henry VII indeed relied on the chamber and his informal surveyors almost to the exclusion of the exchequer, and so in effect did Wolsey. The necessity of better authority than a dead king's word led to the statutes defining the power of the general surveyors, thereby giving them the beginnings of a bureaucratic organization. Tuke's administration limited the usefulness of his office by reducing its flexibility. Cromwell began to reduce it to the status of simply another revenue department, and his aim was achieved when the act of 1542 was passed after his fall. For various reasons, which will have to be investigated later, the court of general surveyors lost its identity in 1547, and the treasurer of the chamber became once more simply a paymaster in the household, unconnected with any department collecting revenues. This eclipse of Henry VII's 'minister of finance' marked the end of household influence in the finances and the triumph of national and bureaucratic institutions. Though not completed until 1554, or at the earliest 1547, the process was clearly outlined in the 1530's—in the act of 1535, the transfer of some household work away from the chamber, and the creation of new departments which reduced the importance and lowered the standing of the chamber machinery of finance.

3. *The new machinery*

The addition of new sources of revenue to the income of the crown naturally raised administrative problems. Such small items as

in wages for an apparitor and messenger, is quoted at the head of his first account, E 351/541, m. 7. A commission under the great seal recited there shows how well the ground was cleared for him (it was dated 6 July 1559 and made at his suit): he was granted a discharge for all payments made since Cavendish's death, and provision was made for future warrants—by the queen, or by six privy councillors (the secretary to be one), or by the lord chamberlain, vice-chamberlain, or secretary for posts, or by the lord chamberlain or vice-chamberlain for the making ready of the queen's houses or for rewards. Mason was ordered to clear outstanding payments due on warrants made out to Tuke or Cavendish.

another escheated estate or an increase in fines for knighthood did not require anything new in the way of machinery, but the huge gains made at the expense of the church—the first-fruits and tenths supposedly transferred from the pope, and the dissolved monasteries—could not be allotted so easily to any existing department without overstraining its resources. It therefore became necessary to create new organizations, and these must now be described.

The act of 1534 which laid down the administrative details concerning the collection of first-fruits and tenths[1] is the more interesting because its provisions were only partially carried out. It was originally intended to utilize existing machinery. The value of first-fruits was to be assessed by commissioners also empowered to take compositions for them and to accept payments, of whom the chancellor and the master of the rolls were always to be two, and it is not surprising to find that the financial officer of the chancery, the clerk of the hanaper, was to keep and account for all the money and obligations which compositions made before them yielded to the crown. Should the king appoint additional commissioners, the proceeds of their labours were to go to the treasurer of the chamber, 'or eles where to whom it shall please the Kinges Highnes...to gyve auctorite by commyssion under his greate seale to receyve the same'. Tenths, to be paid every Christmas from 1535 onwards, were to be assessed by commissioners appointed by the chancellor, and their collection was entrusted to the archbishops and bishops who were to pay the money every year by 1 April to the treasurer of the chamber or, again, to such person as the king should appoint for the purpose. It was clearly thought that the new revenues could be handled by established departments, nor was there any reason to doubt it. The sums involved were as yet unknown, but when they came to be assessed and were found to amount to about £40,000 a year it may still have seemed that hanaper and chamber could deal with them.[2] The real difficulties of organization, the problems of assessment and collection, were settled in the act along lines that were to prove

---

[1] 26 Henry VIII, c. 3 (*Stat. Realm*, III. 439 ff.).
[2] Cf. the estimate given in *L.P.* x. 1257 (xii).

workable and put no additional strain on the treasuries to be used; there appeared to be no need to provide a separate administration for the new revenues. However, the scheme was really rather clumsy; it involved two different agencies for the receipt and account of the money, and first-fruits would have to be divided between two separate treasuries as soon as additional commissioners were appointed from outside the ranks of chancery officials. Cromwell, it may be supposed, had a hand in the making of an act which dealt with his own additions to the revenue; he even corrected at least one draft of it.[1] But he must soon have changed his mind, for a fundamental change, which was certainly his work, was made in the projected machinery before it was put into practice.

On 7 May 1535, before the first payment fell due, John Gostwick was appointed treasurer and general receiver, and also commissioner, of first-fruits and tenths, in accordance with the statute of 26 Henry VIII;[2] he was actually in office by 21 March.[3] Advantage was thus taken of the loophole which the act offered in reserving to the king the right of appointing some other person in the place of the treasurer of the chamber. In addition to his basic duties, Gostwick was also to take charge of other sources of revenue: the issues of lands acquired by the king, particularly those of attainted persons (Wolsey and Rice ap Griffiths) and of suppressed abbeys; the profits of vacant sees and monasteries; and fines for exports, for the escape of prisoners from ecclesiastical prisons, and for the restitution of temporalities. He was also to receive from Cromwell certain bonds of the king's debts, and to see to their collection. For these duties he was to have an annuity of £100.[4]

It is at once apparent that all his income, except the new revenue of first-fruits and tenths, was money that Cromwell himself had been

---

[1] *L.P.* VII. 1380 (2). One might conceivably discover a good deal about his influence from these corrections, but unfortunately it has proved impossible to trace this document at the P.R.O. The reference given in the 'Key' to *L.P.* leads nowhere, and it must be said that the draft appears to have vanished uncatalogued.

[2] *L.P.* VIII. 802 (20).　　　　　　　　　　[3] *Ibid.* 422.

[4] In March 1535 John Husee, Lord Lisle's agent, reported Gostwick's annuity to be £300 (*ibid.*). His information proved prophetically correct. In August 1536 Gostwick was granted an additional £200, the original sum having been found insufficient to meet the expenses of his office (*L.P.* IX. 385, 12). It seems therefore likely that Gostwick was drawing £300 p.a. for a year and a half before he was authorized to do so by patent.

administering for the previous three years, which suggests that the absence of any accounts of Cromwell's after 1534 reflects the fact that he was no longer receiving a well-defined revenue. Gostwick's own accounts confirm and add to this impression.[1] He classified his income as first-fruits, tenths, clerical subsidy, receipts from vacant sees, the bishop of Lincoln's fine for letting 'collectors convicted' escape from his prison, and fines assessed by Cromwell for the making of knights. There is also an item of various sums received from Cromwell and others for immediate and specified employments. Very largely, then, Gostwick was to take over the money which had served Cromwell in his capacity as treasurer, though there was from the first a definite emphasis on ecclesiastical revenues: these formed the bulk of his income, and other matters were merely incidental.

The personality of John Gostwick will help to explain what purpose lay behind the change in the original plan which his appointment implied. There seem to have been two men of that name, brothers or cousins, for one John Gostwick wrote to Wolsey, about 1525, to thank him for his kindness to John Gostwick, his 'germanus'.[2] It is, however, possible to distinguish one of them, an experienced and well-trained financial official of the Wolsey school who had been friendly with Cromwell in the cardinal's household, had secured minor preferment in the king's service, and was now to receive considerable promotion at Cromwell's hands.[3] By 1534 he was in Cromwell's service and was acting for him in various, mostly financial, affairs;[4] nor did he leave that service even after he had been

[1] B.M., Lansd. MS. 156, fos. 146-9.

[2] *L.P.* IV. 231. The writer of this letter describes Cromwell as his own patron.

[3] He appears to have been in Wolsey's service from 1517 (*L.P.* II. 3841, p. 1517; III. 1021, 1451 [20]), and—his 'old and trusty servant' (*L.P.* IV. 2131)—rose to be the cardinal's controller by July 1527 (*ibid.* 3216, 6586 [2]). He was present at the foundation of the Ipswich college, and with Cromwell and others of Wolsey's servants received Ravenston Manor to Wolsey's use (*ibid.* 4461, 5024). In 1525 he was appointed auditor of some crown lands in Yorkshire; he was once described as king's auditor (*L.P.* III. 3214, 18; V. 166, 26). In 1529 he wrote to Cromwell as his trusty and loving friend (*L.P.* IV, App. 233). Gostwick was a native of Willington, Beds.; he repeatedly sat on the commission of the peace for that county even before he became treasurer of first-fruits, and represented it in the Reformation Parliament (*L.P.* IV. 5132; V. 909 [9], 1694; VII. 56; XII. II. 458).

[4] He handed William Elys the letter requesting his resignation as baron of the exchequer; with Richard Cromwell he took an inventory of Lord Dacre's plate; and he handled money under Cromwell (*L.P.* VII. 34, 663, 1011, 1353, 1364, 1469).

promoted to be treasurer of first-fruits and tenths. He remained completely at Cromwell's disposal; left behind in London to look after Cromwell's business, he had to seek his master's permission to go to his home in Bedfordshire, and as late as 1538 this important royal treasurer still had to thank Cromwell for such licence.[1] His relations with Cromwell in matters concerning the king's business are well illustrated by a letter from Cromwell in October 1535 which was in effect a warrant discharging him from certain duties and ordering him to take certain steps:[2] he was authorized to call before him some of the king's debtors whose debts had grown 'desperate' (irrecoverable) in order to make as favourable an arrangement with them as he could. 'And this Subscribed with my hande shalbe vnto you, your heires, executours, & deputies sufficient discharge at all tymes hereafter.' Such language, copying the very words of royal warrants, in a private letter from Cromwell to a royal treasurer and referring to an important transaction with the king's money, puts Cromwell's complete and independent control in a nutshell.

Gostwick, then, was Cromwell's servant as long as Cromwell lived. Rather than commit the new revenue to chamber and hanaper, Cromwell appointed a man from his own household, an experienced civil servant of Wolsey's training, also entrusting to him the money which he himself had administered as master of the jewels—with the exception of that official's strictly departmental business. Not only was Gostwick's income reminiscent of Cromwell's; his payments, too, as long as Cromwell ruled, included all manner of things that were previously found in Cromwell's own payments. An account of the year 1540 enumerated these items, among others:[3] the justices and serjeants; Cornelius Hayes, the goldsmith; Fowler at Calais; Gonson for ships, and for conveying Anne of Cleves; the king's works; the king's tomb; rewards to ambassadors and others; Sadler's diets in Scotland; Wotton's diets in Cleves; suppliers of the great wardrobe. In July 1535 Cromwell noted in his remembrances that he would cause Gostwick to pay certain diets to ambassadors, rewards to Irish officials, and sums for buildings at Calais and Dover.[4]

---

[1] *L.P.* IX. 65, 279, 301; XIII. II. 222.
[2] B.M., Tit. B. iv, fos. 114–15 (*L.P.* IX. 647); printed in Merriman, I. 433.
[3] SP 1:159, fos. 260–4 (*L.P.* XV. 642).   [4] *L.P.* VIII. 1077.

Dockets of four warrants paid by Gostwick and waiting to be signed include a varied number of payments similar to those already given.[1] It would be tedious to list the payments which Gostwick made by Cromwell's orders; examples of the kind indicated can be found throughout the years 1535-40.[2] When it is remembered that in 1535 Cromwell began to be too busy to attend in detail to the duties of a treasurer, and that apparently he ceased to act as one by about April 1536,[3] his intention with regard to Gostwick's office becomes plain. The new treasurer was to take over the income and expenditure hitherto handled by Cromwell himself; he was to be Cromwell's personal paymaster in matters of state. Cromwell may have been responsible for the insertion into the act of 1534 of those reservations which afterwards enabled him to secure Gostwick's appointment, for it is, on the face of it, very likely that he hoped from the first to have full control of the new revenue. Though his clerkship of the hanaper would in any case have given him control of a part, that was so patently an unsatisfactory arrangement that a better solution was found in the appointment of a separate treasurer for first-fruits and tenths who was in Cromwell's pocket.

In consequence of this marked example of Cromwell's personal and masterful handling of the administration, the treasurer of first-fruits and tenths had for the time being no properly organized department at all. He had his clerks and servants whom he paid,[4] but he presided over a treasury which was fed by agencies outside his control. The value of benefices was assessed by commissioners who produced, in the *Valor Ecclesiasticus*, a tax return of lasting value which could be used as occasion arose for the determining of first-fruits. Compositions for these were made before independent officers who were, to begin with, the chancellor and master of the rolls, Audeley and Cromwell. Gostwick's accounts show that these two alone were engaged in taking compositions in the first year of the new revenue (1535),[5] while in the following year a certain John Hales was added to their number, no doubt the same Hales who was

---

[1] *L.P.* XI. 381, 516.
[2] E.g. *L.P.* VIII. 1109-10, 1148; IX. 65, 125, 151, 252, 279, 341, 451, 558, 836; X. 28, 1052; XI. 1163, 1448; XII. I. 1079; XII. II. 256, 260, 577; XIV. II. 53.
[3] Above, p. 140.   [4] *L.P.* XI. 385 (12).
[5] B.M., Lansd. MS. 156, fos. 146-9.

appointed clerk of first-fruits, with powers to value and take compositions, on 3 February 1537.[1] Except that Christopher Hales took Cromwell's place as master of the rolls in 1536, these men continued to supply the treasurer's income in first-fruits. Gostwick received both cash and bonds; in July 1535, he appealed to Cromwell for someone 'to sue the processe of suche obligacions and specialties as be commytted to my charge', the clerk of the king's attorney having departed without letting him know how matters stood, 'so that I am not hable to aunswere nether to the Kinges grace nor your Maistership concernyng thesame'.[2] Normally he therefore relied on the attorney general for the collection of his debts, though later he reported that he was personally active in daily calling on debtors in London for first-fruits and other debts, adding that he himself had committed some to ward for non-payment.[3] There was nothing in his patent to permit such high-handed action: very probably he was overstepping the limit of his authority and relied on Cromwell to back him up. On the whole, however, his work about first-fruits was confined to the storage and disbursement of the money after he had collected on the bonds received from the commissioners.

The procedure for tenths was different. Their collection went by dioceses and was under the control of the bishops who paid the money to Gostwick, as the account quoted shows. However, as the treasurer of first-fruits did not preside over a court of record and could not keep rolls, issue process, control the bishops, or call them to account, all the administrative business concerning tenths was done in the exchequer. In 1535 the new bishop of Salisbury, Nicholas Shaxton, wanted to be discharged in the exchequer for the

---

[1] *L.P.* XII. I. 539 (5). He would thus seem to have exercised the office before he was properly installed, but as a matter of fact his appointment had been under discussion for some time. In February 1536 an entry in Cromwell's memoranda spoke of 'an office to be made for the taking of bonds for the first fruits' (*L.P.* X. 254). In August that year Audeley refused to seal Hales's patent because it would take away his own authority concerning first-fruits (*L.P.* XI. 296). His appeal to Cromwell seems to have succeeded in getting the terms of the patent changed, for Audeley continued to accept compositions for first-fruits for another two years (1536–8). His letter hints that this business was profitable to the commissioners. This John Hales is not identified by *L.P.* with the John Hales who was a baron of the exchequer and one of the general surveyors (XIII. II. p. 152 n., and index), and Audeley's way of speaking of him supports this. He was perhaps the well-known John Hales of Coventry, later so important a theorist and economist, but a new man in 1537.

[2] SP 1:94, fos. 223–4 (*L.P.* VIII. 1123).   [3] *L.P.* XIII. II. 222.

revenues of his bishopric in the previous half year;[1] in 1536, complaints were addressed to Cromwell that the books for the tenth out of the exchequer were full of errors.[2] Accounts for tenths were rendered into the exchequer where they were enrolled on the king's remembrancer's memoranda roll. Though the bishops did the work, the knowledge of what needed doing does not seem to have resided in their diocesan organization but in the exchequer. In January 1540, a privy seal addressed to the treasurer and barons of the exchequer declared that in the absence of the bishop of London, Bonner then being on an embassy, the dean and chapter of St Paul's were to collect the tenth, pay it to Gostwick, and account for it in the exchequer; the king's remembrancer was to direct 'sedules sealed vnder our seale of our said Eschequire' to the dean and chapter, 'conteynyng all such Somes of Money, whyth lettres suffyent whythin the same, whereby the sayd Dean and Chapter may be sufficiently lernid and Instructed to collect, gather, and receue the sayd Annuell rent and pencion'.[3] When things went wrong, Gostwick could not act directly. On 1 December 1539, he complained in the exchequer court that the abbot of Bury St Edmunds, responsible for the collection of the tenth in Norwich diocese, had retained the money and failed to render his account into the exchequer, 'in Contemptum & decepcionem eiusdem domini Regis ac contra Leges suas; vnde predictus Iohannis Gostwyk petit Auisamentum Curie in premissis'.[4] It was not until 29 November 1540 that Sir John Baker, chancellor of the recently established court of first-fruits and tenths, came into the exchequer and collected the records which till then had been kept by the king's remembrancer.[5]

The business organization of the treasurer was thus left in a very rudimentary state. For six years he worked under a system which made him dependent on other officers and departments for everything except the actual accumulation and paying out of the money. This absence of a proper department is surprising enough in an age when so much bureaucratic organization was growing up, but the

[1] *L.P.* VIII. 766. [2] *L.P.* X. 413, 435.
[3] E 159/318, m. 26.
[4] *Ibid.* Communia, Michaelmas Term, Recorda, m. 35.
[5] *Ibid.* 319, Communia, Michaelmas Term, Recorda, m. 24.

reason for it must be sought in the treasurer's immediate dependence on Cromwell. That this was so is amply confirmed by what Gostwick himself described as his 'first accompt after the Court was established in the said yeare 26°', an account which covered the period from 1 January 1535 to Christmas 1540.[1] For all the years before the actual court was set up, Gostwick had rendered no official account. We know that no such account survives; we may take Gostwick's word for it that none ever existed. Yet he undoubtedly kept some form of check on his receipts and payments, for he was able, in 1540, to draw up a detailed balance for those six years, and on several occasions before 1540 he had to render unofficial accounts to Cromwell. In 1536, replying to a request 'to knowe what money remayneth, Aswell in the Mynt, in Robert Lordes handes, & myne', Gostwick wrote that he knew nothing of the mint for which Stephen Vaughan would answer,[2] but that there was some £6,470 in cash in the hands of the jewel-house officials, of Robert Lord, his servant, and of himself.[3] At other times, he sent proper accounts to Cromwell—a statement, for instance, of the receipt of the tenth for two years, or a brief declaration of what remained in his clerk's hands.[4] Though no account was made to the king until 1540, Gostwick was strictly controlled, but he accounted to Cromwell only and no report of the affairs of his office ever went further than the lord privy seal who kept the income of the treasurer of first-fruits and tenths as firmly in his own hand as he had held the swollen revenues of the master of the jewels. It was for this reason that no organized department was set up for first-fruits and tenths; to have done so would have meant giving more independence to the treasurer than Cromwell was willing to grant.

[1] B.M., Lansd. MS. 156, fos. 146–9. This is a copy made in 1609, which may account for the mistake made in the heading. It was the office of treasurer, of course, and not the court of first-fruits and tenths, which was established in the 26th year of Henry VIII. On the other hand, it is possible that Gostwick himself antedated the use of the term 'court', now that the office had actually become one.

[2] It may be noted in passing that the mint, like all other financial departments, was kept under close surveillance by Cromwell, though there is no sign of any active or reforming interest in it. One example of his power over it is the appointment of Vaughan, his friend and servant, as its undertreasurer. Gostwick's words make one suspect that Vaughan was put in as Cromwell's personal agent.

[3] SP 1:112, fos. 68–70 (*L.P.* XI. 1220). Lord had rendered Gostwick an account to this effect which was forwarded to Cromwell (*L.P.* XI. 1220, ii).

[4] *L.P.* XII. II. 567; XIII. II. 222.

Gostwick's appointment continued Cromwell's treasurership by delegation; in this way Cromwell had, throughout his supremacy, large sums immediately at his disposal for the expenses of the government.

The sums involved were indeed not small. In June 1536 Gostwick drew up an estimate of his income in which he quoted the round figures of £30,000 for 'the Annuall Rent or Tenth of the Spiritualtie to be payde in Aprill next comyng', and of £10,000 for 'the furst ffructes by estymacion, Due and to be due at the feest of Thannunciacion of our Lady'. At the same time he expected to collect £12,592 from debts and other sources.[1] The actual receipts for the years 1535-40 totalled £406,103, an average of over £60,000 a year, but of this £130,711 was irregular income, handed over by Cromwell and others and ear-marked for special purposes: it was money for which Gostwick was paymaster rather than treasurer. The totals given for first-fruits (£90,069) and tenths (£156,251) show that the estimate of 1536 erred on the conservative side for the former and hoped too much for the latter; together, the two yielded the expected average of £40,000 a year. First-fruits, in the nature of things, varied considerably from year to year; tenths started at £32,018 and decreased steadily to £18,412, a consequence of the dissolution of the monasteries.[2] Cromwell, therefore, continued to be in nearly immediate control of sums comparable to those he had himself administered as master of the jewels, with the difference that Gostwick's income was revenue in the true sense, while Cromwell had drawn on reserves of capital.

It may be added that Gostwick's income derived mainly from two sources, for in addition to first-fruits and tenths he also administered the clerical subsidies which had thus been withdrawn from the chamber. As we have seen,[3] they had not been administered by Cromwell, and the £130,711 which Gostwick received from Cromwell and others allegedly by the king's express commandment

---

[1] SP1:104, fo. 295v (*L.P.* x. 1257).

[2] B.M., Lansd. MS. 156, fos. 146-9. Gostwick's last account, from Christmas 1544 to the day of his death on 15 April 1545, shows a quarter's receipts of £29,940 (E 336/27), but it would be wrong to multiply by four in order to arrive at a year's income: the year's first-fruits and tenths had both been due to be paid in the period of the account.

[3] Above, p. 145.

can have come from any source at any time during the six years; there is no reason for identifying that money with the fine for the *praemunire*, which in any case was some £12,000 less.[1] The extent to which Gostwick acted as a privileged paymaster is illustrated by the fact that not only plate but even cash was diverted to him by the court of augmentations from the monastic spoil.[2] Wherever possible, Cromwell used him to cover expenses and he therefore wished him to have a steady reserve of ready money. However, such details apart, Gostwick was the treasurer responsible for the king's revenue from his spiritual subjects.

Cromwell's control over the office, which caused its arrested development, was not limited to Gostwick's immediate responsibility to himself, or to the fact that the treasurer generally made payments by his orders. He himself often interfered in the concerns of the office. In particular, as long as he was master of the rolls his correspondence included a good deal on first-fruits and tenths. The bishop of Bath sent him a 'book of the taxes' of his diocese (which Cromwell passed to Audeley who presumably had more time and was by statute equally qualified to handle such matters),[3] and his agents frequently reported to him about the compositions they had taken.[4] Some trouble arose over the first-fruits of Latimer and Hilsey at Worcester and Rochester, and the correspondence which ensued shows how deeply Cromwell concerned himself with these matters. Gostwick informed him that the two elects had sent for him, saying that by Cromwell's orders they were to compound with him for first-fruits; as he knew nothing about it he asked for orders. A few days later Cromwell's private receiver, Polsted, reported that he had accepted Latimer's own bond because the bishop had been unable to find sureties. The business was complicated by the absence of reliable accounts of the 'profits of their promotion', and all the details were communicated to Cromwell. Hilsey wanted to know what he was supposed to do since Gostwick had no instructions to

---

[1] Dr Dietz made the identification (*Eng. Gov. Fin.* 227).

[2] GD 15, no. 9. *Ibid.* no. 100 shows that these transactions were made on Cromwell's initiative (cf. *Bull. I.H.R.* XXII. 35 ff.).

[3] *L.P.* IX. 383, 450.

[4] *L.P.* VIII. 248; X. 363. Perhaps it should be pointed out that Cromwell would, of course, often delegate his powers to subordinates.

take his sureties and Polsted did not know how much they were to amount to; the whole affair illustrates the way in which officers of the crown were mixed up with Cromwell's household servants in the government of the country, as well as the limits of efficiency which the best run civil service often encounters. Soon after, Polsted acknowledged receipt of his instructions concerning Hilsey, and Cromwell himself settled Latimer's problem in a letter probably addressed to the receiver of the profits of the vacant see of Worcester; one can almost see the lord privy seal cutting the knot of confusion so carefully tied by his subordinates.[1] Even after he had ceased to be personally responsible for the taking of compositions, Cromwell might still order an ex-prior to pay arrears to Gostwick or come and show cause why he should not;[2] and bishop Rowland Lee's dispatch of the tenth of his diocese might be communicated to him.[3]

All this underlines Gostwick's status as Cromwell's personal treasurer in affairs of state. On the other hand, Gostwick himself has left it on record that he occasionally managed to escape this control. In a summary of his financial position, drawn up at the time of Cromwell's fall, he wrote:

May it please your moost Excellent Maiestie to be aduertised That I, your moost humble seruaunt Iohn Gostwyk, haue in my handes Whiche I Treasured from tyme to tyme, vnknowne vnto Therl of Essex, Whiche if I had declared vnto hym He wolde haue Caused me to Disburse by commaundement, without warraunt, as heretofore I haue don—x M li.[4]

This confirms that he usually made payments by Cromwell's orders only, though he frequently obtained a royal warrant later,[5] but the more interesting statement is that he managed to withhold £10,000, or about one-fortieth of his income in the years 1535-40, from Cromwell. It is, on the whole, a difficult thing to believe; one cannot

---

[1] *L.P.* IX. 203, 272-3, 342, 359-60, 372, 470.

[2] *L.P.* Add. 1341. [3] *L.P.* XV. 562.

[4] B.M., Royal MSS., App. 89, fo. 127. The document can be dated by another (*ibid.* fo. 128) which says that the £10,000 was in Gostwick's hand on 8 July (1540).

[5] Sometimes he asked for one (*L.P.* IX. 65, 125, 451); Cromwell's notes include entries for Gostwick's warrants to be signed (*L.P.* IX. 836; XII. I. 1079); and drafts of such warrants, drawn up in Cromwell's office, survive (*L.P.* XI, 381, 516). Later he seems to have had his payments authorized by warrants signed by Cromwell, not by the king (*L.P.* XIV. I. 1269). When Cromwell fell, £15,828 had been paid out by Cromwell's orders only, for which no warrant had as yet been obtained (cf. the declaration handed to the new lord privy seal, Southampton, B.M., Royal MSS., App. 89, fo. 127).

really see what Gostwick hoped to gain by doing this in the years when Cromwell was safely in power, and only two explanations will satisfy the known conditions of Gostwick's complete dependence on Cromwell, and of Cromwell's supremacy right into 1540. Either Gostwick had been deceiving the lord privy seal, the money had been destined for his own pocket, and he now hoped to anticipate the discovery of his peculations which the inevitable investigation of Cromwell's affairs might bring about; or he was trying to curry favour by attacking the fallen minister, and the money was simply what he would ordinarily have had in hand at that particular moment. This second interpretation is to some extent supported by the fact that after revealing the existence of the surplus Gostwick immediately named expenses to be charged against it; he would in any case have had to keep some money for these payments. On the whole it seems probable that Gostwick was defaming Cromwell's administration so that he might play the just steward; the method was the more suitable because Cromwell had indeed been in the habit of authorizing payments for which warrants would be produced later as a mere formality. In that case Cromwell probably knew all about the £10,000. However, the possibility that Gostwick was speaking the truth cannot be ignored entirely, and it is easy to believe that no single man could be sure of controlling so many departments so completely and consistently as Cromwell attempted to do.

Naturally, the removal of Cromwell from the helm caused difficulties. The treasurer of first-fruits and tenths had been so much Cromwell's personal servant that without him he was useless and unusable. It was therefore decided to set up a proper new department, a court of first-fruits and tenths, by act of parliament,[1] a step which was certainly not even contemplated till after Cromwell's fall; it was the work of his successors—perhaps of Lord St John, the future marquess of Winchester and lord treasurer. They were faced by a treasurer without responsibility to any immediate superior and no longer fitting into the scheme of things, and it must have seemed best to add him to that scheme by incorporating him in one of those fully organized financial departments which Cromwell had himself

---

[1] 32 Henry VIII, c. 45 (*Stat. Realm*, III. 798 ff.).

championed in his later years. The bill originated in the house of lords where it was introduced on 15 July 1540, five weeks after Cromwell's arrest and a clear three months after the beginning of the session.[1] It cannot have taken long to draft an act which arranged for no new business to be done, and which for its administrative detail had such models as the courts of augmentations and of wards. Once introduced, the bill was rushed through both houses in six days, being concluded on 21 July.[2] Nevertheless, the court does not seem to have started work until November; on the 29th of that month, its chancellor, Sir John Baker, replaced as attorney general only three weeks earlier,[3] collected the relevant records from the exchequer,[4] and Gostwick did not render that famous first account of his until Christmas 1540.[5] The impression is that the court was set up in a hurry; it was, or so it would appear, conceived in the emergency created by Cromwell's fall and embodied in legislation before the actual administrative changes could be organized.

The court of first-fruits and tenths represented no new principle. It provided for the revenues from the church a machinery already in use for the confiscated monastic lands and for wards' lands, and adopted in full two years later for the general surveyors. Here again there was to be an organization complete in itself, independent of the exchequer, and using the procedure of the duchy of Lancaster council. A court of record, equipped with a privy seal and consisting of a chancellor, treasurer, attorney, two auditors, clerk, messenger, and usher, was set up, to be in charge of all matters connected with first-fruits and tenths. The chancellor, or officers commissioned by him, replaced the lord chancellor and master of the rolls in the taking of compositions and Cromwell's informality in the taking of declared accounts. The seal of the court was to be the only weapon for issuing process, and the exchequer was expressly forbidden to interfere. All the work of recording and supervising the collection of tenths hitherto done in the exchequer was transferred to the new court, though the actual collection itself remained in the hands of the bishops.

---

[1] *L.J.* I. 156b.
[2] *Ibid.* 159b.
[3] *L.P.* XVI. 305 (18).
[4] Above, p. 196, n. 5.
[5] Above, p. 198, n. 2.

Thus it was not until 1540 that the financial department for first-fruits, tenths, and clerical subsidies—the department of clerical revenues—was properly set up. It is, however, true to say that Cromwell had created a kind of rudimentary department for the same purpose, keeping it under his tutelage. Since he was looking for a treasurer of state personally subordinate to himself and available to carry on the very direct control of ready cash which his own treasurership had provided, he could not allow the new revenues to be put under a full department of state. Rather he copied the older methods of a half-informal treasury controlled only by the personal attention of king or minister; from 1535 to 1540, Gostwick's treasurership was in the direct line of descent from the treasurers of the chamber and Cromwell's own mastership of the jewels. What Cromwell had done was to secure the administration of a specific type of revenue—that coming from the church—in the hands of one specific treasurer; after his fall it was both possible and necessary to complete his work by setting up a full revenue court for this section of the finances.

The dissolution of the monasteries and the annexation of their property to the crown raised much bigger issues. The houses had to be suppressed, or their surrender had to be accepted; surveys and valuations had to be taken; the monks had to be disposed of; the lands had to be administered, their rents collected, expended, and accounted for; their disposal by grant, lease, or sale had to be supervised; there was the litigation which always attaches itself to property. The monks had departed, but behind them they had left duties and obligations which the government was determined to meet. There were leases to be carried over and debts to be paid.[1] The monks had to be pensioned off, or sent to collect 'capacities', their licences to become secular priests, though the actual issuing of these was the task of chancery.[2] A questionnaire drawn up by the duchy of

---

[1] 'The said Commyssioners shall take the notes of all leases made, and the same to be examyned, So that it may be knowen howe long the seid leases shall contynue or indur.... Item, the said Commyssioners...to pay all true dettes of euery house, being vnder the value of xx li'' (DL 5/6, fo. 204v).

[2] Cf. E 36/116, fos. 50–3.

Lancaster describes some of the difficulties encountered by the commissioners.[1] What was to be done with monks who wished to continue in religion when there were no houses of their own order left near? How much of their personal belongings, as for instance bedding, were the monks allowed to take away with them? Were slate and tiles to be removed from roofs, or only lead? Were bells to be taken from steeples, and who would take charge of the bells and lead? 'Who Shalbe Admytted to serue the Cures of such churches As belonge to the seid Houses Wherof is no priest inducted but at Wyll?' What living or pension was to be given to the late 'governors', and were they to be inducted to benefices straight away or would the king decide further? What was to be done with monks and lay almoners too weak or old to be moved? The commissions which dissolved the monasteries took their tasks seriously, and if these detailed queries are any guide it does not seem likely that there was much cruelty or undue severity in the way in which the king's officers went about their difficult business. But no one existing department was capable of supervising such large and varied duties, in addition to what it was doing already. The task called for the administrative abilities of a political office like the secretaryship, the experience and powers of the general surveyors in administering the royal lands, the financial organization of—let us say—the treasurer of the chamber, and the equity jurisdiction of chancery. The nearest thing in existence was the council of the duchy of Lancaster, but the new department would have more and heavier tasks.

The problem was solved by the setting up of 'the Court of Thaugmentacions of the Revenue of the Kinges Crowne', a court of record equipped with both a great seal and a privy seal. The court was given charge of all dissolved religious houses and their property, except those that the king would preserve incorporated, a sign of those higher ideals for the use of the lands which the needs of the government and the land hunger of the gentry were to render unrealizable. It was also to take over the administration of all lands purchased by the king which had hitherto been in the hands of the general surveyors;[2] the king's revenues were being augmented not only from monastic property, and all such augmentations were logically made

[1] DL 41/12/11. [2] Cf. above, p. 182.

the sphere of one department. The court was to be governed by a council of chancellor, treasurer, attorney, and solicitor, and was to employ in addition ten auditors, seventeen particular receivers in the shires, a clerk, usher, and messenger. The organization of the duchy of Lancaster, with its receiver general and particular receivers, its council, law officers, and auditors, even down to the title of the chief officer, was closely followed. In 1539 another act assigned to the court all monasteries dissolved and surrendered since the wholesale measure of 1536, except those that came to the king by attainder,[1] and confirmed all exchanges and purchases of land made in the king's name since 5 February 1536, that is, since the beginning of the session which passed the original act.[2]

The powers granted to the court were complete. All gifts, grants, and leases of the lands under its survey were to be written by the clerk of the court and sealed with its own seal. The chancellor had authority to make leases for twenty-one years without warrant, though no reversions were to be granted without special authorization, a wise precaution intended to limit speculation and peculation. The clerk was ordered to enrol grants and leases and keep a register of appearances, decrees, and orders. These are all details which illustrate the term 'court of record'. All fees taken were to be as in the duchy. The chancellor's control over subordinate officials was secured by giving him power to take recognizances by way of surety and to issue writs of *scire facias* on them under the seal of the court; he was to hear pleas in the chancery manner, unless trial by jury was involved in which case the plea had to go to the king's bench. The privy seal of the court was to be used in issuing process, and exchequer interference was explicitly prohibited. The act set out in detail the manner of auditing and declaring the accounts both of the treasurer and the individual receivers, but it was left to the chancellor and council of the court to allot spheres of action to receivers and auditors. Separate schedules secured to the treasurer, auditors, and accountants the same allowances as were customary in the duchy,

---

[1] In 1537, Norfolk wrote to Cromwell for confirmation of the report that the receivers of the court were not to meddle with the lands acquired by the recent attainders (*L.P.* XII. II. 53). Attainted lands were strictly speaking the province of the escheators, but at least larger groups had gone to the general surveyors since Henry VIII.

[2] 31 Henry VIII, c. 13.

ordered a yearly return of the profits of the court and state of its charge, and reserved monastic foundations in the county palatine of Lancaster or founded by dukes of Lancaster to the duchy—at the king's pleasure.

The court proved itself modern and up-to-date when it came to the distribution of lands among local officials. As we have seen, the general surveyors preserved the honorial structure of the lands they administered, with the result that rents from any one outlying county went into the hands of different receivers, a wasteful and inefficient system.[1] The duchy, being one huge honour with its headquarters at the Savoy in London, had no comparable problem to solve. If augmentations had followed the older practice, they would have kept the possessions of individual monasteries intact, no matter where they lay, and collected from one receiver for each monastery. Instead, however, they adopted an organization by counties, putting all augmentation lands in each county or group of counties under one receiver, and appointing the receivers each to a specified auditor. The divisions, as listed in the treasurer's account, were as follows:[2] Lincolnshire; Oxfordshire, Buckinghamshire, and Berkshire; Hampshire, Wiltshire, Gloucestershire, and Bristol; Essex, Hertfordshire, and Bedfordshire; Northamptonshire, Warwickshire, Leicestershire, and Rutland; Herefordshire, Staffordshire, Shropshire, and Worcestershire; Dorsetshire, Somersetshire, Devonshire, and Cornwall; Middlesex, London, and Kent; Durham and the archdeaconry of Richmond; Northumberland, Cumberland, and Westmoreland; Nottinghamshire, Derbyshire, and Cheshire; Surrey and Sussex; Huntingdonshire and Cambridgeshire; Yorkshire; Norfolk and Suffolk. To these fifteen groups in England were added two in Wales—the dioceses of Llandaff and St David on the one hand, and those of St Asaph and Bangor on the other. This much more rational organization gave augmentations a securer control of the lands in their charge and, under an efficient minister, made it less likely that lands should 'disappear' through appropriations and oversights, an ever-present danger while an underpaid and only half-developed bureaucracy was faced with the land hunger of gentlemen willing to bribe. From 1536 to 1547 each county thus harboured

[1] Above, pp. 166 f.   [2] E 323/2B, pt. 1.

several receivers: one for augmentations who collected from the various monastic lands there,[1] bailiffs and stewards of chamber lands who contributed to such large blocks as Warwick lands or lands bought from the duke of Suffolk,[2] a receiver for the duchy, officials of the court of wards, and collectors of the clerical tenth—not to mention the receivers for parliamentary tenths and fifteenths, or subsidies, appointed as need arose.

The court of augmentations was thus fairly thoroughly organized from the start, though it is not surprising that additional orders had soon to be framed. A list of such details has survived in a roll, written by a clerk whose hand is familiar on Cromwellian drafts; to judge from the contents, it cannot be much later than the first setting up of the court, for it mentions such matters as debts left by the dissolved monasteries and legal cases concerned with the new lands, all of which must have arisen very quickly.[3] Both legal and administrative reforms were included. The court was to have 'auctorite and pow[er to] here & determyne all Matiers between parties onywise touching ony Lordshipp, Landes, tenementes, &c now beyng, or that hereafter shalbe, within the Surveie and Gouernance of thesame', a point sufficiently obvious, one would have thought, not to require restatement. But in fact the original act did little to clarify the legal and jurisdictional powers of the court of augmentations; it paid more attention to making it an efficient instrument of revenue administration. Another paragraph elaborated possible cases within the court's authority—abbey lands where the king or private persons laid claim to title or reversion of title; but if the title pretended had arisen since the land had been alienated by the crown without reserving the fee simple, the case was to go to the common law. The court of augmentations was to be exclusively concerned with matters affecting the crown, a term which then included actions between party and party over property acquired at the dissolution and not yet given away. These legal points were put on a statutory basis in the first great codification of the state and law of

---

[1] E.g. Bedfordshire, *Lists and Indexes*, XXXIV. 1.   [2] *Ibid.* 317 ff., 316 f.

[3] E 163/11/49. The modern heading ('Project for an Act apparently for the establishment of the ct. of Surveyor General') is misleading; the document deals only with augmentations, though some of its points were later embodied in that section of 33 Henry VIII, c. 39 (for the court of general surveyors) which concerned augmentations.

the crown lands, undertaken when the court of general surveyors was set up in 1542.[1]

The administrative details are, perhaps, of greater interest in the present context. The method for making acquittances on recognizances was laid down: the chancellor to write in 'vacatt', the clerk of the court adding the 'Wordes of the consideracion and Cancellacion of thesame Recognisance', and the treasurer or receiver to whom the debt or redemption was paid signing his name. Provision was made for the treasurers and receivers to pay for purchased lands and to cover lawful debts resting on abbey lands before they came to the crown; the frequent repetition of such orders suggests that the government were readier with promises than with action when these claims were raised by the creditors. The chancellor and court were to give notice of the place, day, and time of each audit, 'and thesame to be publysshed in foure markett places in the Schyre where the Audite shalbe kepte'. Lastly, stringent penalties were devised for defaulting leaseholders who failed to pay the 'Rente reserved by lettres patentes in the name of the tenth', and for bailiffs and receivers trying to deceive or evade the auditor.

With such detailed and gradually more complete orders, Cromwell and the government attempted to give the court of augmentations full and free charge of its own concerns, building up in a few years an organization capable of handling the biggest single accession of revenue and real property that has ever come to the English crown. How efficient and active the court was from its first days may be illustrated from the negotiations between it and the duchy of Lancaster in 1536.

Section 24 of the act establishing the court of augmentations assigned all monasteries in the county palatine of Lancaster and all those of which the dukes of Lancaster were founders to the duchy instead of the court, if the king should please so to decide;[2] soon after, a warrant to the chancellor of the duchy ordered him to take charge of all such houses.[3] The draft of this document, though written by a duchy clerk,[4] was corrected by Sir Richard Riche,

---

[1] See preceding note.   [2] *Stat. Realm*, III. 574

[3] DL 41/12/10, an undated draft.

[4] *Ibid.* 11, a paper definitely drawn up in the duchy office, was written by the same clerk.

chancellor of augmentations; it seems that the court, knowing what needed doing, supervised the drafting. However, the arrangement envisaged in the warrant was unsatisfactory: houses founded by dukes of Lancaster were scattered all over England, and in the event officials of duchy and court were likely to run across each other to the detriment of the work. On 5 July 1536 a meeting was therefore held 'at the Whithall at Westminster in the Kinges Courte', between the chancellors of the duchy and the court, there being present with them the treasurer and attorney of augmentations on the one side, and the attorney, receiver general, auditors, and clerk of the duchy on the other.[1] At this meeting a number of articles were agreed to. In the first place, 'vpon the matter moved betwene bothe the said Chancellors concernyng the Auctorities of the Suppression of Religious howses', it was decided that the duchy would confine itself to the county palatine where its authority was not to be questioned by the court, while augmentations would dissolve all other houses, even if founded by dukes of Lancaster. The officers of the court would certify to the auditors of the duchy the value of such dissolved duchy foundations and deliver to them all rentals, accounts, and other records found. Two short paragraphs made sure that uniformity would prevail in the terms of leases: Riche, of augmentations, clearly wished Fitzwilliam, chancellor of the duchy, to understand that all leases must carry a repairing clause (excepting only tiles and timber), and that leases already promised by the king were to be construed as comprehending only 'the demeanes that be temporall which the gouuerners had in their owne handes'. Fitzwilliam also agreed to compel the lessee of Conishead to find 'a ffryer and oone officer...to ryng the bell ther accustomed whan nede shall require accordyng vnto the old custome for the sauffgard of passensers ouer the sandes in those partes'; while the future owners of Cartmel and Cokersand were to find guides over their neighbouring sands. The agreement was given official sanction in a sign manual warrant to the chancellor of the duchy which outlined his revised sphere of action.[2]

The young and barely established court had not only faced and

---

[1] DL 5/6, fos. 204v–5.

[2] DL 12/7, no. 39. The warrant is dated 11 July, 29 Henry VIII (1537), which is likely to have been a mistake for 28.

overcome the ancient duchy; the officers of the latter were not even able to do this novel work without the assistance of the experts. They therefore now drew up a questionnaire of twenty-two 'Articles matters & Causes concernynge the Dissolucion of the Religiouse Housez within the Countie Palatyne of Lancaster Assigned by the Kynges Highnes to be dissolued And the same to be ordered by Mr Chauncellour of the Duchie of Lancastre & the Council of the same', to which reply was made by John Onley, king's attorney in the court of augmentations.[1] The questions are very mixed, ranging from general points affecting the whole operation to the fate of an individual church, and it is certainly surprising to find the duchy, supposedly sovereign within the county palatine, taking advice on the personal belongings of the dispossessed monks, or the removal of slate, tile, and lead. But these were again points on which it was desirable that the duchy's practice should not differ from the court's, and in which the duchy was therefore prepared simply to follow instructions. Purely duchy matters—to judge from notes added to the questionnaire and the entry 'not moved ne Answered As yett' in the list of replies—were, however, settled by Fitzwilliam himself; it was he who ordered Cartmel Church to continue as a parish church, and who agreed that the parishioners of Cartmel should have 'the Sute of Coopys' which they claimed as a gift under an old will.

It was, however, Onley who told the duchy that they could have no schedule of houses to be dissolved, but that the king would personally mark them 'in the bryeff certyfycat', whereupon the chancellor would have to instruct his commissioners; that, if they wanted letters missive to the great monasteries ordering them to take in dispossessed monks, they would have to go to Master Secretary and the signet clerks; what they were to pay by way of pension to abbots and priors; what they were to do with corrodians, almoners, and discharged servants; and what monastic debts were to be paid. In general he warned them that

they vse to put A Discreccion to the commyssioners in all such Causez & other lyke to be vsed ordered & done, As to them Apon thexecucion therof shall seme conuenyent for the avoydyng of Claymour of the people,

---

[1] DL 41/12/11-12.

& suche other Idemnytiez As they may perceyue by their discreccion. And thynketh that it wyll the easyer be allowed when it is done than when it is putt in questyon.

The chancellor and attorney read his replies, expressed approval, and ordered the duchy commissioners to act accordingly. A bare six months old, the court of augmentations had got fully into its stride, its organization was complete, it had laid down rules and standards, and—most significant of all—it was prepared to allow the commissioners some discretion where hardships or local feeling made it necessary. Clearly, the department was already working well, a tribute both to its design and its staff, and most of all perhaps to those who designed and staffed it.

The court of augmentations marked a new departure in administrative method. Admittedly it was modelled on the duchy chamber of Lancaster, but the idea of copying the organization of one large honour for the management of the vast monastic property acquired by the crown between 1535 and 1540 was something of a revolution. The establishment of the court meant the end of an era in administration, the era of special, undepartmentalized officers with, usually, a household background, the era of barely bureaucratic arrangements depending on individuals for their efficiency. The early Tudor chamber, Cromwell's mastership of the jewels, and Gostwick's treasurership of first-fruits and tenths, had all been such comparatively makeshift expedients. These things were now to be superseded by thoroughly organized departments of state—courts capable of administering sources of revenue without aid from outside, and of exercising considerable powers of jurisdiction, in rivalry (to some extent) with the common law courts. The treasurership of the chamber was a very different thing under an energetic minister like Heron and under a cautious, careful civil servant like Tuke—under an active king like Henry VII and a lazy king like Henry VIII; the court of augmentations might vary in the thoroughness and honesty of its work, but its organization and potentialities were the same no matter who was its chancellor, no matter who ruled at the top. This setting up of a court for monastic lands announced that from now on 'household' government in the finances was to be at an end and that a national bureaucracy would take over. The earlier departments, general surveyors and first-fruits, had to wait a few years before they were as fully equipped as augmentations, even though the former in particular had achieved a high degree of independence by 1535; but these delays were due to the highly personal government of Cromwell himself whom a half organized treasurer of first-fruits suited admirably. There was no question what the new policy was to be: augmentations, and later the court of wards, proved that.

That it was Cromwell who designed the new organization on the model of the duchy is a point which cannot be proved directly and may possibly be considered a point not worth proving. His outstanding position at this time, and his interest in administrative matters, cannot be in doubt, nor has it ever been suggested that he was not responsible for the policy of confiscating the monastic lands which made the court of augmentations necessary. The least that must be said is that he is more likely than anyone else to have stood godfather to the new plan; if there is individual responsibility to be allotted, it must be to him. His hand is obvious in the appointment of the officers of the court. Even the commissioners for the dissolution, so narrowly controlled by the court itself, did not escape his attention: their commission was first drafted by Thomas Wriothesley, Cromwell's chief clerk, and corrected by Cromwell himself.[1] As vicar general, Cromwell had, of course, superintended the commission which carried out the great visitation of 1535; now that the act was passed and the dissolution decided on, he concerned himself with the appointment of the commissioners who had to carry it out. The link was there from the first.

His influence was noticeable also in the choice of the higher officers of augmentations. The act granted no powers of patronage, even as regarded receivers or auditors, to the chancellor of the court, and all appointments were to be made by the king, but it has already been seen that in 1536 royal appointments would, to say the least, be affected by Cromwell's wishes.[2] The chancellorship went to Richard

---

[1] E 36/116, fos. 50–3 (*L.P.* x. 721, 4). Wriothesley headed it 'The Mynute of the Commyssion', and that minute here meant draft is clear from the fact that Cromwell corrected it.

[2] Cf. above, p. 122.

Riche, the solicitor-general.[1] Riche was a lawyer of great ability and skill, with considerable ambitions and no scruples at all.[2] It is significant that he began to rise in the royal service about the time when Cromwell began to secure his own supremacy, and when Riche turned against him at his fall Cromwell hinted plainly enough that the turncoat owed everything to him.[3] Riche obtained a clerkship of the common pleas and king's bench in March 1532, and was made attorney general for Wales and Chester in May that year.[4] In October, he was doing some of the king's legal business, and a year later he became solicitor general.[5] In April 1535 he was appointed one of the surveyors of liveries, an office of some importance in the financial administration, for which preferment he gave Cromwell £40 and his prayers.[6] He owed his rise to services rendered, particularly to the well-known part he played in the tragedies of Fisher and More when he acted for Cromwell or, at any rate, in the interests of Cromwell's policy. Though the evidence does not permit any assertion that he was simply Cromwell's tool, his relations with the minister were those of a follower and (at this time) faithful subordinate. He was too careful to arrogate a position to himself which he did not hold, but could claim to be something more than a servant.[7] By 1536 he had become a leading legal and administrative official of the crown, occupying a fairly prominent position in the government presided over by Cromwell. His elevation to the headship of the new court, an office which would call for great administrative, legal, and financial abilities, was thus the culmination, for the time being, of a steady advance under Cromwell's aegis and must have been due to Cromwell.

[1] He was sworn of the office on 19 April 1536, a bare fortnight after the dissolution of the parliament which had established the court (*D.N.B.* XVI. 1010).

[2] Cf. his life by A. F. Pollard in *D.N.B.*

[3] Merriman, II. 265: '...what Maister Chauncelor of the augmentations hathe bene towardes me god and he best knowyth; I wil ne Can accuse hym; What I haue bene towardes hym your Magestye right well knowyth...'.

[4] *L.P.* V. 909 (32), 1065 (21). The clerkship was a sinecure; the work was done by a certain John Cooke who wished to buy the office in April 1534 (*L.P.* VII. 394), but had to be content with a joint appointment made in February 1536 (*L.P.* X. 392, 32).

[5] *L.P.* V. 1445, 1466, 1470; VI. 1383 (8).   [6] *L.P.* VIII. 490, 632 (34).

[7] *Ibid.* 456, 563. One of Riche's more unpleasant traits was a feigned humility (cf. for example, *L.P.* XIII. I. 1465, though the calendar does not indicate the full flavour of his unctuous modesty). Though not particularly noticeable for piety he almost always headed his letters with the word 'Ihus'' (for 'Jesus').

The treasurership of the court went to Thomas Pope, described in one place as a servant of lord chancellor Audeley.[1] However, he was introduced to Audeley by Cromwell,[2] and himself declared that all he had ever obtained had come from Cromwell.[3] Pope was a tried civil servant with experience of both legal and financial matters, having been keeper of the change and money in the Tower of London and one of the clerks of the star chamber since late in 1534.[4] He resigned as treasurer before 17 March 1540[5] and was succeeded by Edward North who had been clerk of parliament until 1539 when he made way for one of Cromwell's own secretaries, Thomas Soulemont. This suggests that North's appointment, too, may have been due to Cromwell who may well have promised him promotion if he vacated an office to which Cromwell wished to appoint a personal servant.

Cromwell's influence may be traced also in the appointment of the other two chief officers of the court, the attorney and solicitor. In 1532, the former, John Onley, was reporting to Cromwell, then at Calais, on legal affairs in London and seems to have been able to call together the king's legal counsel.[6] A report on a riot in which members of the influential Fitzwilliam family were attacked was addressed to him, and he had an act passed in parliament in his favour.[7] Audeley, himself Cromwell's creature, described Onley as his friend.[8] Despite his obscurity he appears therefore to have been a lawyer of some standing, and he had certainly been in intimate contact with Cromwell early in the latter's official career. When he died, about December 1537, and the office—ostensibly in the king's gift—fell vacant, it was Cromwell and not Henry who as a matter of course was appealed to for favour and preferment. Sir Francis Bryan requested the office for a Mr Molinex,[9] but Audeley suggested that the solicitor of the court, Robert Southwell, be promoted, and that his office be filled by John Lucas whom he described as a lawyer of the Temple.[10] Southwell obtained his promotion. He was a member of a Norfolk family, connected with the Howards, but even more closely connected with Cromwell's family.[11] His brother Richard

---

[1] *L.P.* x. 573.   [2] *L.P.* xv. 351.   [3] *L.P.* xiii. ii. 106 (ii).
[4] *L.P.* vii. 1498 (12), 1601 (33).   [5] *L.P.* xv. 351.
[6] *L.P.* v. 1455. He cannot be traced further back.
[7] *L.P.* vii. 1120; x. 1087 (11).   [8] *L.P.* xii. ii. 1160.
[9] *Ibid.* 1177.   [10] *Ibid.* 1160.   [11] For Robert Southwell cf. *D.N.B.* xviii. 701 b.

acted as tutor to Cromwell's son Gregory, while Robert was in Cromwell's service in 1535,[1] not long before he obtained the office in augmentations. His successor as solicitor was not Audeley's protégé Lucas but a certain Walter Henley, or Hendle, who had been a commissioner for the suppression of the monasteries in several counties,[2] but is otherwise obscure. Altogether, the appointments in the court of augmentations demonstrate Cromwell's influence and confirm that it was he who organized the new department.

But while Cromwell would organize, he also maintained his very personal government. He designed a new kind of department for the administration of revenue which was meant to stand on its own feet, and yet he showed no inclination to let it slip from his control. He kept in touch with the commissioners who were suppressing houses, even though they received their orders from Riche. One of them reported on the surveys he had made, sent a statement about them to Cromwell, and asked whether a letter from Riche and Onley, ordering his return to another nunnery where he had previously been active, was sufficient warrant for him to do so without confirmation from the lord privy seal.[3] Even the duke of Norfolk, busy in the north after the pilgrimage of grace, received instructions on the suppression from the court of augmentations, but he told Cromwell all about his activities.[4] Cromwell's influence over the court was presumed by a country gentleman who asked him to have Riche order the commissioners to spare 'his' priory of which he had been seised nearly two years.[5] Although the routine work of the court was in the hands of the chancellor and council,[6] Cromwell could not be stopped from interfering. He does not, indeed, seem to

---

[1] *L.P.* VIII. 539.   [2] *L.P.* X. 721 (6).

[3] *L.P.* X. 1215. The same man, George Gyffard, reported similar business in another letter, in which he also speaks of the king's anger at his daring to report favourably on some houses (*ibid.* 1166). He recommended another house to Cromwell, trusting in his 'indifference' (fairness). This letter draws a valuable distinction between the attitudes of king and minister to the monasteries.

[4] *L.P.* XII. I. 478.   [5] *L.P.* X. 1038.

[6] A good deal can be learned about the working of the council from a large number of documents—receipts, orders to pay, minutes, etc.—which once undoubtedly belonged to Pope, afterwards to Riche, and were transmitted through him to the Manchester Papers now deposited at the P.R.O. (GD 15/1–114). One interesting point is that almost all business seems to have been done in full session, many of the documents bearing the signatures of all the officers except the treasurer to whom they were addressed.

have ordered Pope to make payments without warrant, but he backed up warrants with personal letters which considerably speeded up payments.[1]

His hand lay heavy on the treasurer of the court because that officer came in close contact with his more personal financial organization. Pope had to hand specie, jewels, and relics over to Gostwick.[2] In this connexion Cromwell wrote him a letter which proves his own activities in such matters:[3] 'my frende Iohn ffreman' had delivered certain plate to Gostwick 'by the Kinges hieghnes commaundement, at my mediacion', and Cromwell found it necessary to rebuke Pope because he had refused to give Freeman (one of the receivers of augmentations) a written acquittance. The lord privy seal kept an eye on even small details of the financial administration, for there is no question of personal motives, despite the word he used to describe Freeman. (Cromwell always signed himself as his correspondent's friend in letters to inferiors; in this letter, too, he was Pope's 'louyng ffreend'.) He wrote because something had gone wrong in the administration. 'I doo sumwhat marvail that you gyve him not a discharge, And Therefore thought me to Requyre you that ye shal, as it apperteyneth, deliuer vnto the said ffreman an acquitaunce thereof.' Cromwell was not even above carrying relics from the court of augmentations to the king; there is a note in Riche's hand on the face of a warrant which ordered Pope to hand over to Thomas Henneage a piece of the Holy Cross from Stratford

that the relik above rememberid, named to be a pece of the holy crosse, was delyuered to the kinges magesty at Hamptun Court, the ixth day of Iune Anno xxix Regni Sui, by the handes of my lord Privay seale, as my lord Chancellour & Master Chancelour of the Augm[entacions] can wytnez.[4]

A more important example of Cromwell's interference in the affairs of the court was the commission which he had made out to himself and Riche, authorizing them to sell such of the king's lands as had come to him by act of parliament or surrender, to the clear yearly

---

[1] *L.P.* XII. II. 274; XIV. II. 282.   [2] E.g. GD 15/28-9.
[3] *Ibid.* 100. This letter was missed by Merriman; cf. *Bull. I.H.R.* XXII. 35 ff.
[4] GD 15/28.

value of £6,000.[1] Cromwell kept the control of the king's lands, and therefore of the king's revenue, under his hands; perhaps he was already trying to prevent the wholesale unloading of monastic property which happened after his fall and helped to destroy the financial stability of the crown which he had so laboriously restored.

There are, furthermore, indications that the system did not work so perfectly as its clear-cut appearance might suggest. Although the court of augmentations had been set up in order to deal with the suppressed and surrendered monasteries, it was not fully master in its own house. After the smaller monasteries had been disposed of under the act of 1536, the voluntary or forced surrender of the remaining houses became cause of dispute between various officials. The commissioners sent out by the king's vicegerent were independent of the court of augmentations and responsible to Cromwell alone, so that agents of his interfered in the court's sphere of action. In a letter written on 26 June 1538, Riche enlarged upon the difficulties created by an all-powerful minister prepared to do even routine work.[2] The point at issue was the surrender of St Augustine's, Canterbury, 'the Survey of the possessions wherof', wrote Riche, 'apperteynith to myn office & to suche as ben officeres in the Court of Augmentacions'. Not wishing, however, to 'neclect or be remyse in doyng my dewty', he asked Cromwell to let him know whether he

shall cause any of the officeres of the Court of Augmentacions to make Survey or not; or els, whether suche as your lordship do apoynt for the disolucion of the howsez shall doo the same.

Sometimes, apparently, two separate surveys had been made, and—what was worse—

your lordship knowith right well ther ben sondry Surveys Certified by suche as hath dissolued howsez, apon the whiche yt ys not possible to procede to grauntyng of any lease, vnto suche tyme as a new survey were made.

---

[1] *L.P.* XIV. II. 780 (36). The commission was dated 14 December 1539, but even in the year ending Michaelmas 1539 the two men had sold monastic lands by virtue of a special commission, for a total of £80,222, as Pope's accounts show (E 323/1, pt. II, m. 13 d). If the terms of the later commission applied to the earlier, lands were being sold at thirteen years' purchase—less advantageously than later; probably less than £6,000 worth had been sold. In March 1540 Cromwell also obtained a commission, together with Sir John Daunce and Richard Pollard, the general surveyors, to sell lands under their charge (*L.P.* XV. 436, 38).　　[2] SP 1:134, fos. 249–50 (*L.P.* XIII. I. 1465).

He reminded Cromwell that 'your lordship diuerse tymez hath said to me that your officeres shold not medyll with the survey of the possessions of any howsez, but only with the surrender, dissolucion, & the goodes'. This theoretical division of labour left the officers of the court with the sole duty of surveying the lands, that is, of establishing the facts taken into consideration when the fate of the property was decided.

We must therefore distinguish between three sets of officials.[1] First, there were the commissioners under the act of 1536 whose commission had been drafted by Cromwell,[2] and who dissolved the smaller monasteries and did everything connected with that dissolution. Cromwell had appointed them, but the attorney of the court instructed them in their work and its chancellor prescribed to them the monasteries to be dissolved.[3] These first commissioners had to conceive themselves responsible to Cromwell as well as to Riche and were controlled by both. However, their task ended with the first dissolution. The administration of the newly acquired property fell to the receivers of the court of augmentations. Thereafter, when the attack on the greater monasteries began, the court had no powers to dissolve them, and the work had to be done by commissioners specially sent down by Cromwell (as vicar general, or perhaps as vicegerent in spirituals) to take the surrender. But these lands, too, were administered by the court, even before the act of 1539 regularized the position. Consequently difficulties and even friction arose between the regular local officials of the court and Cromwell's special commissioners. An attempt to allot them separate duties proved unsuccessful, and Cromwell's agents continued to cut across the departmental lines of the court of augmentations, rendering their unreliable surveys and greatly annoying Riche, though he couched his letter in almost abjectly humble terms. Cromwell had established the court, and he exercised a general, and sometimes a very particular, control over it. Nevertheless, he did not consider that the

---

[1] None of them must be confused with the commissions which carried out the great visitation of 1535 and compiled the *Valor*. The same men, of course, may have been on more than one commission.

[2] Above, p. 212.

[3] DL 41/12/12, which gives Onley's replies to the inquiries from the duchy; cf. also *L.P.* X. 1166, 1215.

existence of a separate department dealing with the monastic lands prevented his personal activities in that field, even though at times he made the task of the court very difficult.

Not much can here be said about the court of wards. The prerogative rights of wardship—custody of minor heirs to lands held in knight's service, with custody of their lands and the right to sell their marriage—were by the end of the fifteenth century easily the most remunerative of the feudal sources of revenue remaining to the crown. Henry VII, if not already Edward IV, set about exploiting them for all he was worth; as we have seen, he freely issued commissions for the seeking out of concealed wards' lands, appointed a surveyor of his prerogative rights, and finally—in 1503—appointed a special master of the wards to control both the direct exploitation of wardships and their sale to interested parties.[1] The second method quickly became the more usual and also the more profitable of the two; before the end of the century, monastic lands having been sold, the court of wards was the main centre for speculation in lands (and persons), and a hotbed of intrigue and corruption, so that even the upright Burghley could not altogether escape the taint.[2] It does not appear that quite the same amount of buying and selling and peculation went on under the early Tudors, but that impression may very well be due to the absence of private correspondence permitting a glimpse behind the scenes. Wardship was highly burdensome to the tenants, their widows and children, and whenever possible they evaded it; it was highly profitable to the crown and to intending purchasers, and repeated attempts were made to secure the king's rights. The seeking out of wardships and tightening up of the machinery were steps automatically taken by every minister or king pressed for money.

In view of this, the organization for securing the revenue from wards was naturally important. The methods used by Henry VII are described for us in a document that probably belongs to Wolsey's

---

[1] Cf. above, p. 29.
[2] Cf. J. Hurstfield, 'Burghley as Master of the Wards', *Trans. R. Hist. Soc.* (1949), 95 ff.

administration; the writer, while speaking of the king in the third person, addresses himself to 'your grace', and the disorderly state which, he maintains, prevails in the office fits the 1520's better than the 1530's when some order had been restored through the efficient administration of Sir William Paulet, master from 1526.[1] The author of the memorandum alleged the existence of grave shortcomings. In Henry VII's time there had been a master, general receiver, and auditor for wards, with particular receivers in every shire; each term the master used to inform the auditor of the wardships due and existing, and every year the particular receivers rendered their accounts to an officer well informed about what was to come in. But the last such record found ended at Michaelmas 1509, since when nothing like it had been produced, to the great loss of the king. The writer suggested his remedies. Let the officers of those days again be appointed, with 'some able person of the Chauncery or of the Eschequor' to keep the records of wardships new and old in a place accessible to the master and auditor. Also, let the master stop the sales and leases of wards' lands for the present, though custody of the heir's person might still be sold; it was always held that the crown lost by selling these lands instead of administering them directly, though it is doubtful whether the government was capable of direct administration at this time.

It is noticeable that neither Henry VII nor the author of these notes envisaged any truly bureaucratic organization. The appointment of even an individual officer to administer wards was delayed until 1503, and naturally he was treated in accordance with the whole administrative policy of Henry VII: he obeyed the king directly and the king controlled him. With Henry VII's death the system immediately went out of action; there could be no better proof for our repeated assertion that these methods of 'household' government suffered severely from their impermanence and dependence on an active king. Wolsey's correspondent, too, was satisfied with such imperfect tools; he recognized the need for some central repository of records so as to prevent the concealment of wardships and facili-

---

[1] I have to thank Mr J. Hurstfield for confirming this impression. The document is SP 1:159, fos. 47–8; its dating into 1540 in *L.P.* xv. 503, is certainly wrong. It has nothing to do with the creation of the court of wards in that year.

tate their discovery, but he could go no further than the borrowing of some clerk in the great departments of state. He saw nothing insufficient in a master of the wards who accounted to the general surveyors, had to apply to the privy seal office when he wished to act against refractory officials or subjects of the crown, and went to someone else's office at Westminster to read up the facts about his department.

Very different was the solution found in 1540. The first sign of action in the matter is an entry in Cromwell's notes in April that year—'The establishing of a law for the Court of Wardes'—followed by an entry on another slip of memoranda, 'to remember Mr Parys for the entry to his office of the receiver general of the Wards, and to know whether the bill shall be conceived after the order of the Duchy or after the Augmentations; whose receipt will be very great.'[1] At this time, then, Cromwell was engaged in the drafting of legislation for the reorganization of wards, and unlike his predecessors he planned to erect a court—a full bureaucratic department. The bill which resulted was introduced in the lords on 3 June 1540, a week before Cromwell's arrest and fall, though it was retained by the commons for six weeks, at a time when Cromwell's attainder and the Cleves divorce took precedence, and did not pass until 23 July.[2] In view of these facts it may be said that the court of wards, unlike those of general surveyors and first-fruits and tenths, was planned by Cromwell himself, in imitation of his highly successful court of augmentations. Since he was still, seven years after coming to full power, prepared to undertake administrative reform, it is not altogether impossible that he even had such plans for the other sections of the financial administration as were put into practice after his fall; but there is no evidence. At any rate, the court of wards was his; it is in his administration and his mind that we must look for the change from the old haphazard methods to the new bureaucracy.

The court thus established need not be described at great length, for it differed from the other courts only in so far as the kind of

---

[1] *L.P.* xv. 438 (1 and 2). The receiver general of the duchy and the treasurer of augmentations differed mainly in that the former ranked below the law officers of his department, while the latter ranked above.

[2] *L.J.* 1. 141 a, 160 b.

revenue administered made differences necessary.[1] It was to be a court of record with one seal, for the issue of process—the exchequer being once again explicitly prohibited from interfering; the court had no great seal, and all sales and leases were to be made under the great seal of England upon a bill signed by the king and countersigned by the master.[2] The officers were a master, attorney, receiver general, two auditors, two clerks (a difference arising from the vast amount of record keeping involved in the work of this court), a messenger and usher; the particular receivers and feodaries (or surveyors of wardships in the counties) were to be appointed by the council of the court. For the rest, the act defined the court's sphere of action, dealt with the master's powers of discipline, and ordered all accounts and other papers to go to the new court instead of the exchequer. The net revenues received were to be paid to the treasurer of the chamber or where the king might otherwise direct; the court was not intended for use as a paymaster's office in the manner of augmentations. It had quite enough to do in the collection of revenue and in the administration of the lands and bodies subject to it. In 1542 another act added the cognate business of liveries and interpolated a surveyor of liveries between the master and the attorney of wards.[3]

In this way the feudal revenue of the crown was also reorganized in the course of the far-reaching reforms in the finances undertaken between 1534 and 1542. The keynote of these reforms was a great increase in bureaucratic form; ultimately, though not at first everywhere, the informality of special treasurers, the 'household' methods of the chamber system, were replaced by departments of state designed to be independent of chance and change. This line of reform was initiated by Cromwell in his courts of augmentations and wards and his treatment of the general surveyors; it was completed soon after his fall by men trained in his school. But it would be wrong to let the story finish here, though the tale of reform in the 1530's, which is our proper subject, is actually concluded. The

---

[1] 32 Henry VIII, c. 46 (*Stat. Realm*, III. 802 ff.).

[2] This had been common practice before the court was set up, as the chancery warrants (C 82) prove.

[3] 33 Henry VIII, c. 22 (*Stat. Realm*, III. 860 ff.).

further history of the financial administration down to 1554 is so much a part and a result of the work of the 1530's that it must be related, however briefly.

4. *The restoration of exchequer supremacy*

As was pointed out earlier, the history of financial reform in the sixteenth century was in great part governed by the needs for a simpler treasury than that provided by the receipt of the exchequer, for a readier system of audit not hampered by the precautions of a fossilized bureaucracy, and for a new form of record which would be drawn up on businesslike lines. Henry VII solved his problem by the development of household finance and the use of individual treasurers and officials responsible directly to himself. The bureaucratization of this system, which began with the acts for the general surveyors of Wolsey's rule, led under Cromwell to a break with household government and the creation of a number of co-ordinate departments of state for the finances. By 1542 this new order was complete. There were then six main revenue-collecting departments, each covering a specific section of the king's income: the exchequer (ancient revenue), the duchy of Lancaster (its own lands), the court of general surveyors (the lands acquired by Henry VII and Wolsey), the court of augmentations (lands acquired since 1535), the court of first-fruits and tenths (ecclesiastical revenue), and the court of wards and liveries (feudal revenue). Though the exchequer retained its time-honoured methods, the other courts employed the 'modern' machinery first introduced in the duchy of Lancaster, which equipped them with effective treasurers handling cash on instruction by warrant, with a straightforward audit, and with accounts drawn up in a manner useful for balancing.

What this bureaucracy lacked was a unifying factor in its multiplicity of departments. Cromwell had intended that he himself should be this, and while he lived there was no need for an organized ministry of finance, but the privy council which supposedly took over at his fall proved unequal to the task. In the general decay of good government which characterized the 1540's, expenditure increased, efficiency declined, corruption grew apace, and before long it became again very necessary to overhaul the financial machinery. Cromwell's reforms had created too many departments, as was only natural since he had made them as need arose; now the time of stocktaking was at hand—extravagance could be pruned and final order could be produced. The man behind this work was William Paulet, marquess of Winchester, lord treasurer from 1550 to 1572; he had the assistance of Sir Walter Mildmay, for forty years from about 1545 a leading civil servant of the time.

The first attempt to simplify the financial structure was made shortly before Henry VIII's death. A commission of inquiry assembled on 1 April 1546, to consider the state of the revenue and its various courts;[1] they decided to amalgamate the courts of augmentations and of general surveyors. By November–December the organization of the new court had got as far as the appointment of the auditors,[2] though there was a difficulty in the way. The old courts rested on acts of parliament and could not therefore be abolished without parliamentary authority; the trouble that could arise from a precipitate setting up of the new court is well illustrated by an undated warrant to the old court of augmentations, which had to be replaced by a warrant made out to the new court 'being not yet established by Act of Parliament, which hath not authority to execute the same until the old Court be annulled'.[3] A bill to authorize the reform was introduced in the lords on 15 January 1547 and reached the engrossing stage there,[4] but the death of Henry VIII dissolved the parliament and nothing further was heard of the bill. The new court therefore rested, for the few years of its existence, solely on the patent of 1 January 1547 which gave the details of its organization in as ample a manner as the acts establishing earlier revenue courts had done.[5]

At last the land revenue of the crown was united under one department. When the first rush of the dissolution was over, it became apparent that Cromwell had in fact simply added more lands

---

[1] *L.P.* XXI. I. 1166 (71). The commission was dated 30 June 1546, but covered activities since 1 April. [2] *Ibid.* 338, 534.
[3] *Ibid.* 647 (13–14). [4] *L.J.* I. 284b, 290a.
[5] This patent, filling fourteen membranes of the roll for 38 Henry VIII, pt. 5 (C 66/790, mm. 15–28), is very inadequately summarized in *L.P.* XXI. II. 771 (1).

to the foundations built by Henry VII from his personal property and the spoils of the Wars of the Roses. The patent of 1547 therefore took a logical step when it combined the two courts which administered all the Tudor lands—leaving out the duchy because the duchy was always in a class by itself. The case for reform was strongly reinforced by what was happening to the revenues of the two old courts before the amalgamation: these were declining and the courts may be supposed to have lost much of the land they were administering, so that their separate existence had even less to recommend it. It is quite commonly supposed that augmentations in particular ceased to have much to do as the monastic lands were squandered, and that this process had gone far before the death of Henry VIII. The facts do not altogether support this view. Though lands were busily sold in the years 1545-7, the figures of receipts from land revenue in the court of augmentations show a surprising steadiness, if not rise.[1] £32,739 in the year ending Michaelmas 1545, £59,255 a year later, £48,303 in 1547—these are hardly signs of a declining capital. Yet—if the normal sales-terms of twenty years' purchase be supposed—lands to the approximate value in rent of £8,250 and £3,500 were alienated in 1545 and 1546. The receipts may have included sales of valuables (especially lead) and perhaps arrears, though as a rule these were totalled separately; we may suspect more energetic exploitation behind these higher receipts from reduced capital. The fact remains that the court of augmentations, though far from the glory of its early days, was yet equally far from bankruptcy; it remained the busiest and most important of the financial departments. The chamber, on the other hand, as has already been shown, was declining rapidly. The history of its lands might be worth investigating, though this cannot be done here; it may be suspected that they had vanished more completely than had monastic lands. Certainly other chamber revenues, in particular the chance of new lands, had been cut off by Cromwell's reforms. In this decline of the chamber, and with it of the court of general surveyors, the main reason for its amalgamation with augmentations must therefore be sought.

The new 'Courte of the Augmentacions and reuenues of the

---

[1] All these details are derived from the treasurer's account, E 323/4.

Kinges Crowne' was to take charge of the lands of the old courts, of any to be acquired in future, and of the charities, hospitals, and gilds lately dissolved. The statutory establishment of the old courts, which stood in the way of a simple abolition by prerogative action, was defeated by a fiction: the courts were declared to have ceased to exist as they were 'voide of officers'.[1] The new court consisted of a chancellor, to be head officer and keep the great and privy seals with which it was equipped; two general surveyors, to be second officer between them; a treasurer, two masters of the woods (north and south of the Trent), an attorney, a solicitor, two surveyors of woods, a clerk, ten auditors, two auditors of prests and foreign accounts, eleven receivers, one surveyor and the necessary stewards as well as one woodward to each county, a keeper of the records of the court, one usher, and three messengers. It had a rather swollen establishment which made the plea of economy look a little silly.

Since the patent is not in print, a little more detail than has been thought necessary in the earlier courts may here be given. The work of the court was to differ in no particular from that performed by its predecessors. Existing leases were declared valid. The council of the court was to seal all writings concerning the lands under its survey with its own great seal, by direct royal warrant, except that leases of lands to an annual value exceeding £6. 13s. 4d. were to pass the signet, privy seal, and great seal of England as heretofore.[2] The chancellor of the court had fees for sealing commissions and process as accustomed, as well as half the fee for every great seal of the court (one mark). The chancellor and general surveyors sitting together could make leases for term of twenty years; they were to take the accounts of the officers of the court, the particular accounts being declared before them by the auditors yearly by 1 March, and the general account of revenues being similarly declared by 1 August,[3]

[1] It is probable that the officers of the old courts had been told to resign to give reality to the fiction and evade the problem of parliamentary authority.

[2] This may have been a concession to lord chancellor Wriothesley's protest of 16 October 1546 (*L.P.* XXI. II. 273). He thought it bad for the 'estimation' of the chancery that the new court was intended to rely exclusively on its own seal; i.e. he feared great loss in fees for himself and his clerks.

[3] The feast of St Peter is mentioned; I have taken it to be that of St Peter ad Vincula, since that coincides with Lammas Day. If SS. Peter and Paul were meant, the date would, of course, be 29 June.

and the signature of the three officers providing a sufficient discharge; they could direct warrants for payment to the treasurer of the court, make rules for the ordering of the court, take and cancel recognizances for debt and commit to ward, assess fines and award process under the privy seal of the court, buy land without warrant, pay monastic debts under £200, and inspect concords in the common pleas. They were to make an annual report to the king of the state of the court, and sit at Westminster in term time. The clerks of the petty bag were to certify inquisitions to them, as was done in the exchequer, taking 3s. 4d. for each transcript.

The treasurer's work is described in detail, though it amounted simply to looking after the receipts and payments of the court. He was no longer to pay monastic pensions, the receivers in the relevant counties being charged with this task; and he was to present his account annually before the chancellor, general surveyors, and two auditors by 30 April. The clerk was to keep a book of all that passed in the court and enrol all leases made, rendering this roll—complete to the preceding Michaelmas—by Easter each year. Records of leases survive, but there is no record of proceedings except the documents in each case;[1] it is unlikely that anything resembling a plea roll was ever kept, especially as the methods of the court, approximating to those of conciliar courts like star chamber or chancery, hardly favoured such a record. The clerk was also to keep 'a faire boke or legier' for recording the lands on charge and their disposal by lease or grant, and was to certify such disposals every four months to the auditors; this was the most practical step suggested in the patent for preventing the losses of revenue which insufficient organization allegedly caused in the old courts.

The two auditors of the prests were an important innovation. They took the accounts of wars, buildings, ships, ordnance, and of all sums delivered in prest, as well as the accounts of two departments which had hitherto accounted to the general surveyors (the hanaper and butlerage) and of the great wardrobe, hitherto accountable in the exchequer. As auditors of these foreign accounts they were to have a long and important history;[2] in the main, however, they were

---

[1] Cf. Giuseppi, *Guide*, under 'Augmentation Office', I. 138 ff.
[2] Cf. M. D. George, 'Notes on the Origin of the Declared Account', *E.H.R.* XXXI. 41 ff.

designed to secure the repayment of money 'prested' or lent out by government treasuries. A complicated system of interdepartmental borrowing and advances made to individual officers served to keep government going throughout the century, and it had always been difficult to secure prompt and complete repayment. On the establishment of the court of general surveyors in 1542, these officials were made responsible for the task; they were authorized to sue out process in whatever revenue court had made the loan.[1] This unsatisfactory method, by which special officials could secure repayment only by going the round of all departments, was now replaced by a control of these debts centralized in two auditors; the treasurers of augmentations and first-fruits, and the tellers of the exchequer were ordered to render monthly certificates of debts owing in their departments, in order to enable the auditors to pursue their quest. The fact that these officials were also entrusted with the foreign accounts hitherto handled by the auditors of general surveyors and exchequer reflects the insufficient specialization of these earlier auditors; those of the new court of augmentations were to be responsible for land revenue only.

The appointment of a keeper of the records is interesting because neither of the parent courts had had one; he was charged only with the custody of the records and was to leave the profitable making of copies from them to the clerk of the court. The patent concluded by naming the first holders of the leading offices, all appointments being for life; on the whole, the men who had held the respective offices in the dissolved courts were reappointed, the treasurership and clerkship going to the officials of the old court of augmentations. The appointment seems to have been made on 2 January 1547, the day after the date of the patent; at least, Sir John Williams was reappointed treasurer on that day.[2]

The amalgamation of crown lands in the survey of one court instead of two also led to a simpler and more efficient arrangement of local collection. With the absorption of the older organization into the new and the creation of a single authority for crown lands, the methods of augmentations also prevailed for the erstwhile chamber

---

[1] 33 Henry VIII, c. 39, sec. xxxvii.
[2] E 323/3, m. 1.

lands, and their honorial structure was at last ignored. To take an example: the first account of the receiver for Bedfordshire of the new court of augmentations lists all the lands in the shire within the survey of the court, though naturally it did not break up the lesser units and retained a division according to source: lands of monasteries in the county, crown manors, parcels of Bedfordshire lands belonging to monasteries in other counties, lands of St John of Jerusalem, Richmond and Buckingham lands in the county, Wolsey's possessions there, attainted lands (by name).[1] The only land revenue to remain outside this arrangement was that from collegiate lands and chantries which accounted separately until the reforms of 1554;[2] the reason must no doubt be sought in the fact that, though the chantries and hospitals had in theory been dissolved and annexed to the crown before the new court was set up on 1 January 1547, very little had been done to carry the confiscation into effect.[3] The general organization of county receivers was worked out before these additional lands came under the court of augmentations; since the gradual dissolution from 1547 onwards added the lands piecemeal, it seems to have been thought easier to collect their revenues separately. The further alterations undertaken in 1554 united all crown lands in the county in the hands of one receiver, duchy and wards' lands alone being excepted all the time.[4]

So much, then, for the reforms of 1547, an essential preliminary to the more far-reaching steps taken seven years later. By combining the courts of general surveyors and of augmentations, the reformers virtually abolished the former and transferred its business to the latter, with the result that they ended the career of the king's chamber in national finance. They thus produced a single department responsible for the revenue from crown lands and made a beginning at reducing the confusion to which Cromwell's lavish creation of separate courts had led under his less capable successors. They also succeeded in putting the internal organization of the court on as rational a basis as possible. The one thing they did not achieve—they did not try very hard—was the economy which they claimed to be

---

[1] SC 6, Edward VI, 1–5.   [2] *Ibid.* 6–10.
[3] A. F. Pollard, *Political History* (Vol. VI), 17 ff.
[4] SC 6, Philip and Mary, 2 (for the year ending Michaelmas 1554).

pursuing. Even from the words of the patent itself it is reasonably plain that administrative efficiency was a more compelling reason, and the constant lack of funds in the chamber gave the necessary final stimulus.

The real troubles, then, remained—the wasteful overstaffing of offices, the lack of proper control throughout the administration, the lack of contact between departments. Nothing, however, was done until 23 March 1552 when a commission was appointed 'for the Survey and examinacion of the state of all his Maiesties Courtes of Revenue', consisting of Lord Darcy (lord chamberlain), Thomas Thirlby (bishop of Norwich), Sir Richard Cotton (controller of the household), Sir John Gates (vice-chamberlain and captain of the guard), Sir Robert Bowes (master of the rolls), and Sir Walter Mildmay (since 1547 one of the general surveyors in the court of augmentations).[1] This was in fact the committee of council fore-shadowed by Edward VI himself in the plan for dividing the council which he drew up early in March 1552; he there provided for seven men to 'loke to the state of all the courtes, specially of the new erectid courtes...and therof shal make certificat'.[2] The patent itself mentioned nine members,[3] but from the commission's report it appears that only the six listed above actually assembled; nothing is known about the reasons for which Sir William Petre, chancellor of first-fruits, and John Gosnolde, solicitor of augmentations, stood down, but it is interesting to note that their absence reduced the official and expert element on the commission to one—Mildmay. It may be suspected that the preponderance of outsiders, while partly the result of the prior occupations of such men as the lord treasurer and the chancellor of augmentations, was also welcome as ensuring a fair and impartial investigation. They sat for eight months, taking evidence, and returned their certificate, together with a long and detailed report, on 10 December 1552.

---

[1] B.M., Harl. MS. 7383, fo. 1.

[2] *Literary Remains of King Edward the Sixth* (ed. J. G. Nichols, 1857), 501.

[3] *Cal. Pat. Edward VI*, IV. 353: Darcy, Thirlby, Sir John Gates, Sir William Petre, Sir Robert Bowes, Sir Thomas Wrothe, Sir Richard Cotton, Mildmay, and Gosnolde.

This report is divided into three parts.[1] In the first place, it gives a full account of the royal revenue for the year ending Michaelmas 1551—'the certaynties and casualties answerable to his Maiestie in the saide courtes, Asalso the Payments allowances and Deduccions Issuynge and paied out of thesame'—which provides the best picture available of the Cromwellian revenue courts as a means for supplying the needs of the government and for creating a reserve. This is followed by 'diuerse and sondrie notes and remembraunces... tendinge to thincrease of the kinges Revenues, the diminishinge of the chardges nowe borne out of the same, And the well and assured yerely aunswering of the said Revenue to his Maiesties Cofers'. This offers precise details about the abuses current in the courts, about shortcomings in organization, and about methods of procedure. Lastly, there are a few brief notes referring to plans for fusing the courts: this, in some ways the most important section, is crossed out in the certificate but not in the report.[2]

Revenue was still divided into certain (of fixed annual amount) and casual (varying year by year), a division which was significant to men trying to arrive at a reliable total for the future and apparently unable or unwilling to take an average over a number of past years. Expenditure was also of two kinds—that deducted by individual receivers as charged upon their office before they paid their receipts to the central treasury of their court, and that paid out from the centre. In the exchequer, for instance, the casualties, which included the customs, vastly exceeded certain revenue; in augmentations, fed largely by land rents, the position was reversed. The income of the court of wards counted entirely as casual. The total income was

[1] The original report seems to have been a roll of which only three membranes survive (E 163/12/19); a very fine copy in book form, made a little later and signed with reasonably accurate imitations of the commissioners' signatures, is B.M., Add. MS. 30,198. This lacks part III of the report. The best copy, though it is unsigned, is B.M., Harl. MS. 7383, which was probably made straight from the roll returned by the commissioners and may have been made by them; it is contemporary and will here be used. I shall quote it as 'Report'.

[2] Report, fo. 1. From this certificate, prefacing the actual report, are also taken the dates mentioned in the previous paragraph. Part III is preserved on the surviving membranes of the original roll, proving that it was part of the report; perhaps it was crossed out and not transcribed into the later copy (Add. MS. 30,198) because its recommendations were never carried out.

given as £271,912, of which £183,998 was certain.[1] The details of receipts demonstrate the precision with which different sources of revenue were allocated to different departments—the principle of Cromwell's reform. The exchequer or ancient revenue consisted of certainties (fee farms, ulnage, farms for terms of years on the ancient demesne, the farms of the counties) and casualties (fines, issues, and amercements in the common law courts, lands seized for alienation without licence, specialties for the shipping of wool, the temporalities of vacant sees, and the customs). The duchy of Lancaster administered the income and incidents from its lands: rents and farms, court fines, wood sales, respite of homage, felons' goods, approvement of Ashdown forest, anchorage of ships, wrecks, the profits of its seal. In augmentations, the land revenue was classified in twelve auditors' and receivers' circuits.[2] Casualties came from the fines for leases made in the court, and the foreign accounts, the province of the auditors of the prests (hanaper of chancery, hanaper of augmentations, butlerage, and the great wardrobe). First-fruits and tenths was credited only with its particular revenue; the clerical subsidies which Cromwell had transferred there continued to be part of the court's income,[3] but there appears to have been nothing from that source in 1550-1.[4] The revenues of the court of wards and liveries are equally plainly derived from departmental sources: wards' lands, courts and leets, wood sales, various fines.[5]

If receipts were classified in kind, payments also had advanced

---

[1] *Report*, fos. 36v *seqq*. The figures are as follows:

	Certain	Casual
Exchequer	£7,562	£31,786
Augmentations	£144,825	£14,370
Duchy of Lancaster	£16,568	£1,486
First-fruits	£15,042	£8,521
Wards	—	£21,749

Since accounts were rarely passed within a year of their being due, the commissioners must have worked on incomplete books. Comparison with other evidence shows that they did remarkably well in the circumstances in arriving at totals near enough the same as those given in other accounts.

[2] *Ibid*. fos. 13 *seqq*. The groups differed from those of the pre-1547 court of augmentations (above, pp. 206 f.). One of them was the duchy of Cornwall, the last survivor of the honorial structure of the court of general surveyors.

[3] They are included in 1542-3 (B.M., Lansd. MS. 156, fos. 133 *seqq*.) as well as 1554-5 (E 101/520/28).

[4] *Report*, fos. 27 *seqq*.   [5] *Ibid*. fos. 28 *seq*.

towards such appropriation since Cromwell's day. The two chief paymasters of the early 1540's were the treasurers of augmentations and the chamber, with the treasurer of first-fruits in reserve; here, too, the reform of 1547 had had an effect. In 1552 nearly all departments returned an expenditure on fixed affairs only; this was true of the duchy (the fees of its officers), first-fruits (fees of its officers, salaries of the judges, learned counsel, and a few other royal officials), and wards (fees of its officers, repairs, and similar items within its survey). Surpluses in first-fruits and the duchy went to the royal household; in 1550–1 these amounted to £19,864 and £6,000, the latter apparently a fixed sum. The exchequer paid many fees and annuities in allocations on individual receivers; the receipt itself paid some more, as well as the fees of the exchequer staff and large sums to the cofferer of the household (£6,000) and to the great wardrobe (£2,475). That left all the casual government expenditure to the treasurer of the chamber who still paid a little on special warrants in addition to payments in the household, and more particularly to augmentations. Here many fees and annuities were paid, the cofferer received £10,000, and all the items of defence were listed. The court was both in its income and its payments, in their size as well as their character, easily the most important financial department. The royal finances still rested on land revenue and the modern accounting methods, both first introduced by Henry VII in his chamber reforms, and retained as the basis of Cromwell's great bureaucratic structure.

The total expenditure amounted to £235,398, which left a surplus of £36,513, or—with those payments marked 'in revertion', that is due to fall back to the crown when the present recipients died—£78,523. But the second figure was merely one of hope and the first was very small, for further expenses had to be charged against it. These were largely unknown and unknowable, beyond the fact that they were very heavy: additional sums to the great wardrobe and the household, the admiralty and ordnance, the king's purse and new year's gifts, and in particular the cost of defending Calais and Ireland.[1] The revenues of Calais, for instance, fell short by £5,500 of its ordinary expenses; the difference as well as the total cost of its

[1] *Ibid.* fo. 40 v.

defence had to be supplied from the 'king's coffers', the reserves.[1] The spurious surplus of regular income over regular expenditure was more than swallowed up by such items, and though no figures are given it is clear that the crown failed by a long chalk to pay its way.

Having established this somewhat obvious truth, the commission next considered reforms and economies which might help to balance the budget, and their notes and recommendations, filling twenty-three folios, front and back, in the manuscript, make up the second part of the report. In general, they complained of excessive fees and alleged that many officials were receiving more than was authorized by patent or precedent. The troubles were many. There were extravagance and exploitation of crown office for private gain, though the increase in salaries, however much deplored by the commission, represented only a natural and inevitable movement in an age of disastrous inflation. There was an over-elaborate structure with insufficient knowledge and hard work behind it to secure efficiency. Many individual points needed further attention, which was scarcely to be wondered at since most of the departments were still barely ten years old. The complaints only describe the growing pains of the new bureaucracy. Cromwell had begun its construction, and while he lived his dynamic and unceasing activity had kept things going smoothly; there was not, in 1552, anyone capable of taking his place, nor had there been for twelve years. Of course the machinery creaked badly; but it was obvious to the commission itself that the shortcomings they had enumerated were only symptoms of a deeper trouble, and that their recommendations hardly touched the problem. The real question was not how each department could be made a little less wasteful and a little more efficient, but how the whole structure of financial administration was to be improved.

These doubts and questions led to part three of the report, 'A Brief Declaracion of the chardge' on the revenue for the fifth year of Edward VI (1551–2) in fees and diets, 'with certeyn divises for the diminishment of the same'.[2] The main task set the commissioners had been to consider the superfluous charges with which the

---

[1] Report, fos. 41 seqq.
[2] Ibid. fos. 61 seqq.

courts of revenue were burdened,[1] and their more penetrating conclusions naturally took the form of searching out possible savings in
officers' salaries. They put the total of these at £18,526, a notable
sum yet far from explaining the insolvency of the crown. That they
were aware of the need for administrative reform is indicated by the
fact that they began by discussing the number of departments it was
desired to retain. Administrative policy was developing along the
lines laid down when the courts of augmentations and general
surveyors were amalgamated in 1547. If all the courts were to
continue, the commissioners could foresee a possible saving of
£6,431, to be achieved by reducing salaries to the level of 1547 and
by abolishing a number of superfluous offices. The exchequer could
do with fewer customers, and first-fruits with only one auditor; in
augmentations, there was no need for surveyors of lands, masters
and surveyors of woods and woodwards, a solicitor whose work could
be done by the solicitor general, and the treasurer of the chamber
'whos place the thesaurer of this Courte might well supplie'. No
doubt it was held that his household work might be done by the
cofferer and his national payments discharged in the court of
augmentations.

This proposed no radical reforms, apart from the extinction of the
treasurer of the chamber, but the other two suggestions went much
further. By combining the existing departments into two courts,
£6,905 might be saved; the small increase on savings in the first case,
due to the fact that some surviving officials would have to be paid
more, sufficiently indicates that the commission were thinking as
much of administrative reform as of retrenchment. First-fruits and
wards were to be annexed to the exchequer; all their offices were to
be extinct, except those of the feodaries, since it was probably
thought wiser to keep specialist officers for their complicated tasks,
and much additional work was to devolve upon the clerk of the pipe,
the auditors of the exchequer, and the king's remembrancer, who
would all be concerned in the audit of the additional accounts.
Augmentations and the duchy were to become one court of the
king's revenue, to handle all the king's lands (except the very few
anciently answerable in the exchequer) with an establishment cut

[1] *Literary Remains of Edward VI*, 501.

to the bone.[1] This reform would have completed the steps taken in 1547 and given the finances a good logical construction. Pure land revenue, the basis of the royal finances, in one department, every other source traditional or new in another—the bureaucratic principle would have been fully answered and the administration greatly facilitated.

The commissioners had, however, another suggestion to make: if all revenue courts were fused into one—'as in the tyme of diuerse his maiesties Progenitours hathe ben vsed', a comment which indicates either how little medieval household finance was understood even by 1552, or how great an influence exchequer officials exercised over the commissioners—£10,242 could be saved. This reformed exchequer was to have its old officials and the court of wards' feodaries, as in the second plan; in addition two auditors of the prests and five additional auditors of revenue (to bring the total up to ten) were to be appointed. All land revenue was to be collected by the sheriffs, and it was suggested that two new officers in the exchequer, to be called general surveyors or any other name—a hint that the hostility of the exchequer to Henry VII's chamber machinery had to be placated by verbal concessions—be appointed to play within the exchequer the part which Henry VII's surveyors had played outside it by taking accounts of lands, prests, butlerage, hanaper, great wardrobe, and Calais and the Marches. This was intended to relieve the officials of the upper exchequer of some of the new work without destroying the departmental supremacy of the court as Henry VII's reforms had done; furthermore, officials concerned with the additional labour were to receive higher fees.[2]

The report produced some further suggestions for economy, among which there appeared the inevitable item of reduced expenditure in the household so familiar from the reign of Elizabeth, and also some points for the increase of revenue—a revision of the customs rates last fixed in 1507, and the typically small point that the abolition of augmentations would increase the profits of the seal

---

[1] A chancellor, general surveyor, attorney, treasurer, clerk, ten auditors of the revenue and two of prests, ten receivers, two messengers, an usher, and a keeper of records.

[2] The barons, clerk of the pipe, king's remembrancer, lord treasurer's remembrancer, clerk of the pells, the tellers, and the auditors.

because the seal of the court was much cheaper than the great seal of England. It concluded with a sonorous paragraph:

Finallie, aftre ordre taken in the premisses, It were conveniente to devise vppon a certayne yerelie Revenue mete for thonorable maintenaunce of the Kinges maiesties Estate [by creating a surplus in that obscure depository known as the king's coffers; the lands, manors, castles, forests, and the like, to be set aside for the purpose] might be so annexed in perpetuitie to thimperiall Crowne of this Realme as then might remayne inviolable vntouched and vndismembred for ever.

That was a pious hope which, however, well expressed the ideal of an administrative system still firmly bound to the traditional methods. The continued solvency of the crown and the covering of unexpected expenditure were to be assured by basing a reserve on the revenues of certain fixed lands. It was still the old rigid system of allocating specific revenues for specific purposes, rather than the freer and more adaptable method of lumping the surplus of the departments together in one liquid reserve, a method practised—as far as we can tell—by Henry VII and especially Cromwell.[1] The need for reform brought to the fore the desire for the safety of the old ways; the administrative measures proposed mark the gradual triumph of the old exchequer. The old bureaucracy and the new had this much in common: they could neither of them abide the irregularities which the personal government of such men as Wolsey and Cromwell produced. Cromwell had, however, based his personal government on a highly developed bureaucratic structure, and this structure was now to be absorbed into the older system, transforming it. With this long, painstaking, and generally honest as well as sensible report in hand, the government proceeded to set about the reform of the financial machinery. They were possibly aware that the commission had been greatly influenced by the conservative views of exchequer officials, especially in part three;

---

[1] In 1537, a document written by Cromwell's clerk Sadler embodied orders to the revenue departments to make a full return of their receipts and issues, 'by meanes wherof the Kinges Highnes maye knowe his estate, And by meanes therof maye establishe all his affaires, And therby be putt an order howe a certain tresure yerely maye be laid vp for all necessities' (SP 1:199, fos. 105–8; *L.P.* XII. I. 1091, where it is wrongly described as a paper for the council).

whether or to what extent they agreed with the civil service in putting safety and economy before speed and flexibility in administration must now be seen.

Soon after the submission of the report in December 1552, the council drew up a list of ten items—'A Remembraunce of thinges worthie examination for the kinges Maiestie'.[1] They all concerned financial matters: a check on the profits of land sales and of the sales of lead and bell metal from dissolved monasteries;[2] accounts to be taken from purveyors, victuallers, and other paymasters of prest money; a strict examination of 'the somes of money demaunded of the kinge for the fall' (that is, in compensation for debasement), 'for therin is thought to be moche deceipte'; a re-examination of sales, gifts, and exchanges of land, to see whether the king was receiving what he ought from them; a check on bonds entered into for purchases of land and woods, for the same purpose; if the yield of monastic plate and jewels were examined, 'the kinges maieste shold think the travaile of his Commissioners well emploied that way'; an account to be called for from the 'factors' (agents) employed by the king and his father in the purchase of alum, copper, fustians, and other goods needed in the war. Point three read:

That execucion may folowe the trauaile of the Commyssioners lately appoincted for the Courtes of Revenue so as the faultes may be redressed and the superfluous charge diminyshed, as ther shalbe cause.

But the troubled last year of Edward VI was not a convenient time for administrative reform, and even less so the interlude before Mary sat firmly on the throne; on her accession, notes were prepared outlining measures of economy among which 'Augmentacions and other nue Courtes' were again mentioned, and soon after the whole 'Remembraunce' drafted for Edward in 1552 or 1553 was virtually copied out for his sister, with the paragraph about the 1552 recommendations left unaltered.[3]

[1] SP 10:5, fos. 154r–v.
[2] This latter point engaged the government's attention at intervals in 1552 until a commission was set up under Northumberland to investigate it (*ibid.* vol. 16, fo. 156). Mildmay sat on that body, too.
[3] SP 11:1, fos. 5, 56r–v.

The reforms were thus planned under Edward VI, and it was only the accident of death that made them the 'Marian' reforms; the queen can claim no credit for them. Even before the boy died, his ministers had managed to take one essential step by submitting to the parliament of March 1553 two acts designed to carry out the recommendations of the commission. The act of 6 Edward VI, c. 1, gave effect to the commissioners' desire to bind all the king's revenue officers in heavy bonds for prompt payment and rendering of accounts; it appointed dates for the paying in of receipts (Easter receipts by 20 June, Michaelmas receipts by 20 January) and for the presentation of accounts, and dealt in detail with the duties of the treasurers and auditors of revenue courts.[1] Such detailed provisions were probably futile; they were in any case undermined by the second chapter of the same statute which provided 'for the dissolving uniting or annexing of certayne Courtes latelie erected by the King that dead ys'.[2] This, of course, was the act which made Winchester's real plans possible. It declared the patent of 1 January 1547 valid, since doubts had arisen about it, and further empowered the king to change, dissolve, unite, or otherwise deal with, the revenue courts as he pleased, by letters patent. An interesting note of caution was sounded in sections iii and iv which ordered that such patents could not authorize the levying of debts contrary to law, or the hearing of cases by officers of the courts to be established except where the king was party. The triumph of augmentations, announced in the second list of orders which were discussed above,[3] had clearly provoked a common law reaction against these encroachments of statutory or prerogative courts. During the passage of the bill in the commons obvious vested interests managed to add a proviso saving to the officers of the existing courts all fees, annuities, and the like enjoyed by 27 March 1553.[4]

Though Edward's death delayed matters a little, the reformers

---

[1] *Stat. Realm*, IV. 161 ff. Exchequer officials were exempt: they were to act as hitherto. An exception made for bishops as collectors of the clerical tenth was remedied by 7 Edward VI, c. 4, for binding them in sureties.

[2] *Ibid.* 164 f. Introduced in the lords on 14 March 1553 and sent to the commons on the 20th; committed to the master of the rolls on the 24th; passed with a proviso on the 30th (*L.J.* I. 435a, 437a; *C.J.* I. 25a, 25b, 26a).

[3] Above, pp. 207 f.   [4] Cf. above, n. 2.

went ahead with their plans. Even before Mary's first parliament met, Sir Richard Sackville, chancellor of the court of augmentations, surrendered his office into the hands of a commission presumably appointed to handle the change-over: lord treasurer Winchester, Sir Robert Rochester (controller of the household), Sir Robert Southwell (master of the rolls), Sir Francis Englefield (chancellor of the duchy), and Sir Thomas Moyle and Sir Walter Mildmay (general surveyors of the court of augmentations).[1] This was on 17 October 1553; on the 24th the parliament met, but it had a good deal of more important business to do, and the bill to give Mary the same powers of dealing with the revenue courts as Edward had enjoyed[2] was not introduced in the commons until 27 November.[3] After a second reading on the 29th it was committed, oddly enough, to Sir John Baker, chancellor both of the court of first-fruits and of the exchequer; this may well account for the addition, in a separate schedule, of a section saving all annuities and fees in courts other than augmentations which alone had been mentioned in the original bill. On 4 December the bill went to the lords—back, presumably, since the royal assent was given on the next day.[4] On that same 5 December a commission granted to Sir Edmund Peckham, treasurer of the mint, made possible the administrative changes contemplated.[5] He was to take into his hands all the money remaining in, or hereafter to come into, the receipt of the exchequer and the treasuries of all other revenue courts, including the hanaper, and the fines collected for compounding for offences against the queen's person. In other words, he was to be temporarily in charge of all the revenue of the crown, so that the needs of the government would continue to be supplied even though the agencies normally engaged on the task were in the melting-pot. On 19 January everything was ready and commands were issued to the chancellor to make writs of

---

[1] *Cal. Pat. Philip and Mary 1553–4*, 300.

[2] 1 Mary, St. 2, c. 10 (*Stat. Realm*, IV. 208 f.). The act was even more careful about the judicial powers of the revenue courts than Edward's had been; it confined them to revenue cases.

[3] *C.J.* I. 31 b. The relevant part of *L.J.* is missing.

[4] *Ibid.* 31 b, 32 b.

[5] *Cal. Pat. Philip and Mary 1553–4*, 72. From the fact that he was paid 26s. 8d. a day for the work involved from 16 November onward, it appears that that was the true date on which the measures of reform got under way.

certiorari to augmentations and first-fruits to deliver and certify their records into chancery, to make letters patent for the dissolution of these courts, and to grant writs of *mittimus* for delivery of the records into the exchequer.[1] On the 20th, Sackville was hurriedly reappointed, 'during pleasure', so that everything was in good bureaucratic order and form when it came to the dissolving of the court.[2] On the 23rd, the letters patent dissolving the courts of augmentations and of first-fruits were issued, and on the day after further patents united the dissolved courts to the exchequer.[3] On the 25th and 26th Gardiner, as lord chancellor, appeared in person in the exchequer for a solemn ceremony in which he presented the two patents and the court ordered their reading and enrolment.[4] The two chief financial departments created by Cromwell had ceased to exist, and at the same time the end of chamber finance was in effect proclaimed; the exchequer was ready to resume its old place at the head of the financial administration.

These, then, were the reforms of 1554: the courts of augmentations and of first-fruits and tenths were amalgamated with the exchequer, while the duchy of Lancaster and the court of wards continued as independent financial departments. The principle advocated by the commissioners of 1552 was adopted; economy and better organization were to be achieved by cutting down the number of departments in existence. On the other hand, the actual steps recommended in the report were not taken. Neither were all financial departments reunited in the exchequer, nor was a logical division made into exchequer and land revenue office. The amalgamation carried out in fact had, to tell the truth, neither example nor logic to recommend it. If the nature of the revenues administered and the precedent of 1547 had been considered, it should have been taken into account that the courts dealing with the profits from lands had something in common; but the duchy, eminently such a court, remained untouched. The amalgamation of 1547 brought together matters so naturally akin that their separation until then was only

---

[1] *Ibid.* 73.   [2] *Ibid.* 67.

[3] The only original extant is the patent of annexation for augmentations with the schedule (E 163/13/2), but all relevant documents are enrolled on the memoranda rolls, and more accessibly on the dorse of the close roll, 1 Mary, pt. 7 (C 54/500, mm. 3–6).

[4] E 159/333, mm. 75, 80.

due to the sudden and large increase of property which the dissolution of the monasteries had meant; that reform was mere common sense. In 1554, on the other hand, it is quite obvious that the best possible compromise was arrived at, rather than that a deliberate plan was fully carried out. The chances are that the government hoped to take to heart the commission's last recommendation and make do with one financial department, and that opposition of one kind or another forced them to leave out the duchy and wards.

That this was so in the case of the duchy is largely confirmed by an exchange of views a year later, in 1555, between the privy council and a committee of officials, respecting further savings that might be made in the financial administration. What matters here is article 10.[1] It appears from the officials' reply that the council had proposed to incorporate the duchy into the exchequer, to have the fines and profits from the lands in the name of the king and queen (presumably instead of the duke of Lancaster), and to cut down its 'waste Officers'. With the last two points the experts declared themselves in agreement, but on the first they had this to say:

Wee thinke not good to alter the Court of the Dutchy because all the Tennantes of the same hold theyre landes by meane tenure, except it be in the County of Lancaster, and haue bene since thereccion of the same Court allwayes ordered by the same in all theyre Causes.

This argument—that, no tenancy-in-chief being involved, the honour of Lancaster had better be kept intact and separate to avoid confusion by cutting across the custom of 150 years—must, it may be supposed, have been put forward also two years earlier and proved sufficient then to save the duchy from losing its identity. The point had, however, rankled with the council who in their 'replication' once more

---

[1] The document is B.M., Tit. B. iv, fos. 129–131v, 'An answer to certen articles propounded for diminishing the charges & the safe answering the Revenew of the Crowne, with the replication to the said answer in Latin'; there is a copy, *ibid.* fos. 135 *seqq.* A later discourse by an exchequer officer refers to this disputation as a 'Consultacion held betweene the pryvy Counsell and Officers' (*ibid.* fo. 272). The original statement of the council is lost; all we have are the answers of the experts consulted and the council's further replies to these. For the fact that the English part is by the experts and the Latin by the council, cf. Sir Julius Caesar's copies of the Latin section headed 'A Conclusion made by the Counsell...' (B.M., Add. MS. 12,504, fo. 164), and of the English section endorsed by him as 'The Subcommittees opinion' (*ibid.* fo. 166). Article 10 is in Tit. B. iv, fos. 130v–131.

asserted that they were yet of the opinion that the lands and possessions of the duchy could well be handed over to the exchequer—
'possunt bene redduci ad scaccarium'; the 'Coloni et Tenentes'
would enjoy their rights as well in the exchequer as in the duchy
court. They put the common-sense point of view of the administrator: the scattered duchy lands could more easily, cheaply, and
profitably be administered by the sheriffs in their counties, and, the
lands having come to the queen united with the crown, 'non
videmus' why they were to be treated differently from other crown
lands. What they failed to see—or preferred to ignore—was that
ordinary tenants so far escaped the burdensome obligations of
prerogative wardships to which only military tenants-in-chief were
subject. Thus the duchy of Lancaster remained outside the reforms
of 1554 because of the opposition of the civil service and the
interests of its tenants, and more conservatism and further chances
have preserved it separate to this day.

No word can be got on the reason for the failure to include the
court of wards in the scheme. Here there was no old department;
in the fifteen years of its existence the court had hardly won any
loyalties among its clients so as to make its disappearance a matter
for sorrow, and even if we pursue the career of the master of the
wards back to 1503 we shall find no interests likely to be affected by
a change in status except those of the court's own officials. It may
be that the peculiar nature of its work—the mixture of land and
personal matters, its character of stock exchange plus slave market
plus marriage agency—made it unsuitable for inclusion in the
exchequer; but the commissioners of 1552 had not thought so.
On the other hand, it may be to the point to remember that the
mastership of the wards was among the personally most profitable
gifts the crown had to bestow; to abolish such an office would have
been cruelty indeed and not to be expected in particular from
Winchester who had held it from 1526 to 1554. Perhaps the most
obvious reason, however, for the separate survival of the court is the
appointment on 1 May 1554 of a new master—Sir Francis Englefield,
a good Catholic and special favourite with the queen.[1] It seems
unnecessary to look further for more strictly administrative reasons

---

[1] *Cal. Pat. Philip and Mary* 1553–4, 249.

for what was done when so excellent a Tudor reason lies ready to hand. At any rate, the court of wards continued independently until the abolition of feudal tenures at the Restoration made its revival after the Interregnum superfluous.

That brings us back to the courts that were amalgamated with the exchequer and to the reforms as they were actually devised. They were embodied in eight documents, four for each court.[1] On 23 January 1554, both augmentations and first-fruits were dissolved, the former for the interesting reason—which constitutes a kind of admission that had been avoided in 1547—that much of the land under its survey had disappeared. On the next day,[2] the courts were united, transposed, and annexed—as the patents have it—to the exchequer, 'there to be and contynue as a membre and parcell of thesame Courte of theschequere'. Their revenue was to come under the survey of the exchequer in manner and form there used and according to 'suche articles ordinaunces and devises as in a scedule vnto theis our lettres patentes annexed and signed with our hande is further lymtted appointed mencioned and devised'. These schedules, duly signed by the queen on every membrane of the roll into which the sheets were stitched together,[3] form the next pair of documents. Finally, writs were issued to the exchequer, authorizing it to receive the records of the dissolved courts; the fact that this was done on 25 January for first-fruits (ten sacks of assorted papers were involved) but not until 12 February for augmentations, suggests that the affairs of the more complicated court were not quite settled when the dissolution was ordered.

The really significant part of all this—the point which indicates what the reformers intended—is that vague phrase about the manner and form used in the exchequer and its detailed elaboration in the schedules attached. To take augmentations first: there are four points on which we must concentrate. It was ordered that the revenues of the lands should be collected by counties, and that the collector should be the sheriff or some other person. The sheriff had been

---

[1] For references to the documents as enrolled on the close roll, see above, p. 241, n. 3.

[2] The transcript on the close roll says 23 January for augmentations and 24 January for first-fruits; the intrinsically improbable discrepancy is removed by the original (E 163/13/2).

[3] Extant for augmentations only, E 163/13/2.

recommended as a suitable person by the commissioners of 1552,[1] but though the employment of an existing official would have meant an obvious economy, when the point was argued anew in 1555 opinions differed. Once again, the council pressed for it; once again, its official advisers demurred, saying that the sheriff had enough to do as it was and was 'otherwise charged and more largely than he maketh good Accompt of'.[2] The council stuck to its guns and came back rather neatly by ascribing the sheriffs' inefficiency to lack of pressure from the 'Officiarij Scaccarij'. They added five good reasons for using the sheriffs: they were the traditional collectors of revenue; they had always been less dilatory than receivers; their short tenure of office prevented fraud and the system by which one year's deficit burdened the next year's revenues; the sheriffs were knights and gentlemen, whereas receivers were mostly 'homines nullius estimacionis'; sheriffs' appointments were public and official, while receivers got their places by influence and intrigue. Some of these points are sounder than others, but none sufficed; as was generally the case in these reforms, the experts triumphed and the land revenue continued to be collected by county receivers.[3]

A second and even more fundamental point concerned the audit. Here it was made plain enough that the accountant, whoever he should be, was to follow the ancient course of the exchequer by appearing publicly in court in the Hilary Term and taking his oath as was usual. He was to finish his account by 24 February, and then —having had it engrossed and signed by at least three officers and an auditor—was to take it to the pipe office by 20 March, for further process if necessary. The account was to remain with the clerk of the pipe. This was not as explicit as it might have been, but it was certainly and justifiably interpreted by conservative officials as obliging accountant and auditor to obey the old course. In the reign of Elizabeth it was declared that the auditor, having finished the account, should pass it through the offices of the queen's and lord

---

[1] Report, fos. 64–6. They recommended some fee, which the schedule echoed in the grant of a 'taile of Rewarde'.

[2] B.M., Tit. B. iv, fo. 129.

[3] From Michaelmas 1554 onwards the 'ministers' accounts' are rendered in one document county by county group, for all the lands in the shire which had belonged to augmentations, the chantry lands being included (e.g. SC 6, Philip and Mary, 2).

treasurer's remembrancers to the pipe office where it should remain readily accessible; and the writer was right in his interpretation of the schedule, for only in this way could the exchequer make sure of getting in outstanding sums on any closed account. Instead of which, auditors were taking accounts privately and without oath, made up the accounts after a new fashion (in English and with many details that should have been left to the 'particulars' or supporting papers), and recorded debts in such a manner that they alone knew them to be debts. The writer scouted the idea that the new methods were cheaper to the accountant.[1] The argument was still raging in the early seventeenth century, when a complaint was raised that the retention of accounts by the auditors contrary to the rule cut out the offices of the two remembrancers and the pipe with their indispensable functions in cases of outstanding debts.[2] In other words, the intention had been to sink augmentations and all its works in the time-honoured methods of the exchequer, though apparently no one ever meant to have land revenue accounts enrolled either on the great roll or among the foreign accounts;[3] instead of which the auditors simply continued the methods of the dissolved court, constituting themselves sole authorities on debts to be collected. This was the more surprising because the men who did this were in the first place the old auditors of the exchequer, those of augmentations having been pensioned off. It may be concluded that they much preferred the rapid and simple methods of the new bureaucracy, even though these did not offer quite as many safeguards against abuses.

The abolition of the court of augmentations further rendered homeless its many records; of these, orders and decrees as well as

[1] A protest, 'Touching accompts taken by Auditors & leviinge of the Queenes debtes due thervpon' (B.M., Tit. B. iv, fos. 68 seqq.).

[2] Ibid. fos. 4–10v. 'Debts' in this sense means sums with which the accountant was charged and which he had not produced by the time of the declaration of his account, or more commonly the deficit on the year's balance for which he remained personally responsible until it was cleared.

[3] The whole controversy turned on the question of debts and their recovery, and this may give a special colour to our knowledge of what it was all about; but it can be said that there is no sign in the schedule of any intention of simply adding the new revenues to the sheriffs' traditional charge and passing it through the same account and audit, with all the usual detail ending in the enrolment on the pipe (cf. also Giuseppi, Guide, I. 74).

cases pending were to remain with the king's remembrancer, while sealed evidences, rentals, court rolls, and other muniments were to be put into a special repository to be appointed by the lord treasurer. This instruction seems simply to have been carried out. Late in 1554 there is a reference to a book of decrees of the late court of augmentations then in the custody of the queen's remembrancer.[1] The new record department is known as the augmentation office, an offshoot from the pipe office whose clerk appointed its keeper;[2] there is no sign among the records preserved there of proceedings after the amalgamation. Most of its documents were acquired before the dissolution of the court; the augmentation office was little more than a storehouse of evidence, and not an executive department of any sort, as is sometimes asserted. Some of the papers belonging there are now to be found in the records of the Land Revenue Office. The receivers' accounts, directed—as has already been said—by the schedule to remain in the pipe office but retained in the hands of the auditors, now form an important part of that despair of the Public Record Office, the Special Collections.[3]

One other detail must receive mention. The abolition of the court removed the auditors of the prests. It was therefore declared that the accounts taken by these officials were to return to the exchequer, there to be taken by the auditors as they had been before the erection of the court of general surveyors, a statement which disguised the fact that they had been taken by the general surveyors for forty years before these were part of a court and had not been near the exchequer for some sixty years. This order proved impossible of fulfilment, presumably because the work involved was too heavy and specialized to be treated as a small part of the tasks handled by already over-burdened officials. Elizabeth was forced to revive the office of two auditors of the prests, assigning to them the works, navy, ordnance, prests, hanaper, wardrobe, and butlerage.[4]

Altogether, then, the intention of the schedule was to abolish all traces of augmentation methods, though its purpose was weakened

---

[1] E 159/334, Recorda, Michaelmas, m. 238.
[2] Giuseppi, *Guide*, I. 140.   [3] *Ibid*. 342 ff.
[4] On 19 January 1560 (*Cal. Pat. Eliz.* I. 299). The further history and general importance of these auditors is described in Mrs George's article, *E.H.R.* XXXI. 41 ff.

by a clause which—as the changes 'cannot perfectlie be established without exercise proof and experience of thesame'—permitted the exchequer to review the regulations as necessary. In practice, the development was towards a somewhat uneasy imposition of augmentation methods on the exchequer background, because the methods were quicker and more businesslike. The process started at once and was moreover pushed through, in some cases, against the wishes of the council; since the old exchequer officials spent much time in the reign of Elizabeth lamenting the evil ways of the land revenue, they cannot have been behind the initiation of it all, and we may justifiably suppose that the lead was taken by the auditors themselves— especially as the complaint that they retained accounts was voiced even before the dissolution of the court of augmentations[1]—with the backing or even guidance of, perhaps, the lord treasurer and, more probably, Mildmay, not appointed chancellor of the exchequer until 1566 but always active about the finances. Expert opinion—the best of it—was for the new methods; the council, hoping to save salaries, tried to insist on the schedule of 1554 and later, when it had very probably forgotten all about it, found itself supported by the exchequer staff who wanted things done in the proper exchequer way. They had a few minor successes—this is not the place to pursue the matter further; generally speaking, however, the land revenue added to the exchequer in 1554 always remained in a different category from the rest of the revenues.

This was even more true of the other dissolved court and its affairs. The schedule concerning first-fruits and tenths is much shorter and simpler, and, as far as appears in the record, was obeyed to the letter. An officer in the exchequer was appointed with the title of remembrancer of first-fruits and tenths;[2] he was to keep the records of the dissolved court, take compositions for first-fruits, and be responsible for all the paper-work concerning both kinds of taxation. He was to collect first-fruits and pay them into the receipt, whereas the tenth and clerical subsidies were paid directly to the

---

[1] Report, fo. 53.

[2] To be held at first by two men, later by one. This was to provide for the officials of the old court: the first appointment went, on 12 February 1554, to Thomas Argall and Thomas Godfrey who had been its keeper of records and clerk respectively (E 159/333, m. 79).

tellers by the collectors of these revenues, that is the bishops in their dioceses. This revived a distinction between the two sources of the remembrancer's revenue which went back to the first days when the crown had imposed these taxes on the Church, and which derived from the natural difference between occasional *ad hoc* payments made to one central officer and an annual tax collected by local receivers. In effect the court of first-fruits simply entered the exchequer whose chancellor and seal it was to employ instead of its own,[1] and whose tellers replaced its treasurer. The name remembrancer was borrowed from the old exchequer; it had none of the precise significance which it had for the two officials who kept 'memoranda' rolls, but it marked the fact that like them the new remembrancer was in charge of certain records and presided over a department charged with the searching out and enforcement of debts. As far as is known, the provisions of the schedule were carried out and the new office immediately got under way; it rendered accounts which were declared before the lord treasurer and a baron of the exchequer and signed by two auditors, but do not seem to have passed for further estreat or enrolment.[2] More even than the land revenue, the revenue from the church remained self-contained and separately administered within the reformed exchequer, of which none the less it was emphatically a part.[3]

One last point about these reforms may be discussed because it throws light on the administrative methods and thought processes of the time. Ostensibly the whole business was designed to secure great savings in salaries; at the same time, as has been seen, the statute under which Winchester proceeded guaranteed some compensation to dispossessed officials. Some were drafted into the new scheme, like the two remembrancers of first-fruits to whom this meant, in effect, promotion. The receivers of augmentations also managed to survive when the original plan of using the sheriffs was abandoned. But Sir John Baker, chancellor of first-fruits, received

---

[1] One clause in the schedule assured the chancellor of the exchequer of the same fees for dealing with first-fruits and tenths business as the chancellor of the late court had had.

[2] Cf. E 101/520/28, account for 1554–5. Signed by Winchester, Edward Saxilby (baron), and Thomson and Hyde (auditors).

[3] Some time during Elizabeth's reign some alterations in the office were made; cf. Thomas Fanshawe, *Practice of the Exchequer Court* (1658), 84.

a life annuity of £233. 6s. 8d., dated from Christmas 1553.[1] This was to compensate him for a salary of £133. 6s. 8d. and the fees he had had of the seal of the court. It may have been fair to him but was in fact detrimental to the crown which compensated him for fees hitherto paid by the public. Augmentation officials did equally well; all of them, including auditors, usher, and messengers, but not receivers, and including even that William Berners whom the commission of 1552 had virtually accused of self-appointment to the pay-roll,[2] received full compensation for their official salaries by a warrant of 4 May 1554.[3] The clerk of the court, with a salary of £40, was compensated to the tune of 200 marks, which indicates who must have profited from the seal of augmentations. Though because of the reforms two new auditors were required in the exchequer to bring the number up to the seven allowed for, there is no sign that auditors of augmentations were used; of the two appointed early in 1554 one had been an exchequer auditor before the reforms and must have had his appointment renewed for some unknown reason, and the other was a new name.[4] Even when alternative employment was found, these annuities continued to be paid: a record of the fees of Sir Walter Mildmay, chancellor and undertreasurer of the exchequer, in 1568, still included £200 as compensation for his office of general surveyor in the court of augmentations.[5] Little can have been saved in salaries and expenses, at least until all the old office-holders died; the unavowed motive for reform—administrative efficiency—bore better dividend than the supposedly major premise of economy.

So much for the actual reform of the revenue courts which pro-

---

[1] *Cal. Pat. Philip and Mary 1553–4*, 5 (12 February 1554).

[2] Report, fo. 53. He was accused of having obtained a patent as auditor of the treasurer's account, in contravention of the ordinance establishing the court.

[3] B.M., Tit. B. iv, fos. 139–40. This is an original, apparently ready for use, but, though supposed to be given under the queen's sign manual, it is not signed by her. A copy in a hanaper register (Add. MS. 38,136, fos. 16v *seqq.*) shows, however, that it was delivered into chancery on the 30th.

[4] John Thomson (16 Feb. 1554: *Cal. Pat. Philip and Mary 1553–4*, 6) was an auditor of the exchequer in 1553 (SP 10:18, fo. 69); John Swift (30 March 1554; *Cal. Pat. Philip and Mary 1553–4*, 229) held no auditorship when that list of financial officials was drawn up.

[5] B.M., Lansd. MS. 171, fo. 344, a transcript which erroneously describes him as an auditor of that court.

duced in 1554 a very different exchequer from its medieval predecessor. It is not true to suppose that the dissolved courts continued their separate existence in the reformed exchequer, but on the other hand they were far from losing their identity completely. Their methods certainly survived. It now remains only to consider what the new exchequer amounted to and in what manner it overcame the various problems faced but never fully solved by earlier reformers. The basic troubles were, to say it once more, insufficient liquidity of resources, the impossibility of making a proper survey and casting a balance from the traditional exchequer records, and a clumsy audit. Henry VII's solution had revived household government at the wrong time and therefore did not last; Cromwell's overburdened the machinery with too many departments which he alone could control. Winchester, building very much on the foundations laid by both these men, and especially on Cromwell's revolutionary turning away from the household, offered a solution of enduring effectiveness, even if in the process he had to come to terms with the demands of traditional and old-fashioned methods.

The Elizabethan exchequer cannot here be described in detail, and there is the less need because the task was performed three hundred and fifty years ago by the then queen's remembrancer, than whom few men can have known more about the ins and outs of the department.[1] Nor can we follow here all the further working out of the 1554 reforms—the protests and counter-protests which poured in upon the lord treasurer from the officials who thought themselves and the queen's service harmed by the new ways; not even the thirty years' war which Robert Hall and Chidiock Wardour, clerks of the pells, waged against Robert Peter and Sir Vincent Skinner, writers of the tallies, can find more than a passing mention here.[2] But one of Wardour's main grievances is the first point that must attract attention in any consideration of the true character and purpose of

---

[1] Thomas Fanshawe, *The Practice of the Exchequer Court*, first published in 1658 but written late in the reign of Elizabeth, probably for the information of lord treasurer Buckhurst who succeeded in 1599.

[2] There is a large package of papers in this dispute at the P.R.O. (E 407/71), and many more among the Lansd. MS. at the B.M. (e.g. vols. 106, 168, 171) and at Hatfield.

the reforms: the altered state of affairs in the receipt of the exchequer expressed in the new powers enjoyed by its so-called auditor.

From January 1554 all but a small part of the crown's revenue flowed into the receipt, so that for the first time since Henry VII expanded his resources the king's money was collected in one place. The income of the duchy and of wards formed an exception but one too small to affect the point. All this money was collected by the four tellers who were accountable for the particular sums they had received. There was no division of function between them and each took whatever happened to come in when he was on duty, except that general receivers and bishops paid the clerical tenth to allotted tellers.[1] At last the exchequer administered again the revenues of the crown; at last there was an end to the old game of going from court to court to find a treasury capable of bearing some particular charge, a game which provides some disgraceful reading in the bad days of the collapse after Cromwell's fall. No change in the government could now make any difference to the bureaucratic organization of a reservoir of treasure.

With this went two things. It was easier to control income and expenditure when all was in the hands of one department, and it was possible to demand comprehensive balance sheets. The 'Declarations of the State of the Treasury' ceased in 1552. Their place was taken in part by the Declaration Books (Pells'), an incomplete series of half-yearly declarations made by the clerk of the pells, and fragmentary until the restoration of the issue roll in 1597 gave the clerk independent records on which to base his return. More important were from the beginning of Elizabeth's reign the Views of Account rendered half-yearly by the tellers, in which the officers who actually handled the money declared what had passed through their hands both in receipts and payments.[2] The only control over them was vested in the writer of the tallies, because of the peculiar manner in which payments into and out of the exchequer were made. A description of the reign of Edward VI (one Mr Felton is mentioned as writer of the tallies) will explain the first.[3] The accountant paid in his

---

[1] B.M., Lansd. MS. 171, fo. 429.
[2] For all these records cf. Giuseppi, *Guide*, I. 193.
[3] B.M., Lansd. MS. 171, fo. 209.

money and received a teller's bill on parchment testifying receipt; a few years later this bill was no longer given to him but 'thrown down a pipe' on to the board of the receipt.[1] The rest of the process was designed to guard against fraud from every direction and to produce the tally which the accountant would bring to his account in the upper exchequer, in order to receive his discharge. On the bill being presented at the receipt, a tally is cut, that is, notches noting the amount paid are cut into it; this with the teller's bill tied round it, must be given to Mr Felton's clerk who copies the amount from the bill on to the side of the tally, enters the tally in a register, and delivers it to 'Mr Ryve in the same office' who, after comparing tally, bill, and roll, 'strikes' (splits) the tally, gives half to the accountant, and throws the other half into a chest in the window behind him. At the account in the upper exchequer the tallies produced are joined with the stocks from the chest in the window; the king's part then goes back into the chest, while the accountant takes his to the clerk of the pipe for his 'quietus est' or acquittance. The clerk kept these tallies until he had warrant to burn them; in 1834 the disposal of the tallies and stocks left behind by the dissolved exchequer burnt down the houses of parliament.

The later document already mentioned adds that the clerk of the tallies kept the tellers' bills, the 'foundacion of all this buildinge'. With tellers' bills and a record book of tallies in his possession, the clerk was in a good position for controlling the tellers' receipts; their issues were also under his eye because until 1597 he alone kept entry books for writs of great and privy seal, authorizing payment,[2] and because of a rule laid down early in Elizabeth's reign that the tellers had to obtain a *debentur* from him for every payment made.[3] It was he also who certified the tellers' Views of Account every half-year throughout the reign of Elizabeth,[4] and a little later he added to all these means of controlling the tellers the locking up of their money, keeping the key at the lord treasurer's pleasure.[5] Having by stages

---

[1] E 407/71, no. 71. The arrangement seems to have been a cross between an old-fashioned speaking tube and the equally old-fashioned cash trolley still sometimes seen at drapers'.   [2] Giuseppi, *Guide*, I. 187 f.

[3] B.M., Lansd. MS. 171, fo. 429. This account also states that the tellers' bills were no longer handed to the accountant.

[4] Giuseppi, *Guide*, I. 193.   [5] B.M., Lansd. MS. 171, fos. 430r–v.

been promoted to such a position of control, the writer of the tallies added to himself the title of auditor of the receipt.[1] He had practically usurped the place of the early Tudor undertreasurer who had dominated the receipt and rendered the 'Declarations of the State of the Treasury'; this officer, since 1543 always also chancellor of the exchequer, was much too busy in the upper exchequer to attend to the detailed work in the lower which had been his sole sphere in the days before the reforms.

The main effect on the lower exchequer, therefore, was to make it a true central treasury in which, moreover, business methods had become—temporarily, at least—speeded up and modernized. In the upper exchequer no such unity can be found. It will be best to give a brief outline description of that department, based on a general acquaintance with the matters discussed; a detailed elaboration or reduction to the record would be out of place. The reformed exchequer as a board of audit is divisible into three. In the first place, there were the accounts taken in the traditional manner. These were the accounts which had been in the exchequer before 1554 and had then been the sole province of its auditors; they went through all the usual stages, including the two remembrancers' offices, and ended up by being enrolled on the old rolls (the pipe, customs' rolls, and so forth). Secondly, there were the accounts of the land revenue. Whereas the auditors were assigned in open court and always afresh to accounts of the first class, they were permanently assigned to certain counties for the land revenue;[2] every Michaelmas term they set out upon their circuits to take receivers' accounts which in the Lent term they then declared before the lord treasurer, chancellor, and one or two barons.[3] The account, as has already been noted, was retained by the auditor, with the result that he alone knew if any debts remained outstanding upon it; but since neither Winchester

---

[1] A document of October 1572 speaks of the 'Scriptor Talliarum or contratall' now called th'Auditor of the Receipt' (B.M., Lansd. M.S. 171, fo. 410).

[2] *Ibid.* fos. 426r–v. By orders made by the court on 10 July 1559 the auditors were granted a special increase in salary in riding fees for the business of the land revenue; the seven auditors were also allotted to seven circuits among nineteen receivers (*ibid.* vol. 3, fos. 203 *seqq.*). The total saving over the old court was estimated at £1,063.

[3] *Ibid.* At first the chancellor seems to have played no part; cf. SC 6, Philip and Mary, 2, the account of Bedfordshire for 1553–4, signed by Winchester and two barons (Brooke and Saxilby).

nor Burghley seem to have objected to this practice until hard pressed
by the exchequer officials, it may be supposed that the method had
the advantage of ease and speed without the drawback of corruption.
No further record was made; after 1554 the only complete total of
the land revenue is to be found in the tellers' accounts where it is
mixed up with the old revenue and the customs in one item. The
abolition of the court of augmentations makes it much harder to
know what was happening to the crown lands.

Lastly, there were the Declared Accounts taken by the auditors of
the prests, whose early history has been worked out in an article
already referred to.[1] The accounts of first-fruits and tenths were
taken by the auditors of the exchequer until the reappointment of
auditors of the prests who were specifically charged with these
accounts also.[2] The proper division of the reformed exchequer is not,
therefore, as it is sometimes made, into pipe office, augmentation
office, and remembrancer of first-fruits, a classification which has
some little meaning only when the storage of records is considered;[3]
the significant classes are accounts taken according to the ancient use
of the exchequer, accounts of the land revenue taken 'augmentation-
wise' (both these by the same auditors), and declared accounts of the
'foreign' revenue and prests taken by the auditors of the prests after
the fashion first employed by the general surveyors of the king's lands
and later more generally throughout the new courts.[4]

One point alone now remains. In the receipt the reforms threw up
the auditor as its new head in practice, though in theory, of course,
the lord treasurer, represented by his deputy, the undertreasurer,
continued to preside. In the exchequer of audit, too, certain changes
took place among the officials. It is from the reforms of 1554 that
we must date the modern history of both the lord treasurer and the

[1] Mrs George, *E.H.R.* XXXI. 41 ff. Cf. B.M., Lansd. MS. 171, fo. 424; the auditors
of the prests take 'th'old great Accomptes of the Exchequere' (Ireland, Berwick, mint,
loans, wars, ships, provisions, hanaper, ordnance, works, and such like), and 'declare the
same nowe before the Lo: Treasurer, the Chancellour & vndertreasurer only, and be
never entered in the Court of th'Eschequere nor examined nor wrytten vpon there as
they were wont to be'.
[2] E 101/520/28. (Thomson and Hyde, auditors of the exchequer, signed this account
which covered the years 1551–7); *Cal. Pat. Eliz.* I. 299.
[3] Even Prof. W. C. Richardson, in the most recent study of Tudor finanoial administration, fell into this error: *Tudor Chamber Administration* (1952), pp. 433 ff.
[4] For a few details, cf. Giuseppi, *Guide*, I. 118 f.

chancellor of the exchequer. As president of the reformed exchequer, the lord treasurer was in a position to be what he had never before really been—the minister of finance. Throughout the middle ages, the existence of household finance, the activities of wardrobe and chamber over which he had no control, had limited his effective power, and the period from Henry VII's reforms through Cromwell's ministry down to 1554 had seen him in practice only the holder of a dignified position. With Winchester's tenure of office and the Marian reforms the lord treasurer recovered a truly important standing in the administration. With Winchester and Burghley begins the line of the great modern lord treasurers who were usually chief ministers and handed the leadership of the ministry down to the first lord of the commission which replaced them in the later seventeenth century. Involved in this was the growth of a new department, the treasury, out of the lord treasurer's private office and staff of clerks. By the middle of the seventeenth century fiscal policy was being made in this new treasury, and the exchequer had become merely a pay office, with a formal board of audit attached—in so far as it was not a court of common law and equity.

The 1554 reforms promoted the treasurer to real instead of nominal importance; they did even more for the chancellor of the exchequer. After Cromwell had given the office a spell of rather personal importance, Baker—by combining it with the undertreasurership—acquired a standing in each part of the exchequer; this double power was one of the pillars on which the future greatness of the chancellor rested. But the reforms of 1554 had a more striking effect still. Both schedules of annexation frequently mentioned the chancellor as the second officer of the exchequer after the lord treasurer, associating the two, with the barons, in all things to be done in connexion with the new revenue. This was something new for an officer who had hitherto had no standing at the exchequer except as the keeper of its seal. A later agreement between the lord treasurer and Sir Richard Sackville 'referred vnto him [the chancellor] the oversight order & rule of the Court of first ffruictes & Tenthes of all composicions bondes matters & causes of the same'.[1] He thus assumed many new

---

[1] B.M., Lansd. MS. 171, fo. 413 v (cf. Fanshawe, *Practice*, 20). The date cannot be established for certain. The MS. speaks of 'the late Lo: Tre's', and Fanshawe of

duties, a fact which was specially recognized on 10 July 1559 when Winchester and Sackville signed an order authorizing the tellers to pay the chancellor (Sackville) larger fees. Because of the annexations the chancellor 'emongest others is greatlie charged with business and attendaunce bothe in Terme and out of the Terme muche more then the Chauncellors of Theschequire were accustomed', and he was therefore to receive £100 in diets and £40 for attendance in the vacations.[1] The rise of the chancellorship of the exchequer is in a way another illustration of the well-known fact that sixteenth-century administration aimed at a proper division of functions, for it was accompanied by the virtual extrusion of the barons from the administrative work of the exchequer; they turned into common law judges pure and simple.[2] It only remained for Sir Walter Mildmay, in his long tenure (1566–89), to establish the chancellor's practical influence, for James I's chancellors, especially Sir Julius Caesar, to raise him to the dignity of a leading officer of state, and for the treasurership to be put in commission—and the modern office was ready to appear under Sir Robert Walpole.

The exchequer reforms of 1554 thus rounded off the development which began with the revival of strong government in the late fifteenth century. More particularly, they completed the bureaucratic revolution of the 1530's by turning the informal control exercised by Cromwell over a number of co-ordinate departments into a bureaucratic organization exercising a similar control over departments now embodied within it. It was the earlier reforms which really set the pace and defined the aims; Cromwell invented, Winchester developed and completed. Few of the gains in administration made in the previous seventy years were really lost, though the receipt, even when reformed, was still nothing like as flexible as Henry VII's chamber or Cromwell's mastership of the jewels. The reforms were more conservative in intent than in execution, and even the prolonged battery of reactionary exchequer officials hunting

---

Burghley, but it must have been while Sackville was chancellor, i.e. between 1558 and 1566, before Burghley succeeded Winchester. From a reference to privy seals of 2 Elizabeth (B.M., Tit. B. iv, fo. 74), it may well have been 1559.

[1] B.M., Lansd. MS. 168, fo. 174, a certified copy from the original in the receipt.

[2] W. S. Holdsworth, *Hist. Eng. Law*, I. 236.

their fees never reduced the new business altogether to the ancient course of the exchequer. The reforms represented a remarkably efficient compromise between the highly speeded up administration of Thomas Cromwell and the safety of the old ways. They provided the government of Elizabeth with a workmanlike tool in its pursuit of solvency, and seventeenth-century governments with a reasonably efficient basis for further reform in detail. The preservation of such out-dated relics from an illiterate past as tallies, and of involved processes designed to protect the king against his officers, and the officers against their king, was a disadvantage which Winchester and his men did something in their practice to minimize; in their theory and ostensible intent they paid it all a deference which to some extent detracts from their high achievement and convicts them of being less thoroughly efficient than Henry VII had been, or more particularly Thomas Cromwell who laboured to create a new bureaucracy; for both these men had done their best to get round the ponderous 'ancient course of the exchequer' which the reforms of 1554 in some degree served to perpetuate into the nineteenth century.

CHAPTER IV

PRIVY SEAL, SIGNET, AND SECRETARY

The financial administration supplies more, and more detailed, instances of the reforming activity of the early sixteenth century than does any other aspect of government. The story of the clerical organization of the seals is less plain; though the changes are in reality as marked, they are neither so easily seen nor so complete and indisputable when discovered. This word of warning is necessary; it does not, however, alter the fact that there is a story to tell. The clerical organization of the middle ages centred, as has been outlined, on the three seals and their keepers—on great seal, privy seal, and signet, on chancellor, lord privy seal, and principal secretary. Of the three, the great seal was on the face of it the most important which alone could give the royal will the fullest expression; the privy seal acted as a sort of general clearing house, receiving orders from the king's officers and transmitting them for execution; the signet office with the king's secretary at its head did the most confidential work, being nearest to the king and entrusted with the writing of his letters. In actual fact, however, the great seal was by this time so firmly bound in routine and so securely wedded to its rules of warranty that it had no original force left outside matters of law; in the administration of England it was the least significant of the seals, though none the less, in its formal capacity, quite indispensable. The privy seal, on the other hand, was the true centre and mainspring of fifteenth-century government, even though it had long left the household and was therefore to suffer when the revival of active household government under Edward IV and Henry VII enlarged the sphere of the signet. This last seal was yet closely linked with the household, as was its keeper, the secretary, and as late as 1529 it could still seem that the normal medieval development might take place, producing yet another seal of state to take the place of the privy seal. Either that or a simple stagnation of things was to be expected during Wolsey's administration when the state of affairs produced by Edward IV and Henry VII was not sensibly changed.

The organization of chancery and the great seal did not require the attention of a reformer. The fall of Wolsey removed the last great chancellor of the medieval type; his successor, Sir Thomas More, enjoyed legal affairs, and the fact that he could not approve of the policy pursued by the king assisted his retirement from politics. Sir Thomas Audeley, who succeeded him in 1532,[1] was even more evidently nothing but a lawyer and a judge; he had neither the ability—though he was no fool—nor the character to play a major part in government or attempt to rival Cromwell whose rather subservient partisan he was. Despite an occasional relapse, 1529 was the date when the office of chancellor finally fell upon one of its two constituents: the greatest officer of state chose to be the greatest judge in the realm and leave administration to others. The development long marked in the seal at last affected its keeper, and this in turn reflected further on the part played by the seal. The great seal continued to be indispensable, but it also continued to be of no original importance in administration. It had lost its link with the council long before when the latter adopted the privy seal to give effect to its decisions; in the sixteenth century it was also to lose most of its administrative work in connexion with a parliament that after 1529 escaped by degrees from tutelage into independence, at least as far as administration went. The seal's routine was complete and reform of its large organization superfluous; whenever chancery was thereafter attacked by reformers, they concerned themselves with its shortcomings as a court. The legislation of the time necessitated the appointment of two new clerks, but these were not reforms so much as additions.[2] The only trace of a change in the actual organization is to be found in the appearance, in 1536, of a clerk-examiner of letters patent. A warrant delivered into chancery on 29 April 1536 is annotated

[1] Keeper of the great seal, 29 May 1532; lord chancellor, 26 January 1533.

[2] The act of 25 Henry VIII, c. 24, necessitated the appointment of a clerk of dispensations and faculties, to prepare confirmations under the great seal of licenses granted by the archbishop of Canterbury (Lyte, *Great Seal*, 266); the office went to Cromwell's friend and servant Vaughan (C 66/663, m. 37; the abstract in *L.P.* VII. 587, 13, does not make the nature of the appointment plain). Vaughan, not to be handicapped by the fact 'quod...in Curia Cancellarie nostre educatus seu in cursu eiusdem eruditus non existat', was appointed from outside; it is safe to conclude that he owed his office to Cromwell. The office of clerk of the leases (Lyte, *Great Seal*, 274) was granted to John Croke, one of the six clerks, on 11 June 1534 (C 66/665, m. 27); he, too, was a friend of Cromwell's who in 1529 appointed him an executor of his will (Merriman, I. 63, n. 1).

'R Cupper exa[minavi]t paten",[1] and Cupper's name thereafter becomes ever more frequent in the files. His duties presumably resembled those of the examiners of letters patent first officially appointed in 1547.[2] He first appeared in the chancery while Cromwell was master of the rolls; it was pointed out above that the master of the rolls was in practice head of the administrative side of chancery,[3] so that this reform may conceivably have been sponsored by Cromwell.

Apart from these minor details, however, chancery pursued its even course: formal though important duties in administration and a highly dynamic activity in jurisdiction were signal indications of its true role in modern England. Not so, however, the lesser seals. In the ministry of Cromwell, in the period of administrative revolution which marked the 1530's, both the signet, the latest arrival among the royal seals, and the all-pervading privy seal entered upon the decline which in the end reduced them to archaic elements in government, served by the ill-paid deputies of sinecure clerks and maintained in a pointless existence by the forces of tradition and vested interests.

1. *Cromwell and the lesser seals*

The two lesser seals were the subject of deliberate reform on two occasions in the time of Cromwell's ministry. His personal responsibility is indubitable in the orders which he issued for the regulation of the signet office on 20 June 1534;[4] it is less easily demonstrated for the act of 1536 for the clerks of the signet and privy seal.[5] The signet office had developed a fairly precise structure in the fifteenth century. The number of clerks had become fixed at four; there were always a few underclerks 'serving a kind of apprenticeship', and there may have been servants to 'do the rough work of the office'.[6] However, its organization was far from complete. Compared, for instance, with any of the departments of finance, it was simply

---

[1] C 82/708/41. Cupper was neither a six clerk nor a clerk of the petty bag in 1535 (SP 1:105, fo. 24); that he was a chancery clerk is proved by a note addressed to him on the back of a warrant in 1540 (C 82/772/2).

[2] Lyte, *Great Seal*, 266.　　　　　　[3] Above, pp. 129 ff.

[4] DL 42/133, fos. 1–1 v (cf. App. II, D, p. 439).

[5] 27 Henry VIII, c. 11.　　　　　　[6] Otway Ruthven, *King's Secretary*, 113.

a collection of individual clerks, doing their work in common and in attendance on the secretary whose special staff they were. Even such servants as there were appear to have belonged to the clerks individually rather than to the office as a whole: Wolsey permitted each signet clerk to stable three horses and bed two servants in the royal household.[1] This lack of proper bureaucratic form was, as a matter of fact, largely due to their remaining part of the household. When Cromwell took the office of secretary, and therefore charge of the signet and its clerks, he seems to have discovered quickly that his staff were not as familiar with order and routine as they ought to have been. The rules which he laid down only three months after entering upon office—evidently a case of the new broom sweeping clean—did not, of course, attempt anything so revolutionary as to break the household link of the clerks, but they did attempt to organize the four clerks into a genuine office, to give them the equipment of a bureaucratic organization, and to make them work according to a proper office routine.

In the first place, Cromwell took care that the work of the signet should not suffer through the inattention or unavoidable absence of its clerks. Two of the four clerks were to be on duty every month, beginning with Thomas Derby and William Paget on 1 August, to be followed by Thomas Wriothesley and John Godsalve in September. 'Acording to the olde ordre and custume vsede hertofore in the saide office', they were to employ themselves in dispatching the king's business, and also in seeing to the furnishing of the king's hall, a reminder that both secretary and signet office were still, in theory, linked with the household; the hall was, however, by this time the most formal and, as it were, official, part of the court where suitors of the crown awaited their turn. Next, the fees received for the sealing of documents were to be pooled, and one of the clerks was to be appointed to receive them. Clerks not on duty were not to interfere with the work of those whose turn it was and who were to have the 'advauntage' of all writing done. All documents passing the signet were to be registered in a special book by the clerk in attendance, and at the end of each month the total entered was to be used in calculating the share of the sealing fees due to each clerk. The clerks

[1] *H.O.* 198.

were to see to it that no unauthorized person did any writing in the king's hall, and no letter was to pass the signet without being examined by one of them who was to sign his name on the document as proof of his examination. Finally, it was appointed that at the end of every month the incoming clerks were to attend on the secretary to receive their share of the fees, and that they were to take up their duties on the first day of their month. There were, then, orders that dealt with the clerks' duties: a duty roster was to be adhered to, and clerks were prohibited from working for the signet during their month off duty, so that all the officials concerned should share fairly in the writing fees which made up the better part of their income and which, unlike the sealing fees, were the perquisite of the man who had actually done the work. Perhaps it was for the same reason that outsiders were to be prevented from writing in the hall. It was also, however, a point of efficiency so to organize the staff that some clerks should always be available for extraordinary duties while the routine work was not neglected, and similar care for efficiency was shown in the demand for the signatures of the examining clerks. Secondly, Cromwell was concerned with the fees taken in the office. A pointed distinction between writing and sealing fees allotted the former to the clerk who did the writing,[1] while the latter were to be put into a common pool. The last order brought together these two aspects; the taking over at the end of each month was to be combined with the paying out of each clerk's share of the sealing fees. Cromwell wished to increase efficiency in the signet office by ensuring regular attendance and preventing slackness at work, while at the same time safeguarding the interests and regularizing the takings of the clerks.

The signing of documents by the clerks responsible for their preparation was no new idea. By the reign of Edward IV signet letters were commonly signed, though the signatory might be the secretary or an underclerk in place of the clerk himself; letters to the chancery remained as a rule unsigned while those to the privy seal were signed.[2] By the time of Cromwell's immediate predecessors both classes of documents were normally signed.[3] On the other hand,

---

[1] If a clerk's servant wrote the document (as is contemplated in the fifth rule), his master presumably took the fee.　　　　[2] Otway Ruthven, *King's Sec.* 26 f.

[3] PSO 2/4, files for 21–23 Henry VIII; C 82/616/2, 629/6, 653/18, 666/13, 669/5, 679/4.

many documents to which the signet was affixed went without a clerk's signature, in particular the many warrants and letters under the sign manual and signet which are strewn over the files of chancery warrants. It may be supposed that a bill signed by the king was considered sufficiently authenticated. Yet even this practice was not without exception, and a signet bill is occasionally found with the sign manual at the top and a clerk's signature at the bottom. One file of chancery warrants, for instance, contains two signet bills with the sign manual and a clerk's signature, authorizing the issue of a congé d'élire and of the royal assent to the election of an abbot;[1] in the same file there are three other documents for the same purpose which but for the absence of a clerk's signature are identical with those first mentioned.[2] All these warrants are made up in the form proper for signet warrants, with the address on the outside and the heading 'by the king'. There seems no reason why John Godsalve should have signed two of them and not the other three, and in all probability there was no reason. Cromwell's ordinance turned a normal practice into a standing regulation, and after he had made it signet warrants both to the privy seal and to other departments were always signed. However, it must not be supposed that there had been much irregularity before; the exceptions which have been cited were apparently confined to documents rather different from the routine work of petitions embodied in letters under the signet.

On the other hand, the interesting idea of a tour of duty appears to have been new. The orders were given on 20 July; the system was to come into operation on the 1st of the following August. It was described, not as a general principle, but with specific reference to certain named persons, and mention was even made of the advanced age of Henry Conway which rendered it necessary to join two other clerks with him, the three to be considered as two for purposes of organization. All this suggests an *ad hoc* enactment. Some such organization was highly desirable, if only because signet clerks were not used only for their routine duties, the writing of warrants to the privy seal; it was as well to have some of the clerks free from these duties and available for such other tasks as the writing of the king's correspondence or the drafting of council and parliamentary

---

[1] C 82/701/8, 13.   [2] *Ibid.* 701/6, 7, 14.

business, while making sure that the office routine did not suffer. Moreover, the growth, about this time, of a group of assistant writing clerks probably made the constant attention of all four clerks superfluous.[1]

However, despite the undoubted desire for the advantages of a rigid organization, the order was not carried out to the full. The information supplied by the few signet warrants surviving for Cromwell's time[2] can be augmented from the larger number of petitions addressed to the king, signed by him, and used as warrants to the privy seal and chancery, a number of which were endorsed by the signet clerk on duty who sent them off. A bundle of such petitions shows that Wriothesley was on duty during certain months when by the regulations he should not have been. He seems to have adhered to the roster in 1534 and 1535 but was, for instance, endorsing documents in June 1536, not one of his months; after that, his attendance on the signet constantly broke the rule.[3] The chancery files, too, indicate that the new regulations were only obeyed at the start. Thus Paget was on duty in February 1535,[4] and Godsalve and Wriothesley worked in March and May 1535,[5] which accorded with the rota laid down in July 1534. But Wriothesley appears also in October 1535, which marks a break in the system,[6] and when God-salve is found endorsing petitions in April, May, June, and July 1536, it must be concluded that the duty roster had been abandoned.[7] The reason is not far to seek. With Wriothesley (as we shall see)[8] practically doing the work of an assistant secretary of state, Derby appointed to a clerkship of the council in 1533 and active as clerk of the privy council in 1538,[9] and Paget away on embassies for a great

---

[1] It is very difficult to deduce anything from the handwritings on signet warrants because clerical hands in both the signet and privy seal offices varied little. It is certain, however, that during this period we find both warrants apparently written by the clerk who signed them, and warrants written by someone else. The names under a warrant are always genuine signatures, like those on privy seals and unlike those on chancery documents.

[2] There are none for the privy seal and ten in the chancery files.

[3] PSO 2/4. All but four of the thirty-four documents in the file for 25–29 Henry VIII are endorsed by Wriothesley; one bears Godsalve's signature, and three are not endorsed at all.

[4] C 82/693/25.
[5] Ibid. 694/12, 698/11.
[6] Ibid. 703/7–9.
[7] Ibid. 727/40, 46, 728/18, 23, 31.
[8] Cf. below, pp. 307 ff.
[9] Cf. below, pp. 334 f.

part of the period under review,[1] the routine work of the office had to be done by whoever happened to be available. In practice this generally meant Godsalve. On the whole, it therefore appears that Cromwell's order was adhered to for a year or so and had then to be given up because the multifarious employments of the signet clerks made it impracticable. There may at first have been some hope in Cromwell's mind that he might be able to prevent the clerks of the signet from being employed outside the signet office in duties which retained them for more than a month at a time; if this was so, he had to acknowledge himself defeated by the necessities of the king's service and the tempting advantages of using clerks so fully dependent on himself—the secretary—for work which might otherwise have been done by men (for instance, household officers) over whom he had less control. With the failure of the duty roster, the most far-reaching of Cromwell's attempts to further the bureaucratic organization of the signet office went by the board. However, the idea of such a parcelling out of the work survived, being reasonable in itself, and in 1557 the clerks themselves came to a permanent arrangement. By then the work that actually fell to the share of a clerk had dwindled to such an extent that it was thought sufficient for one of them to be on duty to supervise the writing clerks, and consequently every clerk was to confine his attendance on the signet to three months in the year.[2]

The problem of signet registers is complicated by the fire of 1619 which destroyed most of the early signet and privy seal records.[3] Like the privy seal office, the signet office never made enrolments, but it seems to have kept warrants and dockets as early as the fifteenth century.[4] No registers survive earlier than Cromwell's order, though this is no proof that none were kept. On the other hand, the phrasing of his order suggests the introduction of a new rule: it speaks of 'a boke to be made for that purpose', and the emphasis is on the need for a record of documents sealed to enable the fees to be pooled and divided at the end of each month.[5] The keeping of a register was therefore considered necessary because of the division of labour and the details about fees which were laid down

---

[1] Cf. *D.N.B.* xv. 60.   [2] Evans, *Principal Secretary*, 198.   [3] *Ibid.* 199 n.
[4] Otway Ruthven, *King's Sec.* 114 f.   [5] For the full text cf. App. II, D, p. 440.

in other parts of the same direction: it was an additional order emerging from Cromwell's other orders. For that reason it very probably constituted an innovation. Although no signet registers survive for the period of Cromwell's secretaryship, he himself, very early in his career, possessed a book of all documents which had passed that seal 'since the signet came to my hand',[1] so that this part of his orders seems to have been carried out immediately. The earliest register which we possess is that of Ralph Sadler which begins on 1 April 1540.[2] The keeping of registers became essential when, in 1540, two secretaries were appointed each of whom was to know what passed the other's signet;[3] perhaps it was only then that signet clerks began regularly to record the documents they sealed. All that is certain is that Cromwell wished to add the keeping of entry books to the organization of the signet, that he himself had among his papers a book of writings sealed with the signet, and that such registers were kept by his successors.

Something of a problem is suggested by the very book in which Cromwell's orders for the signet office are preserved.[4] It contains a mixture of things. The fly-leaf is covered with attempts at the signature of John Godsalve, one of the clerks of the signet, and the book is nearly all in his hand. Cromwell's orders are followed by copies of grants and the like (fos. 2–16 v), the first two of which are headed in large letters 'De indigena fienda pro extraneo et liberis' and 'Aliter de indigena pro extraneo fienda'; some others are given marginal descriptions, as 'Licencia', 'Nonresid'', 'Plea', 'Presentacio'. In many cases the grantee's name is given by initials only and the dating clauses are not transcribed. This section is therefore, not a book of copies kept for record, but a precedent book. Many of the documents to which the entries refer were issued a short time before Cromwell's order. Thus there is the denization of Luke Hornbolt, the painter (fo. 4) of 22 June 1534,[5] Christopher Mount's annuity (fo. 12) of 26 June 1534,[6] and the wardship granted to Thomas

---

[1] *L.P.* VII. 923 (xxxv).   [2] B.M., Add. MS. 35,818.

[3] Cf. the warrant of their appointment, *L.P.* XV. 437.

[4] DL 42/133.   [5] *L.P.* VII. 922 (14).

[6] *Ibid.* 922 (25). This is annotated in the register as 'delyuered to Mr M'es Seruant the xjth of ffebruarij', which suggests that a grant might easily take five months to go from the signet office to the chancery.

Wentworth (fo. 12) on 13 May 1534.[1] It follows that some of the
entries were made at the same time as Cromwell's orders were
entered, the former having perhaps been transcribed from an earlier
book. When Godsalve made up his private precedent book he would
naturally preface it with the latest (and as far as we know, the only)
departmental orders. The precedents are followed, after a few blank
pages, by a register of documents signed by the king, with notes of
delivery to various recipients and covering the period from 9 January
1541 to 30 September 1543 (fos. 23 ff.). This part is clearly the
register of an individual signet clerk. It does not contain only
documents sealed and paid for; petitions presented to and signed
by the king come within its scope and these were not sealed. While
it is not, therefore, exactly the kind of register which Cromwell
envisaged in his orders, it is evidence of the same desire for the
keeping of records which, as far as we know, Cromwell inspired in
the administration. In Pollard's words, his 'recording habit...was
inveterate and invincible'.[2]

The other orders could not by their nature leave any trace behind
them. But together with those that did they show that in organizing
the signet office Cromwell was particularly concerned with its
efficiency and a fair distribution of its fees. The routine work of the
office was not to suffer neglect because signet clerks were habitually
and with increasing necessity employed on business of state by the
secretary, their departmental head, who was about to extend his
field of activities so greatly. The careful preservation of departmental archives was another most important point in rendering
bureaucratic organization complete. As for the fees, it was desirable
that all clerks should be able to make an honest living from their
appointment, in the interests of the clerks themselves, in the interests of suitors to the seal, and for the sake of harmony in the
office. Cromwell's ideas bore fruit, some of them possibly at once
and others later.

No similar orders for the privy seal office survive, if ever they were
made; it may, however, be presumed that Cromwell as lord privy
seal desired to see similar efficiency and fairness there, too, the more
so as he was as personally attentive to the one office as to the other.

---

[1] *L.P.* VII. 761 (20).   [2] Pollard, *Wolsey*, 67, n. 1.

As secretary he countersigned signet warrants, continuing a practice certainly common under Gardiner;[1] more important, he took so much personal interest in the signet office that he countersigned, in July 1534 (long before he was lord privy seal), a privy seal for the grant of an annuity to John Godsalve,[2] and later a warrant appointing a signet clerk was addressed to him by name and title.[3] No habitual practice of counter-signatures prevailed at the privy seal, but some warrants under that seal bear his name beneath a clerk's, and this is evidence of an attention to business which would be unusual for anyone but Cromwell. He countersigned a privy seal written and signed by a signet clerk, presumably to cover the irregularity;[4] the clerk's name was erased and Cromwell wrote his over the blank space on a pardon to the bishop of Lincoln for letting prisoners escape;[5] he signed the warrant for the restitution of Bonner's temporalities at Hereford (perhaps as vicegerent rather than as lord privy seal), and a privy seal to the collectors of the wool custom in London on behalf of the merchants of the staple.[6] Even clearer proof of Cromwell's personal activity in the office is to be found in two privy seals dispatched respectively from Thruxton (Hampshire) and Donnington Castle (Berkshire) in August 1539 which were signed, not by a clerk of the privy seal, but by Thomas Soulemont, Cromwell's private secretary, 'in absentia', as he was careful to add, 'clericorum priuati sigilli de mandato domini priuati sigilli'.[7] Cromwell was travelling with the court at the time,[8] and while the privy seal office was fixed at Westminster (where it had been since about 1360)[9] the seal was with its keeper and the work went forward away from the office by his personal intervention. This detailed attention to the business of both the seals and their offices whose

---

[1] Gardiner signed nearly all extant signet warrants of his secretaryship, and the practice had become sufficiently established for a deputy to act for him during his absence; on 22 March 1532 Edward Foxe signed a warrant 'in absentia Reuerendi domini Secretarij' (C 82/653/18). All but one of Cromwell's extant warrants bear his signature: *ibid*. 674/4 (this, as is pencilled on the document, belongs to 1534, not 1533 as its date pretends), 681/26–7, 688/5, 700/28, 701/1; the exception is 700/14.

[2] *Ibid*. 685/33. [3] *L.P.* XIV. II. 435 (2).

[4] C 82/743/2. [5] *Ibid*. 748/10.

[6] *Ibid*. 749/55; E 159/318, Communia, Easter Term, Recorda, m. 13.

[7] C 82/757/9, 13.

[8] He dated a letter from Donnington Castle on 16 August 1539 (*L.P.* XIV. II. 83).

[9] Tout, *Chapters*, v. 72 f.

more than nominal head he was must be remembered when the second great measure of reform is considered.

The act of 1536, 'concernyng the Clerkes of the Signet and Privie Seale',[1] began with a statement of the principle underlying it: clerks of the signet and privy seal had no wages except the profits of their labours, and it was therefore desirable to prevent their being cheated of these. It was then enacted that from 15 April 1536 no manner of writing was to pass the great seals of England, Ireland, the duchy of Lancaster, and the principality of Wales, or by process out of the exchequer, unless it had first been examined by the king's principal secretary or a clerk of the signet. Within eight days of receiving a warrant signed by the hand of the king, the master of the wards, the general surveyors, or any other royal officer, the clerk of the signet was to make out a warrant to the keeper of the privy seal, such warrant to be subscribed by him and sealed with the signet. Within eight days again, the clerk of the privy seal was to make out his warrant to the lord chancellor or other officer whose province it was to carry out the instructions. The penalty for disobedience was to be £10, half to the king and half to the informer. Immediate warrants[2] were permitted in exceptional cases, but fees were still to be paid to the signet and privy seal, on pain of a like fine. Provisos excepted some routine or minor matters, and a scale of fees payable to the clerks of the signet and privy seal for the writing of documents was appointed. Here again, a penalty of £10 was imposed on any clerk taking higher fees. Finally, there were some more provisos, the most important of which permitted the lord chancellor to remit the fees of all three seals 'as hath ben accustumed'.

The system here described was not altogether new, and the significance of the statute will be better understood after considera-tion of an earlier draft, much longer, more detailed, and with some important differences from the act as passed.[3] That it was prepared for that particular act and session is certain from the general agree-

---

[1] 27 Henry VIII, c. 11.

[2] Immediate warrants were petitions addressed to the crown and approved by the sign manual which were used as warrants to the great seal, thus cutting out the signet and privy seal.

[3] SP 1:101, fos. 292–302. Listed in *L.P.* x. 246 (5).

ment of the provisions and from the mention of the date on which it
was to come into operation as 27 Henry VIII (April 1535 to April
1536), with the day and month left blank. There must have been
a draft between this and the final form, for the scale of fees, which
mentions the same kind of documents as does the act itself, leaves
blanks where the amounts ought to be. The biggest difference is in
the preamble. This establishes that the act of 1536 gave statutory
force to a customary practice, laid down (though this is not mentioned
in act or draft) at least as early as 1444.[1] It has been doubtful whether
the council ordinance of that year had been observed and was merely
being re-enacted in 1536, or whether the practice had been forgotten
and was stated afresh in this statute.[2] The preamble of the draft
makes it plain that the system of 1444 was supposed to be in working
order, and that the authors of the act knew themselves to be but
confirming an older practice which, however, was not being well
observed; they declared the statute to be necessary because of late
'many malicious, lewde, and crafty persons' had managed to commit frauds by exploiting the non-observance of the established rule.
It was further asserted that the kings of England had heretofore
decreed that nothing should pass their great seals or out of the
exchequer by way of levying forfeitures or payment of sheriff's
rewards without

furst beyng examyned by their principall Secretaryes as personages moost
nere of their moost honorable counsaill and which by dayly and contynuall
view and sight ought best to knowe the true caractes and Signes of their
moost noble handes.[3]

The secretary was to give the warrant signed by the king to a clerk
of the signet who would keep it and write a warrant to the lord privy
seal. He, in his turn, would examine the warrant and leave it with
a clerk of the privy seal who would make out a warrant to the
chancellors of England, Ireland, or the duchy, or to the treasurer and
chamberlains of the exchequer. The procedure is here set out at
greater length than in the act, with details which show that the
secretary and lord privy seal were expected to carry out their
departmental duties in person.

The body of the draft did not differ greatly from the act as passed.

[1] Lyte, *Great Seal*, 90.   [2] Evans, *Princ. Sec.* 195 ff.   [3] SP 1:101, fos. 292 v–293.

It specially prohibited all unauthorized persons from making any writing by warrant of the king's sign manual, and from procuring the passage of such a document, which recalls point five of Cromwell's orders to the signet office; chancery clerks passing a grant by immediate warrant were afterwards to obtain the usual signet and privy seal warrants within three months; according to the draft, clerks of the signet and privy seal were to act within one month after receiving their warrants, and not eight days, as in the act. Apart from these minor points, the main changes made during the revision of the draft touched the angle from which the problem was viewed. The draft intended to abolish fraud and abuse and was mainly concerned with devising a fool-proof system of bureaucratic organization; almost as an afterthought, and with a special brief preamble explaining how desirable it was for the clerks to get an honest living from their work and for suitors not to be overcharged, it appended a scale of fees. The afterthought was so marked that at first only the principle was inserted without the details of figures which presumably still needed working out. In the event, the scale of fees became the core of the act which was ostensibly passed in order to assure the clerks of their income.

This different attitude is important. It would appear that an act designed to reform the bureaucracy was so amended in the result that its first purpose became the protection of that bureaucracy. One obvious reason for this was the fact that if the strict rules were not obeyed—if grants were made by immediate warrant to the chancery —the clerks of the signet and privy seal were liable to lose their fees, and (as we shall see) the practice of these years did nothing to discourage immediate warrants. It is likely, therefore, that the section of the act which proved of the greatest importance at the time was section iv which ordered fees to be paid at every stage, even for immediate warrants. Suitors were, in fact, made to pay fees at every stage even when they obtained an immediate warrant, as is shown by a signed petition delivered into chancery on 2 September 1540 which has on its dorse a brief note from a clerk of the signet to a clerk of the chancery, asking him 'to passe this byll by this warraunt, receyving the ffees for our office and the privie seale for the same'.[1] A man

---

[1] C 82/772/2.

whose grant passed by immediate warrant would thus pay a lump sum into chancery, and the signet and privy seal clerks would draw their share from there. It may also have been thought wiser not to confront a parliament, which undoubtedly contained many who had at one time or another profited from immediate warrants, with a statement that they were 'malicious, lewde, and crafty persons' who, if they had not actually forged the king's sign manual, had been the cause of 'manyfold other enormities and inconveniences'. Hence the shifting of the emphasis. The alteration which reduced the time allowed to a clerk for writing his further warrant to a quarter of the time granted originally was obviously in the interests of suitors and may have been made to placate opposition. However, despite the interest which attaches to this change of mind, fundamentally draft and act did the same thing. This act of 1536 mattered, not because it safeguarded the interests of the clerks, but because it gave statutory force to the established order of making a grant under the great seal. Though, on the face of it, its purpose was to prevent people from evading the fees due to the clerks by taking their signed bills straight to the chancery, administrative efficiency and the prevention of fraud remained as much in the minds of the framers of the statute as the payment of fees.

The most important aspect of the act remains to be discussed. In laying down a sequence of seals through which grants of the crown under the great seal had to pass, the statute did no more than confirm an ancient and supposedly existing practice. But it did something quite new when it decreed that orders from other departments of state, and orders to seals other than the great seal, were also to observe a rigid routine of this kind. Officers like the master of the wards or the general surveyors, even we must suppose the council itself, who had hitherto had their commands authenticated by means of a simple fiat directed to the privy seal, are explicitly instructed to approach the signet instead; the office of that seal will see to it that the necessary privy seal is issued. The privy seal retains its 'original' force: it alone is fit to do certain things. But between it and the king's officers the signet is now interpolated, even as it stands between the privy seal and the king's bounty. The meaning of all this is that the signet has come of age: it has 'gone out of court'. The common fate of medieval seals has overtaken it; in the theory of this statute the signet has followed great and privy seal out of the king's personal administration and has entered that of the state. It has ceased to be the king's private seal and is instead to act as the first of the seals of state, reserving thereby to the secretary and his staff the first and most important scrutiny of all orders, whether administrative or concerned with the bestowal of the royal patronage. Owing to other developments of the time, discussed below,[1] the significance of this step has been overlooked; as things turned out in the end, all matters except grants under the great seal evaded the competence of the lesser seals, and the act of 1536 mattered only inasmuch as it dealt with such grants. It would not, however, be right to ignore its more original intentions. It not only standardized a routine of office procedure; it also planned to substitute the signet for the privy seal as the central seal of administration. This may be differently expressed by saying that as far as the act was concerned the signet ceased to be part of household government: once again we meet the cardinal principle of the administrative revolution of the 1530's. In view of what we shall have to say about the new activity of the secretary, it is important to remember that at this point it was intended to concentrate formal control over administrative processes in his hands through his control of the signet.

It must be said that in our view the responsibility for this act and its intentions can be assigned. Yet Cromwell's part in it, though perhaps it hardly needs proving, ought not to be taken too readily for granted. It cannot be proved by any of the more direct and convincing methods. Cromwell was in charge of the signet and privy seal, and it has been seen that he took this responsibility seriously: it is therefore highly unlikely that an act concerned with these offices could have been passed, at the height of his power, without the active participation of the man who above all others interested himself in the details of parliamentary legislation.[2] The fact that the earlier draft was so greatly revised before it passed is no proof that

---

[1] Pp. 293 ff.

[2] The evidence for this interest cannot be discussed here at length; it lies in many an entry in his remembrances and in the corrections which he made in the drafts of bills. This kind of activity is one of the few agreed points about Cromwell which there is no reason to doubt (cf. Merriman, I. 102; Fisher, *Pol. Hist.* v. 296).

it did not also originate with Cromwell; some acts changed almost out of recognition in a long process of redrafting under his hands.[1] On the other hand, it is of course possible that the first proposal came from someone else, and that Cromwell confined himself to the change of approach which has been noticed. However that may be, it is inconceivable, on the grounds alleged, that Cromwell should not have been squarely behind the act as passed; it ought to be considered as one of his administrative measures.

The case gains strength from a comparison of the act with Cromwell's orders to the signet office. The statute itself repeated his injunction to the clerks to sign their warrants, and with its scale of fees it supplemented the earlier direction for the payment of signet clerks. The draft provided a further link when, rather needlessly, it guarded against unauthorized persons doing the work of the clerks, recalling the purport of the fifth of Cromwell's orders. This, one may conjecture, was one of the clerks' special grievances which they had drummed into the secretary. Both the orders and the act did two things: they attempted to reform the bureaucratic organization on more bureaucratic lines and to protect the interests of the civil service. They appear as part of one policy—the policy pursued by Thomas Cromwell towards the secretarial offices. The sequence of warrants established by the act was nothing new; in the manner of Tudor statutes it enforced by the law what had hitherto been more or less powerful custom. Nevertheless, the very fact of parliamentary enactment meant that a more definite and more businesslike organization was to be observed in the routine of the signet and the privy seal offices. Moreover, but for the revolutionary discarding of central seals in the control of the administration which followed upon the reforms of Cromwell's later years, the act would also have been seen to mark the triumph of the signet over the privy seal.

The two documents have one other point in common: they are both interested in the seals only as stages in the process by which documents are issued under other seals, and they pay no attention to their independent existence. All the orders about writing and sealing fees could only apply to documents in any of the bureaucratic chains,

---

[1] For an example of this sort of thing, cf. my 'Evolution of a Reformation Statute', *E.H.R.* LXIV. 174 ff.

for when the signet was used for authenticating the king's own correspondence no fees would, of course, fall due. The act was even more single-minded: it attempted to deprive the privy seal of all its independent and original work, and treated both seals simply as instruments which had to be affixed to documents giving effect to decisions taken elsewhere and to be transmitted elsewhere again. This might imply that the lesser seals had ceased, or nearly ceased, to be used in an independent capacity; on the other hand, it might merely mean that Cromwell directed his organizing activities to that part of the work of the offices which was most obviously organizable and in need of organization. Which of these answers is correct can only be established by an investigation of the seals in both capacities during the 1530's. It may, however, be said at once that this concentration on the formal duties of the seals accurately forecast the future; though the keeper of the signet, the secretary, became the leading executive minister of the crown, the signet never in fact replaced the privy seal as the central seal of administration, and though the lord privy seal governed England for five years his departmental seal was to decline even in that period. The day of seals was past; government now relied on personal action and the signed letter rather than the formal processes of a less than semi-literate society.[1]

2. *The signet*

We will begin by discussing the signet and its use in the 1530's, and in the first place the signet as a seal of warranty to other departments of state. In theory all grants under the great seal required a signet warrant at an early stage in the proceedings; either the process was started by such a warrant, or one was made out on the basis of a petition approved and signed by the king. Such petitions are technically known as signed bills, but as that term includes other documents signed by the king and used as warrants we shall here always refer to them as signed petitions. If the theory were right—the theory which was elaborated in the preamble to the draft of the act

---

[1] This was not an entirely new thing but can be traced back, like most of the developments in the offices of the lesser seals, to the reign of Richard II (Tout, *Chapters*, v. 60 f.); nevertheless, Tudor practice operated on so vastly increased a scale and so much more consciously that in effect it constituted an innovation.

of 1536—we should expect to find that warrants for the privy seal were mostly warrants under the signet even before that act gave statutory sanction to the procedure; we should certainly expect such warrants after 1536. However, the extant warrants to the privy seal tell a different story.[1]

For the year 21 Henry VIII (1528–9) there survives one file of eighty-two documents, for 22 Henry VIII one of sixty-five, for 23 Henry VIII one of twenty-one, and for the years 25–29 Henry VIII one of thirty-four. This in itself indicates that some of the records are missing; the year 24 Henry VIII is quite unrepresented, and the others are far from complete. The year 25 Henry VIII alone, for instance, produced among the chancery warrants 196 privy seals each of which ought to be matched by a corresponding signet warrant in the privy seal files. The fragmentary state of the record prevents full and final conclusions, but even so it justifies some reliable though partial deductions. To begin with, there is a rapid decrease in the number and regularity of the documents preserved by the privy seal as we approach the time of Cromwell's secretaryship, while their composition is even more suggestive. Of the eighty-two documents in the first file fifty-six are warrants under the signet; in the second file the number is forty-three out of sixty-five, and in the third sixteen out of twenty-one. In general terms it therefore appears that the privy seal could expect about two-thirds of its warrants to be sealed with the signet. The fourth file, which contains what remains for Cromwell's secretaryship, does not include one genuine signet warrant. There are three signed bills sealed with the signet (nos. 7, 17, 18); even they differ from others of their kind in being endorsed with the place and date of issue by a signet clerk. Otherwise the file contains only signed petitions, forwarded as warrants and endorsed with a note about their being dispatched to the privy seal, with place and date. These notes are all signed by, or in the hands of, signet clerks. Before Cromwell's time the forwarding of signed petitions as warrants for the privy seal only was so unusual that but one survives in the files analysed.[2] For the last two years of Cromwell's tenure of office there are no warrants preserved at all. But with his

---

[1] The warrants for the reign are in PSO 2/4.
[2] File 21 Henry VIII, no. 119.

fall and the appointment of the earl of Southampton as lord privy seal a great change comes over the files. From June 1540 onwards, warrants to the privy seal consist of monthly bundles, usually with covering notes signed by a clerk of the privy seal, of warrants under the signet and nothing else. From that moment, therefore, the records assume the appearance which a theoretical knowledge of the procedure would lead one to expect.

It is, of course, possible that all these facts are merely the result of the accidental preservation of some records and destruction of others, but that would be to suppose too large a working of coincidence. The absence of signet warrants under Cromwell could be so explained, but hardly the satisfactory and complete survival of such warrants after his time. Probably we have here something like a true picture a little distorted by the absence of what is lost, but yet essentially correct. It seems less incredible that there were very few signet warrants to the privy seal from 1534 to 1540, than that just those warrants should be lost when so many were preserved before and after that period. It may therefore be suggested that the evidence permits the tentative conclusion that the signet practically ceased to be used as a seal of warranty to the privy seal during Cromwell's supremacy. The signet office continued a practice begun in the last year of Gardiner's secretaryship, when Cromwell was often deputizing: it forwarded the signed petitions received from the secretary directly to the privy seal, and it was the rule that the signet clerk carrying out this duty should endorse the petition to that effect.[1] At the same time such carelessness prevailed about the keeping of warrants that none at all survive for the better part of the period when Cromwell was lord privy seal, unless indeed such care was used that signet warrants were kept separate and lost in bulk, an improbable contingency which may be allowed but can never be proved or disproved. All this happened at a time when it had only recently been enacted by parliament that the traditional routine should be carefully observed.

There can be only one explanation: the personality and personal

[1] The fact that the file preserved at the privy seal office contains almost only the name of Wriothesley does seem to be due to an accident of preservation. Signed petitions which got as far as the files of chancery warrants are endorsed also by other clerks of the signet.

government of Cromwell. In charge as he was, and in strict control, of signet and privy seal, he found it unnecessary to insist on the details of the bureaucratic process; what counted, as it so often does in a government dominated by one man, were efficiency and speed, and not the letter of the law. Since, as has been shown, fees continued to be paid even when the regulations were evaded by the use of immediate warrants, the ostensible purpose of the act was not necessarily offended by the practice of cutting down the administrative process. There was the less need for attention to the regular routine, and, as far as the evidence goes, it was ignored freely enough. Signet clerks were frequently employed on other work, for their chief was so much busier than he had ever been, and the signet was, temporarily, used only rarely for its proper function of authorizing letters under the privy seal. That this was due to Cromwell alone is clear from the sudden change which occurred at his fall. His successors could not take the risks which were endemic in his conception of his office, and when he fell the system which had been given the authority of parliament was at last put into full operation. It was not worked out after Cromwell but under him, for it appeared fully grown immediately he had gone. Secretaries Wriothesley and Sadler could insist on the writing of warrants instead of the forwarding of petitions, and the new lord privy seal could have them carefully filed, only because the system had already been organized. Despite the irregular practice of the 1530's, it was the regular theory propounded in those years that really mattered. The first was incidental to Cromwell and vanished with him; the organization stood.

The privy seal office was not the only place to which warrants under the signet might be directed. Sometimes it would be bypassed, and signet warrants made their way into the chancery files; but their number is small. How they reached their present whereabouts is not clear. When one is addressed to the chancellor, it is of course certain that the privy seal was being left out deliberately, but there is only one such warrant in the ten years with which we are concerned;[1] all the others found among the chancery warrants are

---

[1] C 82/653/18. This warrant (22 March 1532) was signed by Derby as clerk of the signet, and by Edward Foxe in Gardiner's absence, which may account for the irregularity of sending it straight to the chancellor.

properly addressed to the lord privy seal and order him to write warrants for the great seal. Most—not all—bear the livery clause, giving place and date of their being handed into chancery, which is proof that they are filed in the correct place. None exist for the period of Cromwell's tenure of the privy seal, but there are some that he countersigned as secretary.[1] Perhaps this ought to make us qualify what was said above about the virtual cessation of the signet as a seal of warranty, but the small number of warrants surviving even outside the privy seal records leaves that conclusion essentially untouched. Probably, the normal procedure was employed more frequently at the beginning of Cromwell's secretaryship, and it decreased as his government became more personal and un-challenged. That is what one would expect, and these signet war-rants in the chancery files for 1534-5 support such a view. Why some warrants addressed to the lord privy seal should have been delivered into chancery is a question to which no answer can be given: none is to be found in their subject-matter, nor do we possess any means of discovering whether they passed the privy seal office and what happened to them there if they did. They appear to be freaks, due perhaps to pressure of work at the privy seal, or simply to chance. They were not rarer or more common than usual in the 1530's.

Among the warrants to the exchequer in this period there is one under the signet. It is dated 7 August 1538, and is actually cast in the form of a privy seal.[2] However, it is 'yeven vnder our signet' and signed by Godsalve, and therefore a genuine signet warrant, which proves that warrants under that seal might be addressed directly to the treasurer and chamberlains of the exchequer. Its solitary state also proves how very unusual such a cutting out of the privy seal was. A somewhat different story is told by the warrants to the duchy of Lancaster. There signet warrants were not uncommon in the earlier years of the reign,[3] but none can be found after June 1532.[4] Under Cromwell, warrants to the duchy were, with a few

---

[1] C 82/674/4, 681/26-7, 688/5, 700/14 (of July 1535 but not signed by Cromwell), 701/1.

[2] E 404/101.

[3] Thus there are twelve in DL 12/11, between 1509 and 1515.

[4] DL 12/8/24, a draft patent of 7 June 1532, marked 'per warrantum sub Signeto'.

exceptions, either signed petitions or privy seals; after him, the latter clearly predominated. The petitions may have gone directly from the signet office to the duchy; but as only one is endorsed as being thus dispatched,[1] it is more probable that they went to the privy seal and were forwarded to the duchy from there. The chancery of the duchy was one department over which Cromwell's various offices gave him no direct control, and the great decline in the number of warrants marked 'per consilium ducatus', which composed the bulk of the warrants in the earlier years of the reign, suggests that Cromwell used his control over signet and privy seal in order to exercise some indirect control over the duchy. It is possible that here, in a department technically independent of him, Cromwell allowed the correct routine to be followed, so that duchy grants were ordinarily authorized from the privy seal office. Direct warrants therefore disappeared, and the duchy council lost that independence of action which it had apparently enjoyed under Wolsey's rule. This enforcement of the regulations continued after Cromwell's fall; as far as the duchy was concerned, the act of 1536 operated.

A last class of warrants under the signet must be considered— warrants authorizing expenditure by officials of the household. Their 'diplomatic' appearance differs from that of the normal signet warrant: they have the address written on the face of the document, are not signed by a clerk, and are signed by the king (usually with a stamp). We have already discussed the warrants to Cromwell as master of the jewels;[2] similar warrants were made out to the keeper of the great wardrobe,[3] the great master of the household,[4] the master forester of the forest of Windsor,[5] and to many others. Expenditure of the king's treasure outside courts of record was ordinarily authorized by warrants sealed with the signet and also signed by the king to ensure strict control of payments; though that control was appreciably lessened when it became common to use a stamp for the sign manual, as was the rule during Cromwell's ministry. Once again, Henry VIII maintained only the appearance

[1] DL 12/12, loose document of 28 April 1537.
[2] Above, pp. 142 ff.
[3] E 101/420/1; 418/1, a bundle of twenty-one warrants to Andrew Lord Windsor, keeper of the great wardrobe.
[4] B.M., Add. MS. 9,853, fo. 21 v.   [5] *Ibid.* fo. 24 v.

of a practice which had given real power to his father, and once again
it would be easy to overestimate his part in the government from
a merely theoretical knowledge of business methods. The signet, on
the other hand, had to be impressed (*en placard*) by its staff, and
possession of that seal therefore gave the secretary a valuable weapon
in controlling expenditure. Unlike warrants to departments of state
which kept records, these warrants to individual officers have
naturally failed to survive except by accident, and it is impossible to
say what precisely the practice was concerning them. We know that
Cromwell obtained warrants to cover payments made to himself,
that he filed them and either produced them at the account (if there
was one) or left them to be confiscated with his papers; we know that
the treasurer of the chamber insisted on them, declining any longer
to pay on verbal commands; we have also seen that the treasurer of
first-fruits and tenths complained after Cromwell's fall that he had
been forced to disburse money without warrant, though for him,
too, Cromwell on occasion obtained a warrant after payment had
been made. It therefore seems that warrants were ordinarily
expected, and also that they were ordinarily issued. Their importance
as well as their number was bound to decrease somewhat when
national finance came to be dominated by revenue courts which
disbursed their money mostly by their own authority and accounted
for it afterwards, even though they often still paid on warrants; the
signet warrant for expenditure lost all importance outside the household with the restoration of the supremacy of the exchequer where
payments were authorized by other means of which the lord
treasurer's warrant (afterwards treasury warrant) was soon the most
important. The destruction of household influence in administration resulted in the decline of the seals which the household had
produced.

These warrants for payment which ordered action and not a
further warrant for action serve to introduce the second group of
documents issued under the signet: it was the seal with which the
king's correspondence was sealed. The evidence for two representative years, 1534–5, shows that the king ordinarily corresponded under
the signet, for in that period twenty-three letters were certainly thus

sealed.[1] Normally, they were what might be termed proper signet letters: written by a signet clerk, with a dating clause mentioning the signet, headed with the phrase 'by the king' and Henry's signature, and addressed on the outside. The signature was sometimes added by a stamp[2] or might be missing even in a letter which was definitely sent.[3] In one letter to Cromwell the signet was not mentioned, but something that looks rather like it was applied and still survives.[4] Letters which were not provably sealed with the signet are either drafts without the final clause (which, when added, must have turned them into letters under the signet) or belong to the king's diplomatic correspondence with foreign powers, most of these being in Latin and written by the king's Latin secretary, Peter Vannes.[5] These had nothing to do with the signet office as far as the writing went, but it is of interest that they were not authenticated by the king's normal seal. The signet is not mentioned in their dating clause, nor was it affixed *en placard* by way of authentication, even if—though this is very unlikely—it was used to seal the letters when folded. The royal signature, written either at the top or at the foot like any normal signature, must have sufficed as proof of genuineness. Instructions to ambassadors went out in the form of ordinary signet letters[6] and were written by signet clerks. In these years, they are mostly in the hand which also wrote the additional instructions sent over Cromwell's name, the hand of Wriothesley,[7] suggesting that instructions which appeared to be coming from the king were also prepared in Cromwell's office and submitted to the king for approval and signature.[8]

---

[1] *L.P.* VII. 338, 375, 494, 526, 684, 845, 1033 (1, 2), 1144, 1688; VIII. 25, 43, 92, 592, 594, 623, 783-4, 921; IX. 527, 838, 1038, App. 7. Wherever possible, the letters quoted in this and the succeeding paragraphs have been checked with the originals, as the calendar often gives no indication of the sealing.

[2] E.g. *L.P.* VIII. 25, 43, 92.   [3] *L.P.* VII. 684, 845.

[4] *L.P.* VIII. 592. On the face of it, it is of course unlikely that when the king wrote to the secretary and keeper of the signet that seal should be used; some even more personal seal—a signet ring?—ought always to have taken its place.

[5] He countersigned some of them; *L.P.* VIII. 522; IX. 532.

[6] E.g. *L.P.* IX. 838, 1038. *Ibid.* 443 was all ready and signed by the king, but there is no dating clause.

[7] E.g. *L.P.* IX. 838 (the king's instructions to Gardiner) and 848 (Cromwell's supplementary instructions sent at the same time).

[8] Cf. p. 284, n. 4. An interesting comparison can be made with the practice under Elizabeth. In March 1562 certain instructions were sent to Nicholas Throckmorton,

The evidence is similar for a later year when Cromwell was more fully independent, a fact which may be reflected in the comparatively small number of letters sent out under the king's signature in 1539.[1] Letters definitely given under the signet were in English and addressed to persons within the realm or English ambassadors abroad.[2] Those not so sealed were all addressed to foreign courts and were written either in Latin or French.[3] It may be concluded that the signet was used freely, not to say regularly, to seal the king's personal correspondence, but that letters not written in the signet office did not mention the signet, did not use it for authentication, and are likely never to have come near it.

The preoccupation with the signet as a seal authorizing the issue of documents under another seal, evinced in Cromwell's orders and the act of 1536, was not, therefore, due to its being used only in that capacity. On the contrary, everything suggests that as far as its formal use went it tended to be ignored in the 1530's, while it was used regularly as the king's personal seal. As such, however, it was not in need of formal organization. Its use enabled the secretary to exercise some control over the king's correspondence, and this control was increased by the habitual employment of signet clerks to draft Henry's letters which quite possibly he never saw until they were submitted ready for his signature—and not necessarily even then if a stamp was used.[4] In its administrative function, however, the signet needed organizing. Cromwell's orders and statute were

resident ambassador in France. The original (B.M., Add. MS. 4,160, fos. 42–3) is a proper signet letter, but the draft was corrected by Cecil and endorsed by his secretary (*Cal. S.P. For. 1561–2*, no. 926); again we see that what was clearly an official letter ostensibly emanating from the crown might originate in the secretary's private office.

[1] There are twenty-three in the index to *L.P.* xiv, compared with thirty-six in 1535 (*L.P.* viii and ix).

[2] *L.P.* xiv. I. 92, 280, 406, 487, 711–12, 744; II. 574.

[3] *Ibid*. I. 364, 441–3, 462, 1156; II. 221, 307, 387, 415.

[4] In 1536, Sadler wrote to Cromwell, to excuse himself for delaying the return of letters on which he was to have got Henry's signature: 'I doubt lest his Grace will cause me to tary here veray long, wherefore I thought good...to sende all the lettres that be stamped by this berer. I thinke also it wolbe harde to gette any Billes signed at this tyme.... As ye knowe, his Grace is always loth to signe, and I think he deferred the reding of the Instructions at masse tyme because he was not willing to signe' (Ellis, *Orig. Letters*, 3rd ser., II. 9 f.; *L.P.* x. 76). Obviously Henry never saw the stamped letters.

designed to establish a rigid bureaucratic system, though in his own practice Cromwell seems to have allowed the orders to fall into disuse and paid little heed to the details of the statute. The fact that he disregarded the system which, if we are right, owed its statutory confirmation to himself, is no proof that the arguments for his authorship are fallacious. The new state needed bureaucratic organization, but the minister needed freedom of control and action, and when the two came into conflict it was only natural that the personal element should triumph. The other element, that of systematic organization, was, however, the one to survive. Cromwell might have done as Wolsey did: he might have been content to exercise such detailed control that the weaknesses of an imperfect organization—the opportunities it offered to neglect, laziness, and corruption—could pass unnoticed or unremarked. Though he sometimes did so, he went a step further by providing a better system to be put into practice when he was no longer there.

Thus, whether the reorganization of the signet office and the attempt to restrict the signet to its formal functions testified to a deliberate intent or were due to the fact that in that sphere organization could be applied, and though Cromwell himself did not practice what he preached, the later development of the seal rested on the reforms of the 1530's. Several pointers in that direction have already been mentioned; in particular, the use of the seal for warrants for payments came to mean less as household treasurers ceased to play a part in national finance. The records of the signet office prove that in later times, with the exception of the king's letters to his lord lieutenant in Ireland, the staff dealt with only two things: they wrote the king's bills which were based on petitions submitted and signed with the royal sign manual, and they copied them into the signet warrants for the privy seal.[1] Their work was so purely formal that in fact they did it twice over and need not, but for the demands of an obsolete routine, have done it at all. Certainly the signet never followed up the more hidden meaning of the act of 1536; it never came near to taking the place which the privy seal had occupied in the later middle ages, and the details of administration were attended to by new staffs—the households of the secretaries of state which developed

---

[1] Giuseppi, *Guide*, II. 133.

into departments of state—with new means which did not involve the use of seals so much as the signature of a minister. It was a fundamental change in administrative methods which is reflected in the archives in the growth of the state papers. The memory of the signet's old power remained alive for a little longer, and the early Stuarts tried to revive its possibilities as a weapon of autocracy.[1] That this attempt to turn the clock back proved thoroughly unsuccessful is in itself a sign that the bureaucratic and formal aspects of the seal had triumphed over its original force. The old seals survived into the nineteenth century, essentially in the form and doing the work which had been laid down for them in 1536; despite Cromwell's high-handed practice, the reforms of 1534 and 1536 established the place which signet and signet office were to hold thereafter in the administration of England.

3. *The privy seal*

As has been shown, it was the intention of the act of 1536 that the privy seal, like the signet, should be used in the strict order established by tradition and the council ordinance of 1444, with the addition that this routine should apply to all the work of the privy seal. As, in theory, nothing was to leave the privy seal unless a warrant under the signet had been obtained, so—in theory—no action was to be taken by the chancellors of England, Ireland, and the duchy of Lancaster, or by the treasurer and chamberlains of the exchequer, unless they had had a warrant under the privy seal. But once again it would be rash to suppose that this process was properly observed merely because it was embodied in an act of parliament; the truth can only be discovered by a study of the files of warrants to the chancery which contain a varied assortment. There are occasional warrants under the signet, bills and fiats signed by the king, warrants from the lord treasurer, fiats for protections signed by the deputy at Calais, petitions countersigned by the general surveyors of the king's lands.[2] By far the greater part of the warrants,

---

[1] Cf. Evans, *Princ. Sec.* 202 f.

[2] One month (June 1529, C 82/616) can provide examples of all these: signet warrant—2; bills signed by the king—22, 24; treasurer's warrant—1; petitions signed by the general surveyors—12, 13; fiats signed by the deputy at Calais—7, 25.

however, are privy seals and signed petitions, and it is with these two classes that we must here concern ourselves. If the system had been working properly we should not, of course, expect any signed petitions but only privy seals, for petitions should at best have been used as warrants to the privy seal itself and by rights should never have got past the signet office. On the face of it, every petition found among chancery warrants must represent an evasion of the privy seal; though theoretically it is possible that the privy seal office might simply have forwarded a petition received from the signet office, there is no reason why this should have happened. Some of the petitions ask definitely that they may be signed and used as direct warrants to the chancellor,[1] and even where there is no such request signed petitions found to have been delivered into chancery cannot have been anything but immediate warrants employed to cut short the cumbersome process of warrant upon warrant which every grant was supposed to follow. A large number of such petitions over a longer period will therefore indicate a large-scale evasion of the rules, a smaller number a stricter adherence to them.

In the last months of Wolsey's rule (to go back further would take us beyond the necessary limits of this study without adding to our conclusions) petitions regularly and considerably outnumbered privy seals.[2] In October 1529 Wolsey fell, and there suddenly appear eighteen privy seals to two immediate warrants.[3] This proportion was kept up for quite some time, with signed petitions almost disappearing at times and always in a minority: for the first year after Wolsey's fall, from November 1529 to October 1530, 315 privy seals are matched by only thirty-six petitions.[4] Similar proportions continued for three years after, with the number of petitions slightly on the increase, but in 1534 there are only 178 privy seals as against 111 petitions, and in 1535 the latter actually outnumber the former. In 1536 there is a considerable drop in the number of petitions, but for the rest of Cromwell's government they are again very numerous. A table will make this plain.

<hr>

[1] E.g. C 82/646/3: 'that this bill signed with your most gracious hand maye be a sufficient and ymmediat warraunt vnto your Chauncellour of England'.

[2] The figures, with privy seals first, are: May 1529—2, 18; June—6, 11; July—3, 21; August—8, 13; September—4, 10 (C 82/615-19).

[3] *Ibid.* 620.   [4] *Ibid.* 621-34.

Year	Privy seals	Petitions	Ref.
1531	309	27	C 82/637–650
1532	253	39	C 82/651–663
1533	201	82	C 82/664–677
1534	178	111	C 82/678–691
1535	117	139	C 82/692–705
1536	277	89	C 82/706–719
1537	216	185	C 82/720–733
1538	185	177	C 82/734–747
1539	149	243	C 82/748–761

The same tendency continued at first after Cromwell's fall, largely because of the time-lag between the signing of a warrant or petition and its delivery into chancery; although Cromwell was arrested on 10 June 1540, four petitions countersigned by him by virtue of his commission to sell crown lands survive in the August file.[1] Things took several months to sort themselves out, and until September petitions continued to outnumber privy seals. But in November the numbers were forty and thirteen, in December sixty and one,[2] and in the following year the new proportion was steadily maintained.[3]

These figures tell their own story. During Wolsey's chancellorship the privy seal had been ignored in a somewhat high-handed fashion. Since high-handedness was one of the chief accusations against him, it is not surprising to find that his successors in office were careful to avoid it, with the result that immediate warrants became the rare exception. Nevertheless, they were too obviously useful in avoiding long delays, and the caution inspired by the cardinal's fall could not last for ever. Evasions of the privy seal were again becoming more frequent when Cromwell's appointment as secretary led to a rapid revival of Wolsey's practice; in February 1535 immediate warrants for the first time again outnumbered privy seals.[4] In 1536, however, partly no doubt as a result of the legislation of that year, and partly perhaps because as lord privy seal Cromwell would treat the privy seal with

[1] C 82/771/8, 20, 23, 29. These petitions are rather a special case; they had to pass through augmentations and were delayed by the surveys and valuations which a sale necessitated. There was nothing like them in 1529.

[2] *Ibid.* 774 and 775.

[3] A few examples will show this: January 1541—58, 0; March—47, 2; July—41, 6; November—39, 1; January 1542—35, 0 (*ibid.* 776, 778, 784, 788, 790).

[4] *Ibid.* 693; 12 privy seals and 15 petitions.

less contempt, there was a temporary return to a more strict observance of the regulations. But this was not to last, and during the remainder of his rule Cromwell allowed the privy seal to be evaded more and more. It became ever more usual for grants, especially of monastic lands, to be made on a petition signed by the appropriate authorities and approved by the king's countersignature. Neither the signet nor the privy seal was then called upon to make out warrants, and tradition as well as the statute of 1536 were sedulously ignored.

Cromwell's fall created a situation somewhat similar to that of October 1529, with this difference that business standing over from before his arrest delayed the full effects for several months. In the end matters developed as one would expect them to: no one was now prepared to ignore the regulations in so sovereign a fashion, and consequently the civil service reasserted itself. The privy seal office managed to secure that matters again passed through its hands in the ordinary way, just as the signet office had re-established the proper routine once Cromwell was gone. There was, however, a difference in the routine before and after Cromwell. In the interval between Wolsey's and Cromwell's ministries the proper course for making a grant under the great seal was followed in the majority of cases but without full obedience to rules or special care in the keeping of warrants, while after 1540 the routine was always observed punctiliously. From that time the privy seal files are full of signet warrants and the chancery files full of warrants under the privy seal. Again it becomes clear that the organization of the system which took effect in the very month of Cromwell's arrest was completed during his rule, though he had not himself enforced it. Worked out under him, it became manifest on his fall.

So much for warrants to the chancery; those to the duchy of Lancaster yield little of interest. It has already been noticed that under Cromwell its warrants tended to be from the central offices rather than by order of its own council, and it has been suggested that Cromwell was here trying to exercise an indirect control over a department where he had no directly controlling powers.[1] On the whole, it is noticeable in these files, too, that during his rule there

[1] Above, pp. 280 f.

was no strict adherence to the act of 1536, and privy seals are found freely mixed with signed bills.[1] After Cromwell's fall, privy seals vastly predominated, as they did in the chancery and no doubt for the same reason. Here, too, the organization came to full flowering only after the removal of the man who was prepared to ignore the rules, even though he may have perfected them himself.

As far, therefore, as the privy seal was a seal of warranty to other seals, its business was to be organized and it was always to take its place in the chain which ran down to the great seal and to parallel institutions. Cromwell, in practice, was ready enough to see these rules evaded by the use of signed petitions as immediate warrants, while making sure that the clerks were paid even when no work was done, but after his fall the rules were enforced. Cromwell treated the privy seal in exactly the same way as he treated the signet: he concerned himself with the formal and routine business of the seals, organized it for them, and then ignored the organization created in the interests of his personal ascendancy, and more particularly because an organization designed to prevent abuses was superfluous while he was there to keep his eye on things.

As a seal of warranty the privy seal acted as a distributing centre for the orders of the government; as the act of 1536 put it, it issued warrants

to the Lorde Chauncellour of Englond, Lorde Kepar of the Great Seale, Chauncellour of the Duchye of Lancastre, Chauncellour of the Kynges Landes of Ireland, Threasourer and Chamberleyns of the Eschequyer, and Chamberleyns of any his Counties Palantynes or Pryncypalite of Wales.[2]

Its peculiar power and special position, on the other hand, derived from the fact that it was also a receiving centre for orders from various officials. The act mentioned writings received under the signature of the king, the master of wards, the general surveyors, or other officers, and the true extent of this function of the privy seal is apparent from the files of warrants addressed to it. For 21 Henry VIII (1529–30) the following warrants survive:[3] fifty-five signet letters, one signed

---

[1] Warrants to the duchy are in DL 12/6–8, 11–12. They are not arranged chronologically, and these bundles cover nearly the whole of Henry VIII's reign.
[2] *Stat. Realm*, III. 543. [3] PSO 2/4, file 3.

bill, one signed petition—all these were warrants from the king; seven warrants on behalf of the council; two from the general surveyors; three from the master of the wards; four from the deputy at Calais; one from the chief baron of the exchequer; three from the surveyors of forfeitures and casual revenues; two from the cofferer of the household. The council, general surveyors, master of wards, and surveyors of forfeitures ordered privy seals for appearances before themselves; the deputy at Calais asked for the issue of 'protections', the chief baron for an attachment, the cofferer for orders to sheriffs to pay him the assignments due to the household by acts of parliament.[1] Notes of similar orders to the privy seal can be found among the state papers.[2]

Privy seals directed to the exchequer belong more or less to the same category. At this time the exchequer received its orders for payments by two kinds of warrants: the large majority were chancery writs of *liberate* and *allocate*, usually on patents and obtained by the recipients of the money as a matter of course, while less regular payments or such as were not based on some written grant were authorized by privy seal.[3] If privy seals had at one time threatened to drive chancery warrants entirely from the exchequer,[4] that tendency had been checked and the less formal warrant was now reserved for special government payments of which the exchequer had at this time few enough to make. Thus there are among the privy seals for 25 Henry VIII orders for the payment of sheriffs' rewards, of the king's offerings, of the money due to the cofferer of the household for the St George's feast of the Garter, and of rewards to household officers and others from goods confiscated by customers and other exchequer officials.[5] This division between chancery and privy seal warrants holds good before, during, and after the time we are discussing; no reform attempted to touch the routine of the privy seal office in that respect. Since the day-to-day expenditure of the government was not covered by the exchequer, there was no induce-

---

[1] 1 Henry VIII, c. 16, amended by 14 &15 Henry VIII, c. 19 and 22 Henry VIII, c. 18.
[2] *L.P. Add.* 716, 854, 1179 (general surveyors); 644, 875 (the king's wards); 876 (the king's woods).
[3] Warrants for issues for the years 21–31 Henry VIII (1529–40) are in E 404/97–103.
[4] Tout, *Chapters*, v. 57 f.
[5] E 404/99, file 1, nos. 69; 70; 73; 68, 71, 72, 76, 77, etc.

ment to meddle with the process of issues from it. These warrants to the exchequer, since they were not authorized by any warrant and had become matter of routine, were a little different from all the other orders received at the privy seal which were for letters carrying into action details of administrative work and not authorizing action on the part of another seal. Nonetheless, they were addressed to another government department and resulted in direct action, not in a document under another seal. In a way they stood between the privy seals which were only interpolated warrants for the work of a great seal, and those which ordered some specific administrative step.

These last, on the other hand, were the result of the fact that all departments of state which had no seal of their own had to apply to the privy seal for authentication of their orders. If the treasurer of the chamber wished to recover a debt he had no power to act directly. He could either get the surveyors of the king's casual revenues to sign a fiat to the privy seal summoning the debtor to appear before the treasurer;[1] if the question concerned land revenues, he would have had to go through the general surveyors. Alternatively, since he could not give his orders the force of a warrant without which the office would refuse to act, he could approach the lord privy seal privately, for instance asking his lordship

to directe the Kinges lettres vnder his privie seale to Charles Jakeson to content and pay vnto my handes to the Kinges vse the some of xxx li' due to his grace at daies expired by obligacion, or elles that he appere before me Immedialtly vppon the sight herof vppon payne of Cli',[2]

setting out the terms of the requested privy seal in his letter instead of embodying them in an official warrant. In either case, however, it needed an instrument under the privy seal to give effect to his actions. In 1533 Cromwell himself asked for a privy seal to 'Iohn lyngen the Elder, Squir, to Apper personally octabis Trinitatis' before himself, and added under his signature an autograph request 'that thes pryvye Seales may be hadde with spede'.[3]

[1] PSO 2/4, file 3, nos. 107A, 110, 117. These surveyors appear to be another name for the 'legal counsel', and the attorney general was one of them.
[2] SP 1:239, fo. 73 (*L.P. Add.* 945); similarly, *ibid.* fo. 43 (*L.P. Add.* 932).
[3] SP 1:238, fo. 107 (*L.P. Add.* 855).

Another note in the same affair, signed by him about the middle of 1534, reads:

M^d to have A pryve seale dyrected to Iohn lyngen the Elder, Squir, to Apper before Master secretarie, returnabull Crastino Animarum: Makyng mencion that At his last Apparans he obstinatly departed without lycens.[1]

Cromwell was acting on behalf of a friend,[2] but even so this paper proves that the privy seal was the seal to employ for a summons, even for a man who as the king's principal secretary controlled another of the king's seals. This work of the privy seal was obviously more important than its routine in the chain of warranty and gave it its central position in medieval administration. Its standing was marked and augmented by the fact that it was the seal normally used for the authentication of its business by the king's council.[3]

The records indicate that these orders from other departments continued to come in certainly up to 1533, but—as has already been seen—there are few surviving warrants for the time of Cromwell's supremacy, and they are signed petitions. Nevertheless, a fiat from the general surveyors in 1536, preserved among the state papers, proves that this side of the privy seal's duties had not disappeared altogether before that date.[4] The scantiness of the material in the privy seal files makes it difficult to argue anything about the later 1530's, but what is very striking is that when the files of warrants again become very full and possibly complete, in June 1540, they contain nothing but warrants under the signet ordering the issue of further warrants. Such unanimity, kept up for month after month, hardly looks like an accident of survival. The consequence of Cromwell's administration seems to have been the disappearance of all those orders from other officers of state which gave to the privy seal its peculiar function of a bureaucratic centre, a clearing house of incoming and outgoing departmental business.

What was the place of the 1536 statute in this? It was pointed out above that in effect it deprived the privy seal of its varied warrants

---

[1] *Ibid.* 239, fo. 75 (*L.P. Add.* 947).

[2] *L.P.* vi. 607, Sir Thomas Englefield to Cromwell, thanking him for having a privy seal sent on his behalf to John Lyngen. The handwriting of the two notes of Cromwell's is quite unlike that of any other document known to have come from his office; perhaps Englefield had the notes prepared and gave them to Cromwell to sign.

[3] Above, p. 17.   [4] *L.P. Add.* 1179.

from executive officers and transferred them to the signet. One would therefore naturally expect these warrants to disappear from the privy seal files. But a negative proves little, and unfortunately no files of warrants for the signet survive at all. We cannot therefore tell for certain whether all this important business was in fact transferred from one seal to the other. What we do know is that the warrants under the signet that appear in the files of the privy seal have nothing to do with administrative orders; they direct the issue of warrants to the chancery only. One way or another, therefore, the administrative warrants have disappeared by 1540; they are not to be found at the privy seal, and if ever they existed—and are lost—at the signet, it is a little surprising to find that they were not further translated to the very ample extant files of warrants for the privy seal. For, to make it quite plain, there was no question of literally replacing the older seal by the newer; the signet merely entered the chain, and the effective order—the order which would be obeyed—was still supposed to be sealed with the privy seal. Our evidence for the existence of warrants for such orders simply peters out between 1533 and 1540.

This might be due merely to the defective state of the records, were it not that there are in fact good reasons why a change of this sort should begin to show in 1540. The privy seal had been necessary because other officers of state had no seal of their own, but the reforms of the 1530's gradually replaced these officers by the new courts which were better equipped. Let us rehearse the facts as we have already presented them. The court of augmentations had both a great and a privy seal of its own, the former for leases and grants of lands under its jurisdiction and the latter for process out of the court, that is for such administrative purposes as summons or orders for local inquiries which had up to that time required the ordinary privy seal. The later courts were given less complete independence, but they needed the privy seal no more than did augmentations. Wards and general surveyors had their proper seals under which to issue process, so that they were independent of both exchequer and privy seals; on the other hand they could not bestow the lands under their survey except through the great seal of England, to move which they had to approach the privy seal in the manner laid down by the

1536 statute. The court of first-fruits and tenths was given a seal with which to issue attachments to sheriffs or orders to the exchequer concerning the revenue which it administered; it too did not need the privy seal to cope with the administrative work involved. Debts to the crown, though assigned to the sphere of the court of general surveyors, were to be sued by them in whatever court they happened to arise in and by process under the seal of that particular court. All this was part of that detailed and bureaucratic organization of state departments which has been described as the new principle in the financial administration. In consequence the privy seal lost nearly all its customers; in addition to the obvious officers involved, such others of its users as the treasurer of the chamber and the surveyors of forfeitures were also swallowed up by the court of general surveyors.

There remained the most important of all institutions using the privy seal, the council, which did not acquire a seal of its own until 1556,[1] and which certainly continued to employ the privy seal until then. The records of the privy council show that summons to appear before it was still often, though by no means always, made under the privy seal. The best part of the council's business was done by letters signed by the councillors present, and in the first year for which records survive (August 1540–August 1541) only thirteen privy seals are noted.[2] On the other hand, there are eleven notes of summons by some other means, usually an ordinary council letter,[3] and the privy seal was never used to authenticate any of the many other acts of the council. There was, therefore, some use of the privy seal after 1540, and though it amounted to little it is nevertheless odd that no warrants from the council at all should have been preserved at the privy seal office. Nor were all the new revenue courts established by the time (June 1540) that departmental warrants disappeared from the privy seal files. It is more than unlikely that orders for the privy seal should have been given by word of mouth, for the privy seal office could not act without some permanent warrant with which to protect itself in case of trouble, and the council as well as other

---

[1] Cf. *E.H.R.* XLIII. 195.

[2] *Ordinances and Proceedings of the Privy Council*, ed. Sir H. Nicolas, VII. 5, 59 (three), 84 (four), 120 (two), 123, 186, 187.

[3] *Ibid.* 10, 24, 82 (three), 84, 98, 103 (three), 192.

officers had certainly in earlier years been in the habit of issuing written fiats.

One can only conclude that such few warrants as were received—whether they were departmental fiats or signet warrants in accordance with the act of 1536 (and if a guess may be hazarded, it is that the act was ignored and these administrative orders never passed the signet)—were filed separately from signet bills for warrants to the great seal, and are lost. This would hold good for orders from the council until 1556 and from other officials until the new courts gave them seals of their own, for until then it is difficult to see how they could have done without the privy seal. The careful preservation of signet warrants, filed monthly and endorsed by the clerk on duty, makes one suspect that there was a purpose behind such discrimination. May it not have been that the dual role of the privy seal was being recognized, that its work as a link in the chain of warranty was being separated from its independent and 'original' work? With the latter already much reduced in amount and constantly decreasing, the main work of the office, and therefore the main concern of its organization, must have been with the former. Therefore, signet warrants were treated with care and attention, while departmental warrants, getting fewer all the time, appear to have become things of little consequence. Though for a time the privy seal must have continued to receive warrants of various kinds, the general development, indicated and helped by the new courts with their seals, was towards making it no more than a stage in the chain from petition to grant under the great seal.

It might be argued that such a development must have been coming for a long time, but there is enough evidence to show that it goes back no further than our period of administrative revolution. In 1533 there were miscellaneous warrants in the files; by 1540 they had disappeared. It was noticeable that the act of 1536 not only ignored the privy seal except as a warrantor to other seals, but also interpolated the signet even in the case of departmental orders. Moreover, Cromwell's personal government in all branches of the administration undermined the importance of the privy seal to individual officers; a study of his correspondence shows that he was in the habit of doing by personal letters a good deal that would normally have required a privy seal. Thus, for instance, he was requested by the treasurer of the chamber to help in the recovery of debts,[1] ordered an appearance before himself and the council,[2] and ordered an arrest and release,[3] all matters which ordinarily demanded the issue of privy seals. After Cromwell's fall his habit of personal government caused considerable confusion, and, in order to prevent the machinery from running down, those letters of his had to be admitted as valid; it was decided that all those should be allowed that dealt with the king's business, 'of the which [the king] being advertised a privy seal shall be directed'.[4] Evidently it was realized that only privy seals could legalize the late lord privy seal's private letters by means of which the administration had so often been set in motion and kept going in the years of his supremacy, a sufficient comment on the effect which this practice must have had on the work and importance of the seal.

The privy seal, then, declined during Cromwell's administration and in consequence of the reforms then carried out in the government. The seal itself was more strictly organized for its formal routine business, while its more important work as an original instrument shrank to almost nothing. The one exception to this rule was its use by the conciliar courts. Not only had the council habitually employed the privy seal to order appearances, but its descendants—the courts of star chamber and requests—continued the practice.[5] Star chamber came to rely more on the great seal, moved by warrants from the clerk of the court, but the court of requests did all its business under the privy seal, the issue of orders being authorized by signed endorsements on various documents in the particular cases, so that warrants were not required and cannot be expected to exist. The privy seals demanded by the court were so frequent, and the connexion between court and seal was so strong, that the senior clerk of the privy seal was appointed clerk of the

---

[1] *L.P.* XII. II. 1048.

[2] *Ibid.* App. 41. As early as 1534 one of his correspondents offered to fetch a man due to appear before the council without the formality of a privy seal (*L.P.* VII. 692).

[3] Merriman, II. 62 (letter no. 191).

[4] *L.P.* XVI. 655 (March 1541).

[5] Cf. I. S. Leadam, *Select Cases in the Court of Star Chamber 1477–1509* (Selden Soc.), xix–xxi; *Select Cases in the Court of Requests* (Selden Soc.), xxi.

court of requests.[1] The privy seals issued from the court, and therefore probably other privy seals issued for similar purposes by the
orders of other departments,[2] were 'informal letters' rather than
writs of privy seal;[3] like signet letters they were headed 'by the king',
were addressed on the outside and not on the face of the document,
and began with the phrase, 'Trusty and well beloved, we greet you
well'. The dating clause was peculiar in omitting the regnal year.
These were ephemeral documents the preservation of which was not
contemplated. As the seal of the conciliar courts, the privy seal
continued to be important. The developments which began with the
reforms of 1536–42 hardened its formal use as a seal of warranty into
statutory routine and destroyed its importance in administrative
matters, but they did not touch its judicial functions which grew in
scope as the conciliar courts looked likely to become part of the
regular judicial machinery of the land. But as the seal of requests
and, at first, star chamber, the privy seal was also in danger of
formalization; had the courts survived, it would have had to undergo
something like the development which gave the great seal such vast
judicial importance by the side of a purely formal administrative
routine. The parallel is very close and only ceased when the Long
Parliament abolished the prerogative courts. The outstanding fact,
however, is that the privy seal ceased to be the administrative seal
par excellence; nor was it replaced by the signet, as medieval precedents might lead one to expect, and as the act of 1536 seems to
have intended. The new moving spirit in the administration was the
secretary of state, and he acted by personal letter—by 'state paper'—
rather than by a formal document under any seal.

4. *The principal secretary*

The place of the secretary before 1534 has already been discussed.[4]
Men like Pace, Knight, and Gardiner were officials of standing and
influence, men whom proximity to the king's person enabled to

---

[1] W. Lambarde, *Archeion* (1635), 230.

[2] I have been unable to find any. In the nature of things, they would normally be
lost. Those surviving among the records of the court of requests are almost all orders to
magistrates to render certificates; these would be returned with the answer. The orders
for appearances were not returned and are lost—at least at the central archives.

[3] Cf. Tout, *Chapters*, v. 115.   [4] Above, pp. 31 f., 56 ff.

dispense favours and affect events, but all this was on a small scale. They were not ministers—neither technically officers of state nor great men in the council. Indeed, the fact that no proper governing council existed helped to keep them from exercising greater influence; as we shall see later, the rise of the secretary and privy council tended to go hand in hand.[1] In April 1534 Cromwell replaced Gardiner, and the office of secretary suddenly took on a completely new guise. Cromwell made it the centre and driving force of the administration.

From 1534 onwards, every aspect of the government of England is reflected in the correspondence of the king's principal secretary, but the details are to be found in thousands of letters which we have neither space nor inclination to quote. In 1592, Robert Beale, Walsingham's chief clerk, wrote a 'Treatise on the office of a Councellor and Principal Secretarie to her Majestie' in which he enumerated the business which lay within the secretary's sphere of duty;[2] he listed religion, control over the councils established in the borders of the realm, the defence of the kingdom by land and sea, the affairs of the king's dominions beyond the sea (Ireland and the Channel Islands: in Cromwell's time Calais would have had to be added), English merchants abroad, the royal revenues and finance in general, the royal household, foreign affairs and intelligence. A comprehensive catalogue indeed, but no more comprehensive than a list of Cromwell's activities which might be compiled from his correspondence and remembrances. In certain respects Cromwell did even more than the great Elizabethan secretaries would have thought their office justified; thus he supervised both religious and financial affairs more closely and completely than any secretary ever did again. Burghley became lord treasurer in order to control the finances; Cromwell, ruling before the restoration of exchequer supremacy, achieved the same effect through the secretaryship. On the whole, however, it can be said that the sphere of action which Cromwell established for himself had sixty years later become the secretary's standard employment. He made the office into something to be described almost as a premiership—even if after a few years he

---

[1] Below, pp. 352 ff.
[2] Printed as an appendix to Conyers Read, *Mr Secretary Walsingham*, I. 423 ff.

acquired the title of lord privy seal without adding to his activity; he laid the foundation and erected the scaffolding which the Cecils and Walsingham could easily use in building the finished structure. The secretaryship came to be the linch-pin of administration because Cromwell exploited it in a novel and unlimited manner; by the end of the century the position had been reversed to the extent that a man who wished to govern would do so through an office whose wide scope had already come to be traditional.

What was the ingredient that Cromwell added to the office—apart, of course, from force of character? A case has been made out for supposing that the secretary's greatness rested chiefly on his knowledge and conduct of foreign affairs.[1] Cromwell took his share of diplomacy,[2] but while in this sphere he may have enlarged and improved upon his predecessors he did not create anything new. Foreign affairs had been the usual, indeed the natural, field for men trained in correspondence and languages, and possessed of the sovereign's immediate confidence. Cromwell also attended to the other traditional pillar of the secretaryship, the custody of the signet and management of its work; this, too, was nothing new. His great addition to the office was government at home: he made the secretary supreme in the internal administration of the state. Judging only from the things he did or supervised, one is tempted to call him the king's sole executive minister. Was there any need for any other minister—for anyone else concerned with both the making of policy and the working of the administration—when one man took charge of finance, the civil service, police, economic policy and administration, the control of parliament and council, the preparation and carrying out of legislation, the ecclesiastical affairs of the age of the Reformation, and foreign affairs? There were, in fact, other ministers: members of the inner council like the duke of Norfolk, heads of departments like Paulet, master of wards, or Riche, chancellor of augmentations, but they were one and all under the authority of Cromwell as secretary and later as lord privy seal. On this all-embracing activity the new secretaryship grew up, to be the most

[1] Higham, 'Note on the Pre-Tudor Secretary', *Essays...presented to T. F. Tout*, esp. p. 366: 'More and more the secretary controlled the various threads of diplomatic intercourse, continually increasing his power in council by his knowledge of foreign negotiations.'   [2] Merriman, I, ch. 12.

powerful active element in the state. Despite a king who was so far from negligible that his share in affairs is commonly overrated, Cromwell was a prime minister who kept a strict control on his associates and subordinates, and in addition personally attended to much business in the smallest detail.

It would not, of course, be true to say that no similar pre-eminence had ever been known in the king's government. From the Angevin justiciars onwards, there were offices under the crown which offered the widest scope to their holders, and by the end of the fifteenth century one officer of state had emerged as the head of the official hierarchy. The lord chancellor had reached a position of eminence which he was to retain, in theory at least, until the present day. Wolsey used the office to make himself supreme in a way which differed little from Cromwell's supremacy, however much their tasks, attitudes, and precise activities may have differed. We have already seen that there is good reason to suppose that Cromwell deliberately avoided it with all the prestige and power which it traditionally carried, preferring the comparative obscurity of the secretaryship which only his exploitation made great.[1] Partly no doubt it was wise to remember that Wolsey's fate offered little encouragement to follow in Wolsey's footsteps, while comparative obscurity probably suited Cromwell's temperament rather better than the pomp and circumstance of an ancient office, but there were more cogent reasons. The chancellor had become so burdened with the routine duties of a judge that it was increasingly difficult for him to be also an administrator and controller of policy. Wolsey himself had greatly increased his judicial work by expanding the court of star chamber, and even he found it hard to combine the two aspects of his office.[2] The time was rapidly approaching when the lord chancellor would be above all else the head of the judicial machinery of the realm.[3]

Furthermore, and arising out of this fact, the chancellorship as an office of state did not really answer the purpose which Cromwell had in mind; even its administrative duties were circumscribed and

---

[1] Above, p. 123.   [2] Pollard, in *E.H.R.* xxxvii. 533 f.
[3] After Wolsey only one chancellor tried to free himself from some of his judicial duties in order to have time for politics—Wriothesley, and he failed (Pollard, *ibid.*).

defined. It did not, for instance, offer control of the financial administration, and Wolsey never exercised any form of bureaucratic supervision over that vital part of government. No man who aspired to be the king's chief councillor could afford to ignore foreign affairs and diplomacy. But while Wolsey had built his power on these and on the majesty of a judge and cardinal, allowing the administrative machine largely to run itself under the impetus given to it by Henry VII, Cromwell desired to erect his power on a foundation of administrative control in all its details; his collection of offices has proved as much. In a sense, the position to which he aspired was new; not only was general control of the administration theoretically with no single person except the king, but the very idea of government which it was to embody reflected the new condition of the state and the trend towards centralization. The Renaissance, it is said, created the international complex which gave Wolsey his chance of shining in the field of foreign affairs; it also saw, if it did not produce, the growth of the paternal state which raised the great administrator to unquestioned supremacy in the commonwealth.[1] In all the 'advanced' states of Europe—in Spain and France as well as in England—the secretary of state came to the fore as the executive agent of the new type of government.[2] It was only common sense to choose an office new to the highest honours when the end in view was one never before accomplished. The reign of Henry VIII marked a transition in the field of ministerial pre-eminence with a startling directness very different from the usual evolutionary obscurity of these things; the last medieval chancellor was followed by the first modern secretary of state.[3]

It has often been noted that the rise of the secretaryship can be measured by the act of 1539 which appointed the order of sitting in the house of lords.[4] The chief secretary is there mentioned as one of

---

[1] Cf. the significance of this word in the 1530's and 1540's (e.g. S. T. Bindoff, *Tudor England*, 1950, p. 129). Cromwell's political philosophy might be reduced to the words 'empire' and 'commonwealth', but this is scarcely the place even to touch upon so vast a subject.

[2] Cf. R. Doucet, *Les institutions de la France au XVI* siècle* (1948), 159 ff.; W. S. Holdsworth, *Hist. Eng. Law*, IV. 57, 66 f.

[3] Though Cromwell is never called secretary of state, the slight anachronism may be permitted in order to make plain what his 'principal secretaryship' amounted to.

[4] 31 Henry VIII, c. 10.

the great officers of state, following the lords chancellor, treasurer, president of the council, privy seal, great chamberlain, constable, marshal, admiral, grand master or steward of the household, and king's chamberlain. This was promotion indeed for an officer whom the Eltham Ordinances of 1526 had placed in the fourth group of those entitled to 'bouge of court', on a level with the vice-chamberlain of the household.[1] The act does more than mark the rising importance of the secretary: in 1526 he was still completely a household official,[2] while in 1539 he had become an officer of state attached to the household. His importance was now such that, if a baron or a bishop, he was to take precedence of all other barons and bishops, and that he was to sit with the other ministers of state in the house of lords even if he was a commoner. The act was not passed specifically to exalt Cromwell who was provided for by name as the king's vicegerent in spirituals and took precedence over all other members of the house; it was a question not of doing something for Cromwell, but of marking the height to which he had raised the office of principal secretary. He had made him 'not merely either the king's private servant or an administrative official, but a minister of the crown with definite political views, representing one among many factions between which the crown had to choose'.[3] The political importance of the secretary must not, however, be exaggerated; it attached to the man and not the office. What mattered was the ministerial and administrative development.

By the manner, then, in which he exploited and used the office of principal secretary, Thomas Cromwell created the modern secretaryship of state; in some ways this achievement, however personal and personally restricted it was, proved to be Cromwell's leading contribution to the administrative revolution. Modern government has come to centre round the secretaries of state and ministers designed to copy them. But as might be expected, this development did not take place all at once, and Cromwell's place was but ill filled by many of the secretaries that followed him. Though the secretary never dropped back into the relative obscurity from which Cromwell had

---

[1] *H.O.* 162 f. The lord privy seal was placed two ranks higher (*ibid.*).
[2] Evans, *Princ. Sec.* 29.   [3] *Ibid.* 33.

raised him, though he never ceased to be an officer of state, few sixteenth-century secretaries were Cromwells. Once again, bureaucracy was the answer: before every secretary, no matter what his personal qualities were, could automatically become the chief administrative officer, he had to possess an organized department. These departments grew out of the personal staffs of the Tudor secretaries, though they did not grow to full stature until the seventeenth-century.[1] But like Elizabeth's secretaries after him, Cromwell used his private staff of clerks and assistants in the government of England; in this, too, he initiated an important administrative development. A word must therefore be said about his private office.

This private office was an important organization in the government of the 1530's, yet—it has regretfully to be admitted—it is not likely ever to emerge from obscurity. Quite clearly it did a vast amount of the work required in ruling England. The correspondence through which Cromwell so largely governed was written and received, endorsed, classified, and filed away by his private clerks. Their handwritings are quite familiar, though as they are clerical hands they too often lack very distinctive features; but where we know a name we cannot assign a hand, and familiar hands have no known owners. Their names run in and out of the record of the time which they assisted so much in shaping, but they are mostly little more than names: Richard Cromwell, John Williamson, Thomas Soulemont—to list some of the leading members of Cromwell's staff; Henry Polsted, Thomas Thacker, Thomas Avery, William Johnson, William Body—these are some of the second rank, picked at random. An interesting list of his household in the late 1530's no doubt includes his office staff; it also includes much more and it is impossible to disentangle the one from the other.[2] The office with its organization defies reconstruction; everything appears as far too fluid, with different people doing the same or different business without any distinct division of labour. It is a vague picture of an office doing its work with considerable efficiency and apparent absence of organization, though at a guess this appearance is due rather to lack of evidence than the facts of the case, if they could be known; the one certain thing about the office is the outstanding

---

[1] Evans, *Princ. Sec.* 152 ff.   [2] *L.P.* XIII. II. 1184.

importance of Thomas Wriothesley—more than chief clerk, perhaps, but definitely a subordinate and not the head of the office; Cromwell alone was that. But Wriothesley's name and handwriting appear so often that there is no question about the special position he occupied both towards his master and within his master's private office. In this appointment of a 'private secretary', in the vagueness of the outline, and in the comparatively small number of men employed, Cromwell's office was a portent of the future: these features are notable in the description of the secretary's office written in 1592 by Nicholas Faunt, a clerk of Walsingham's.[1] Here again Cromwell invented, and nowhere more so than in the place he assigned to Wriothesley. The secretaries of Wolsey's time had no staff under them except the signet office; the nearest thing to Wriothesley's place under Cromwell was Cromwell's own place on Wolsey's staff, but that was much less formal and 'official'. The organization outlined in the revolutionary 1530's was to become standard administrative practice.

In the course of the seventeenth century the signet office became clearly divorced from the secretary's office, doing different work, but that was due to the progressive crystallization of the latter. Under the Tudors the signet clerks not only continued to be freely at the secretary's disposal but were also often employed indiscriminately with the secretary's own clerks.[2] Here, too, Cromwell started the later practice, as is shown by a document which gives a glimpse into the way in which the two staffs were intermingled. When the administration of the northern borders was reorganized after the pilgrimage of grace, a paper was drawn up appointing the officers of the 'west-marches fforanempst Scotland' and listing the men who were to assist the deputy warden. In one copy of the paper the names are bracketed in groups, with names written against the brackets by someone other than the clerk who wrote the document.[3] These names are: Taverner, Huttoft, Jermyn, A. Roke, Godsalve, Derby, and 'T. S.'. They were undoubtedly the clerks deputed to write out the commissions of the gentlemen against whose names they were

---

[1] Evans, *Princ. Sec.* 152 f. [2] *Ibid.* 156.
[3] B.M., Calig. B. iii, fos. 246–7. Calendared, rather insufficiently, in *L.P.* XII. II. 249 (7).

placed, those letters missive which the duke of Norfolk delivered to the commissioners a few days later.[1] Of them, Godsalve and Derby were clerks of the signet. Taverner and Huttoft both obtained this position some time later but did not hold it about June 1537 when the document was drawn up. Huttoft was appointed to succeed Derby in October 1539,[2] and Taverner's signature first appears on signet warrants in 1540;[3] but as no warrants survive for the years before, and as Wood says that he was made 'one of the clerks of the signet in ordinary' in 1537,[4] he may have been in office earlier. However, the four clerks of the signet in 1537 are known (Wriothesley, Derby, Godsalve, and Paget), and Taverner must have been an underclerk. Both Huttoft and Taverner had been trained on Cromwell's private staff; Taverner had been his 'client' as early as 1533 and had worked for him, mostly as a propagandist of reformed views, ever since,[5] while Huttoft described Cromwell at about this time as his lord and master and wrote to Wriothesley in terms which suggest that the latter may have been his immediate superior.[6] The other three men held no position in the official bureaucracy. Jermyn was almost certainly that brother of Germyn, servant of bishop Rowland Lee, to whom Cromwell 'showed favour' in 1537,[7] and the favour probably consisted in his being taken into the lord privy seal's service. Anthony Roke was at one time servant to Katharine of Aragon,[8] but had entered Cromwell's service by the latter half of 1536 when Gostwick, in the north fighting the pilgrims, wrote urgently for his services.[9] He seems to have been transferred from Cromwell's staff to Wriothesley's by the beginning of 1538,[10] though he continued to belong to Cromwell's household.[11] 'T. S.', in the circumstances, cannot have been anyone but Thomas Soulemont, apparently the king's French secretary in 1536,[12] but described as Cromwell's secretary as late as March 1537.[13]

Thus a certain piece of work was being shared out among two

[1] *L.P.* XII. II. 248. They were presumably given under the signet.
[2] *L.P.* XIV. II. 435 (2).   [3] PSO 2/4, file for June 1540.
[4] Anthony à Wood, *Athenae Oxonienses* (ed. Bliss), I. 420.
[5] *D.N.B.* XIX. 394.   [6] *L.P.* XII. II. 546.
[7] *L.P.* XIII. I. 152.   [8] *L.P.* XI. 1082, 1436 (2).
[9] *Ibid.* 791.   [10] *L.P.* XIII. I. 20, 44, 151.
[11] *L.P.* XIII. II. 1184 (iii).   [12] *L.P.* XI. 1400.
[13] *L.P.* XII. I. 1096.

clerks of the signet, two underclerks of the signet who had been promoted to the royal service from Cromwell's personal staff, and three clerks who were still on that staff. At the same time, the omissions from the list are interesting. Why were two clerks of the signet included but not the other two? The addition of two under-clerks argues that it may have been intended to use the full strength of the signet staff. Paget can be accounted for: he was normally employed on embassies abroad and may have been out of the country at the time.[1] But no such reason would account for the omission of Wriothesley who was not only in England but had actually drafted some of the documents concerning the government of the northern border.[2] The reason why he was not ordered to write out some of the commissions, as were Derby and Godsalve, must have been that he was in a position different from theirs: his standing must have been higher. His duties, such as the drafting of the scheme, were those of an undersecretary rather than of a clerk, and he may have apportioned the other clerks' tasks. It cannot be claimed with confidence that it was he who wrote their names against the brackets; there is not enough of the writing to be definite; but it is possible. Moreover, two of the clerks at least, Huttoft and Roke, who were Cromwell's servants in name, treated Wriothesley as their master in fact, and others were presumably in the same position. Wriothesley appears to have been in charge of Cromwell's office, running it for him, though very much under his eye.

That is all that can here be said about Cromwell's private office. It did much of the work required in the administration of England; it was employed indiscriminately with the royal secretariats, more especially the signet office; its staff could hope for promotion into the more lucrative royal bureaucracy; and Cromwell had appointed Wriothesley to be his private secretary. It was therefore the proto-type of the Tudor secretary's private office from which grew the great departments of state of the future.

The career of Thomas Wriothesley deserves a brief discussion, not so much because it illustrates Cromwell's control of the clerical organization—which it does, but that is not our present concern—as

---

[1] *D.N.B.* xv. 60. [2] *L.P.* xii. II. 249 (2, 4, 5).

because it describes a typical instance of the new civil service at its most successful. All these matters—decline of the seals, rise of the secretary, creation of a new staff around the secretary—are aspects of one fundamental change, the change from a bureaucracy trained in the church or the king's household to a bureaucracy trained in a minister's household and then employed in the service of the state. As a rule, these new civil servants obtained preferment under the crown, but they depended on the favour of the great ministers of state, that is, in the main on the secretaries. The system is known as the clientage system. It did not originate in the 1530's, for Wolsey's household, for instance, had produced a number of leading officials of the crown, and isolated examples of laymen making good in this way could no doubt be found a long way back. But it was in Cromwell's household that we can first see it grow beyond haphazardness, as it was in the later secretaries' households that it was to develop most fully. Whether Cromwell was deliberate or not in practising it hardly matters; it is enough to say that the men whom he trained and systematically transferred to the king's service were the forerunners of a long line reaching down to the civil service reforms of the nineteenth century.[1] Wriothesley is an eminent early example both because he was so obviously an important civil servant and nothing more under Cromwell, and because he ultimately rose to hold the offices of principal secretary and lord chancellor. Outside the church his career cannot be matched before 1529; in the later sixteenth and in the seventeenth centuries many could be found who did as well. Once more we see the revolution at work, and this time at the very base, the admittedly rather obscure base, of the whole machinery—the minor executives themselves.

Here we are only concerned with Wriothesley the civil servant. He was apparently in Cromwell's employ as early as February 1524 when he was not yet nineteen and just down from Cambridge;[2] documents in his handwriting prove him to have been a clerk in Wolsey's household from about that time onwards. There are references to him, in 1529, as servant to the cofferer of the household

---

[1] Cf. D. Mathew, *Social Structure of Caroline England* (Oxford, 1948), 3 f. Dr Mathew ascribes to Thomas Cromwell the beginnings of the bureaucratic structure which he sketches. [2] *D.N.B.* XXI. 1063.

and as messenger for the king,[1] but nothing further can be found about him in these capacities; possibly another Thomas Wriothesley was meant—the name was not unique. By May 1530 he was a clerk of the signet,[2] and it was there that his official career began. He now, of course, came under the secretary, Gardiner, and may have been his servant in the technical sense; certainly he acted as messenger for him.[3] Nevertheless, it would seem that he did not lose his contact with Cromwell. In January 1531 he received the grant of an annuity from the abbey of St Mary, York,[4] a grant which was in the gift of the archbishop of York and therefore, York being vacant, in the king's. Since the administration of vacant sees was at the time in Cromwell's hands, it seems reasonable to suppose that Wriothesley owed his annuity to him. There are a few drafts of Cromwell's letters in Wriothesley's hand for this period some of which—private letters to Wolsey—could not have been drafted by him in his official capacity as clerk of the signet.[5] There are also plain indications in the latter half of 1533 that Wriothesley was working for Cromwell.[6] Altogether it seems likely that he continued his association with Cromwell's secretariat despite his clerkship of the signet and official service under Gardiner. When Cromwell became secretary, Wriothesley of course became once more fully his servant. His handwriting appears constantly on Cromwell's letters as well as the king's, on the backs of signed petitions, on the face of signet warrants, and on many another document.

Wriothesley continued to hold his clerkship of the signet until he became secretary, Thomas Knight succeeding him on 14 April 1540,[7] but it seems that his position at the signet office did not remain unchanged. We have seen that in Cromwell's orders of 1534 he was named simply as one of the four clerks who took his turn with the others. In September 1536 it was remarked that he was in Cromwell's special favour and a good man to approach if Cromwell needed persuading.[8] In 1537, he had acquired a new importance, and Lord Lisle's agent reported him to be in a position where he could do much for suitors to Cromwell—where he could 'please and

---

[1] *L.P.* IV. 5979, 6489.
[2] *Ibid.* 6600 (11).
[3] *L.P.* V. 723.
[4] *Ibid.* 80 (25).
[5] *L.P.* IV. 6368, 6571.
[6] *L.P.* VI. 928, 1067.
[7] *L.P.* XV. 611 (17).
[8] *L.P.* XI. 460.

displease'.[1] The impression is that from being merely a favourite leading servant he had graduated into a position of some independence. By 1537 he was correcting, and therefore supervising, documents drawn up by other clerks of the signet, as though he held a superior position within the office.[2] Taking this together with the fact that he was described in June 1537 as 'principal clerk of the signet under my lord privy seal',[3] and that the evidence for his having attended to the routine of the signet office gives out about the same time,[4] one may feel justified in concluding that by the middle of 1537 he had ceased to be an ordinary clerk of the signet and had acquired some pre-eminence among his colleagues.

Wriothesley's signature does not appear on signet warrants only; he also signed privy seals. The first example extant belongs to early September 1536,[5] after which date his name is found at least as often as that of any other clerk until he signed his last privy seal on 30 March 1540, probably a day or two before he took over the secretaryship.[6] Yet we can be quite certain that he was never appointed to a clerkship of the privy seal, for the clerks were enumerated in a grant of April 1537 where their names are given as Richard Turner, Robert Forthe, Thomas Jefferey, and John Hever.[7] Though four was the usual number of clerks more might be appointed, and other men are known from signatures on privy seals to have worked in the office. Jefferey, for instance, employed an underclerk, Reynoldes, who signed in his master's frequent absence, and undoubtedly there were several such underclerks. But it may be taken that a grant of the reversion of a clerkship which gives the present holders would list all persons properly appointed to the office, so that Wriothesley was certainly not a clerk of the privy seal several months after he started signing privy seals. Nor is it credible that he should have been employed there as an underclerk; one cannot

---

[1] *L.P.* XII. I. 492; II. 555.

[2] E.g. SP 60:4, fos. 98–101 (*L.P.* XII. II. 378, 2 and 3). These instructions are certainly the work of the signet office, and Wriothesley's corrections are numerous and material.   [3] *L.P.* XII. II. 163.

[4] The last signed petition which he endorsed as a clerk of the signet bears date of June 1537 (PSO 2/4, 25–29 Henry VIII, no. 30), and there is a surveyor's bill similarly endorsed for April 1538 (C 82/736/33).

[5] C 82/716/3.   [6] *Ibid.* 764/77.

[7] *L.P.* XII. I. 1103 (15).

imagine the lord privy seal's confidential private secretary, and a clerk of the signet too,[1] taking such an inferior position in the privy seal office, and in any case underclerks were the private servants of the clerks.

But if Wriothesley was not a clerk, and could not have been an underclerk, of the privy seal, how did he come to do as much work in that office as any of the full clerks there employed? The answer, we suggest, is to be found in a medieval precedent. From its early beginnings the staff of the privy seal office had usually included a man who was not a clerk of the privy seal, and apparently had no hope of ever becoming one. That was the keeper's personal clerk, 'an important person in a modest way', who would be employed to write for the seal in the keeper's absence.[2] Essentially, this description fits Wriothesley. He was Cromwell's personal servant and clerk, and he was not employed at the privy seal office until Cromwell had taken over the keepership. His work in that office, unlike his work for the signet, was clearly the result of his relationship with Cromwell, and of Cromwell's tenure of the office of lord privy seal. Cromwell must have put him in the privy seal office as his personal clerk; he must have made him his personal representative there. He can have had no reason to do this unless he wanted someone he could trust to look after the privy seal office for him. He could not exercise day to day supervision over the clerks and did not, on the other hand, want to let the department slip from his control. Wriothesley therefore acted as the lord privy seal's representative in the privy seal office.

It therefore appears that Wriothesley occupied a triple position in the civil service. He was chief clerk of the signet, the lord privy seal's representative at the privy seal, and private secretary to the lord privy seal and principal secretary, Cromwell. It was an unprecedented position, and not one which found any imitators. But that was due to Cromwell who made Wriothesley his understudy in every clerical office he controlled; what was to be less unique and more

---

[1] *H.M.C., Hatfield MSS.*, VII. 419, Gell to Cecil, to the effect that the clerkship of the signet was 'more esteemed and more valuable' than that of the privy seal. In the fifteenth century the position was reversed (Otway Ruthven, *King's Sec.* 135). Whatever the truth for the reign of Henry VIII, clerks of the signet were much higher in the social and official scale than underclerks of the privy seal.

[2] Tout, *Chapters*, v. 78 f.

typical was the bureaucratic flavour of the whole thing. Thomas Wriothesley was manifestly the most successful civil servant of his day, in a way the head—not officially, of course—of the civil service in the later 1530's. The very fact that such a position was possible shows that we are dealing with a new kind of government in which bureaucracy has become the guiding principle.

Wriothesley's career under Cromwell was rounded off when he became principal secretary, and with this appointment and its significance we may conclude this chapter. For the period of administrative revolution not only witnessed the rise of the secretary of state; it also saw the second most important event in the history of that office—its division between two holders. Though Cromwell raised the secretary to a high advisory and executive position, he found it necessary to attain to a higher dignity still when he was created a peer. The title of 'master secretary' was good only because of what its holder had put into the office, and the better office and nobler title of lord privy seal seemed desirable when master Cromwell became Lord Cromwell of Wimbledon. He continued as principal secretary after his promotion, for he was several times addressed in both capacities.[1] Perhaps he did not want to lose the profits of the secretaryship; perhaps, again, he feared to put a possible rival in the place that had made him great. At any rate, when during the ups and downs of the last months of his ministry he at last gave up the secretaryship, its power, scope, and newly won dignity were markedly curtailed.

The precise date of this event is doubtful, for like Cromwell his successors were appointed without a patent; but they entered upon office when the bureaucratic Cromwell ruled, and a warrant was drawn up defining their duties.[2] This warrant, by which Thomas Wriothesley and Ralph Sadler were named joint secretaries, has usually been dated into April 1540 because they first appeared officially as secretaries on the occasion of Cromwell's creation as earl

---

[1] *L.P.* xii. I. 1098; xii. II. 445.

[2] The warrant (SP 1:158, fos. 153–4) is extracted in *L.P.* xv. 437 and printed in *St. Pap.* I. 623, and by Evans (*Princ. Sec.* 360 f.) from Brit. Mus., Stowe MS. 163, fo. 170. The latter MS., a later copy, differs in spelling and one or two minor details from the original.

of Essex on 18 April 1540, and because Wriothesley's cousin, the chronicler, specifically mentioned the month in his account of the event.[1] This evidence is further corroborated by the fact that Wriothesley signed his name as a clerk on a writ of privy seal as late as 30 March 1540,[2] and by Sadler's register of the signet which begins on 1 April.[3] The office continued as one, exercised jointly by the two holders: each was to have a signet and to keep a book of what passed through his hands, but both were to know both sides and pool the fees; they were to share the profits. Relinquishing the exalted rank given to the secretaryship by the act of 1539, they were to take precedence after all peers spiritual and temporal and also after the four executive officers of the household—the treasurer, controller, master of the horse, and vice-chamberlain. This was a distinct decline, amounting almost to a return to pre-Cromwellian status.

The division of an office which had always been held by one person is a fact which deserves a satisfactory explanation. Neither a desire to reward two faithful servants, nor the hope of two additional allies in the council (reasons usually adduced), fully accounts for Cromwell's action—if indeed it was Cromwell's, for which there is no evidence. Both these motives could have been answered more easily by the grant of different offices, without so startling an innovation. Nor would they explain why the division became common practice, only temporarily abandoned by the Cecils who wished to govern through the secretaryship. The work may have become too much for one man, but that seems unlikely in view of the fact that Cromwell had himself held the office together with his other posts for so many years. Perhaps Cromwell feared to raise a rival for himself: but a glance at his relations with the secretaries after April 1540 shows how thoroughly he kept them under control. While Cromwell was in power there was never a rival to him in the administration, and hardly one on the council. Such a fear would have been unnecessary and does not, therefore, offer a sound reason for the appointment of two secretaries.

These are what might be called political explanations; perhaps

---

[1] *L.P.* xv. 541; *Wriothesley's Chronicle* (Camden Soc.), i. 115.
[2] C 82/764/77.   [3] B.M., Add. MS. 35,818.

a better answer can be found in an administrative point. Wriothesley, as we have seen, had been for at least two years Cromwell's 'under-secretary of state'; under the minister he had controlled the various secretariats through which Cromwell worked. Sadler, on the other hand, had been for many years practically the king's private secretary. He was on Cromwell's staff as late as September 1535,[1] but from the beginning of 1536 to the date of his promotion, he was, as a gentleman of the privy chamber, in attendance on the king and acted as intermediary between Henry and his minister.[2] The promotion of these two men made no difference to their spheres of action, and Sadler continued to report to Cromwell Henry's views and instructions, as he had done before.[3] Cromwell's reply to one such letter is in Wriothesley's hand; he used the secretary who was with him to write to the secretary who was with the king.[4] The intention seems to have been to have one secretary permanently in attendance on the king, and the other permanently in attendance on the lord privy seal.

This seems the most convincing motive yet suggested for the division of the office of principal secretary; nor is it weakened by the fact that the warrant appointing the two secretaries explicitly decreed that both were to have lodging at court and were to accompany Cromwell whenever he was at court. Nothing was said about the contingency that Cromwell might be out of court, a frequent one in practice, but it seems likely that the double appointment was made precisely for this contingency. The king needed a secretary and Cromwell an assistant; the office was divided for sound administrative reasons. It must be remembered that for at least four years the king had had no secretary regularly to write his letters, read him his incoming correspondence, and present papers for signature; one of the most obvious routine duties of the office could not be carried out by a man whose work for ever took him away from court. The appointment of two secretaries remedied this serious defect in the bureaucratic organization of the 1530's, and the king ceased to depend on gentlemen of the privy chamber. In a way, then, this step of 1540 also

---

[1] L.P. IX. 466.
[2] L.P. X. 76; XI. 501, 1124; XII. II, App. 44; XIII. I. 1375; II. 178; XIV. I. 236, 579.
[3] L.P. XV. 468, 719.   [4] Ibid. 469.

assisted the general turning away from household government, in that it provided an officer of state to resume doing work that household secretaries or other household officials had been doing, though in practice members of the chamber were too near to the king to be kept away from affairs of state. The theory is supported by the fact that the privy council of these years was in the habit of splitting up, some of its members attending the king and some the lord privy seal;[1] it must have seemed highly desirable to have a principal secretary with each part, to prepare its agenda and carry out its decisions.[2]

From 1540 there were, therefore, two principal secretaries, though it was not until the reign of James I that the practice became invariable. Two parallel secretaries with ostensibly identical duties and powers naturally could not dominate the administration as Cromwell had done, and as William and Robert Cecil were to do who again acted without a colleague and rival. Not only in order of precedence but also in true power the office declined when it was divided and when Cromwell gave it up. But the decline was more apparent than real, though it underlines what was said earlier about the part personality continued to play for some time in the standing of the office. In the last resort, these measures of down-grading the secretaryship were the result of Cromwell's own higher standing as lord privy seal, and of the highly personal flavour which he gave to his administration. The office of principal secretary was not permanently depressed. In the 1530's a profound change came over the clerical organization of the English government. The rise of the secretary completed a development that was based on the formalization and decline of the lesser seals and the gradual replacement of the older civil service, lay (household) or clerical, by a new kind recruited through ministerial patronage and training. The centres of medieval administration sank to the rank of formal, unnecessary, and wasteful survivals, and in their place new organizations, new methods, new classes of records, and new ministers made their appearance.

---

[1] Below, p. 324.

[2] If this interpretation is correct, it seems to show that Cromwell's influence was as strong as ever two months before his fall, supporting a point I have made elsewhere ('Thomas Cromwell's Decline and Fall', *Camb. Hist. Journal*, x. 169 ff.).

CHAPTER V

THE PRIVY COUNCIL

It has already been shown how the small official council of Richard II developed into the magnates' council of Henry IV and Henry V, how it collapsed in the Wars of the Roses, and how Edward IV and Henry VII restored an earlier type of council—a fluid and indeterminate body of advisers and executive servants from which all elements of opposition were carefully excluded. Within that body there was an inner ring of more confidential councillors, and this inner ring assumed some permanence and institutional organization in the first years of Henry VIII. Wolsey, however, interrupted what promised to be the growth of a more restricted and more powerful council than any seen since the Lancastrian failure, and during his rule conciliar activity concentrated on the judicial business transacted in the public sessions held in the star chamber. The small council attendant on the king, the potential makers of policy and controllers of the administration, ceased to play any part in affairs; indeed, for all practical purposes they ceased to exist. On the other hand, the characteristic government of the later Tudors was the privy council, an organized board of—normally—less than twenty members, most of them leading officers of state and household, travelling with the sovereign and meeting very nearly every day. It concerned itself not only with the traditional conciliar duty of advising the crown on matters of policy, but attended in detail to executive and administrative matters which it usually debated and decided as a body and not necessarily with reference to the king (or queen) who were, in fact, potential rather than permanent heads of their privy councils. Elizabeth never attended its meetings.[1] Although most of the medieval council's judicial work devolved upon the court of star chamber, the privy council retained a proportion of it—either work of importance to nation or king, or work pressed upon it by suitors who saw in it their best hope of rapid and con-

---

[1] J. B. Black, *The Reign of Elizabeth* (Oxford, 1936), 170.

genial justice. The crown, of course, reserved to itself the decision in matters of importance, and the sovereign might occasionally attend council meetings, but it was more usual for him not to do so, awaiting the opinion of the board which was tendered as the advice of the whole body and not of its individual members; in the routine of government, moreover, the council had a wide discretion and independence. It was a true institution, not a mere group of individuals.

1. *The making of the privy council*

Though the term privy council was often employed as early as the fourteenth century, no separate council was meant by it; the name exemplified the special 'secretness' or closeness to the king of his more intimate advisers. There were two kinds of councillors only inasmuch as some were more important than others, not—as was to be the case under Henry VIII and after—in the sense that some belonged to a special and more important branch of the council from which others were excluded.[1] All the king's councillors were of one kind, even if they did different work; no 'organic division' on the lines of their work was carried out or even contemplated.[2] A very different kind of privy council emerged on 10 August 1540 when nineteen men, described as 'his Highnes Pryvey Counsaill whose names hereafter ensue', met to appoint a clerk and provide for the keeping of a register.[3] Here the separation had taken place, and these nineteen composed a separate conciliar body to which other councillors did not belong; the separate body was, however, older than this first entry in its register, for it is quite plain that what was new then was the order made and not the organization making it. The problem how that body, that privy council, came to be organized has puzzled the various general historians of the institution: Dicey seems to have been content with the notion of a gradually evolving privy council without bothering about details, while Miss Gladish, for instance, solved the problem by a categorical and unproven ascription

---

[1] Baldwin, *King's Council*, 105, 110-11.
[2] *Ibid*. 112 f.
[3] *Ordinances and Proceedings of the Privy Council*, ed. Nicolas, VII. 3.

of the reforms to Henry VII.[1] The question has been tackled in special studies, but it has rarely been seen in its true light. If we were to inquire (as usually we are asked to do) how an inner ring of more intimate councillors grew up within the council, we should soon be lost in the mists of antiquity; naturally every king who had a council worthy of the name relied more especially upon a select few in the making of his policy, particularly once the medieval council, as a body, had settled down to its terms and vacations and the formal meetings of a quasi-court, a fashion in which government could not be carried on. What we must really discover is how that inner ring, that informal group of advisers and administrators, developed into a formal board of government. The problem became real only with the first of the Tudors, since Henry VII swore as many of his servants as possible of the council until there were a hundred or more men who at one time or another could claim to be members of the 'whole council'. This somewhat amorphous assembly concerned itself with routine or judicial business, while a distinct group of more intimate or 'privy' councillors advised the king and administered the realm. The privy council was formed when this loose group of 'councillors attendant on the king' turned into an institutional board, and it is here that the problem lies.[2]

Three views have been advanced in its solution. Pollard argued for 'the definite organisation of the privy council' in 1540; though he admitted the existence of an inner council of the same membership, at least from 1537 onwards, he preferred to reserve the name of privy council for that body which started to keep a record of its proceedings in August 1540.[3] Turner attacked this and other views expressed in Pollard's articles but did not provide any definite answer of his own, except that he would almost deny the existence of the privy council proper before the reign of Elizabeth. He seems to

[1] A. V. Dicey, *The Privy Council*; Dorothy M. Gladish, *The Tudor Privy Council* (1915), especially p. 10. The account of the rise of the privy council in Holdsworth, *Hist. Eng. Law*, IV. 56 ff., is the least satisfactory part of his heroic but doomed attempt to write the constitutional history of the sixteenth century by way of a gloss on his text, and entirely from printed materials.

[2] For the sake of clarity, the terms council attendant and privy council will here be used for the unorganized and organized bodies respectively, though there was no such rigid distinction in sixteenth-century usage.

[3] A. F. Pollard, 'The Privy Council under the Tudors', *E.H.R.* XXXVIII, especially pp. 42–4, 60.

have thought that the privy council developed gradually from a group of councillors composing either an administrative council or the court of star chamber at will.[1] It would be better to speak of the continued existence of the undifferentiated medieval council, that 'whole council' since stressed by Mr Dunham, from which both these institutions descended. The last-named scholar tentatively decided that the gradual evolution of the privy council became manifest on some date soon after Wolsey's fall, though he held that it may have existed earlier.[2] These three views have one thing in common: they consider the privy council to be the result of an evolutionary process so gradual that no date, not even an approximate one, can be given for its origin. Even Pollard used a definite date only as a *terminus ad quem*, believing it to be the earliest known on which we may speak of the privy council. Of necessity, therefore, as it seems to me, they underestimated the difference between the informal group of intimate councillors who accompanied Henry VII on his travels and in his government, and that thoroughly organized institution which we know as the Elizabethan privy council. The view which will be put forward here is that the difference between these two kinds of council, however superficially unimportant, is profound in the sense that the one permitted great variations in the methods of government while the other standardized them; over-poweringly great ministers were possible under the one system but not under the other. The history of the reign of Edward VI is no argument against this view, for the councils of Somerset and particularly of Northumberland were rapidly reviving the conciliar characteristics of the fifteenth century; they hardly belong to a discussion of Tudor methods of government. If we are right, the change from the unorganized to the organized condition matters; it marks not just a rather vague stage in the development of an institution but draws a line between two different attitudes to problems of government and administration—between the medieval attitude of relative vagueness and the new, 'modern', attitude of bureaucratic organization. The argument to be here advanced is that

[1] E. R. Turner, *The Privy Council 1603–1784*, I, chs. 2–3, especially pp. 59 ff.
[2] W. H. Dunham, Jr., 'Henry VIII's Whole Council and its Parts', *Huntington Library Quarterly*, VII. 39 ff.

there was no privy council in 1532 but that there was one in 1540, and that the privy council was deliberately and consciously organized some time between 1534 and 1536.

It must first be established that nothing fairly to be described as the privy council existed before the early 1530's. The activities of a small council in the years 1509–12 may be ignored, partly because they were so evidently the temporary result of Henry VIII's youth and inexperience, and partly because their immediate cessation upon Wolsey's rise to power proves that that council lacked institutional organization, the essential characteristic of the privy council. It has been argued that Henry himself, not to mention some of his contemporaries and a later generation, thought that he had an institutional privy council at the beginning of his reign,[1] but it is not advisable to rely on the use of the term which was employed loosely and might imply no more than the existence of a group of more intimate councillors.[2] This business of nomenclature is a difficult one; generally speaking little can be deduced from the contemporary use of any term outside official documents, but when names and titles occur in letters patent or similar papers they ought to be given more weight than the common parlance of men's letters deserves. It will be well here to deal with a passage which is often quoted to support the theory of an earlier privy council,[3] Sir Robert Wingfield's assertion that he had been of it since about 1520.[4] The calendar misquotes him, for what he actually wrote was:

I am oon of thoose which hath ben sworne of the kynges Cowncell above xx[tl] yerys past; & feyth, of his pryve Cowncell above xiiij yerys I haue Contynuyd,

leaving little doubt that he was not thinking of the privy council as an organized institution but merely of himself as one of the more intimate councillors.[5]

---

[1] *Hunt. Lib. Quart.* VII. 35 ff.

[2] Cf. *ibid.* 32, where Dunham points out the difficulty of relying on terms whose significance was far from rigid at the time. This really disposes of his own arguments in favour of an earlier privy council.

[3] *Ibid.* 38; Pickthorn, *Henry VIII*, 216.   [4] SP 1:90, fo. 137 (*L.P.* VIII. 225).

[5] He wrote another letter (*L.P.* VII. 1525) in which there is a suggestion of his being

Nothing was done during Wolsey's rule to give greater coherence and reality to conciliar organization at the centre, though it is commonly asserted that the famous provision in the Eltham Ordinance of 1526 for the establishment of a council in attendance on the king marks just such a step. It would be more correct to say that the ordinance recorded the minister's victory over the king's wish for a true council of his own. Twenty men were to compose this council, but by allowing the necessary absence of all the more important officers of state the council was reduced to a committee of ten and then to a subcommittee of five, while finally it was provided that two councillors were always to be present, 'except the King's grace give lycence to any of them to the contrary'.[1] A council attending on the king which might consist of two of the lesser councillors was clearly no privy council, and the hope expressed that by this order 'the King's highnesse shall always be well furnished of an honourable presence of councillors about his grace, as to his high honour doth apperteyne' has the flavour of subtle irony. In any case, there is no evidence that even this modest reform was actually carried into effect during Wolsey's supremacy;[2] as far as is known, no body consisting of the councillors named was ever put together, let alone allowed to meet and act. There was no privy council before 1529, and even the informal council attendant had been shouldered out of its place by the autocratic cardinal.

Wolsey's fall naturally altered this, and as soon as he was gone the inner council came to the fore. Council meetings were now frequently mentioned in ambassadorial reports; the king often referred foreign envoys to his council, and they often met it without seeing the king first.[3] The council discussed such widely differing aspects of the king's affairs as the divorce and the fate of Wolsey's colleges at Oxford and Ipswich,[4] while a report that Henry had complained in a rage that Wolsey was a better man to govern than any of them

---

sworn of a privy council: 'It is above xiij[ti] yerys synst I was fyrst sworne of the kynges Councell, and afftyr of his pryvat Councell, being his vicechambyrleeyn', but he probably meant only that he became an intimate councillor by virtue of his office, and the oath he was thinking of was that of the vice-chamberlain. For his general unreliability cf. also Pollard, *E.H.R.* xxxviii. 45, n. 1.

[1] *H.O.* 159 f.   [2] Pollard, *E.H.R.* xxxvii. 359.
[3] King refers to council: *L.P.* v. 40, 105, 287, 773; ambassadors meet the council: *ibid.* 45, 216, 251, 653, 1013, 1633.   [4] *L.P.* iv. 6307, 6666, 6679.

indicates that details of the administration were now again being handled by the council.[1] The absence, for a time, of any one outstanding councillor naturally allowed the council attendant as a group more scope and gave it greater weight. There is, however, no reason to suppose, with Mr Dunham,[2] that Henry was deliberately consolidating his intimate councillors into a board of government. The king simply returned to the practice of the early years of his reign, asking advice of several men where he had long been wont to rely on one, and sharing out the duty of supervising the administration which Wolsey had discharged alone and which the king was as reluctant as ever to take upon himself. This reluctance was one of the chief factors in the rise of Cromwell; it gave his chance to the one man able and willing to administer the realm in the Wolsey manner.

The events of the autumn of 1532, when Henry went to France, show the nature of the council attendant at this time. A council was left behind in London which governed the country and daily met as a body to do so[3]—typical characteristics of the privy council—but its membership, which included judges and civil servants as well as churchmen and nobles and officers of state,[4] was very different from that of the fully developed privy council. The council in London was only a temporary body, sometimes not free to act without reference to the councillors with the king,[5] consisting of what may be called the second rank of the council, and organized as an institution only because the king and his leading ministers were out of the country; on their return it simply ceased to exist. Its members became again members of an undifferentiated body of councillors; only two of them, lord keeper Audeley and the earl of Sussex, were later to be privy councillors. The inner ring, the council attendant, was with the king, forming no more than a group of individual councillors who, for instance, corresponded with the temporary board in London as individuals.[6] There was no institutional privy council in 1532 when Cromwell's rise to power once more bade fair to jeopardize the existence and influence of the councillors as a body.

[1] *L.P.* IV. 6738.
[2] *Hunt. Lib. Quart.* VII. 41 f.
[3] *L.P.* V. 1473.
[4] *Ibid.* 1408.
[5] Instructions had been left for this council (*ibid.*), but it had to ask special permission to open letters from Scotland (*ibid.* 1450).
[6] *Ibid.* 1408, 1421, 1427, 1430, 1444, 1450, 1473, 1542.

On the other hand, the privy council existed by 1540. Not only is there proof of organization in the order for the keeping of a register, there is also evidence that the inner circle had become a board with a definite membership, an institution to which some councillors belonged while others did not. Now at last there appear references to 'ordinary councillors'—members of the council who were not members of the inner ring. A list of them was drawn up early in 1540, and work was delegated to them in that year by the privy council itself.[1] This body shows full corporateness. When one privy councillor died another was immediately called in his place.[2] In October 1540 Henry himself told his ambassador with the emperor to pretend that he had sought advice from

oone of our Counseil (though not of our Pryvie Counseil) but a man of gravitie and learnyng, and oone that hathe great intelligence with our nere Counsailours and suche as be aboute Us.[3]

Evidently, the king by this time thought of his privy council as a body institutionally divorced from the council as a whole or the group of 'ordinary councillors'. Admittedly, not all its members were always present at its meetings, and it could even split up, part going with the king and part staying in London, but the same was true for the privy council of James I when no one doubts its institutional completeness.[4] Neither under James nor under Henry did these parts include anyone not known to have been a privy councillor. On 21 October 1540 the 'Lords of the King's Privy Council at London' wrote to 'his privy council here' (at Windsor), as the contemporary endorsement has it,[5] and the men who signed this letter together with the privy councillors who met at Windsor on the same day[6] number eleven out of the total membership of nineteen. The register proves that round about that time more or less the same small group of five met every day at court, the remainder presumably sitting at London or individually employed elsewhere.[7] On the last day of the month nearly all the privy council assembled at court; the absentees were Cranmer, busy at Canterbury,[8] Hertford who attended nearly

---

[1] *L.P.* XV, p. 5; XVI. 127, 146.
[2] Nicolas, *Proceedings*, VII. 57 f.
[3] *St. Pap.* VIII. 456.
[4] Turner, *Privy Council*, I. 92 f., 97.
[5] *L.P.* XVI. 181.
[6] *Ibid.* 180.
[7] Nicolas, *Proceedings*, VII. 68–74.
[8] *L.P.* XVI. 221, 469.

21-2

always but missed a spell in October–December 1540[1] (he may have been ill), and Sandes, who was captain of Guisnes as well as lord chamberlain and does not seem to have been in England until the beginning of November.[2]

Turner's argument against the existence of a true privy council at this time depends mainly on the facts that the section of the council which followed the king and kept the record was not of a fixed composition, and that it was rivalled by the council at Westminster which did similar work.[3] But no one has argued the view, which he set himself to disprove, that 'the councillors with the king made up a smaller, exclusive council'. The councillors with the king and those at Westminster together composed one privy council of fixed membership (Turner's own examples show that), a council which could split into two parts as administrative convenience demanded. Under Henry VIII the privy council with the king kept the record; under James I, that at Whitehall took over that task.[4] In neither case does this prove that the other part did not deserve the name of privy council, but only where its centre of gravity lay. We have seen that the whole privy council would assemble at court if need arose; on the other hand, when the king went on his winter progress in 1540 he took with him only four privy councillors, leaving two to hold the fort at Windsor and allowing the rest to disperse to their homes, though he occasionally ordered them to assemble at London if business made it necessary.[5] By 1540 the privy council was an institution none the less real because it was flexible.

It follows that at some time between 1532 and 1540 the group of councillors attendant became the privy council. The question when the informal became the formal is very difficult to answer because the difference between them is simply that one was organized and the other was not; as Mr Dunham puts it, it is difficult to say 'just when a group of men, bound together by a common duty to aid their king in the conduct of government, changed from a number of individuals into an organ of government'.[6] Nevertheless, this change took place,

---

[1] *L.P.* XVI. 159, 325.
[2] *Ibid.* 243.
[3] Turner, *Privy Council*, I. 21 ff.
[4] *Ibid.* I. 22.
[5] Nicolas, *Proceedings*, VII. 89.
[6] *Hunt. Lib. Quart.* VII. 39.

and it may be possible to trace it, for it must be said again that the change is really important because it marks the transition from the casual arrangements at the king's pleasure which characterized medieval practice in the council to bureaucratic organization, even though membership remained at the king's choice.

Signs of development are to be found in the increasing activities of the council in the course of the 1530's. Its work in the years 1533–40 is not so obscure as the absence of registers might lead one to believe. Though the evidence is to some extent fragmentary, it is possible to reconstruct a tolerably complete picture from notes and references extending over the whole period; where there is evidence for certain activities at several points throughout those eight years, it is permissible to assume that such activities took place in the intervals when the evidence fails us. References to the council multiply, and for 1533 the index to the *Letters and Papers*, with twenty items, for the first time becomes reasonably complete on the subject. The five references in the index to volume IV (1524–9) and the two in that to volume V (1531–2) do not, indeed, represent the total of mentions in the text, but they indicate that the council is not mentioned often and could appear of little importance to the editors of the calendar.

As has been said, the council of 1529–32 regularly occupied itself with the discussion and execution of both foreign and domestic policy, in a manner which almost suggests the work of the fully developed privy council. The interesting point is that to all appearance Cromwell's arrival on the scene did not interfere with these activities on the part of the council. Ambassadors were often before it, to declare their business, discuss points at issue, and receive information. Chapuys' testimony is particularly strong for the earlier part of the period because his reports were then fullest. The council informed him of the king's proposed marriage to Anne Boleyn, though his answer was so unsatisfactory that they had to refer back to the king.[1] Matters of trade were discussed frequently.[2] He had a long meeting with the council in May 1534 when he was informed

---

[1] *L.P.* VI. 720, 805.   [2] *Ibid.* 975, 1018, 1112, 1125.

of the passing of the act of succession and wrangled with Foxe, Tunstall, and others about the obstinacy of Katharine and Mary in refusing the oath.[1] When Mary fell ill, Henry ordered the council to inform the imperial ambassador.[2] On another occasion Chapuys held a discussion with the French ambassador before the council.[3] Other ambassadors, of course, also attended on the council, as did the Scots or the Lübeckers and other German envoys.[4] In 1538 the French ambassador, Castillon, was before the council with considerable and ineffectual frequency,[5] and his successor, Marillac, kept coming up to discuss some trouble that had arisen in connexion with a French merchant.[6] Altogether, the council was kept pretty busy with matters of foreign policy.

It would, however, be wrong to suppose that ambassadors invariably discussed their business with the council, or that the king's foreign policy was necessarily decided in council. Chapuys throws some light on Henry's practice when he reports that he was informed by the duke of Norfolk that the king would see him if the matters about which he had come were of importance; if they were not, the council would settle them.[7] Ambassadors sometimes saw the king alone, or with only one or two of his councillors, or they might discuss matters with Cromwell. Thus after the session in which he had fought the council over the queen's disobedience, Chapuys had a private conversation with Cromwell in which he tried to put his more intimate thoughts.[8] Cromwell might sometimes prefer to take the lead in council rather than conduct foreign policy on his own, as for instance in the negotiations with Castillon already referred to, but it was most usual for him to hold conversations with foreign ambassadors away from the council; references to such conversations can be found in the vast majority of ambassadorial reports scattered over the years of his supremacy. The examples of council activity which have been given indicate what the practice was. While negotiations were carried on by the king or Cromwell, the more formal business as well as the lesser matters were dealt with by the

---

[1] *L.P.* VII. 690.
[2] *L.P.* VIII. 189.
[3] *L.P.* XI. 7.
[4] *L.P.* VII. 662, 888; XIV. I. 1092.
[5] *L.P.* XIII. I. 623, 629, 843, 855, 909.
[6] *L.P.* XIV. I. 1261, 1301, 1316; II. 656, 743, 779.
[7] *L.P.* VII. 726.
[8] *Ibid.* 690.

council. If an ambassador was to be given the impression of a government united on major aspects of its policy such as the anti-papal legislation, or if he was to be solemnly informed of certain steps taken, or, on the other hand, if his business was of comparatively little importance (temporary difficulties, for instance, in the wool and cloth trade), he would see the council. The real decisions in foreign policy were made by the king, or sometimes by Cromwell, and the important discussions in which the diplomacy of the time was carried on were held with them.[1] Though the council seems to have discussed foreign policy more frequently than it had done in Wolsey's time, there was no essential change: it still did not greatly influence such matters.

There are some indications that towards the end of our period the council came more to the fore; perhaps this is one sign of that reorganization of the council which we are endeavouring to trace. It has already been seen that Castillon, in 1538, negotiated with the council, though it was usually Cromwell who spoke at these meetings. Interesting evidence is provided by the reports of the ambassadors of the Schmalkaldic League who visited England twice in 1539.[2] During their first embassy they arrived in London to find the king absent, and therefore presented themselves to Cromwell. Later, the king heard their message in a formal session of the council, and further negotiations were carried on with Cromwell and a part of the council, either at St James's or at Cromwell's house. They had no further conversations with Cromwell alone. Their embassy was largely concerned with the question of an alliance between England and the League, and the report makes it clear that the king's main intention was to prevent the conclusion of any definite agreement. The meetings were constantly put off, because Cromwell was ill or because the councillors were busy in parliament,

[1] By way of example we will give an analysis of the evidence for the two years of Cromwell's highest power, 1534-5. During these years Chapuys' reports are frequent and full. He saw the council hardly at all (*Span. Cal. 1534-5*, 170, 219, 479); the king as rarely, though the matters discussed were more important (*ibid.* 569, 599 f.); Norfolk occasionally (*ibid.* 61 ff., 279, 339 ff., 485); Cromwell very often indeed (*ibid.* 125, 219 ff., 294 ff., 301, 413 ff., 423 ff., 432, 436 ff., 454 ff., 465 ff., 476 ff., 488 ff., 534, 553 ff., 590 ff.). It was, moreover, in his conversations with Cromwell that Chapuys regularly discussed all the points affecting relations between England and the emperor.

[2] These reports are printed by Merriman, I. 272 ff.

and most of the time was spent in discussing the insufficiency of the ambassadors' powers. The use of a council committee may have been intended as a further check on Cromwell who would undoubtedly have liked to come to an agreement. The envoys fared differently on their second visit when they saw the king or Cromwell or both together, but no one else. Though the question of the alliance was discussed at length, many minor points and difficulties were also brought up, but the subject of the second embassy was not so different as to account for the difference in treatment; the real difference was that by this time Henry's mind was made up and the delaying tactics of the previous visit were unnecessary. The council was used to check Cromwell when his policy was in opposition to the king's as yet vague leanings, but by the end of 1539 the minister had himself realized the failure of the Lutheran alliance and was again working on the same lines as Henry.[1] Without ascribing too much importance to the part played by a few councillors in these negotiations, we may nevertheless see in it a sign that the council, which had handled a good deal of foreign policy since Wolsey's fall, was becoming more important in that field as Cromwell's position became insecure.

Diplomacy was by no means the only point on the council's agenda. Affairs at Calais, for instance, were often discussed. A representative from that town was hauled before the council in 1534 but could report that on the whole the deputy and his council had come off well.[2] In the same year there was 'the greatest fume' when the king and council took up a Calais proclamation, though the trouble blew over.[3] The council was present when the king, seconded by Norfolk and Cromwell, declared his regard for the deputy to the commissioners who had in 1535 investigated matters at Calais, and it was in the council that the ordinances drawn up by them were discussed.[4] They approved them, and the debate turned on the question whether it would be wiser to embody them in an act of parliament or in a council ordinance emanating from the king. In 1537 Calais cropped up again, and Lord Sandes, the captain of Guisnes, personally reported on the state of the town and its en-

---

[1] Cf. Merriman, I. 256 f., 264 ff.   [2] *L.P.* VII. 310.
[3] *Ibid.* 386.   [4] *L.P.* VIII. 912; IX. 766.

virons, first to the king and Cromwell, but later to a full session of the council.[1]

It will be useful to compile a list of the matters known to have engaged the council's attention in the period 1533–40. The evidence is scattered through the state papers; brought together here, it will indicate the wide scope of the council's business. The council proposed to prohibit great assemblies of armed people, discussed the dower lands of Queen Katharine, investigated the navy and sea fortifications, authorized the issue of a pamphlet justifying Henry's second marriage, discussed the general council of the Church and relations with the emperor, was very busy considering a message brought back from France by a special envoy, debated and settled parliamentary business and the succession, corresponded with Reginald Pole, was informed at once when a courier arrived from the Netherlands even though the letters he brought were for the king and Cromwell and the latter was absent, itself authorized the dispatch of messengers, and was called by the king to discuss letters received from Cromwell in which he reported diplomatic negotiations.[2] The varied nature of the council's concerns appears clearly from the few notes of business transacted, or to be transacted, which survive. In 1533, Cromwell put down some memoranda which included several decisions regarding the troubles in Ireland, a letter to Lord Dacre, 'the Supplycacyon of the Sergauntt for the rescus', 'the byll put Ageynst my lorde darcye for the kynges maner of Rowthwell and of the decaye of xxx plowes', and another petition alleging wrongful imprisonment and the embezzling of lead.[3] In 1537, lists of matters to be put before the council mentioned the defence of Calais, Berwick, and Carlisle; the gaining of diplomatic friendships by marrying off at least one of the royal princesses; the navy; measures to preserve the peace at home; letters to local magistrates and noblemen to make sure that they spent at least some time in their own counties; an attempt to restrict commissions of the peace to men of 'worship and wisdom'; the council of the north; provisions for the king's household; the granting of a general free

---

[1] *L.P.* XII. II. 802.
[2] *L.P.* VI. 720, 1510, 1571; VII. 1; VIII. 666, 826; X. 635, 1069; XII. I. 125, 444, 1009; XII. II. 1280 (*passim*); XIV. I. 236.   [3] SP 1:76, fo. 137 (*L.P.* VI. 551).

pardon in the hope that the profits of the seal would make up for all other losses.[1]

These lists speak for themselves. The council was kept fully occupied about many different aspects of the government: foreign affairs, home affairs, defence, affairs of the king's dependencies overseas, the household, petitions, administrative projects. These were matters of political or administrative importance; there must be added the cases decided or discussed before the council, and the appearances ordered of men concerned in such cases which were political and criminal as well as civil. Even the state papers supply an impressive list of these, and we can only wonder what the full extent of this kind of work would appear to have been if we possessed a complete council register.[2] Reports abound of the council's busyness. In April 1536 they sat every day, discussing letters from France, and in the end could not come to a decision despite a session lasting from early morning until nine or ten at night;[3] very often they were so busy with affairs of state, despite daily meetings, that they had no time to spare for suitors.[4] There is then no question of the council being eclipsed by Cromwell's rise to power; in the scope of matters brought before it, it resembled the future privy council rather than the shadowy and ill-attended body of Wolsey's time.

The crisis of the pilgrimage of grace shows the council in greater independence than it achieved in normal times. It was no doubt thought advisable for Cromwell, whose rule in general and control over the council in particular the rebels made one of their chief points of attack, to remain rather more in the background. For some part of the time that the troubles lasted he was in London, looking after the administrative details of the fight against the pilgrims, while the king and the councillors with him conducted policy. He was never unseated, for at no time was he left uninformed of what went

---

[1] *L.P.* XII. I. 815; II. 177.
[2] Cases before the council: *L.P.* VI. 818, 1059; IX. 191, 411; X. 765, 1101; XI. 166, 300, 365; XII. I. 152, 837; II. 1018, 1325; XIII. I. 615, 735; II. 6, 387, 1246; XIV. I. 1271; II. 351; XV. 56, 128; *Add.* 1018, 1030. Appearances before the council: *L.P.* VI. 945; VII. 480, 641, 694; VIII. 43; IX. 150, 369, 670, 760; X. 1027; XI. 158, 226, 696, 1232; XII. I. 80, 782, 1182; II. 691, 694, 817, 886, 1118, 1134, 1208, App. 41; XIII. I. 307, 1117; II. 4, 18, 110; XIV. I. 358, 800, 1114; XV. 105, 252 (ii), 406.
[3] *L.P.* X. 748, 752.
[4] *L.P.* X. 789; XIII. I. 91, 659, 1149; II. 605, 703; XIV. I. 381.

on, and his advice and action were in constant demand. It is, how-ever, significant that most of the reports from the north were addressed not to the king or Cromwell but to the council. The duke of Norfolk usually wrote to 'my lordes' or 'my veray gode lordes of the kynges most honorable counsell',[1] though he might also write concurrently to Cromwell.[2] When Paulet and Kingston wanted money they addressed themselves to Cromwell and the council; as Cromwell was not then with the king, the council answered alone— but it ordered them to apply for the money to the lord privy seal in London.[3] Replies to letters from various commanders in the field and instructions to them were ordinarily written and signed by the council as a whole.[4] Though Cromwell was usually one of the signatories and might even, in at least one council letter, employ the first person singular,[5] the council acted as a body and the conduct of affairs was not left to Cromwell alone. The occasion was an unusual one, and as has been said there were sound reasons for making it appear that Cromwell was no longer in charge; moreover, the fact that the whole council signed these letters and received the reports does not prove that policy did not really continue to be in the hands of Henry and Cromwell. However, the fact remains that as early as 1536 the council had developed to a pitch where it could meet regularly to decide very vital issues and was capable of administering its decisions. The council of the 1530's was an active body which dealt with many aspects of the government; unlike Wolsey, Cromwell made no attempt to govern without a council. The true relations between the minister and the council's actual powers are another matter which will be discussed below.[6]

This increase in the activity of the council marks its increasing importance; it also suggests an increasing formality and precision about it as an institution. However, no particular point can be found

---

[1] *L.P.* XI. 775, 825, 909, 921, 1242; XII. I. 319, 321, 382, 398, 468, 594, 651, 916.

[2] Cf., for example, *L.P.* XII. I. 318 (Norfolk to Cromwell) and 319 (Norfolk to the council), both written on 2 February 1537. *Ibid.* 293: Norfolk wrote to Cromwell that there was no news except what he had written to the king in a letter which would first come to Cromwell's hand.   [3] *L.P.* XII. 803, 823.

[4] *Ibid.* 701, 788, 799, 836; XII. I. 291, 332, 333, 505, 558, 636, 667, 846, 864.

[5] *Ibid.* 846.   [6] Pp. 353 ff.

in this access of work at which the council attendant may be said to have ceased and the privy council to have begun. The two did the same kind of work, and signs of a definite change from one to the other can only be looked for in details which depend on whether one is faced with the loose group or the organized board. It is far from easy to be certain where such differences lay. The distinction between the medieval council and the 'incipient privy council of Tudor times' has been defined as 'the distinction between a council which met only at Westminster during term, and a council which met all the year round and sat with the king wherever he might be'.[1] This is an important point which helps to elucidate the separation of privy council and star chamber, but it does not provide a clue to the distinction between the incipient and the established privy council, between the informal inner ring and the fully developed institution, for when these two met at all they met all the year round near the king's person, wherever he was. The difference between them lies in the simple fact of organization, a somewhat intangible factor in the absence of some definite order referring to the thing organized. However, since organization there was, the fact ought to show somewhere in the result, and it may be suggested that differences can be traced in two points of procedure and two points of personnel. The two points of procedure will be taken first. The privy council proper, or part of it, attended the king without intermission, and it met so regularly and frequently that one might say it sat almost every day. The council attendant travelled commonly with the king and met fairly often, but its practice lacked that very regularity and obedience to rules which would be the consequence of institutional organization; if signs of development can be found in the history of these two characteristics, it may be taken that procedure had been tightened up at some time—that organization had taken place. In the absence of council records before 1540 we cannot be certain what the practice then was, but what evidence there is may be collected in the hope that it will at least indicate probabilities.

In the years 1528–32 Henry sat frequently enough in the council to suggest that it was then often with him,[2] but for the first years of

[1] Pollard, *Wolsey*, 111.
[2] *L.P.* IV. 6738; V. 105, 216, 287, 773, 1013. Cf. also *L.P.* V. 1633; VIII. 826, 912.

Cromwell's ministry there is no evidence of any regular practice. In June 1534 the council was reported to be coming to Hampton Court in order to meet the ambassadors from Lübeck;[1] the privy council proper would have been at court in any case. Early in 1536 signs of a more frequent and regular attendance begin to accumulate. In April that year the council sat at Greenwich, that is at court,[2] and the same applied a year later.[3] On thirteen days between October 1536 and April 1537 the council is known to have met at court,[4] and the presumption that it was often sitting there between the recorded meetings is strong enough to amount to certainty. When, in September 1537, the king moved from Hampton Court to Esher, he reduced the number of his attendants' followers and ordered those lords of the council who were present to inform Cromwell and the lord chancellor to do likewise on coming to court;[5] it looks as though a regular council was accompanying the king on progress. By early October Cromwell had joined Henry at Esher where Lord Sandes saw both them and the council.[6] In January 1538 the council was again sitting at Greenwich, and it was still with the king three weeks later.[7] The following year the king conferred with the council at Waltham while Cromwell was in London.[8] It was possible for the king at Windsor to tell some of his councillors to order others to assemble in London, but the letter which communicated the order proves the constant attendance on the king of at least a substantial part of the inner council; moreover, the councillors with him behaved as an institutional council, deliberating apart and as a board, which suggests that the existence of two halves of the privy council acting side by side was nothing new in 1540.[9] The evidence is not conclusive, but it offers a strong suggestion that from 1536 onwards there was a council permanently attending on the king: about that time the organization seems to have tightened up.

Nothing more definite can be said about frequency of meetings, but the same strong suggestion is to be found. In November 1535

---

[1] *L.P.* VII. 888.   [2] *L.P.* X. 748.
[3] *L.P.* XII. I. 1009.
[4] *L.P.* XI. 701, 788, 799, 885, 1228, 1237; XII. I. 291, 332, 333, 505, 558, 636, 667.
[5] *L.P.* XII. II. 774.   [6] *Ibid.* 802.
[7] *L.P.* XIII. I. 91, 241.   [8] *L.P.* XIV. I. 236.
[9] *L.P.* XIV. II. 183.

Cranmer had to deliver a document to the bishops because the council was not sitting,[1] but from the year after references to frequent meetings multiply. Daily meetings were noted more and more often, and the reason why they were reported was usually that they prevented the council from hearing suitors;[2] these frequent meetings were concerned with policy and administration, not with the hearing of petitions, and were thus meetings of a genuinely governing council. It is of particular interest to note that in 1538–9 informed observers reported daily meetings with obvious surprise; what was to become the ordinary practice of the privy council from 1540 onwards was two years earlier still something new and unusual. But it had begun.

A more regular attendance on the king, and a great increase in the number and duration of meetings therefore make it seem credible that some definite step had been taken by the beginning or middle of 1536 to organize the inner council on more effective lines. Better proof of what happened can, however, be found in two aspects of the privy council which are concerned with its personnel: it had a clerk of its own, and its membership was fixed and limited. Admittedly, neither a clerk nor a register was an absolute necessity in the organization of the privy council; Mr Dunham has reminded us of the history of the modern cabinet to warn us not to ascribe too great an importance to these formal details of organization.[3] There were meetings of the privy council in the later sixteenth century from which the clerk was excluded and for which therefore no record survives. Nevertheless, unlike the cabinet the privy council had its clerk, and that clerk had a history.

In investigating that history, Pollard came to the conclusion that we must distinguish between a senior and a junior clerkship of the council, remunerated with 40 marks and £20 respectively, the former of which grew into the clerkship of the (council in the) star chamber, while the latter developed into the clerkship of the privy council.[4] Further evidence to support this view can now be produced. In January 1533, Thomas Derby was appointed to the junior

---

[1] *L.P.* ix. 741.
[2] *L.P.* x. 748, 789; xiii. I. 91, 659, 1015, 1149; II. 703; xiv. 381.
[3] *Hunt. Lib. Quart.* vii. 39 f.   [4] *E.H.R.* xxxvii. 345 ff.

clerkship.[1] The document which records his appointment is a privy seal warrant ordering the issue of letters patent addressed to the treasurer of the chamber for the payment of Derby's salary; the treasurer was to take a copy in his 'boke of warrauntes' as his only basis for payment. This proves that Derby had no patent of appointment, for if he had had one he would have been paid on the submission of successive writs of *liberate*;[2] in this he was like the clerk of the privy council who was appointed by word of mouth,[3] and unlike the clerk of the star chamber who had a patent.[4]

The calendar conceals another fact of great importance: in this document Derby was actually described as 'Clarke of our Counsaill attending vppon our person'. Five years later, in March 1538, Derby appeared in the accounts of the treasurer of the chamber, who was duly paying him his salary, as 'clerk of the privy council'.[5] Although, as has been said, nothing definite can be deduced from a casual contemporary use of these terms, descriptions employed by clerks of the privy seal and the chamber—officials engaged in the writing of accurate routine documents—carry more weight and greater authority. We cannot tell when 'privy' entered Derby's title as there are no chamber accounts extant between 1531 and 1538; all that can be said is that the man who was officially described as clerk of the council attendant in 1533 was officially styled clerk of the privy council in 1538. The inference, permissible though not indubitable, is that the informal had changed into the formal between those two dates. The critical time is being narrowed down.

There remains, lastly and most decisively, the question of the council's membership. It is clear that well before the privy council emerged as established there were numbers of men of varying

---

[1] *L.P.* VI. 105 (24). The original is C 82/664/25 (see below, App. II, E, p. 441); by ordering Derby to receive back-pay from midsummer 1532 it virtually predates his appointment.

[2] Cf. Sir Brian Tuke's insistence on such writs when paying on patents, above, p. 180.

[3] There are at the P.R.O. three early copies of the first entry in the privy council register (the order appointing a clerk), endorsed as 'the originale of the office of the Clarke of the Consell', which indicates that Paget never had a patent (SP 1:162, fos. 51-6).

[4] Cf. Richard Eden's patent, *L.P.* IV. 6490 (1).

[5] *L.P.* XIII. II, p. 528.

degrees of importance and varying functions who were described as councillors, with a consequent distinction between an 'inner ring' and councillors not belonging to it. In 1533 the 'lords of the council' committed the execution of certain matters to five men, all of whom were king's councillors—Sampson, Foxe, Tregonwell, Oliver, and Carne—a phrase which implies that even then the inner ring was well developed.[1] The name of councillor was bestowed on local gentlemen like Sir Edward Guildeford of Kent or Sir Roger Townsend of Yorkshire, neither of whom ever attended the council proper.[2] Fisher was interrogated in the presence of some men known to have been leading civil servants but not inner councillors; yet they were described as councillors.[3] The chief justice of Ireland and the lord mayor of London were both sworn of the council, but that did not make them members of the active council, the king's government.[4] The most complete list of this outer ring of councillors within the whole body is given in the list of 'the counsellors learned with other of his council at large' who walked in procession at the coming of Anne of Cleves.[5] There we find, among others, the law officers of the crown, as well as many of the leading civil servants of the day: Peter Vannes (Latin secretary), Sir Richard Weston (under-treasurer of the exchequer), Sir John Williams (master of the jewels), Sir John Daunce and Richard Pollard (general surveyors of crown lands), Sir Brian Tuke (treasurer of the chamber), the treasurer of first-fruits, and the officers of the court of augmentations. Clearly, then, the distinction between the inner council and the councillors at large was quite definite by the end of 1539, but it is noticeable that it does not seem to have been so definite before; distinctive titles for that group of councillors who were not of the inner ring are not to be found earlier.

For the early 1530's we have to rely on a few ambassadors' reports if we want to discover who was of the inner council; the evidence is unsatisfactory. In August 1533, Chapuys was told to explain his business to the council; he found them in a house twenty-two miles from London and was entertained with hunting. On that occasion

---

[1] *L.P.* VI. 1490.　　　　　　　　　　[2] *L.P.* VII. 630; XIII. II. 34.
[3] *L.P.* VIII. 867 (i): Bedell, Aldridge, Layton, Curwen.
[4] *L.P.* XIII. II. 504; Add. 1053.　　　[5] *L.P.* XV. 14, p. 5.

the council consisted only of Gardiner, Cromwell, and Richard Sampson, dean of the chapel.[1] A few days later Chapuys met the council at Windsor, and this time there were present, in addition to those three, the duke of Suffolk, the great chamberlain (the earl of Oxford), and others.[2] In May 1534, a council meeting was attended by Norfolk, Exeter, Fitzwilliam, Paulet, Rocheford, the bishop of Ely, and Sir William Kingston, the captain of the guard,[3] which looks like a rather more complete session, though Cromwell was absent. Even more councillors were assembled when some very particular business was toward. On 15 May 1534, Chapuys was called to meet the council at Westminster, at seven o'clock in the morning, in order to be given an official account of the act of succession and the obstinacy of Katharine and Mary in refusing the oath.[4] The occasion was meant to be impressive; there was a Latin harangue from the almoner, Edward Foxe, and an acrimonious discussion between individual councillors and the ambassador; an exceptionally large number had been brought together—fourteen councillors and 'all the principal judges'. The councillors included all the familiar members of the inner ring except Gardiner; the presence of the judges proves that this was not yet the privy council, for their exclusion from the governing body was an essential step in the organization of the Tudor privy council.[5] There was a division between important and lesser councillors, but the former composed still the informal council attendant and not an organized board of government.

Once again a new stage in the development becomes visible in 1536—in the autumn of that year, during the pilgrimage of grace. One immediate consequence was that Cromwell retired from the limelight and the council came to the fore, though Cromwell's eclipse was never more than a pretence. There were also signs of a new permanency in the council's membership. In his reply to the

---

[1] *L.P.* VI. 975. [2] *Ibid.* 1018.
[3] *L.P.* VII. 726. [4] *Ibid.* 690.
[5] Pollard, *E.H.R.* XXXVIII. 59 f. I am not convinced by Turner's attack (*Privy Council*, I. 54 ff.) which seems largely to consist of arguments and examples in favour of Pollard's view. The distinction between these two elements of the council seems to have been familiar to the petitioner who in 1536 addressed his request to 'the ryght honorable lordys and justyces of the Kynges honorable Councell' (*L.P. Add.* 1048).

rebels' demands Henry gave this list of his 'privy council':[1] Norfolk, Suffolk, Exeter, Shrewsbury, Oxford, Sussex, Sandes, Fitzwilliam, Paulet, Foxe, Sampson, and Gardiner. To these twelve must be added, at any rate, Cranmer, Cromwell, and Audeley, all certainly intimate councillors but also men whom the rebels had singled out for attack and whom it was therefore wiser not to mention. The council corresponds very closely with a list of leading councillors which could be derived from earlier evidence, and it is good evidence for a considerable degree of fixity in membership, as well as for a thoroughly official use of the title privy council. More important is what actually happened during the struggle with the north. Some of the councillors were absent in the field, Norfolk and Shrewsbury nearly all the time, and Suffolk, Kingston, Paulet, and Russell for short spells. They received most of their instructions in letters signed by the council as a whole, and these signatures reveal a council organized on lines of a restricted and fixed membership, and not different in any essentials from the later privy council.

The signatures show that on sixteen occasions between 14 October 1536 and 8 April 1537 the following councillors attended meetings of the council: Cromwell (sixteen times); Foxe (fourteen times); Sampson (thirteen times); Audeley and Paulet (ten times); Sussex (nine times); Suffolk, Fitzwilliam, Kingston, and Russell (six times); Oxford (five times); Norfolk, Cranmer, Tunstall, Exeter, Beauchamp, and Sandes (once).[2] Of those that appear only once, Tunstall, as a man of known conservative views, was probably kept from the centre of affairs at this juncture; Norfolk and Exeter spent nearly all these months engaged in battle with the rebels; and Beauchamp (Sir Edward Seymour) was but beginning to make himself felt. The rare attendance of Cranmer and Oxford was no doubt due to the fact that they were two of the three 'inner' councillors appointed with a number of councillors at large to form a resident council in London to attend on the queen while the troubles lasted;[3] Audeley, who was the third, must have found that his lord chancellorship required a more frequent attendance on the king despite his formal detach-

---

[1] *L.P.* XI. 957.
[2] *L.P.* XI. 701, 788, 799, 885, 1040, 1228, 1237; XII. I. 291, 332, 333, 505, 558, 636, 667, 846, 864.   [3] *L.P.* XI. 580 (3).

ment to the London council. This was a by-product of the rebellion when it was feared that communications between the king and the capital might be cut, and is evidence of the desire to keep most of the inner council together and with the king. Cromwell signed every one of these letters, so that, despite the evidence for his occasional absence from the council, it may be taken that he normally attended. All except three of these extant letters are dated from royal palaces— Windsor, Richmond, Greenwich, Westminster—clear evidence that this council attended on the king wherever he went. The three exceptions, two from the Rolls and one from Christ Church (London), prove that the council would occasionally meet at Cromwell's house and further confirm his outstanding position, thinly disguised by the employment of an organized council.

We may therefore now draw up a list of the inner council of the years 1536-7.

Thomas Lord Cromwell, vicegerent in spirituals, lord privy seal, etc.
Thomas Cranmer, archbishop of Canterbury.
Sir Thomas Audeley, lord chancellor.
Thomas Howard, duke of Norfolk, lord treasurer.
Charles Brandon, duke of Suffolk, president of the council.[1]
Henry Courtenay, marquess of Exeter.
John de Vere, earl of Oxford, lord great chamberlain.
Robert Ratcliffe, earl of Sussex.
Cuthbert Tunstall, bishop of Durham.
Edward Foxe, bishop of Hereford.
Richard Sampson, bishop of Chichester.
William Lord Sandes, lord chamberlain of the household.
Sir William Fitzwilliam, lord admiral, treasurer of the household, chancellor of the duchy of Lancaster.
Sir William Paulet, controller of the household and master of the wards.
Sir William Kingston, vice-chamberlain of the household and captain of the guard.
Sir John Russell.
Edward Seymour, Viscount Beauchamp.

To this list of seventeen men there ought to be added George Talbot, earl of Shrewsbury, lord steward of the household, a very old

---

[1] So described several times in 1537-9 (*L.P.* XII. II. 1155; XIV. II. 610 [11-13, 37], 780 [17]). For the fact that the office had little practical importance cf. Pollard, *E.H.R.* XXXVII. 353 f. It was probably kept in being to provide Suffolk with something to balance his ducal colleague's treasurership.

man who was nearly always absent but had been included in the king's list of his privy council with the proviso 'when he may come', and Stephen Gardiner, bishop of Winchester, then absent as resident ambassador in France. There is good reason to think that Cromwell had deliberately rid himself of his most able and tenacious opponent in the council;[1] Gardiner would assuredly have had to be included in the list of inner councillors if he had been in England.

This gives a council of nineteen, the same number as that of the established privy council of August 1540. Moreover, if the ecclesiastical councillors be removed, one arrives at exactly that council which a document of about October 1537 describes as 'to be had at this tyme in the kinges most beningne Remembraunce'.[2] The manner in which that list is written, bracketed together and 'The Conseill' put against it in the margin, shows how definite the segregation of the inner circle had by then become. Pollard has deduced a privy council for January 1540 which includes the same men, except that Exeter and Shrewsbury had dropped out by death and Kingston for some reason unknown had been put among the councillors at large; he has also explained rationally how circumstances changed the council so as to give the nineteen men of August 1540.[3] It will be seen, therefore, that by October 1536 the inner council had achieved a limitation and fixity of membership which goes far to prove that it was already an organized institution. From that time it can be shown that some men belonged to a restricted special council with fixed membership, so that changes could only occur when death or disgrace caused the replacement of one councillor by another. Nothing was left of that indefinite fluidity which characterized the council attendant, and the judges had gone into the outer darkness.

One piece of evidence alone raises difficulties. In the act of 1539 which gave council proclamations the force of law, the king's council is explicitly named,[4] and the body listed there bears no relation to the council which has just been worked out. The council is given twenty-six members: the archbishop of Canterbury, the lords

[1] Cf. *Camb. Hist. Journal*, x. 157.

[2] *L.P.* XIII. I. I. The date of this list must be before 13 October 1537 when Beauchamp was created earl of Hertford.

[3] *E.H.R.* XXXVIII. 43 f.

[4] 31 Henry VIII, c. 8 (*Stat. Realm*, III. 726 f.).

chancellor, treasurer, president of the council, privy seal, great chamberlain, admiral, lord steward, lord chamberlain, two bishops, the principal secretary, the treasurer and controller of the household, the master of the horse, the two chief justices, the master of the rolls, the chancellors of augmentations and the duchy, the chief baron, the two general surveyors, the chancellor and undertreasurer of the exchequer, and the treasurer of the chamber. In practice this body (which is named not to be part of the council but the whole council responsible for enforcing proclamations) would have been difficult to constitute because of official pluralism; Cromwell, for instance, qualified as lord privy seal, principal secretary, and chancellor of the exchequer, and Fitzwilliam as admiral, treasurer of the household, and chancellor of the duchy. What is more extraordinary is the peculiar mixture of councillors. The first fourteen are all great officers who were habitually privy councillors throughout the century; the two justices, the master of the rolls, and the chief baron belonged to the king's legal counsel who were definitely of the second rank and described as councillors at large early in 1540; the remainder were high civil servants and heads of government departments of whom the same is true. No such council ever existed in practice: it never met and was never, it may be asserted, intended to meet. Our understanding of the problem raised by this statutory body depends on our interpretation of the act. If one agrees with Professor Adair that the government intended to have proclamations enforceable at common law and that this establishment of a conciliar 'court' was the work of the house of commons,[1] one would see no more in this than a popular misconception as to who really constituted the council. Such a misunderstanding must have been easy at a time when the privy council had only just been organized and was kept as yet by Cromwell's tight hand from a full display of its powers and composition. If, on the other hand, it be supposed that the government themselves put forward so peculiar and non-existent a group, it must have been because they knew that the leading councillors would often be too busy for the work envisaged in the act, so that the quorum would have to be made up from lesser or 'ordinary' councillors. Whichever view one takes—and the present writer

[1] E. R. Adair, 'The Statute of Proclamations', *E.H.R.* XXXII, especially pp. 42 ff.

confesses to a prejudice in favour of the former—it is evident that the so-called council of this statute did not, in fact, ever exist, and was never thought of as existing. The only councils that were to be found in reality were the organized inner ring of nineteen members, and the vague outer ring of ordinary councillors among whom the legal counsel—judges and law officers—may have formed a half-organized separate group.

The crisis of the northern rebellion ended, but there was no return to the earlier informal arrangement. The council continued to meet and act as a body; though few letters survive signed by it as a whole,[1] further evidence is provided by some of Cromwell's correspondents who state themselves to be answering letters written by the lord privy seal and others of the council.[2] To all appearance, the privy council had been organized, even though the existence of a chief minister reduced its practical influence and sometimes caused it to split into two parts, one of which attended the king and the other Cromwell.[3] We have seen that the privy councils of 1540 and even of James I were equally capable of doing that.

The date of the privy council's establishment has now been traced to the narrowest limits which the evidence permits. It was first shown that it must have been organized between 1532 and 1540; the career of Thomas Derby then made it possible to alter those dates to 1533 and 1538. Now it can be said that everything points to its having been organized before the second half of 1536 when attendance on the king grew regular, meetings became frequent, and membership settled down to fixity and permanence. The presence of the judges at a meeting in May 1534 puts the changes which distinguish the formal board from the informal group after that date, which coincides with a note of Cromwell's, made in June 1534, to the effect that he wished 'to remember the Kyng for the establyshment of the Counsayle'.[4] The phrasing suggests that some fundamental reform was in his mind, and we do not think it rash to suspect

---

[1] *L.P.* XIII. I. 628; II. 968.
[2] E.g. *L.P.* XII. I. 639, 677, 1271; II. 275; XIV. I. 610.
[3] Cf., for example, *L.P.* XIV. II. 183.   [4] *L.P. Add.* 944.

that he was thinking of the changes which became manifest in 1536. It may therefore be suggested with such reservations as the insufficient evidence naturally imposes, that the privy council as a proper board of government was created at some time between June 1534 and the middle of 1536, a period narrow enough to dispose of the purely evolutionary and vague theories about its origin, and to make certain that its organization was a deliberate step of administrative reform.

As is so often the case in these developments in the 1530's, an administrative reform is found reflected on the statute book. The act of 31 Henry VIII, c. 8 ('that Proclamacions made by the King shall be obeyed')[1] has a significance in the history of the privy council which has been overlooked. That it was not a 'lex regia', a vast and threatening weapon of royal autocracy, is no longer in doubt;[2] how it could ever have been so understood is difficult to see. The very preamble declares proclamations to be necessary not only because heresy can best be fought through them and because emergencies require remedies when parliament is not sitting, but also because the king 'shuld not be driven to extend the libertye and supremacy of his royall power and dignitye by wilfulnes of frowarde subjectes'. This odd but revealing phrase, which may safely be ascribed to the commons rather than the government, suggests that the limitations to be imposed on the power of proclamations were much to the fore in the debates. Proclamations had always had legal validity, even though their precise character and power may have been uncertain. The act was to do no more than provide machinery for the punishment of offenders; it says so.[3]

It is here that its interest lies for the present purpose. If indeed it had originally been the government's intention to commit the enforcement of proclamations to the ordinary courts of the realm, the administrative aim is quite plain. But even if that ingenious conjecture (made by Mr Adair) be rejected, the appointment of a conciliar court including many second-rank councillors shows that it was hoped to free the leading councillors from the heavy task of judging breaches of proclamations. Something better and quicker

[1] *Stat. Realm*, III. 726 ff. [2] Cf. Adair, *E.H.R.* XXXII. 24 ff.
[3] *Stat. Realm*, III. 726.

than trial before the council as such was to be provided,[1] not only because offenders would thus meet more certain retribution, but perhaps even more so because the reorganization of 1534-6 produced an administrative council, a council which had to be free to employ its energies in the detailed government of the country. As far as possible it was therefore to be relieved of the burden of jurisdiction which rested upon councillors. The statute is part of the general development which led to the institutional separation of privy council and star chamber. Not that the court of star chamber in any way rested on the statute or derived its powers from it, but the act reflects the same policy and purpose as went to the making of these different conciliar bodies. The differentiation was actually achieved by the setting up of the institutional board of government. The privy council, not the star chamber, was deliberately created; the court simply carried on—in business, place and time of meetings, and institutional character—where the old 'whole council' left off.[2] It is for this reason that Mr Adair's suggestion seems so convincing: if the statute was to achieve the only aims it seems to have had— effective judgement on breaches of proclamations and the relief of the privy council—this second aim could indeed have been best ful- filled by taking such matters away from the council altogether; admittedly, the first might have suffered thereby. As Mr Adair has shown, the solution proposed in the statute as passed did not work out, because the councillors named and appointed were too busy.[3] However, whether one holds to the possibility of transferring all this business away from the council, or considers the compromise which enabled lesser councillors to stand in for some of the leading ministers, the statute was manifestly devised to enable the council to attend more freely to administrative business. Thus it played its part in the organization of the privy council which took place in the 1530's.

This reform is in line with the other administrative reforms of the time. Replacing an informal, fluid, and—as it were—household arrangement dependent on the whim of the king, by a permanent, fixed, and bureaucratically organized board of government which,

---

[1] Adair, *E.H.R.* XXXII. 42.

[2] It should be noted that in membership the star chamber was steadily approximated to the privy council in the course of the century.　　　[3] *Ibid.* 43.

though still fully dependent on the king in its work, had emancipated itself from the whim of the moment as well as from close association with the household, it is one example of the general activity in defining and modernizing the administration, an activity marked in such diverse fields as the financial machinery, the royal seals and the secretaryship, the royal household itself, and—it may be added, though this is outside the scope of the present study—the use of parliament. The period saw a good deal of development in conciliar bodies employed to administer. Efficiently organized councils under active presidents, staffed by a mixture of members of the central council, local gentlemen, and trained government officials, and with permanent clerks of their own, were the answer to the serious administrative problems set by the outlying parts of the realm; in the 1530's, these councils acquired an entirely new importance and effectiveness, that in the west being founded in 1539.[1] There is the well-known note in Cromwell's remembrances:

Item to appoynt the most assuryd & most Substancyall of all gentylmen within everey shyre of this Realme to be Sworn of the kynges counseyle, and they to haue commandement to explore and Inserche to knowe who shall preche teche and speke any thing to the aduauncement of the popis auctoryte, and yf any suche be Indelaydlye to apprehend them and to commytt them to warde.[2]

The intention here seems to have been to create a network of king's councillors for police duties, and though this is rather a different idea from the centralizing of administration in the hands of small councils it shows a similar regard for the principle of government by those sworn of the king's council. Councils were also the instruments used in the reformed administration of the finances. The use of small and centralized boards, organized as institutions with presidents, secretaries, and permanent members, was one of the leading administrative ideas of the time;[3] the reform which we have

---

[1] For these councils cf. C. A. J. Skeel, 'The Council of the West', *Trans. R. Hist. Soc.* (1921), especially pp. 70 ff.; R. R. Reid, *The King's Council in the North*, 147 ff.; C. A. J. Skeel, *The Council in the Marches of Wales*, 65 ff.

[2] B.M., Tit. B. i, fo. 466 (*L.P.* VII. 420).

[3] Mr Dunham seems to have seen something of the significance of these councils (*Hunt. Lib. Quart.* VII. 42), though he did not realize how strong a point they are in the history of the privy council.

discussed here—the making of the privy council—extended the principle to the men who were responsible for the government of the whole realm.

If it be asked whether any one individual can be discovered behind these ideas, the hand of Thomas Cromwell is once again evident. He it was who invented the councils for the financial administration, and his close connexion with them in local government, a field which must not be entered into here, stands out in his correspondence.[1] That he had much to do with the reorganization of the northern council after the pilgrimage of grace appears from his memoranda.[2] All this, as well as the fact so often repeated and proved that while he ruled he exercised an almost unquestioned sway over the administration, goes some way to indicate where we must look for the man who produced from the vague inner ring or council attendant the institutional privy council which dominated government until 1640 and became the ancestor of the modern cabinet. Furthermore, there are two convincing pieces of evidence to be adduced. One is Cromwell's note, already mentioned, that he wished to remind the king of the 'establyshment of the Counsayle', which suggests very strongly that he meant to get Henry's approval for reforms planned by himself. The other point is this. It emerges from the warrant of Derby's appointment that the clerkship of the inner ring had been vacant since 1512, for Richard Eden, who was appointed to the senior clerkship in that year,[3] is mentioned as Derby's immediate predecessor. The vacancy coincided with the period of Wolsey's supremacy and aptly illustrates his attitude to the budding privy council; it ended with the beginning of Cromwell's supremacy. Derby was appointed shortly after he had complained to Cromwell of ill usage and destitution,[4] and Cromwell must have been responsible for getting him the post. The fact that Cromwell chose to revive that particular office to satisfy his petitioner shows that he took care, almost as soon as he came to power, to provide the council attendant with a clerk, an essential part in the organization of all these councils. From the first he furthered the growth of the

---

[1] There are many letters between him and the local presidents scattered over *L.P.*
[2] *L.P.* xii. I. 1314.
[3] *L.P.* iv. 6490 (1). Cf. Pollard, *E.H.R.* xxxvii. 350, n. 7.   [4] *L.P.* v. 1068.

privy council. The supposition that it was he who organized the privy council seems as fully proven as circumstantial evidence can make it, even though unhappily there is no evidence of any other kind.

It would, of course, be absurd to suppose that Cromwell started from scratch. Not only had he the practice of the half-organized inner ring to guide him; what is more interesting in this connexion is that he also had the theory of the Eltham Ordinance before him. A comparison of the council there appointed[1] with that which emerges in 1536 demonstrates remarkable similarities: it is plain that Cromwell in fact rested his reorganization on Wolsey's projected reform, giving it that peculiarly bureaucratic flavour which marked all his administrative work, and which is his chief claim to the title of the man who laid the foundations for the modern administrative system of the country. The ordinance provided a council of twenty, while the organized privy council had nineteen members; the difference is accounted for by the omission, in the event, of Dr Wolman, specially appointed by Wolsey to attend to poor men's causes. By 1534 that task was fully delegated to the court of requests of which Wolman remained an active member until his death, and there was no call to include such a specifically judicial appointment in a body designed primarily for administrative and advisory purposes. Cromwell would appear to have seen that. For the rest, Cromwell's council took over some members from Wolsey's: Norfolk, Suffolk,[2] Exeter, Shrewsbury, Tunstall,[3] Fitzwilliam, Kingston,[4] and Sampson;[5] to these there should probably be added the earl of Oxford since the 'Lord Chamberleyn' in Wolsey's list ought to be the great chamberlain of England, the hereditary office of the Veres of Oxford, Sandes (lord chamberlain of the household since 1523)

[1] *H.O.* 159.

[2] Earl marshal in 1526, president of the council in 1536. The marshal's office went back to the Howards in the person of the duke of Norfolk in 1533 and Suffolk had to be compensated by the continuation of a shadow office.

[3] Bishop of London and lord privy seal in 1526, bishop of Durham in 1536; presumably he was retained because of his high reputation, age, and vast experience. His case underlines the truth of the statement that in the sixteenth century the man still mattered more than the office.

[4] Captain of the guard but also vice-chamberlain in 1526; vice-chamberlain but also captain of the guard in 1536.

[5] Dean of the chapel in 1526; bishop of Chichester in 1536.

being mentioned separately and making a tenth. Audeley had succeeded Wolsey as chancellor, Cranmer as primate of England; Paulet had replaced Guildford as controller of the household. Cromwell himself had taken Wolsey's unofficial place as head of the council and Tunstall's official place as lord privy seal; however, he did not thereby increase the numbers of the council because he must also be counted against the secretary whose office, of course, he held as well. The marquess of Dorset, dead in 1530, had found a successor in a nobleman of rather more recent vintage—the earl of Sussex. The dean of the chapel was still there as bishop of Chichester; his successor's absence from the new council did not affect its size because it had taken two men to replace Wolsey in his clerical and secular capacities. Two doughty and trusty champions of the divorce, Hereford and Chichester, had elbowed out their episcopal brethren of Bath and Lincoln; very possibly they owed their places to the treatises in the king's favour which they published in 1534.[1]

That leaves three men to be accounted for in the respective councils: More, Wyat (treasurer of the chamber), and the vice-chamberlain in 1526; Gardiner, Russell, and Beauchamp in 1536. More's chancellorship of the duchy had gone to Fitzwilliam who was already a privy councillor as treasurer of the household, and he himself was dead; if we like, we may see his mantle fall on Gardiner who had presumably entered the council first as secretary and continued of it because of his general standing rather than for a specific office; in matters of religion, intellectual stature, and—at times—intimacy with the king, the bishop of Winchester came nearer to the martyred layman than any other member of this council. He alone had the ability to pit himself against Cromwell, an ability which was also More's though in his case the pride and will to use it were lacking; the rest were pygmies compared with those three. One of the vice-chamberlains was still a privy councillor in 1536, in the person of Kingston who doubled the office with that of captain of the guard; the other, Sir John Gage, was not yet included, though Kingston's colleague in 1526 had been, at a time when Kingston himself was more definitely captain of the guard. It would therefore be truer to say that the captain of the guard had disappeared from the council

[1] Cf. P. Janelle, *Obedience in Church and State*, p. xxiv.

as a separate officer, while one of the vice-chamberlains continued to be of it. The vacant place was filled quite properly by Russell, a gentleman of the privy chamber and soon to succeed Paulet as controller, who could maintain the strength of the household group on the council. Wyat's successor as treasurer of the chamber, Tuke, however, never became a privy councillor; as the history of his administration has already shown, he marked the transition from treasurers of the chamber who were virtually ministers of state to another kind who were only leading civil servants. The nineteenth member of Cromwell's council, Beauchamp, may have owed his place to the fact that his sister was the queen of the moment or to his own ability as a soldier; however, he too had been of the household for some years and was created a gentleman of the privy chamber in 1536. In any case, more than any of his colleagues he was purely a man of the future.[1]

On the whole, therefore, Cromwell simply organized the loose inner ring which he found in existence on the lines of the government board which Wolsey had planned on paper. Cromwell's chief part in the growth of the privy council was that he did what others had been groping for—not an unfamiliar role for him; but he also reinforced the separate and deliberate organization of a true governmental board. He saw the necessity for practical organization and provided that by reviving the junior clerkship of the council (even if Derby was more of a nominal than a real clerk) and by employing the council as a genuine board of government (even if its power was only apparent). The few changes which he made in Wolsey's list also have their significance. In general the composition remained the same— a mixture of the new nobility, the church, and the household. The council ceased to be part of the household but not of the court; and the household, while it withdrew to its own departmental sphere,[2] continued to be an outstanding government department because of its close link with the sovereign's person. Naturally, therefore, leading household officials were leading privy councillors; not only did this not contravene the general trend of an administration turning away from the household—it even assisted it by weakening the link between the head officers of the household and their departmental

---

[1] For all the details given cf. *D.N.B.*   [2] Cf. Ch. vi below.

duties. The more they were privy councillors and ministers, the less they did the work which their offices supposedly involved. As for the church, it would have been strange indeed if it had not been given full representation in the council of Reformation times—bishops were necessary in the government; it is, however, interesting that though the clerics maintained a strong position on the council they no longer held any of the offices of state which had all gone to lay members. Furthermore, Cromwell excluded Wolman whose presence had seriously detracted from the organized character of Wolsey's council by admixing an element of the old judicial activities which it was the ambition of the privy council to shed, an ambition often expressed but never fully achieved.[1] The dropping of Wolman proves that Cromwell realized the true character of the privy council he was constructing: it was to be as nearly a board of advisers, policy makers, and ministers of state as the contemporary lack of ultimate definition would allow. The exclusion of the treasurer of the chamber points the same way; mere executive ministers of the second rank were to have no place on it.

Cromwell's council reforms were, therefore, not altogether original, though his part in them must not be underrated. It would have been something merely to work out the plans conceived by someone else, but Cromwell added a good deal of his own and in particular the element which we have described as organization or bureaucratization. Wolsey drew up a list of inner councillors to form a separate body from the rest of the council, but quite apart from his reluctance to give reality to the plan, he had no intention of setting up a properly organized institution which would have been independent from himself, nor—since he was not by nature or inclination a reformer of administration but only a sound administrator—was he capable of adding to the inner circle those details which clearly distinguish the privy council from the council attendant—corporate unity, organization, permanence. These Cromwell supplied, so that it was he who created a separate institution out of the inner circle and accomplished the splitting off of the privy council from the larger body, the council at large, the whole council, the old medieval council—whatever we like to call it. At the same time, his

---

[1] Cf., for example, *A.P.C.* XIII. 394; XVIII. 181; XXI. 240.

influence and control prevented the privy council after all from achieving independence. The only record of which a trace survives was kept by Cromwell himself,[1] and Derby's clerkship (held together with a clerkship of the signet and later with the secretary-ship of the council in the west) was something of a farce. The institution was there, for when Cromwell retired for a time to the background, as in 1536, or when he disappeared altogether, the privy council at once became evident and important. While its organization was essential for that more energetic, efficient, and bureaucratic government which Cromwell desired, the establishment of a board of equally powerful members, subject to and dependent only on the king, could not but militate against the supremacy of one minister. Under the Tudor crown, no man of Cromwell's position and ambitions could afford the rivalry of such a body. Elizabeth used that inherent difficulty in order to play off her ministers one against the other, and her privy council became at times the battle-ground of faction. Cromwell did not want a rival faction, but he wanted organized government. He solved his dilemma by organizing the privy council but keeping it in tutelage by the force of his personal rule.

Nevertheless, it was the privy council which in the end enabled his enemies to gather against him. The establishment of the privy council undermined Cromwell's indispensability which rested on his unique administrative ability. What need was there of the lord privy seal now that he had taught the council to govern efficiently and well? The history of the last seven years of Henry's reign suggests a different answer from that so confidently given by Cromwell's rivals, but the king did not discover the truth until it was too late. Then, indeed, he was heard to complain bitterly of Cromwell's death and to reproach his ministers with the fall of 'the best servant he ever had'.[2] Cromwell failed in the end to hold back the full development of the institution he had himself helped to create. There is no evidence for what happened between his fall on 10 June 1540 and that 10 August when the council met to inaugurate its register, but the result shows that once Cromwell was gone the newly emancipated councillors finished the elaboration of the board of government

[1] *L.P.* VI. 551.   [2] *L.P.* XVI. 590, a report of January 1541.

351

which would in itself prevent the rise of another Cromwell. But as long as his position with the king was safe Cromwell could control the privy council, powerfully modifying its nature, work, and competence. On the face of it, it was his own vigour and the king's favour that maintained his position, but in terms of administrative organization he dominated the council through the office of principal secretary.

2. *Privy council and principal secretary*

In the fifteenth century there was no special connexion between the council and the king's secretary. As a rule, the secretary was far too unimportant a man even to be a member of the council, until Edward IV's restoration of royal control in government promoted this most confidential of the king's servants to a place in his council.[1] The signet played no part in council procedure. The council not only employed the privy seal for its work but even used one of the privy seal clerks as its own clerk;[2] as has already been told, it was in the interests of the council that a struggle was waged for the privy seal against the signet.[3] On the other hand, the secretary occupied a peculiar and highly typical position in the Elizabethan and Stuart privy councils.[4] He was reckoned a junior member—the office did not acquire high social standing till the reign of Charles I, or even Charles II—and therefore usually spoke first on any resolution. This was meant to mark his inferiority, for the Tudor privy council gave their opinions in ascending order of seniority; but naturally it enabled a skilful man to exercise great influence on decisions. Of all councillors the secretary attended most regularly and worked hardest; he was 'the one element of permanence and the rallying point of more amateur politicians'. He attended to the correspondence resulting from council decisions and was generally responsible for carrying out the lords' orders; he prepared the agenda and submitted it for consideration; the council's increasing staff of clerks was to some degree under his special authority. In 1550, orders were drawn up to regularize the secretary's control of council business:

[1] Otway Ruthven, *King's Sec.* 75.   [2] *Ibid.* 55.
[3] Above, pp. 15 ff.
[4] For what follows cf. Evans, *Princ. Sec.* 224 ff.

he was to bring all letters to the council, check the register and present it for signature, and take charge of all writings ordered by the council.[1] In his account of council procedure, written early in the seventeenth century, Sir Julius Caesar described the manner in which the secretary acted at meetings: he would stand at the upper end of the table, put forward the business to be discussed, and ask the council's opinion.[2] In short, he acted as any secretary acts towards his committee, and, as any good secretary will, he dominated the council.

Since there is no trace of such influence before the consolidation of the privy council and so much after it, and since both the privy council and principal secretary entered upon their modern career in the 1530's, it will be to the point to inquire if this later relationship can also be traced back to that period of revolution. This means, in effect, that we must seek to discover Cromwell's place with regard to the council and his treatment of it, for he was secretary throughout the critical period, and even *in loco secretarii* from late in 1533 onwards, before he actually acquired the office. This investigation is further advisable because the account which has been given of the active council of the 1530's is incomplete: the council was active, but it had less independence or initiative than a bare recital of its ostensible business would suggest. Cromwell as chief minister was as avid of the reality of power as he was, upon the whole, careless of its appearance; to understand the council of his day properly, it is necessary to discover how he managed to reconcile his personal activity and ascendancy with a council that was busily working on matters of policy and administration. In the first place, all the council business which has been discovered has hardly contained a trace of financial affairs. The collection and expenditure of revenue was apparently not discussed in the council or controlled by it; here Cromwell ruled supreme. Similarly, no evidence had been found that the council concerned itself with the supervision of the government secretariats. To the best of our knowledge, these branches of

---

[1] B.M., Egerton MS. 2603, fos. 33–4.

[2] B.M., Add. MS. 34,324, fo. 239. Cf. also the picture presented by Shakespeare in *Henry VIII*, v. ii. At this otherwise highly unhistorical council meeting (the scene depicted took place in 1545), the chancellor begins the proceedings by calling upon Cromwell as secretary to submit the business for which the council has met.

the administration were left entirely to Cromwell who thus had a free hand in the two departments without which no government can work. However, if it were to be thought that the council controlled all the business which came before it, the facts would greatly modify any estimation of the governmental structure of the time. Cromwell was responsible to the king, and it can be argued that Henry never gave him the freedom of action that Wolsey enjoyed; it may be added that Cromwell does not seem to have wanted so much but was always careful to appear as the king's servant.[1] Was he also the servant of the council? We have seen that it did not cease to play its part in affairs in 1532, as it had done in 1512; we must now show that Cromwell did not allow himself to be governed by it but ruled it.

The first point which arises is simply that of Cromwell's relation to the council: how did he stand in it? The answer to this question will explain why a better organized governing council was created at the very time when the best administrator whom Henry ever employed was at the helm. There is much to show that he wished to be the chief of the council, a title actually once bestowed on him by one of his correspondents,[2] rather than—like Wolsey—a being apart. Some letters about the victualling of Calais show that as early as December 1533 it was Cromwell who was expected to achieve results, even though it was officially pretended that matters were attended to by the king and council.[3] In 1534, when the mayor of Rye sent two quarrelling parties to the council, he informed Lord Rocheford, the warden of the Cinque Ports; Rocheford's father, the earl of Wiltshire, opened the letter in his son's absence and showed it to the attorney general who advised sending the parties to Cromwell.[4] In 1539, a merchant who brought some interesting news from abroad and told the council was sent on to see Cromwell.[5]

---

[1] Cf., for example, Cranmer's letter to Henry after Cromwell's arrest (*L.P.* xv. 770). The words of an Elizabethan dabbler in historical writing suggest that a view was then current which has since been too much ignored. John Clapham (*Elizabeth of England*, ed. E. P. and C. Read, 1951, p. 46) speaks of Cromwell 'who succeeded, or rather exceeded, [Wolsey] in authority'.

[2] E 36/122, fo. 63 (*L.P.* xii. I. 685), addressed to the '[M]ost Worshyffull lorde of the preve selle & cheffe of the kynges consell'.

[3] *L.P.* vii. 4–6. [4] *L.P.* viii. 776.

[5] *L.P.* xiv. I. 718.

A letter from Norfolk and the council could result in a reply to Cromwell.[1] When the earl of Southampton came to court for instructions before leaving on commission for Calais, he hoped that Cromwell would be there with the rest of the council, so that he might be quickly dispatched.[2] Foreign affairs might be discussed in council but, as we have already seen, it was Cromwell who mattered, and the important discussions were with him alone (or with the king). As early as 1534, when the admiral of France arrived on a special embassy, no member of the council was concerned except Cromwell.[3] Cromwell could organize the way in which the council received their information from ambassadors; on one occasion, in 1536, he told Chapuys to speak to the king at length after dinner, and on leaving him to see the council and explain his charge to them 'agreeably to their custom'.[4] The council, it would seem, had established a customary right to information, but we are allowed to understand that Cromwell was doing no more than bow to precedent; while he did not wish to antagonize the council by ignoring it, he knew and insisted that serious business should be transacted in conversations with the king and himself. In council he would often do most of the talking,[5] and ambassadors might meet the council assembled at his house.[6] As late as April 1540, when the battle for the control of the council was well under way, Sadler communicated the king's orders, as a matter of course, that Cromwell was to arrange some business together with the council.[7] He was still its 'cheffe'.[8]

Altogether, it seems that Cromwell was often careful to associate the council with himself. In reports to the king he stressed the fact that he had not been acting on his own,[9] and letters conveying orders or instructions are frequently signed by him and at least a few other

---

[1] *L.P.* VIII. 389.
[2] *L.P.* XIV. I. 596.
[3] *L.P.* VII. 1482.
[4] *L.P.* X. 699.
[5] *L.P.* XIII. I. 623, 855, 909.
[6] *L.P.* XIV. I. 926.
[7] *L.P.* XV. 468.
[8] On the other hand, the internal troubles in the council led one observer as early as June 1539 to doubt the usefulness of appeals to the king and Cromwell only. Husee wrote to Lord Lisle: 'And wher your lordshipp wrytethe that yf you myzt come over you wold shewe the kynges grace and my lorde privy sealle that thing wherby the towne sholde ever be the better, yn my pore opyneon it sholde be good that your lordshipp signefye the kyng of it and the councell whull all the lordes ar here' (SP 3:5, fo. 68; *L.P.* XIV. I. 1144).
[9] *L.P.* XIV. I. 516, 538.

councillors.[1] The council of Calais went so far as to speak of Cromwell's letter signed by the council,[2] and the accuracy of that description exactly illustrates the relations of Cromwell and the council. The appearance of an active and governing council was maintained, but all men knew who the real ruler was under the king. Even when writing on his own Cromwell would often pretend to be merely communicating orders received from king or council. The king, he wrote to the university of Oxford in 1534, was informed of their misdeeds towards the town, and he had been ordered to bid them restore all persons they had dispossessed. He added that the council had determined to make a final award between town and gown. A letter from the commissary of the university to Fitzwilliam, himself a leading councillor, shows that when he and the mayor came before the council they actually saw only Cromwell and the lord chancellor.[3] The council which made the final award was in effect Cromwell himself. It was Cromwell who asked the bishop of Ely to attend the council in the following term if his health permitted, who informed the sheriff of Yorkshire of a council decision to hold an inquisition *post mortem*, who asked the earl of Rutland to examine certain friars and report to 'the kinges highnes or his counsaile', who gave instructions to Wriothesley, then on embassy in the Low Countries, by order of 'his highnes by thassent of his hole Counsail'.[4] Like the secretary he was, he put council decisions—so called—into effect. He wrote letters of summons to appear before the council,[5] and men were often told to appear before him and the council, information of such orders being given in letters addressed to Cromwell personally, further evidence of the special position he occupied in relation to the council.[6] In one of the two surviving letters of his to the council, written in October 1534 when he had stayed in London, he gave instructions for the further examination of a suspected traitor and asked for the findings to be sent to him.[7]

Other people treated him as the head of the council and appealed to him if they wanted to secure or prevent council action. The mayor

[1] *L.P.* xii. I. 639, 677, 1271; II. 275; xiv. I. 610.
[2] *L.P.* xii. I. 560.   [3] *L.P.* vii. 618, 903.
[4] *L.P.* vi. 312; vii. 383; x. 59; Merriman, i. 415; ii. 180.
[5] *L.P.* vi. 1205, 1320; xii. II, App. 41.   [6] *L.P.* vii. 1590; viii. 457, 515, 727.
[7] *L.P.* vii. 1271. The other is *L.P.* xv. 910, written from the Tower after his arrest.

of York asked that suits made by some private persons to the king's council be stayed until he and his brethren could attend; the ambassador with the emperor enclosed a supplication which Cromwell was to show to the council, afterwards doing as he thought best; Sir John Russell asked him to summon before the council some criminals against whom the local magistrates were powerless; a man subpœnaed to appear before the lord chancellor and council in the star chamber excused himself to Cromwell on a plea of ill health; another reminded him of his promise to bring his suit to the consideration of the council; a letter from Antwerp requested that Cromwell show certain parts of it to the council; when Calais informed Cromwell that the appointment of certain officials belonged to the bailly and freemen of the town, the order was confirmed by the king and council to whom Cromwell must have passed the information—in fact, Lisle, the deputy, spoke of certifying the king by letters to the lord privy seal; in a dispute over the ownership of some confiscated property Cromwell was appealed to for a certificate from the council.[1] In all this there is more to be discerned than the influence of any leading councillor; the implied assumption is that to appeal to Cromwell is equivalent to appealing to the council, and that Cromwell's favour will produce the formal favour of the council. This catalogue may make dull reading; but nothing else will serve to show exactly how fully council action meant in effect Cromwell's action—how thinly the pretence of conciliar activity disguised the pervading control of the lord privy seal.

By way of caution, one may point to an interesting letter of June 1539 in which Nicholas Shaxton, bishop of Salisbury, asked Cromwell for assistance against the other lords of the council.[2] His friend, the king's almoner, had spoken to the king about Shaxton's coming to court, the reason for his absence being the common one of plague in his household. The king told him to have Shaxton come after the end of the parliament; in the meantime he was to attend parliament

except I wer forbeden by the cownsell. And therfor, my good lord, It shall nowe be openly known that I am forbeden to come at yᵉ parliament

---

[1] *L.P.* VI. 904; VII. 124, 1084, 1232; VIII. 863; IX. 405; XIII. II. 161; XV. 426.
[2] SP 1:152, fo. 102 (*L.P.* XIV. I. 1157).

by the cownsell, except that by this occasion they be content that I come thyther now agayn....I beseche your lordship to be A mean to the other lordes of the kynges most honorable cownsell that I may knowe thir pleasures herin.

There is less suggestion here than usual that Cromwell could do what he liked with the council, though that may be due to Shaxton's particular trouble of which we are ignorant, and to his desire to make it appear that Cromwell might take his side against the council. It is also to be remembered that in June 1539 Cromwell was temporarily in a very unhappy position.[1] As soon as his power weakened, the council grew in independence.

On the whole, however, there can be no question that the council of Cromwell's time was very much under the control of the king's chief minister. Although the only true head of the council ought to have been the king himself, Cromwell acted in practice like a somewhat despotic prime minister presiding over a cabinet of comparative mediocrities; ostensibly the council governed, but in reality it merely followed Cromwell. He was its leader, even at the time of the pilgrimage of grace when, as we have seen, circumstances compelled him for a time to retire to the background. It is true that one of the messengers sent to the rebels, examined by them as to whom he had seen about the king and whether Cromwell was still of the council, replied that he had seen Norfolk, Oxford, Sussex, Fitzwilliam, Paulet, and Kingston, but that Cromwell had not been to court for some time before he left.[2] His answer, however, was very probably suggested by prudence rather than strict veracity, for he would remember the rebels' specific complaints against Cromwell's person;[3] even if he spoke the truth, Cromwell's absence must have been temporary and the envoy's reply misleading. The real balance of power between Cromwell and the council does not seem to have been much affected. In November 1536, Aske himself reported to Darcy that Cromwell was, still or again, the 'only ruler' about the king,[4] and even at the height of the crisis Henry asked him to hold the envoys from the north until the two of them, together with the council, had examined the matter.[5] While he governed, Cromwell

---

[1] Cf. my paper in *Camb. Hist. Journal*, x. 165 ff.
[2] *L.P.* XII. I. 1013. [3] *L.P.* XI. 585, 860.
[4] *Ibid.* 1128. [5] *Ibid.* 985-6.

was undisputedly the king's chief councillor, and the council did its work under his direction. He showed no desire to do without a council—in this as in other things he may have learned from Wolsey's unfortunate example—but worked through a council which he dominated.

Cromwell's control and rule of the council before and after its reorganization was, however, an aspect of his personal standing and activity. All these matters of reputation and domination had little to do with his office of secretary, though it is well to remember that until 1536 he had nothing better to call himself by and was yet as much the council's master as ever he was later. The secretary might order the council largely because Thomas Cromwell held the office, but in return Cromwell necessarily added this ordering of the council to the secretary's normal duties. Formally the relationship was expressed in his control over the council's business and agenda, and in his firm hold upon the administrative strings through which council resolutions were translated into fact. In other words, Cromwell's use of the secretary's place in the council set the pace for later secretaries; in this, as in most things, he created the true scope of the office. There is not much evidence extant of the way in which he handled the council's business, but what there is—a few memoranda and records of meetings—makes it plain that the council order of 1550 merely put on paper, and made a rule of, what had been the practice of the first great principal secretary. Thus Cromwell notes down such details as that he would have to

advertise the lords of the council that no more allowance is given to purveyors when riding out than fivepence a day for him and his horse, which is sufficient.[1]

This was in 1533 when perhaps he hardly thought of himself as equal yet to the real lords of the (inner) council; two years later the tone of his notes implies a change in his position:

That the perfection of such laws which hath been this two years thoroughly and indifferently examined by a great number of sage clerks of the realm

---

[1] *L.P.* VI. 1609.

may not only be published to the King's council...between this and the next session, but also that all those laws which shall be thought expedient for the good order of the English church may pass by Act of Parliament....[1]

By this time he obviously supervised what business should come before the council and could confidently anticipate its decisions. He seems to have kept a private record of council proceedings, for on the back of a letter dated 28 May 1533 he wrote down a list of matters under the heading 'Remembrancys to be put into my boke for thinges done in the Cownsayle'.[2] This note raises the unanswerable question whether an official register, such as the 'Ellesmere extracts' are supposed to represent, was continued in the 1530's, or whether it was the absence of such a register that induced Cromwell to keep what was apparently an unofficial record, though it must also be remembered that the 'extracts' recorded the meetings of a body very different from the governing council of these days. Cromwell's 'recording habit', already stressed, seems to have asserted itself in this most suitable sphere; at any rate, he was clearly most careful of the council's business.

The most obvious as well as the most effective way of controlling the council was to prepare its agenda in detail. Few notes of that kind survive, but from what is known of Cromwell in general—his wide and detailed control of all aspects of the administration—it seems legitimate to infer that the few known cases of such a prepared agenda represent a reasonably common practice, and that the council would normally find itself debating matters submitted by Cromwell. In 1537, a list of business to be treated in council in Wriothesley's hand shows its provenance; Wriothesley also wrote out a list of the council's decisions on that particular day.[3] Thus the council's clerical work seems also to have been handled by Cromwell's own secretarial organization; clerks of the signet had no business to write council matters, and the clerk used was not even Derby, the signet clerk who also held a clerkship of the council. These little irregularities shoot through all of Cromwell's administration, re-

---

[1] *L.P.* IX. 725.   [2] SP 1:76, fo. 137 (*L.P.* VI. 551).
[3] *L.P.* XII. I. 815-16. Similarly, *L.P.* XII. II. 177. The list in *L.P.* XII. I. 1091, is described as council business in the calendar, but it seems more likely that the notes were meant for Cromwell's eye only.

minding us not to overstress his bureaucratic habits and not to forget the elasticity of sixteenth-century methods.[1]

By far the best example of the manner in which the council's business was prepared and dispatched is to be found in a number of papers concerned with a council meeting of 2 December 1533. It will be advisable to go in detail through the stages before, during, and after the meeting; though the case is exceptional in being so well documented, there is no reason to think that it was exceptional in any other way. The council's agenda must always have undergone some such preparation. Perhaps there was usually rather less formal detail, for the fullness and intensity of the preparation must of course have depended on the kind of business in hand; we may well believe that this meeting provides a gratifyingly full view of the way in which Cromwell, then deputizing as secretary, used and directed the council.

The meeting was a special one, for the council was called upon to consider the new policy towards the church and the pope, and the manner in which it was to be enforced, as well as the measures of defended preparedness which it necessitated. For the present purpose the very interesting points outlined cannot be investigated any further; it is the administrative importance of this council meeting that requires attention. The first thing to happen was that a long list was drawn up by a clerk, enumerating these points:[2]

1. All bishops to be examined individually whether they could find any support in 'the law of god' for supposing that the pope had any more authority in England than any other foreign bishop.

2. The bishops to see to it that sermons were preached declaring the authority of the pope to be void and usurped.

3. Similar sermons to be preached every Sunday at the Cross of St Paul, the bishop of London being made responsible.

4. All bishops to be similarly instructed.

5. The nobles to instruct their households in like manner.

6. The shores and frontiers of the realm to be fortified.

7. 'Som trustie persons' to be sent to Ireland, 'to see that Domynyon establisshed, and also to draw and adhere towardes the king asmany of the grete Irysshe Rebelles as is possible.'

---

[1] There is a note of 'matters to be laid before the council' in September 1539 among the *Hatfield MSS.* (I. 11), but the calendar gives no indication of the business concerned or from whom the note emanated. [2] SP 1:80, fos. 171-5 (*L.P.* VI. 1487, 3).

8. To reform the administration of Wales so that peace should be preserved and justice done.

9. The navy to be overhauled.

10. 'Ordynaunces and munycyons of warre' to be surveyed and repaired.

11. To survey and complete stores of bows, arrows, guns, gunpowder, etc.

12. To send ambassadors to various princes of Germany.

13. Ambassadors to the cities of the Hanse.

14. The same to Nuremberg and Augsburg.

15. The four orders of friars to preach as aforesaid.

16. The friars observant to do likewise.

17. The mayor, aldermen, and common council of London as well as the corporations of other towns to instruct their households against the pope.

18. All heads of religious houses to instruct their convents in the same way.

19. Every bishop to instruct every priest in his diocese in the same manner.

20. 'To remember the merchauntes aduenturers hauntyng the domynyons of Braband, and to staye them.'

21. To discuss the household establishment of 'the prynces Dowagiers' (Katharine of Aragon).

22. To do the same for 'my Lady prynces' (Elizabeth).

It is an impressive list, and also a very mixed one. Its very length suggests that the council would in some cases only be asked to endorse something, or would delegate the work to some individual minister; committees do not seriously consider and dispatch so much weighty business in one session. The first draft was revised, and the second draft[1] is in a hand which is familiar from many Cromwellian drafts, as for instance parliamentary bills; it may be that of a signet clerk. The items of the agenda were rearranged in a more logical order, so that the business to be considered was now set out in grouped topics: propaganda at home to spread the new theory of the papal position in England, in the pulpit (1–4, 15–16) and in private (5, 17–19); the setting in order of the realm and its defences (6–11); embassies to Germany (12–14); and some miscellaneous points (20–22). Two new items were added: (23) the spiritual and temporal peers were to write a letter to the pope, and (24) spies were to be sent into Scotland.

[1] SP 6:3, art. 21 (*L.P.* VI. 1487, 2).

Cromwell now enters the story, to leave no doubt of his personal part in the matter. He went to work on this second draft, correcting and adding to its various heads in his most characteristic manner, and his corrections were embodied in the next stage. The bishops were to make up their minds not only about the pope's authority in England, but also about his powers relative to the general council of the Church, a point also to be included in their preaching. The pope, it had originally been put, had no more authority in England than any other foreign bishop; Cromwell clinched this point by adding 'which is nothing at all'. The friars' orders were not only to be negotiated with but were also to receive 'a strayt Commandement' to set forth the new ideas. If the observant friars would not agree to the order (as indeed they did not), they should be 'stayed and Suffryd to preche in No place of the Realme'. The bishops were not to 'teche' but to 'make specyall Commandementtes' to their diocesan clergy 'to preche and declare to theyr parochans in lyke-wyse'. Points 6 and 7 were elaborated with additional detail. The envoys to the German princes and to the Hanse were to be specially instructed to 'inserche of [what] Inclynacyon the sayd prynces & potenttattes be of'. Not only Katharine's household but that of Mary too was to be settled. Where, in point 23, the scribe had spoken of 'the Pope', Cromwell put 'busshope' (forgetting 'of Rome' in his hurry), and stated the subject of the letter which had been left undefined—'declaryng the wrongs, Iniuryes, and vsupacyons[1] vsyd ageynst the kynges highnes & this Realme'. Whoever prepared the first draft (and Cromwell may, of course, have had a hand in that too), these and other corrections show who supervised the second. They demonstrate Cromwell's complete control of the council's agenda. He made many of the points more definite and detailed, prescribed the lines on which the nobles' letter was to be conceived, and generally sharpened the tone of the draft; the effect of his rescension was severely to curtail the council's liberty of action.

From this draft the actual agenda was drawn up.[2] It is in Ralph Sadler's hand, and in 1533 Sadler was still no more than Cromwell's private and confidential clerk. The final document, therefore, came

[1] Sic.
[2] B.M., Cleop. E. vi, fos. 325–8 (L.P. VI. 1487, 1).

from Cromwell's office. There are some interesting differences from the second draft, particularly three new items: proclamations were to be published containing the whole act of appeals,[1] and the king's provocation and appellation from Rome to the general council were to be similarly exhibited throughout the realm and abroad, particularly in Flanders.[2] Points 5–11 and 17 were omitted; these concerned the setting in order of the country's defences and dependencies, and the propaganda to be spread in private households. It may be supposed that the former task was in any case being attended to by the king's ministers and needed no further discussion in council,[3] while it may well have been thought too dangerous to press the other point. A council which was by no means united on the king's ecclesiastical policy might not take too kindly to a suggestion that its members should advocate that policy in the privacy of their homes, and any attempt to enforce such a measure on all the nobility and municipal officials of England could only end in failure or revolt. The idea was therefore abandoned, to be replaced by the more usual and practicable method of propaganda by proclamations affixed to church doors.

Whether or not Cromwell was behind these further changes, the agenda was written out in his office, and it may be concluded that if he was not alone responsible for its terms and heads he must at any rate have had a considerable say in them. The copy of the agenda which we possess has notes in his hand in the margin; the notes were mostly made after the council meeting, and it is therefore clear that Cromwell kept this paper when the council rose. The chances are that Cromwell went to the meeting with this document in hand and read it out point by point. The alternative, that enough copies were made to give one to every councillor, may be dismissed as most improbable and contrary to the practice of a time when paper was valuable and a clerk's time limited. Someone must have read the agenda to the council and everything points to Cromwell; we ought to imagine him not only preparing the council's business but also

---

[1] 24 Henry VIII, c. 12.

[2] Points 9–11 in the numbering in the MS.

[3] All these items of the agenda were receiving Cromwell's attention in April 1534 (*L.P.* VII. 420).

submitting it to the board, in exactly the manner adopted by later Tudor secretaries in meetings of the council.

A note of the council's decisions at this meeting of 2 December 1533 also survives.[1] It is headed 'Acta in Consilio domini Regis ij^do Decembris', is in a clerical script with additions by lord chancellor Audeley who wrote, for instance, the last three paragraphs, and bears one correction in Cromwell's hand. Audeley had put the 'castel of herf' as the place where the princess Elizabeth was to have her household, and Cromwell substituted 'Hatffelde'. This is no great matter, but it proves that Cromwell went over the record and checked its accuracy.

The memorandum lists the points as they were numbered in the agenda itself, but in order to avoid confusion we shall here keep to our own numeration. The council showed itself more cautious than ready to shoulder responsibility. Point 1 was referred to Sampson, dean of the chapel, and Foxe, the king's almoner, '& other doctours', who were to consult the authorities and report to the council by the end of the week. Naturally, 'as vnto the other vij[2] Articles depending vpon the saied first, the Counsail will be advised therof vntill the retourne of the saied answer'. When they received this answer it was Cromwell who was entrusted with the execution of the necessary steps, as his memoranda of January 1534 show.[3] The three proposals for propaganda by proclamation were committed to Cromwell and Audeley 'to put in executing with all spede'.[4] As for point 23, the letter to the pope, Foxe was ordered to draft this 'according to the purport therof', that is, according to the outline added by Cromwell in the second draft; the council wished, however, to see first two letters previously sent to Rome, one under Edward I and another recently. The spies to Scotland were to be seen to by Norfolk and Cromwell, and as for the embassies to Germany, the council advised that the king of France be first informed by means of a letter sent to

---

[1] B.M., Cleop. E. vi, fo. 329 (*L.P.* VI. 1486).
[2] Corrected from 'ix'.
[3] *L.P.* VII. 48 (2).
[4] The scribe had put Cromwell only, adding in a separate phrase, which presumably represents an afterthought on the council's part, 'with the lorde Chauncellour with hym'. Audeley, not liking this, had crossed out the phrase and interlineated 'my lord chauncellour &' before 'Mr Cromewell'.

the English ambassador resident. The last three points, the households of Katharine, Mary, and Elizabeth, were decided by the king who may have been present at the meeting, though the tenor of Audeley's note, which recorded that Henry had personally ordered certain councillors to attend to the business 'acordyng to suche Instruccionz as shalbe devised for the same', is on the whole against the possibility. Henry may have said so at the council board, but it sounds more as though he had sent word. The fact that this matter came up before the council only to be immediately taken out of its hands again suggests that Henry had little to do with the drawing up of the agenda, a suggestion which strengthens the possibility of Cromwell's sole parentage.

Altogether the council had not done much, considering what a tremendous amount had been put before it. Perhaps that amount in itself had prevented more penetrating attention and action. The council tendered advice, of little moment, on one minor point. A number of details requiring action it had left to its most prominent members of whom Cromwell even then, four months before he formally became secretary, was quite the most conspicuous. But, in order to get the point clear, let it be noted that the council did not instruct the executive officers to do certain things—it merely asked them to see that the problems raised were dealt with. The really serious business on which it was to decide—the question of the church and any possible obstruction from that quarter—it shelved with the feeble pretence that 'the doctours' would first have to ascertain the facts of a controversy which had been decided eight months earlier with the passing of the act against appeals to Rome. The political significance of this reluctance to come to grips with the giant nettle, though interesting enough, cannot concern us here; what matters are the obvious inefficiency of the council as a board of government, contrary to all appearance, and the sway exercised by the deputy-secretary.

Nor was that all. The notes which Cromwell made in the margin of the agenda reveal a little more of the way in which the government was really carried on. The lords of the council had at least shown a desire to get that letter to the pope written, but even in this they had not done well—they had been premature. Cromwell noted that it was 'not yet done ne can welbe done before the parlyament', for of course the presence of all spiritual and temporal peers was required for signature. Point 24 had been left to Cromwell and Norfolk, and it was Cromwell who put down the details of what had to be done: 'for to Send letteres to my lord dacre, my lorde of Northumberland, and Syr Thomas Clyfford', the wardens of the northern marches. The council, and possibly Norfolk too, left to him the administering of certain steps he had put before them in ready form and merely for endorsement. The envoys to Germany, on the other hand, were not to be sent until a higher authority had spoken; that matter stood 'in the kynges arbytrement'. However, a few weeks later Cromwell was noting that he would have to devise the various details of these embassies—who was to go and with what instructions; again it is plain that he did the actual work of government.[1] Point 19 is annotated 'this is all rede doon'; as the point was apparently not discussed in council, Cromwell's note may have been made before the meeting. Against the last items Cromwell noted that the necessary orders had been issued.

If we have gone at considerable length into this council meeting of 2 December 1533, it has been because nothing like the same detail can be found for any other meeting in the 1530's. The four documents available have enabled us to conclude that Cromwell, acting in the place of the secretary whose office he was soon to occupy, supervised in detail the preparation of business for the council's consideration, that even at the start of his career he would be entrusted by the council with most of the executive work involved, and that he could afterwards act quite on his own, except for his dependence on the king. We have given reasons for believing that it was he who actually submitted the council's business and in a way conducted its meetings. Cromwell's control of the council in 1533 is manifest; the council continued to meet frequently and act, ostensibly, with vigour and authority throughout Cromwell's career, and if such a measure of control can be proved at the outset it may be assumed to have been at least as complete in later years of greater power. What is still more to the point, Cromwell's control of the council was typical in form and method of the control exercised by

[1] *L.P.* VII. 48 (i).

the secretary of state in the sixteenth and seventeenth centuries. Not only is there no sign of such management before Cromwell's secretaryship, but the position of the secretary and the condition of the council both suggest strongly that there could be none before 1533. The peculiar interrelation of privy council and principal secretary on which the efficiency of the Elizabethan and early Stuart governments rested, began with the reorganization of the council, the rise of the secretary, and the use made of both by Thomas Cromwell, in the course of the 1530's. Power depended on personality and the royal favour; administrative control, of the council as of everything else, depended on office, and the office chosen was that of the principal secretary.

Thus, in the history of the council, too, the period of administrative revolution is plainly visible. The new kind of council, suitable to the needs of the new kind of state, was created in the 1530's; its organization was completed; and from the first the special efficiency which it was to display in its long period of prosperity under Elizabeth depended on the special position occupied, the special duties carried out, by the king's principal secretary. Bureaucratic detail, firm outline, permanence—these mark off the Tudor privy council from its informal predecessor, the council attendant or 'inner ring'; and it acquired all these between 1534 and 1536. At the same time, the reorganization of the council broke a household link. The leading councillors of Edward IV and Henry VII had been very much personal—that is, 'household'—associates of the king; however much the privy councillors of 1540 and after were courtiers living with the sovereign in his household, they were members of a national institution and not personal companions. Under the Tudors the fact was marked by the distinction made between ministers in the council and favourites without political influence outside it, and though James I might transfer government to his favourites, he could only frustrate, not abolish, the ministerial board of the privy council. Government by the king and the privy council differed profoundly from government by the king and such councillors as he chose to consult, precisely for the reason—institutional organization —which made it possible for the privy council to produce in the end a system of government compatible with the supremacy of parliament. Government by the king gave way to government under the king; where efficiency had depended on the personal qualities of the sovereign, it came to depend on his choice of ministers. The change derived from the bureaucratic reform of the 1530's which created a conciliar board largely composed of office holders, divorced from the generality of councillors, and managed by the king's principal secretary.

CHAPTER VI

THE KING'S HOUSEHOLD

As the administration of England was slipping away from the king's household and transferring itself to national bureaucratic offices and departments, the household itself was left behind and had to be put in order. Up to this time it had played a double part, taking care of the king's person and court, and also supplying officials and even departments for purposes of national government. Though it was deprived of this second of its activities, it retained the first; until the establishment of the civil list in 1782—the final separation between service for the king and service for the crown—the royal household remained one of the institutions of the king's government. If the term be permitted, we might say that in the 1530's it became a department of state, a department specializing in the administration of the king's court. It is well known that throughout, at any rate, the thirteenth and fourteenth centuries the mainspring of government lay in the immediate entourage of the king—in his household, whose officers, high and low, were the real ministers and executive servants of the royal will. It is as well known that, if one wishes to discover the administrative history of the seventeenth and eighteenth centuries, it is useless to look to the household whose officers were the notorious sinecurists, those men whose support in parliament was indiscriminately at the disposal of anyone who controlled patronage, and who were mown down in their hundreds by the economic reform of 1782. No contrast could be stronger than that between the hard-working and none too well rewarded clerks and *laici litterati* of the medieval household, and the clouds of place and fortune hunters who beset a duke of Newcastle or a Lord North. To narrow it down: there is a change from the household described in Tout's pages to the household which emerges from Sir E. K. Chambers's exhaustive description,[1] a change from the household of wardrobe and chamber

---

[1] E. K. Chambers, *The Elizabethan Stage* (Oxford, 1923), I, ch. 2. This detailed and lucid account of the household under Elizabeth makes it unnecessary for this chapter to

to the court looked after by the departments of lord steward and lord chamberlain, of whom the former was responsible for the physical well-being of the sovereign and his entourage, while the latter managed the ceremonial side of court life.

One change did not take place, and only confusion would result from failure to realize this. Until at any rate the madness of George III the sovereign was indisputably the political centre of things, and his court was the place where advancement was to be found, policy was made, government was carried on. Socially, the central position of the court (not nearly so unchallenged before the days of the 'new monarchy') was paramount under the Tudors and Stuarts, lost little even during the great days of the Whig oligarchy, remained strong under Victoria, and has not altogether gone yet; politically, that position, which declined greatly only after George III's failure in America, was perhaps stronger under the Tudors than it had ever been before, even in the days of strong kings. What disappeared in the sixteenth century was the sheer administrative importance of the household. The change has been noted before: it was brilliantly sketched by A. P. Newton[1] who came to the conclusion that when the reign of Henry VIII began 'the Household was still an agency of importance in the management of the kingdom and the usual source of supply from which trained officials could be drawn...when it ended all this was over'.[2] In other words, the household became specialized. Its two sections, the household 'above stairs' (the chamber or lord chamberlain's department) and the household 'below stairs' (the lord steward's department) took over definite duties about the court to the exclusion of all work of national scope; they looked after the king and those with him, but they did not provide officials in the government of England.

Another warning becomes necessary here. One of the effects of the sixteenth-century household reforms was to turn the greater household officers into virtual sinecurists in their department, while

contain a full description of Henry VIII's household—the differences in structure were only such as the differences between a male and married sovereign and an unmarried female would cause.

[1] A. P. Newton, 'Tudor Reforms in the Royal Household', *Tudor Studies*, ed. R. W. Seton-Watson (London, 1924), 231 ff.

[2] *Ibid.* 232.

24-2

they became men who took a leading part in council and politics. It might be objected that one cannot describe as freed from household influence a government in which treasurers and controllers of the household, lord stewards and lord chamberlains, even vice-chamberlains and masters of the horse, were as active as they were, for instance, in the Elizabethan privy council. And what after all is the significance of all that national bureaucracy of which so much has been made when all the major decisions depended on courtiers, and when the careers of such men as secretaries of state or masters of the wards turned on the vagaries, intrigues, and interests of the court? But there is a confusion in such a question. Of course, the court dominated the political scene and through it affected administration: the decisions were not taken 'bureaucratically' but in the clique that surrounded the sovereign. For that matter, decisions are never the province of the bureaucracy—at least not in England—and the modern civil service is none the less bureaucratic because it acts at the behest of a group of politicians. Administration itself, the agents of the executive, no longer belonged into the household. True household government—the government of the middle ages—meant not only government by the king and the men near him, but government in and through departments that were part of the household. In that way, Henry VII's chamber finance was household government, because the treasurer of the chamber, active financial officer of a household department as he was, was also the active financial officer of an organization of national finance. However much of a courtier, however frequently at court, a master of the court of wards may have been after 1540, he presided over a department which had nothing to do with the household. Therein lies the difference. And in proportion as Elizabethan treasurers and controllers of the household, and secretaries too, took the lead at the council table, they weakened their links with the household, until only empty titles remained. It would be as true to say that the great seal was still in the household because the chancellor, a household officer in the twelfth century, tried in the sixteenth to maintain his influence with his sovereign by frequent attendance at court, as it would be to make anything serious of the formal household titles of some great councillors in Elizabethan and Stuart times. Admittedly, successive reformers displayed some desire to make a reality of these old names, but their persistent failure sufficiently describes the true position. The political life of the country centred on the court, but administration rested in the hands of agencies divorced from the household, though often in those of men not strange to court life, and the household concerned itself only with its specialized tasks.

A partial exception must be made for times of war, for the management of wars was still considered a matter so personal to the king that the household was naturally employed in looking to it. Even here, however, specialization set in with the development of the ordnance office as one of the household departments permanently located at the Tower of London—these military sections of the household were 'going out of court'. The subject of this chapter is that central core of perambulating administrators who had really governed medieval England and now ceased to do so; it is the organization of chamber and household[1] which took place in the sixteenth century. As has been seen, the development was not entirely new. The household (lord steward's department) was simply the medieval wardrobe which, having been the centre of national administration, had by the reigns of Richard II and Henry V declined into 'the account department of the household';[2] its officers were described as of the household rather than of the wardrobe and came in time to compose the board of management which under the lord steward regulated the various household offices of supply and the like. This final organization was just what the Tudor reforms added; the essential difference between the fifteenth and sixteenth centuries may be seen when Tout's words that by the time of Henry V there was 'little real distinction between service of the court and service of the state'[3] are compared with the position after the reign of Henry VIII when no household officers 'but the very highest, who held what had become merely sinecure household appointments, played any part in national affairs'.[4] By the end of the fourteenth

---

[1] This word will often have to be used in the narrower sense of lord steward's department.

[2] Tout, *Chapters*, IV. 223 ff.   [3] *Ibid.* 225.

[4] Newton, *Tudor Studies*, 232. I hesitate to agree with the description of the treasurer and controller as household sinecurists as early as 1547; they were certainly expected to take an active part in household management, though it is true that the work tended to

century the household had temporarily ceased to supply a personal administrative machine to the king, independent of the national organization and subject to his autocratic control, but in doing so the household itself had almost—if so to express it were not palpably absurd—gone out of court, inasmuch as service in the wardrobe was equivalent to service in any of the offices of national government. This confusion was not resolved till the reforms of the sixteenth century created a clearly defined household department concerned only with ministering to the physical well-being of king and court. The reform was not unprecedented, nor could one expect it to be, for king and court had always had to be looked after, but as usual the sixteenth century gave fuller bureaucratic form to an existing loose organization. The chamber, more intimately connected with the royal person and staffed by gentlemen who made it an important stepping-stone in a career of personal advancement, was in a slightly different position and had never been so technically administrative a unit as the wardrobe.

Newton ascribed the changes to Henry VIII who, he considered, had 'the aid' of Wolsey and Cromwell;[1] perhaps it is permitted to express an immediate doubt about the king's personal share. Newton saw the decisive measure in the great household ordinance of 1526, promulgated at Eltham and named after that manor, and in the supplementary regulations issued thirteen years later, and in this he was undoubtedly right. We must here above all deal with Cromwell's part in the work, because it received little attention from Newton who thoroughly analysed Wolsey's share, and because in it rather than in the Eltham Ordinance will be found the effective measure of organization. Some of the reforms of the 1530's that have already been discussed played their part in household reform. The destruction of the chamber system of finance, the creation of the revenue courts, and ultimately the restoration of exchequer supremacy, ended

be done by the clerks of the greencloth. For details of the board of greencloth see below, pp. 389 ff. It was the presence of household officers in the privy council which justified that body in concerning itself in detail with household matters (Chambers, *Eliz. Stage*, I. 66 f.). As the century advanced the head officers found their time so much taken up by work of state that they ceased to attend to their household duties; but this development was for a long time not admitted to have taken place.

[1] Newton, *Tudor Studies*, 232.

for ever all possibility of that 'household finance' that had been typical of the middle ages. The development of the office of secretary of state greatly weakened that functionary's link with the household (or, properly speaking, with the chamber); it was in the 1530's that he first became an officer of state. The establishment of the privy council withdrew the board of government from the household, though—to say it again—not from the court. Of course, secretary and privy council continued habitually to be at court; the political exaltation of the sovereign, of which we have already spoken, saw to that.[1] They ceased, however, to be part of the household or personal establishment of the crown; though entitled to lodge and eat at court, they formed no part of the so-called 'ordinary', the regular establishment. Several of these administrative reforms thus indicate that offices which were concerned with national government were being deliberately taken out of the household, which is only another way of saying that a truly national administration was being made in which the household was to have no part. As a corollary the household itself had to be organized thoroughly for its particular province, and that is the development of which the outlines have now been sketched. It is time to turn to the details.

1. *Organization*

It has already been pointed out that Wolsey began to concern himself with reforming the royal household at least as early as 1519;[2] indeed, to judge from the papers he was collecting for the purpose, he was probably at it a year earlier.[3] After a delay of several years he was at last able in January 1526 to produce a detailed book of rules, the deservedly famous Eltham Ordinance.[4] This started by recognizing the chief source of the trouble:

Officers and Ministers of his Householde being ymployed and appointed to the making of Provisions and other thinges concerning

---

[1] The secretary continued to be carried on the strength of the chamber as late as 1689 (Tout, *Chapters*, V. 227), a fact which in no way derogates from his position as an officer of state, though it proves both his continued intimacy with the sovereign and the conservatism of the civil service.   [2] Above, p. 39.

[3] *L.P.* II, App. 58, a bundle of papers analysing expenditure in the household; the last year taken into account was 1516–17.

[4] As Newton pointed out (*Tudor Studies*, 238), the copy used by the Society of Antiquaries in *H.O.* is probably D'Ewes' MS., now Harl. MS. 642, which is not a good

the Wares, the accustomed good ordre of his said Houshold hath bin greatly hindred.[1]

That was the basic problem of household administration, and one principle which underlay all these reforms was to prevent inefficiency in the household by confining household officers to their proper duties. The other difficulty was the swollen establishment of idle and useless mouths, especially in the chamber, who greatly increased expense and caused annoyance by their lawless and riotous behaviour.[2] Here, drastic retrenchment was necessary, so that for instance only twelve out of one hundred and twelve gentlemen ushers were retained, the rest being pensioned off.[3] Economy was further ensured by the declaration of 'bouge of court' (those entitled to food and lodging in the court) which preceded the drawing up of the ordinances,[4] and by the lists of 'ordinarie', or permitted establishment, 'on the king's side' as well as 'on the queen's side' of the household which were drawn up at intervals in the years following;[5] Wolsey himself had a list prepared of authorized stabling for horses and lodging for servants which was nicely graded from a cardinal (allowed twenty-four horses and nine beds) down to grooms of the chamber and similar small fry (who yet kept two horses and a servant).[6] In the household proper, the lord steward's department,

copy and was moreover carelessly transcribed. He judged Bodleian, Laud MS. P. 597 to be the best, but mentioned only one of the three copies preserved at the P.R.O., and that by far the worst of the three (E 36/231). An early seventeenth-century copy is among the records of the Lord Steward's Department (LS 13/278), but the best is in the lord chamberlain's papers (LC 5/178); made about the same time, written on parchment, and definitely 'authoritative', it is clearly the copy used in that department for official reference, for it combined Wolsey's and Cromwell's regulations into one ordinance belonging to Henry VIII's reign—'The Booke of the new order of Household established by our most dread Souer'gne Ma.ᵗˡᵉ...Henry the viijᵗʰ Ordained & made the xvijᵗʰ and xxxjᵗʰ Yeare of his godly and prosperous Raigne'. The fact that it is not contemporary matters the less because it was copied from an earlier book; there are frequent references to a 'Liber Vetus'. The copy which Henry VIII was supposed to sign with his own hand and deposit as authoritative, though it existed in 1539 (*L.P.* xiv. II. 3), must have been worn out by frequent use and replaced by LC 5/178. These various copies have been studied and compared, and it can be said that though small differences exist the printed version in *H.O.* is complete and satisfactory enough, especially as far as Cromwells orders are concerned; as it is by far the most accessible, it will normally be quoted here.

[1] LC 5/178, p. 1.   [2] Newton, *Tudor Studies*, 241.   [3] *Ibid.* 242.

[4] *H.O.* 162 ff., though it is doubtful whether this particular list does not belong to the spate of documents produced after the 1539 reforms; cf., however, cap. 1 in *H.O.* p. 137.

[5] *Ibid.* 165 f. (about 1545), 166 ff. (soon after 1540).

[6] *Ibid.* 198 ff.

the great difficulty of getting the work done was to be surmounted by making household officers attend to their specific duties and no other, and it is here that the more constructive of Wolsey's reforms applied. The lord steward, the treasurer, and the controller of the household were named as head officers; it was their duty to assemble every year to plan for the needs of the following year, to devise the means for obtaining them, and to allot officers to the task of providing them.[1] Absence without licence was strictly prohibited.[2] The accounts of money advanced quarterly to the household were to be kept by the clerks of the greencloth and the chief clerk of comptrolment who had to make up accounts of expenditure every day.[3] The next twenty chapters enjoined strict performance of their duties on the various supply offices of the household as well as on the hall, porters, armoury, and stable.[4] The remainder of the ordinances dealt with the measures of economy already outlined, means to ensure cleanliness,[5] and some odds and ends of which the establishment of a council (cap. 74) was the most important—but that has already been discussed.

Wolsey's[6] Eltham Ordinance therefore did three things. It asserted the principle of retrenchment and gave it reality by the pensioning off of large numbers of probably aged supernumeraries;[7] it outlined an organization for the household and spoke strong words on the subject of performance of duties and the need to prevent household officers from being employed on other tasks; and it gave many and varied directions of great usefulness in the smooth running of the court. It did not provide the detailed machinery which alone could make good intentions effective. The very idea, for

---

[1] *Ibid.* 138 (caps. 2–3).   [2] *Ibid.* 139 (cap. 5).

[3] *Ibid.* It was assumed that the household would be financed by quarterly 'prests' or advances from the chamber, at this time true enough.

[4] *Ibid.* 140 ff. (caps. 6–25).

[5] E.g. scullions were not to go about naked (cap. 37), and dogs were not to be kept in court (cap. 43).

[6] For the fact that Wolsey was really responsible for orders ostensibly made by the king, cf. Newton, *Tudor Studies*, 239; that the reforms of 1539–40 were Cromwell's will become apparent in the course of this chapter. As usual, Henry VIII did not personally attend to the working out of administrative reforms, though his assent was of course required for their enforcement.

[7] Many of the pensions assigned by the ordinance do not seem to have been paid for long, which suggests that their holders may have died off rapidly.

instance, that the supervision of the household could be entrusted to a board meeting once a year, leaving the daily running presumably to individual initiative and mere custom, shows that the purely administrative problem had hardly been tackled at all. The Eltham Ordinance asserted two important principles—economy and specialization—and dealt effectively with some immediate problems, but it did not succeed in creating a bureaucratic organization which would enable the household to stand on its own departmental feet and become what was clearly demanded of it—the business centre capable of running the brilliant Tudor court, the apogee of the social and political life of the nation. Once again Cromwell succeeded to a problem of government which required a 'bureaucratic' solution; once again his peculiar genius for creating efficient administrative machinery on the basis of what already existed was called into play.

As was only to be expected from a leading minister, and especially a leading minister whose mind was exercised over the king's heavy expenditure, Cromwell from the first showed a lively interest in the affairs of the royal household. Mostly this interest concentrated on the cost of its upkeep, which will have to wait till the discussion of the financial side of household management in the second part of this chapter;[1] but from an early date matters of organization engaged his attention. Late in 1532 he was asked by the lord chamberlain to get a warrant signed for the liveries due to a number of pages of the chamber and the wardrobe of beds who were yet unprovided for.[2] In the year after, a first attempt was made to reform certain problems within the court, and the point chosen for attack was the king's privy chamber. This, the inmost and therefore most highly esteemed section of the household, came theoretically under the oversight of the lord chamberlain, but gentlemen of the privy chamber were men of importance and ambition, ready and well placed to rise to higher things, and even the lesser officers hoped for ultimate advancement outside the household. Even an old soldier and royal servant like Lord Sandes, who moreover combined the lord chamberlain's staff with the captaincy of Guisnes and was consequently often away from court, must have found the haughty and lively young men of the privy chamber a pretty handful. Wolsey devoted twelve chapters of

---

[1] Below, pp. 398 ff. [2] *L.P.* v. 1323.

his Ordinance to the privy chamber;[1] he appointed its staff to consist of the marquess of Exeter, six gentlemen (who performed the services about the king's person), two gentlemen ushers (who kept the door), four grooms, a barber, and a page, all named, and gave detailed instructions for their behaviour in which the words sober, reverent, humble, and discreet loom large; it was found necessary to forbid the undue petitioning of the king by those nearest to him, and immoderate dicing and playing of cards in his privy chamber while he was absent.

These orders were found insufficient in two respects: six gentlemen were not enough—for men in that position were not civil servants and were often employed on business of state, especially in embassies—and a mere injunction had little effect in ensuring attendance. A brief order was therefore drawn up on 10 April 1533, 'howe and in what nomber the gentlemen of [the king's] prevy Chambre shall geve there attendaunce vpon his saide highnes daylye'.[2] It appears from this that there were now fourteen gentlemen divided into two groups of seven of whom in each case two stood out as 'senior' to or more important than the rest: Exeter and Sir Henry Norris leading Sir Nicholas Carew, Sir Anthony Browne, Sir Thomas Cheyney, and masters Page and Weston; Lord Rocheford and Sir Thomas Henneage leading Sir Thomas Neville, Sir Francis Bryan, Sir John Russell, and masters Wellisbourne and Henry Knevett. Each group of five was to attend for six weeks at a time, and no more than five chambers were to be occupied at any given moment; the senior gentlemen, one of whom in any case was a lord, seem to have had more liberty in coming and going. In order to control the arrangement, the gentlemen ushers were

to kepe a boke of the comyng and goyng of the saide gentlemen and tentre therin the dayes certayne of departyng and agayne commyng of the saide gentlemen for ther tyme of waiting from six wekes to six wekes, & the

---

[1] *H.O.* 154 ff.

[2] B.M., Add. MS. 9853, fo. 24. The date of this order is in doubt. It is given as 'Wednisday the xth day of Aprill in the xxiiij^the yere of his most prosperous reigne'; 10 April, 24 Henry VIII would be 1533 (the regnal year ran from 22 April), but that day was a Friday, whereas the 10th of April fell on a Wednesday in 1532 and *L.P.* prefer that date (v. 927). I have adhered to the year given, largely because further attempts to deal with chamber matters belong to 1533, but it is quite possible that the weekday is correct; the point is not very important.

saide boke to remayne continually in the gentlemen husshers Chambre
for thentent that it may be had to the comptinghous for the viewment of
the vacat of the saide gentlemen at altimes that yt shalbe thought
Necessary to thofficers of the saide comptinghous to call for the saide boke.

In the same book all gentlemen were to enter the name of the deputy
they were authorized to appoint if sickness or 'any oder reasonable
let' prevented their attendance,

so that the Kinges highnes shall neuer be vnpurvaide of syx gentlemen of
hys chambre at oones and oon lord to serue hym accordynge to thole
numbre of seven.

Not only, therefore, was the staff of the privy chamber given a fixed
tour of duty, but these troublesome gentlemen were put under the
supervision of the counting-house, the body which Cromwell—as
we shall see—was concerned to make supreme in the management of
the household. In effect the privy chamber was partially withdrawn
from the lord chamberlain's insufficient care and put under the more
observant eye of the board of greencloth; though this may have been
necessary and even successful at the time, there is nothing to show
that the latter established a permanent ascendancy over that part
of the royal household. Too detailed an organization of what was
difficult to organize—and gentlemen of the privy chamber were too
important to submit to discipline easily—tended, in this century, to
fail of its purpose. We do not know whether or for how long the rules
laid down were observed, but at least it does not appear that the
privy chamber was for quite some time in further need of attention
from above.

The keeping of a book of attendance bears Cromwell's bureaucratic stamp, and the similarity of the rota arranged in the privy
chamber with the later reform of the signet office[1] also suggests that
he may have been behind this reform. Another attack on household
problems made in 1533 is more surely linked with him because it
survives in a list of his memoranda.[2] Cromwell was apparently
wrestling again with the excess of staff which beset the household,

---

[1] Above, pp. 264 f.

[2] *L.P.* VI. 1609, put quite reasonably into 1533 by *L.P.* The list itself, in a formal
script, gives no indication of its connexion with Cromwell, but another list in E 36/143,
no 5, which is certainly Cromwell's, was written by the same clerk.

for he wanted to know the king's views on the allowance to be made to gentlemen and pages discharged from offices in the household; also, the reforms of the privy chamber already discussed raised the question who was competent to appoint to those 'waiting' (attending) places to dine and sup—the masters of the household apparently were not.[1] One of Cromwell's queries was to result in the issue of a proclamation against vagabonds frequenting the court.[2] The rest of the notes concerned various financial points which will be considered later. In all probability this list is a sign of Cromwell's general activity in tightening up administration which is so marked at the beginning of his ministry; it is not likely that he was at this time contemplating large-scale reforms, though some points—such as the organization of the privy chamber—may have required attention because the Eltham Ordinance had failed to provide a solution. Similarly it cannot be known what Cromwell meant by a note to see to the signing of 'a bill for the King's household',[3] though, very likely, nothing more than some warrant for payment was involved; the fact is evidence of his continued interest and activity in household matters. Such interest and activity really go without saying in one who to the best of his ability engrossed all the work of government, as does the fact that household patronage depended on him: in 1537, William Paulet, himself treasurer of the household, sent one of Cromwell's old servants to him with a letter recommending

his aduaunsement in the kinges service...if Any of the Clerkes of the Kitchen or grene clotth be taken to my lord princes service, for by the Removing of one diuerse shall Ryse; Whereyn gret Labor is made all Redy, Whiche shalbe this mans Hindraunce onles it may pleas your lordship to speke for him....[4]

Prince Edward's household seems to have been the place hunter's best hope; a rumour, in 1540, that it was to be enlarged provoked another request for patronage to the lord privy seal.[5] Some time in 1538 or 1539, Sir William Parr, delicately alluding to 'the late

---

[1] There is no sign of officials known by that name till after the reforms of 1539; Cromwell was here either using the term loosely for any leading household official (cf. Chambers, *Eliz. Stage*, I. 34, n. 2) or giving a hint that the later reforms were already in his mind.

[2] *L.P.* VI. 1610.

[3] *L.P.* VII. 50, 107, 108.

[4] SP 1:125, fo. 242 (*L.P.* XII. II. 945).

[5] *L.P.* XV. 602.

change'—surely the fall of Exeter—begged a place in the privy chamber for his nephew;[1] Cromwell's power over the staff of the household was as great as in spheres less intimately connected with the king's person.

Despite all this obvious interest and power, however, it was several years before Cromwell found time to turn his attention to the household. In January 1537, John Husee, Lord Lisle's well informed London agent, reported that Cromwell would from now on 'keep the Court ordinarily', and that some thought the king's household was to be reformed on the model of that of France.[2] Husee's words are the more valuable in that they leave no doubt that it was from Cromwell's arrival to stay permanently at court that people guessed at the coming reforms; he came to see what needed doing and to do it. Some ten days later Husee reported the details: fifty 'spears' or mounted guard were to be appointed, with £40 a year each, and it was rumoured that further reforms would make for economy and the pensioning of the 'most part'—the old problem of too great a number of hangers-on was yet far from solved.[3] The council was now presented with the plans, and by the end of January 1537 both the question of the bodyguard and the household reforms were 'at a point, though the result is not published'; a week later, with remarkable suddenness, all this business had disappeared from sight—the new spears 'nothing spoken of', the proposed reduction of staff forgotten, and 'for the abridging of the King's house, all those matters sleepeth'.[4]

Cromwell's first attempt to reform the household thus came to nothing. We cannot be certain why it failed, but it may be suggested that the troubles of the pilgrimage of grace were behind both the attempt and the failure. The crisis pressed home the need for economy, and whenever that subject arose in Tudor England the extravagance and costliness of the court was not only the obvious but also the right point of attack. Wolsey, Cromwell, later Burghley and his son, all found it necessary to curb the expenditure of the

---

[1] L.P. Add. 1297. I suggest that this letter belongs to a later year than that given in L.P.   [2] L.P. XII. I. 89.
[3] Ibid. 237.   [4] Ibid. 299, 353.

largest single spending department of the day, and such curbing was to be achieved only by rigorous management and the cutting down of hungry mouths. It appears that Cromwell had hopes to do both in January 1537, though the addition of a life-guard of fifty men rather detracted from the seriousness of the proposed retrenchment. Here again, however, the rebellion may have had something to do with a move to provide better protection for the royal person. At the same time it must be remembered that all the Tudors suffered from a truly *parvenu* love of showy display, a failing from which even the careful Henry VII was not free, while his son was throughout his life downright extravagant. In their efforts at economy Tudor ministers had always to contend with this desire for visible splendour, even if admittedly there was some good politic cunning behind the desire: a visibly splendid king was more likely to impress than a threadbare one. As for the dropping of the proposed reforms, Bigod's rebellion, which broke out on 10 January 1537 and did not end until its fool-hardy leader was captured a month later,[1] must have given the council more important things to talk about than a reform of the royal household. However, these first hints show what Cromwell was likely to do when the time served: he would give the king his new guard, would limit the number of men cluttering up the precincts of the court, and would—this was so far the barest suggestion—reform the management of the household on the French model.

Just over a year later, in March 1538, another attempt was made to put these intentions into practice. Lord Lisle received information from Sir John Dudley who reported that there was to be a great master of the household (as in France), a change in the 'old ordinary' or authorized establishment, and the appointment of the guard under the earl of Southampton, the lord admiral and lately, as Sir William Fitzwilliam, treasurer of the household;[2] his report was confirmed with reservations by the cautious Husee who wrote

ther shalbe an ordre tacken as it is in ffrance and a gran mastre de hostel made, and certayne speres made, which I do skant belyue.[3]

His disbelief was justified; nothing materialized at this time, and it seems that about the middle of 1538 someone had to get out good

[1] Fisher, *Pol. Hist.* v. 414 f. [2] *L.P.* XIII. I. 503.
[3] SP 3:4, art. 108 (*L.P.* XIII. I. 510).

grounds for the creation of a guard; a paper, in Wriothesley's hand and therefore probably part of Cromwell's planning, worked out that the king's existing surplus in revenue enabled him, among other things, to appoint two hundred gentlemen with a salary of 100 marks each to attend on him—a larger number than was ever contemplated in practice.[1] Someone—perhaps Henry, perhaps Cromwell—appears to have needed persuading, for another document of about this time put the case for a guard of one hundred gentlemen armed with poleaxes (to distinguish them from the yeomen of the guard who carried bills and halberds), at a cost per man of £50 a year, of which £10 was allowance for meat and drink.[2] The matter dragged on; in January 1539 talk about these 'spears' had died down, though there was a school of thought which held that they would be established.[3] These were the years when Cromwell's hands were full with organizing the defences of the kingdom, restoring the navy and harbour fortifications, and planning measures at home and abroad against the attack from emperor and, possibly, Most Christian king of which Cardinal Pole's mission was rightly believed to be the spearhead. During such a crisis there was no time to spare for a reform of the royal household, however pressing. At last, however, Cromwell determined to see the business through. On 31 July 1539 he ordered one of his servants to send him 'a book called The booge of Courte, signed with the King's hand'—almost certainly the Eltham Ordinance—and ten rolls concerning the household,[4] and thus equipped he set about his reforms.[5] On 22 December Husee, grown more cautious by experience of such rumours than even his nature was, once more reported that it was said the household was to be altered; five days later he could at last announce that the new order for the household had taken effect on Christmas Eve.[6] Cromwell's household reforms can be dated more accurately than most of the measures of his administration: they were put into practice on 24 December 1539, and the king specially removed to Greenwich—his birthplace where he liked to celebrate Christmas—

---

[1] *L.P.* XIII. II. 1.   [2] *Ibid.* 111.
[3] *L.P.* XIV. I. 29.   [4] *L.P.* XIV. II. 3.
[5] There are several notes in 1539 showing Cromwell busy on the household: *L.P.* XIV. I. 400; II. 548–9.
[6] *Ibid.* 719, 745–6.

in order to inaugurate them.[1] However, the business could not be settled completely at one blow; as late as February–March 1540 there are notes in Cromwell's remembrances 'to take a final end' with the household and the spears, and to see to the finances of the organization.[2]

The fact that some really thoroughgoing reforms were involved comes out most clearly in a manuscript book still apparently preserved in private hands, extracts from which were published in 1913 and 1914.[3] It appears to have been made by William Dunche whose exact employment at the critical time is not known but was probably something subordinate in the household,[4] and its importance lies in the fact that unlike all other extant copies of Henry VIII's household ordinances it is dated to the year of Cromwell's reforms. Its heading —'Anno xxxi^{mo} Regis h viij^{ui}: The booke of the Newe Ordynarye of the Kinges most honerable houshold'[5]—is clear proof that what Cromwell called 'the new ordre'[6] really constituted a complete overhaul of the household establishment, and the table of contents in Dunche's book gives an idea of what Cromwell tackled in straightening out the household.[7] Apart from detailed and careful records of 'bouge of court' and estimates of all charges and expenses in the household—calculations on which the real reforms had to be based —the interesting items are, first, a complete establishment both of the household above stairs, the chamber officers on the king's and the queen's sides, and of the lord steward's department, and secondly, the detailed instructions for the board of greencloth. Although many of the items in Dunche's book were entered in the course of the years following, the title gives sufficient indication of the fact that all these lengthy lists and detailed estimates (many of which appear in the printed *Household Ordinances*) were part of the reforms of 1539–40; small wonder that it took several years to work them out, and that they had so often to be put aside for more urgent business, before in the end—and none too soon, for Cromwell's time was running out—the thorough bureaucratic scheme for the royal household was produced.

---

[1] *Ibid.* 726.　　　　　　　　　　[2] *L.P.* XV. 195, 321.
[3] *The Genealogist*, n.s., XXIX. 12 ff., 94 ff., 144 ff., 238 ff.; XXX. 18 ff., 94 ff., 153 ff., 208 ff.　　　[4] *Ibid.* XXIX. 13.　　　　[5] *Ibid.* XXIX. 12.
[6] Merriman, II. 244.　　　[7] The contents are listed in *Genealogist*, n.s., XXIX. 18 f.

As far as the king's chamber was concerned, the main work of organization had been done in the order for attendance in the privy chamber which has already been discussed. It remained to produce the full establishment, and though Dunche's list must have been drawn up after Cromwell's fall as it gives the office of great chamberlain to the earl of Sussex who succeeded him,[1] it was earlier than 1542 when the earl died and near enough contemporary with the events of 1539 to be used in evidence. It is not the only list extant, though probably the earliest, and it would appear that after Cromwell's reforms records of the 'ordinary' were brought up to date at short intervals.[2] The chamber establishment is worth looking at, especially because it marks a considerable increase on the numbers (where they are given) of the Eltham Ordinance. In 1526 the privy chamber was composed of one lord, six gentlemen, two gentlemen ushers, four grooms, a barber, and a page;[3] in 1533 there were certainly two lords and twelve gentlemen. The new 'ordinary' of 1539 survives more completely. We may leave out the lords whose attendance and identity would vary with the political duties of those privileged to belong to 'the king's side'; the regular officials are more interesting.[4] There were to be three each of cup-bearers, carvers, and sewers, four squires for the body, and two surveyors, all properly speaking belonging to the outer chamber. The privy chamber was now staffed by sixteen gentlemen, two gentlemen ushers, four gentlemen ushers daily waiters (these were more like the yeomen ushers of the Eltham Ordinance), three grooms, and two barbers. Two officers of the Robes, five of the Beds, and a groom porter completed the chamber establishment proper; there were further eight gentlemen ushers quarter waiters, four sewers, four pages, and twelve grooms, all without bouge of court and with much

---

[1] *Genealogist*, n.s., XXX. 18 ff.

[2] Cf. below, p. 392. Another list is printed in *H.O.* 165 ff.; its date is about 1544 or 1545. Similarly a partial list in B.M., Lansd. MS. 2, fos. 34r–v (also about 1545). Cromwell's own list does not survive but the chances are that it existed; though the reforms of December 1539 were pretty complete, Cromwell's notes of March 1540 (*L.P.* XV. 321) show that the details dragged on, and these full lists may not have been ready for issue when he fell, so that the task was left for his successors. The various lists could be used to illustrate the principle of promotion by seniority in the sixteenth-century household (cf. Newton, *Tudor Studies*, 254 f.). E.g. Edward Sulliard, second surveyor of the chamber in 1540, was first surveyor by 1545.

[3] *H.O.* 154.   [4] *Genealogist*, n.s., XXX. 19 f.

less reward, constituting as it were a reserve fund of servants. This detailed list gives a good idea of the complexity of the chamber organization which yet was as nothing compared with the great number of men who staffed the household proper. It also indicates how fully Cromwell secured the organization even of the chamber, and is in marked contrast to the much less thorough methods which seem to have prevailed in 1526.

There may be doubt how many of these officers were newly added by the revised 'ordinary' of 1539 or how many were removed, but it is certain that the gentlemen pensioners or spears were new at this time. Their establishment seems to have struck contemporaries as more important than all the other measures taken; to judge from the frequent references, they were considered to be the essential part of the 1539 reforms. The chroniclers, too, take note of only this detail, though Wriothesley gets the date and fee wrong;[1] Hall mentions, correctly, that a similar guard had existed at the beginning of Henry's reign.[2] Abroad it was thought that Henry wanted to imitate French practice, for the court of that country had two hundred such gentlemen-soldiers in attendance,[3] and the belief may have been true since the French model was mentioned several times in the course of the abortive planning of 1537 and 1538. However, the pensioners who so forcibly struck contemporary opinion were unimportant enough as far as administrative reform went. Generally speaking, they existed for display,[4] though on ceremonial occasions they might fulfil the very necessary duty of maintaining order.[5] They were launched with some difficulty, for even in February 1540 it was not yet certain how and by whom they were to be paid, and they found it hard to horse themselves in a suitable fashion.[6] Their chief value to others than the king lay in the fact that they offered splendid chances of promotion to young men of good family; the more respectable offices

---

[1] *Wriothesley's Chronicle* (Camden Soc.), I. 112. He said that the spears were to have £5 from augmentations; there is no trace of such a payment in the augmentations accounts, and more authoritative records give them £46. 13s. 4d. each (*H.O.* 168 f.). They appear to have been paid by the cofferer of the household (*L.P.* xv. 394, 3), though as a matter of fact there is no record anywhere of their fees being paid; but this is discussed more fully below, pp. 402 ff.

[2] Hall, *Chronicle*, 832. Cf. *L.P.* I. I. 244. The spears established in 1509 must have dropped out of existence in the interval. [3] *L.P.* xv. 179.

[4] *L.P.* xvi. 868, 1088.   [5] *L.P.* xv. 10.   [6] *Ibid.* 195, 217.

there were in the chamber, the better for men hoping to carve a career—in politics, not in the administration. Cromwell was pestered for an appointment to the spears on 28 December 1539, when it was probably already too late, and the man did not succeed.[1] On the other hand, a preliminary list of the spears included four men marked as 'my Lord Privy Seal's men' and one each promoted by Norfolk, Suffolk, and Southampton;[2] of these only Suffolk's man failed of his ambition.[3] Cromwell's outstanding position is fairly illustrated by these figures; it was the man who could help his servants and followers to advancement under the crown who mattered in the 350 years between the first Tudor and the last Hanoverian. Fifty men were at first appointed, with three officers (a captain, lieutenant, and standard-bearer, though the last named may have been taken from the fifty), but on 6 July (1540) three were added on the recommendation of the captain, Sir Anthony Browne.[4] The guard also had a clerk of the check and a harbinger. The wages, especially of the officers, seem soon to have been considered insufficient, and Cromwell himself authorized increases in April 1540 which were still further raised by 1545.[5] It was altogether a surprisingly useless and spendthrift arrangement for which the king may have been largely responsible; perhaps Cromwell had succeeded in getting the numbers reduced from the first swollen estimates. At any rate, for a time the guard served the typical Tudor desire to add visible glory to their court.

As far as the chamber was concerned, then, no actual reorganization took place. For the household proper, however, Cromwell did much more. The chief reform here was a detailed constitution for the counting-house or board of greencloth, the committee responsible for administering the household.[6] The core of Cromwell's reforms

---

[1] *L.P.* xiv. II. 751. [2] *Ibid.* 783.

[3] *Genealogist*, n.s., xxx. 21. The list does not include a certain Bolles, mentioned in *L.P.* xiv. II. 783 as Suffolk's follower.

[4] *H.O.* 213. Dunche's list contains fifty-two men and two officers (*Genealogist*, n.s., xxx. 21).

[5] Thus in April 1540 the captain got 100 marks and the lieutenant £50 (*H.O.* 213), while the captain's fee was doubled and the lieutenant's raised to 100 marks before the end of the reign (*ibid.* 168).

[6] The institution, though less formally complete, was very much older, but the name 'board of greencloth' (after the cloth which covered the table round which they met) seems to have come up under the early Tudors (Tout, *Chapters*, II. 41, n. 1).

was contained in the 'Ordinances appointed for all officers of Household, upon the Makeing an Establishment of the new Booke of Household, made by the King's Majesty in the 31st yeare of his most Gracious Reigne';[1] these are divided according to the various departments of the household, beginning with a long section devoted to the counting-house, continuing through the supply offices,[2] and winding up with a few general directions. The counting-house was to consist of the lord great master, the treasurer of the household, and the controller of the household, as head officers, one of whom at least was to attend every day at its office, with the cofferer, clerks of the greencloth, and one clerk controller, 'to sitt and to have brought before them all the Bookes of briefments of all the Officers of the Household for the day before passed' and to check waste by punishment. This ordinance was devised to give reality to the pious aspirations of the Eltham Ordinance (cap. 2) which defined, on general lines, the supervisory duties of the head officers.[3] Cromwell intended the board to meet every day to consider the details of expenditure in all the offices, probably the only way in which extravagance or dishonesty could be stopped at the source. However, this much more definite order was also more difficult of fulfilment than Wolsey's vaguer decree, for the head officers were well on the way to becoming leading ministers of state; they were invariably privy councillors and, to use a parallel, were almost in the position of our present day lords privy seal or president of the council whose nominal duties have ceased to exist but who play an important part in cabinet. Cromwell admitted the difficulty by allowing two of them to be absent at the daily check, but as in practice none of them tended to be sufficiently active in their household duties he compromised further by ordering the clerks of the greencloth and clerks controllers to take over these duties if none of the great men turned up; all was done that could be done to ensure constant supervision.

Even more important because more effective were the very detailed

---

[1] H.O. 228 ff.

[2] Those mentioned are Bakehouse, Pantry, Cellar, Spicery, Ewery, Kitchen, Larder, Poultry, Pastry, Saucery, Squillery, Woodyard, Porters at the Gate, and Almonry, the last two not being strictly speaking offices of supply.

[3] H.O. 138.

rules laid down for the active officials of the board. They may not have been altogether new, but the very absence of a comparable set of precise orders from the Eltham Ordinance suggests that Cromwell was doing more towards the bureaucratic organization of the household than had ever been attempted before; and it must be remembered that the organization which he provided administered the royal household for two and a half centuries.[1] The cofferer, head clerk of the household and the highest office to be attained by promotion from below,[2] was to attend daily 'at the Greencloth' to offer his expert opinion on the books to be engrossed; he was to advance weekly to the purveyors of each department the necessary sums certified to him by the clerks accountant[3] and to exact an account from the purveyors not later than five days after the end of each month; he was to pay all wages, fees, and board-wages, as well as all other expenses, without delay; within one month of the end of the financial year he was to put his 'Journal' or day-book of expenditure on the greencloth for the accountants to make up their accounts. The clerks of the greencloth and clerks controllers (there were two of each) were charged jointly with the maintenance of discipline and order; they were to punish offenders and search out unauthorized strangers whose presence they had to report to 'the Soueraignes of the House'—the head officers.

By themselves the clerks of the greencloth were made responsible for the careful keeping of all accounts. Each morning, after the board had passed the previous day's expenses, they were to record them

in the Parchment docquett called the Maine Docquet: and the same Docquet, so entred and engrossed, to remaine in the Comptinghouse for record, without taking it away from thence by any officers.

Six days after the end of each month they were to call in the expense accounts of each office, and after the clerks controllers had checked them were to enter the account in their ledger, 'called the Booke of Foote of Parcells'; also they were to prepare the cofferer's annual account book which they were to have presented at the exchequer

---

[1] Newton, *Tudor Studies*, 247, n. 42.   [2] *Ibid.* 255.
[3] I.e. the heads of each office in the household—the clerks who had to account to the cofferer for the money spent there.

yearly in the Hilary term, on pain of losing a quarter's wages.[1] They were further to make out a half-yearly abstract of expenses—it is difficult to say whether of the half-year past or an estimate for the future, though the second is more probable from the language used —which would make possible either a current check on expenditure or more accurate budgeting;[2] and they were enjoined to keep all their books secret till the end of the year, 'without the view or sight of them to any other Officer', an obvious precaution to prevent collusive cheating which would have made the complicated system of several accounts acting as checks on each other rather pointless. The same order was also given to all accountants and the clerks controllers.

These last-named officers were in a way the linch-pin of the whole system—they were simply to provide the check on the activities of all other officers which their designation implied. There had been one of them, with a very junior clerk of the controlment, until the latter was promoted to equality.[3] The fact that this took place about 1533[4] suggests that Cromwell, by then already the administrator in chief, deliberately enlarged the scope and duties of an office whose sole purpose was to ensure honesty and efficiency and whose growth marked the developing 'modern' organization of household administration. He certainly gave them wide powers in 1539. It was their duty to prevent absentees from drawing wages and to enforce the strict rule against the wasteful serving of meals in private chambers which Wolsey had laid down,[5] and to make sure that no servants

---

[1] This was a very necessary provision, for the cofferer's accounts were usually at least a year delayed. E.g. the book for 1534–5 was handed in on 13 February 1538 (E 101/422/1), that for 1537–8 on 27 March 1540 (E 101/540/30), etc. However, either the order was not enforced or the clerks made do on three-quarters of their wages: the first book handed in after the reforms (for 1539–40) was presented on 18 February 1542 (E 101/422/17). There are signs in the memoranda rolls of pressure being put on the cofferer in 1538–9 to get his accounts settled; those for 1534–5, 1535–6, and 1536–7 were presented in the Easter, Trinity, and Hilary terms 30 Henry VIII (E 159/317, Recorda: Easter, m. 16; Trinity, m. 21; Hilary, m. 19d). This may well have been part of Cromwell's preparations for his household reforms.

[2] 'They shall make every halfe yeare a view of the expense of the Household, that it may be seen what the Charge thereof amounteth to for the said half yeare.'

[3] E.g. SP 2:A, fo. 126, a list of household officers, temp. 1516–19. The clerk controller had £40, his assistant £7. 16s.

[4] Newton, *Tudor Studies*, 248.

[5] Eltham Ordinance, caps. 44–5, 52 (*H.O.* 151, 153).

were kept beyond the permitted establishment. For this purpose they were to keep a quarterly 'Check-Roll' of all those who were 'of the Ordinarie and within the Check of the Household' on which they were to enter allowances and deductions of wages, an order in which we may see the origin of those successive lists of household establishment already mentioned. It is specially interesting in view of the fact that even the establishment of the chamber, technically independent of the board of greencloth, was to come under the survey of the clerks controllers. They were further to check daily the stores remaining in all the offices, and without their agreement no fees or wages were to be paid. Finally, they were made responsible for drawing up the book of account which the controller of the household submitted annually to the exchequer, by way of checking the cofferer's account.

The board further disposed of the services of a yeoman and a groom, responsible for seeing the table prepared every morning by eight o'clock and for the safe custody of all books and records: they were to allow none of these out of their hands unless, for some special cause, two or three officers of the board bound themselves to answer for the safe return of the documents.

These were the orders laid down for the board of greencloth, the administrative committee of the king's household, and it will be agreed that they were very full, very thorough, very bureaucratic, and—if obeyed, as to all appearance they were—reasonably sure of achieving the desired result: the safe and steady government on as economical lines as possible of the biggest supply and spending department of the day. But we are not yet done with the board, for some of its members require special attention. One group of them has not so far been even mentioned: the masters of the household. Four of them had certainly been appointed by the time that Dunche's list was drawn up, but that was not until after 9 October 1540 when Sir John Gage became controller;[1] it has, however, generally been taken that the creation of this new office was part of the 1539

---

[1] The list in *Genealogist*, n.s., xxx. 27 is identical with that given in LC 5/178, p. 29, as far as the counting-house is concerned, but is in fact a little earlier, for the clerk of the kitchen, George Stonehouse, of LC 5/178 was still clerk of the squillery in Dunche's list. For the date of Gage's promotion cf. *L.P.* xvi. 137; he had been vice-chamberlain before.

reforms.[1] As the title is frequent after 1540 and does not occur before, and as the only major rearrangement took place in and shortly after December 1539, the presumption is quite safe. The masters were interpolated between the cofferer (himself once described as first master of the household)[2] and the clerks of the greencloth from whose ranks they were recruited;[3] it is reasonable to suppose that they were to assist in the running of the board without specific duties, in fact replacing the truant head officers and making possible the daily check at the counting-house. For that reason, perhaps, no special orders were issued for them in December 1539, though it is also quite possible that they were only appointed after the ordinances had been made. Their duties may be further surmised from the fact that two each were appointed 'for the king' and 'for the queen'; as the only division along those lines applied to the household above stairs, it seems likely that the masters were to act as links between the lord chamberlain's department and the board of greencloth. Together with the powers, already mentioned, of the clerks controllers over the establishment of the chamber (king's and queen's), this surmise underlines what was clearly one of Cromwell's main principles in the reform of the household: he hoped to break down to some extent the separation of chamber and household, and to establish the board of greencloth as the proper administrative organ over the whole of the court. This will become further confirmed when the financial side of his reforms is discussed.[4]

No other motive will so adequately explain the other innovation

[1] Newton, *Tudor Studies*, 248. The title was borrowed from France (R. Doucet, *Les institutions de la France au XVI* siècle*, 126), but the office was not; the French masters appear to have been habitually employed outside the household (*ibid.* 440), while their English counterparts had no duties except to assist in the management of household affairs.

[2] In March 1540, in the account of the treasurer of the chamber (B.M., Arundel MS. 97, fo. 120). This offers some support for the theory that Cromwell created the masterships but is not conclusive proof as the title in the cofferer's case was only one of courtesy; unless indeed Peckham temporarily combined the two offices, for which there is no other evidence.

[3] E.g. Edward Weldon, clerk of the greencloth in December 1538 (*H.O.* 217), master of the household by the end of 1540 (*L.P.* XVI. 394, 5); James Gage, clerk of the greencloth late in 1540 (*L.P.* XVI. 394, 5), was fourth master by December 1541 (*ibid.* 1488, 4). William Thynne, once clerk of the kitchen, who was clerk controller in 1538 (*H.O.* 217) and master by 1540 (*Genealogist*, n.s., XXX. 27; *L.P.* XVI. 394, 5), may be presumed to have passed through the stage of clerk of the greencloth in between.

[4] Below, pp. 404 f.

in the household below stairs, the replacement of the lord steward by the lord great master. As Husee had learned some time before the reforms were made, the household of the English king was to have a 'grand maître' on the French model. The peculiar process of duplication which affected English medieval administration produced hereditary great stewards and great chamberlains on the one hand, and on the other household stewards and chamberlains who were lay officers of knightly rank; in the course of the fourteenth century, one officer of each kind emerged, instead of the previous two who had been considered as the deputies of the great hereditary dignitaries. In the sixteenth century the title of lord steward invariably applied to the household officer who governed the supply departments and presided over the board of greencloth; the hereditary stewardship had disappeared. The household chamberlain, too, acquired greater dignity and the habitual designation of lord chamberlain, though his predecessor, the hereditary great chamberlain of England, continued a purely titular existence.[1] Essentially the two household officers were therefore parallel and on a level; their two departments began to develop simultaneously in the process of simplification which in the later fourteenth century initiated the change from a multitude of household offices into the two sides—ceremonial and businesslike—which made up the sixteenth-century court.[2] This duality proved to be very useful and suitable to the needs of the household, but it left a genuine bureaucratic organization uncompleted. The position in France was rather different: the great master of the household, an officer of little antiquity, was responsible for the 'superintendence sur tous les domestiques' in which he resembled the English steward, but his far wider duties included even 'des travaux artistiques', a task belonging to the chamberlain's department in England. He supervised, in short, 'tout le service intérieur de l'Hôtel du roi'. The office was habitually held by great men who gave it more importance than its sphere of action deserved, and ultimately became practically hereditary in the house of Guise. The French king's chamber, on the other hand, was

---

[1] The office was normally hereditary in the family of Vere, earls of Oxford, until Cromwell interloped after the death of the fifteenth earl in 1540.

[2] Tout, *Chapters*, IV. 160.

in the charge of a *premier chambellan* (after the abolition of the office of *grand chambrier* in 1545) who was merely the head of the gentlemen of the privy chamber (*gentilshommes de la chambre*). He controlled the French equivalent of the English privy chamber and wardrobe of robes—no more.[1] It will be seen that the *grand maître* held a much more commanding position than did the lord steward, and the deliberate borrowing of the title is one indication that Cromwell hoped to organize the household in a more centralized fashion, under the supremacy of one great officer.

In actual practice the changes made were almost confined to the change of name. That was made, no doubt, in the course of the 1539 reforms, but for some reason it was thought wiser to get the alteration confirmed by parliament; it is difficult to see why, but the step is one of the many examples of that desire for parliamentary authority which informs all the work of the 1530's. The bill was presented by the great master designate, Suffolk, on the first day after parliament had reassembled,[2] sufficient proof that the matter had been in hand for some time and had only awaited the meeting of parliament to be settled. The statute declared that

it has pleasid the Kinges Roiall Majestie to alter and chaunge the name of the Lord Steward of his most honorable houshold into the name of the Greate Maister of his houshold or Grand Maistre Dhostel du Roy,

and enacted that the new official was to have precisely the same pre-eminences, authority, privileges, and jurisdictions as the old one had had.[3] The act was repealed and the traditional title restored in 1554,[4] and it would appear that but for this business of nomenclature the whole legislation was rather futile; however, Cromwell seems to have succeeded in putting the supremacy of the lord steward—by whatever name—within the king's household on a firm basis. To quote a later compiler of precedents and author of an eighteenth-century 'Short View of That Great Office of the Lord Steward',

The Management of the Kings Family is intrusted with him...and all his Mandates in the palace Royal must be Obeyed & Observed.[5]

---

[1] For all these details, cf. R. Doucet, *Les institutions de la France*, 122 f., 126.

[2] 13 April 1540 (*L.J.* I. 130a). Though rapidly disposed of in the lords, the bill hung a week in the commons (*ibid.* 131 b, 133 a); as this act cannot possibly have roused opposition, its fate should warn us not to deduce too much from delays in either house.

[3] 32 Henry VIII, c. 39.   [4] 1 Mary, st. 3, c. 4.   [5] LS 13/277.

The clearest proof of his superiority to the lord chamberlain is that promotion from the latter office to the former now became possible: Sir William Paulet, Lord St John, held the chamberlain's staff in 1543 and the lord steward's in 1545.[1] As Tout's tables show, such a thing was unknown in the middle ages when the two were equivalent and served by separate succession.[2] The lord great master was the coping stone of Cromwell's household reforms; he was to be the indisputable head of the bureaucratic organization topped by the board of greencloth which was to encroach more widely than had hitherto been usual or feasible on the sphere of the chamber. Though the title was abandoned by the ministers of Mary to whom the thorough organization of the French court did not, perhaps, outweigh the odium of borrowing from the national enemy, the lord steward of the sixteenth and subsequent centuries owed his position and powers to the clarification and definition carried out in 1539.[3]

That accounts for Cromwell's orders to the counting-house; the remainder of his ordinance can be dealt with more briefly. He gave very detailed and thorough instructions on their duties to the individual officials of the supply offices; these instructions are in the same relation to Wolsey's brief and general notes in the Eltham Ordinance as is Cromwell's organization of the board of greencloth to Wolsey's vague outline of a board of control. Cromwell did not revolutionize the organization of the household—there was no need for that; he simply tightened it up and gave it that firm yet flexible form which enabled it to deal with the problems of an ever-expanding court and ever-increasing expenditure for well over two centuries. The last decrees of 1539 concerned order and decency in court, forbade unlicensed absence, the keeping of unfit servants, and unauthorized possession of hawks and other hunting gear, and ordered the constant attendance of the knight marshal or his deputy for the purpose of policing the court. Finally, a note very characteristic of

---

[1] *D.N.B.*   [2] Tout, *Chapters*, VI. 38 ff.

[3] It is at least possible that the change was intended to do no more than please Suffolk whose dukedom had not provided him with any of the old and most honourable offices, especially after he ceased to be earl marshal in 1533. A mere lord stewardship of the household was not very exalted, and the office of lord president of the council, which he also held, was very recent.

Cromwell's careful, bureaucratic, and recording habit of mind was struck in the order to the harbingers' office: they were always to be ready to provide lodgings not only for the household but also for distinguished visitors, and no billeting was allowed without a written order. At each move of the court, the harbingers were to give to all those entitled to lodging a paper with the name of the householder on whom they were billeted, with the number of beds available and stabling for horses.

Cromwell's reforms of 1539 mark a much more definite step in the organization of the household than do Wolsey's reforms of nearly fourteen years earlier. After 1539, lists of household officials multiply in a fashion which shows that the orders were being obeyed; there is also plenty of evidence that the board of greencloth was much more active than it had ever been before.[1] After several years' work on the problem, held up again and again by its size and the claims of other concerns, Cromwell finally produced a set of ordinances which was to be the basis of household administration until the reforms of Burke and Pitt.[2] His chief achievements were a complete overhaul and virtual reconstitution of the board of greencloth, enlarged by the addition of the four masters of the household and given higher powers by the elevation of its head to the dignity of lord great master; the partial subordination of the lord chamberlain's department to the board; the keeping of careful check lists of the permitted establishment; and the creation of the mounted guard of gentlemen pensioners. He had in fact given the household the organization necessary to enable it to stand on its own feet and administer itself for a good long time, an achievement made possible by the deliberate departmentalization and the decision to cease employing household servants outside the household which have already been noticed. That fulfilled one of the needs of the household—the need for fuller organization; the other—that for solvency and economy—was also greatly advanced thereby. We must now turn to the financial problems involved and to the financial side of the reforms of 1539.

[1] Cf., for example, *H.O.* 208 ff. Some of these orders are earlier than 1539, but the great majority are later.

[2] Cf. Newton, *Tudor Studies*, 247, n. 42: 'Even in the Instructions of March 12, 1783...there are still echoes of the phrases first used by Thomas Cromwell.'

2. *Finance*

That Cromwell showed an interest in household expenditure from an early date is only what one must expect, and it is not surprising that by 1533 he had among his papers estimates for the annual expenditure of household and chamber, and a declaration of the assignments due to the household in October of that year.[1] His memoranda in the same year touch on such points as whether any loan money was to be advanced for household expenses, who in the household was to have monthly wages and who quarterly, the fact that fivepence a day was enough for purveyors riding about their business, and the regrettable fact that the allowances commonly made to servants of the household who were absent through sickness were not enough.[2] The problem of finding money for the household was often present,[3] and Cromwell himself seems occasionally to have transmitted from reserves the cash which enabled the cofferer to pay his way.[4] The most effective way of controlling expenditure was, naturally, to budget for it in advance and stick to the estimate; it is now that genuine estimates appear for the first time.[5] The earliest extant is an 'Estimate Viewe of the charges of the prouisionz of the Kinges housould' for the year ending at Michaelmas 1533 which was drawn up soon after 5 July of that year.[6] There is no direct evidence that this paper was ordered by Cromwell, beyond the dubious point of its being endorsed by a Cromwellian clerk, but the year itself is significant; everything goes to show that Cromwell's accession to power produced another attempt at economy, also noticed by Chapuys,[7] and this estimate looks like being part of it. Other estimates were prepared in the course of and after the reforms of 1539: a very detailed list of the expected charges for food and stores proves by the very roundness of its figures, as well as by the occasional

---

[1] *L.P.* VI. 299; VII. 923 (xl).   [2] *L.P.* VI. 1609.

[3] *L.P.* XII. II. 177, 1151.

[4] He paid him £2,000 on 18 July 1533 (E 101/422/17).

[5] Cf. Newton, *Tudor Studies*, 253 f. Newton had no doubt that in 1526 elaborate calculations were made for the future, but the fact remains that none survive until Cromwell took over.

[6] E 101/421/11. The date appears from the fact that receipts up to that day are given as in hand, while the remainder is estimated.

[7] *L.P.* VI. 19.

use of the words 'by estimation', that it was truly a forecast for the future, not a summarized account of the past.[1] Such a document was certainly required if the new establishment was to achieve real economies. Another estimate, produced in April 1540, will require attention later.[2]

The 1533 paper showed the household to be in a condition of debt and difficulties which was little short of chronic. It gave the 'Charges of the provisionz... with wages of houshold, lyvery costes, and other necessary charges' incurred in the nine months from 1 October 1532 to 1 July 1533 (this included the cost of Katharine of Aragon's household) as £22,550, 'by Estimacion'—which in this case meant a rough-and-ready total. The charges for the three months of the financial year 'yet to come' were assessed at £4,200; here 'by estimacion' must have meant a genuine forecast. Against this total of £26,750 the cofferer had received £8,000 'prest money', that is as an advance and due to be paid back later, while his regular income, the assignments from the exchequer, had yielded £7,248. 13s. 6d. by 5 July and were estimated as likely to produce another £500 by Michaelmas. However, of this total income of £15,748. 13s. 6d., £3,000 had to be deducted from the prests as appropriated to the purchase of storage goods for the next year,[3] so that a total deficit 'owyng to the Kinges Subgiettes for the forsaid provisionz at Mighelmas' of £13,001. 6s. 6d. was envisaged. In this particular case the cofferer's fears do not appear to have been realized, for the completed account showed an income of £27,434 and a surplus of £46;[4] it would seem, therefore, that the usual step was taken of supplying the difference by special warrant.[5]

It will be best to study in the first place the actual balance sheet of household accounts for the decade 1530–40, in order to see what it reveals.[6] There was hardly ever any deficit in the account as

[1] H.O. 192–7.   [2] L.P. xv. 599; cf. below, pp. 409 f.
[3] 'Wax, Lyng, Codd, hay, Oxen, & Shepe for scoryng the Kinges pastures, and in prestes to be given to diuers proviours.'
[4] E 361/8, mm. 40–40d. Figures will normally be given in pounds only.
[5] £3,076 was paid by Tuke in 1534 to cover the year's deficit (below, p. 400); earlier, immediately after the estimate was made, Cromwell supplied the cofferer with £2,000 (18 July 1533—E 101/422/17).
[6] Taken from E 361/8, mm. 37–44d. The figures are given in pounds only; it should be noticed that 'debita' (what the accountant owed) means surplus, while 'superplusage'

ultimately made up, and the surplus was so small that income, it is clear, must have been carefully tailored to fit expenses; but these features were due to the fact that the cofferer received each year enough money to cover the deficit left in the previous year by the insufficiency of his supposedly regular income. His receipts, as recorded in the accounts, consisted of the exchequer assignments fixed by statute (£19,394. 16s. 4d.) and a 'foreign' revenue mostly made up from the previous year's surpluses in the supply departments which were returned to him and amounted to some £1,500–£1,700 a year. The rest was paid by the treasurer of the chamber on those special warrants which Tuke found so heavy a charge on his money.[1] The clear-cut appearance of the accounts gives no idea of the difficulties involved in the system; no doubt the cofferer ultimately received his due, but the treasurer of the chamber was often in no better case and took a long time to pay the whole sum allocated. In May 1537 he reported that the cofferer was behindhand above £2,000 of his warrant for 'superplusage' which amounted to £7,000;[2] but the household was understood to be the first charge on chamber money, and Tuke paid. At times he was prompt: on 7 June 1534 he paid out the full sum due on a warrant of 31 March for the deficit of the year ending Michaelmas 1533 (£3,076).[3] The deficit

(the additional sum needed to balance the account) means deficit. The surplus was paid into the chamber.

Year	Receipt	Expenditure	Debita	Super-plusage
1529–30	£25,872	£25,812	£59	—
1530–31	£24,976	£24,908	£69	—
1531–32	£27,952	£27,947	£5*	—
1532–33	£27,434	£27,387	£46	—
1533–34	£24,296	£24,223	£72	—
1534–35	£23,490	£23,461	£28	—
1535–36	£27,783	£27,690	£92	—
1536–37	£27,672	£27,635	£37	—
1537–38	£22,381	£22,339	£41	—
1538–39	£21,494	£23,303	—	£1,808†
1539–40	£34,093	£32,933	£1,160	—

* Turned into a deficit by payment of £20 pension to Richard Trees, lately receiver of household assignments from the chamber, whose post fell into abeyance when these assignments again went directly to the cofferer.

† The next year's surplus was charged against this deficit, while for the rest the cofferer received satisfaction 'elsewhere in the exchequer'.

[1] L.P. XII. I. 1297; XIII. I. 1288.   [2] L.P. XII. I. 1297.
[3] Indenture in E 101/421/17.

for 1537 was covered by a warrant of 14 March 1538; this time Tuke found it necessary to pay on ten separate occasions between 30 March and 6 July.[1] It is highly significant that the only year with a serious shortage in the account was 1539 when no chamber money came into the household, for reasons which will have to be elucidated later. The system was plainly unsatisfactory.

The actual ups and downs of expenditure are easily explained. In part, no doubt, increases were due to the fatal tendency of all regular expenditure to go up, especially in an age of gradually rising prices, while declining expenditure may have had something to do with efforts at economy. However, in the main the history of household establishments offers a full enough explanation. The increase in 1531–3 may well have been due to the needs of Anne Boleyn coming on top of the full establishment of Queen Katharine, while the decline in the next two years reflects not only Cromwell's first attempt at retrenchment, already noticed, but also the fact that the 'princess dowager's' household cost less to maintain than that of a queen. The steep rise up to 1537 no doubt indicates the higher expenditure on the third queen, together with the needs of the royal children, while the sudden drop in 1537–9 follows plainly from Henry's temporary widowerhood. The difference between 1539 and 1540, however, a difference in expenditure of over £9,000 or forty per cent. of the earlier year's payments, cannot be accounted for so readily; when the time of its occurrence is considered it will be seen that there may well be some connexion with Cromwell's reforms in the royal household, and indeed this is so.

The cofferer listed his expenses under these headings: *Expensa hospicij cum oblacionibus donis & regardis, empcio equorum, Robe valectorum & Garcionum Camere domini Regis & aliorum officiariorum, Vadia per warrantum Regis, Annuitates* (that is, pensions in chamber and household), and *prestita* or advances made to supply departments.[2] The last item varied a great deal with the needs of the household, but it and all the rest except the first were too small to have

---

[1] Indenture in E 101/422/4. For 1537–8, cf. E 159/319, Communia, Recorda, Easter Term, m. 3—indenture of 26 May 1539, recording payments authorized by warrant of 18 December 1538.

[2] The comparison between 1538–9 and 1539–40 is made from E 361/8, mm. 43–44 d, where these details will be found.

much effect on the total. Pensions increased from £197 in 1539 to
£436 in 1540, and the number of those pensioned from twenty-one
to one hundred and six;[1] the difference illustrates one aspect of what
the 'new ordinary' of 1539 meant. But the real difference lay in the
actual household expenditure, the 'diets', which increased from
£20,886 to £29,389, a figure for which neither the expenses of Anne
of Cleves, who can in any case have been a charge on the household
for only a short time,[2] will fully account, nor will those of the gentlemen pensioners, though they must have made their presence felt.
The answer lies rather in an interesting aspect of the 1539–40
reforms—a change in the system of paying household salaries.

It is astonishingly difficult to discover where many of the fees and
salaries of leading household officials were paid in this period. The
lists of 'ordinary' and household establishment often give full
details of salaries due; thus in about 1544–5, the great master
received £100, the treasurer (here surprisingly named by his old title
as keeper of the wardrobe of the household) £123. 14s. 8d., the controller £107. 17s. 7d., the cofferer £100, a master of the household
£50, a clerk of the greencloth £44. 6s. 10d., a clerk controller
£44. 6s. 8d.[3] But there is little trace of these sums in the accounts of
the time. The cofferer's accounts in the 1530's include, as has been
said, an item marked *Vadia*, but these were special fees authorized
by special warrant which in these years amounted to only two or
three sums.[4] It may be supposed that the small fees paid to the lesser
officials of the supply and kindred offices were included in the daily
expenses listed as 'diet', but there is no separate list of payments of

[1] E 101/422/12, 17. All those involved were gentlemen, yeomen, grooms, and pages
of the household.
[2] Arrived in January 1540 (*L.P.* xv. 10), she was not crowned until Whitsun (*ibid.*
401, 485) and was divorced by the end of July (*ibid.* 925). The total assignment to a queen
was about £4,600 a year (*ibid.* 21, 2), but it is not clear how much of this would be
recorded in the cofferer's account and how much would come out of the queen's private
income from her jointure.
[3] LC 5/178, p. 29: 'Rotulus Nominum Officiariorum omnium officiorum Hospitij
Domini Regis Henr. viij^ul.'
[4] E.g. in 1538–9 (E 101/422/12), fees were paid to Thomas Vicarie, chief surgeon
(£20), Robert Tatton, Richard Trees' successor as receiver of household assignments
(£20), and William Dynes or Dyves for his usual year's fee (£3). Tatton's is an odd case:
Trees was granted his £20 when his office was abolished in 1531, yet apparently a
successor to the sinecure and the pension was appointed. It is probable that he had
bought the reversion and that the government honoured the bargain.

salaries, for instance, for the officers of the counting-house. A few household fees were paid in the exchequer, as those of the master of the armoury, the master of the ordnance, the master of the horse, the officers of the jewel-house, the chief carver, the squires of the body.[1] The most regular paymaster of wages was undoubtedly the treasurer of the chamber who seems to have paid all the lesser officials of the chamber establishment, such as grooms and pages, yeomen of the guard, the musicians and minstrels, but can be shown to have paid also the fees of the gentlemen of the privy chamber, while he disbursed to the controller and cofferer of the household sums which do not amount to anything like the salaries given in the list of 1544-5 and were obviously personal annuities only.[2] The treasurer of augmentations paid nothing in household wages, despite the chronicler's statement that the fees of the gentlemen pensioners were charged to his account.[3] On the whole, then, the truth is that some fees are untraceable, especially those of the lord steward and the officers of the counting-house, but that the great majority of wages were paid by the treasurer of the chamber; the cofferer was responsible, before 1539, for the maintenance of the serjeants and lesser officers of the household offices whose rewards may have been in kind and not in cash, as is suggested by a rather obscure paragraph in Cromwell's ordinances which, making certain that they took their fees in daily instalments, supports the suggestion that these items were included in the daily return of household expenditure.[4]

What can be said with confidence, however, is that the reforms of 1539 made an attempt to dethrone the treasurer of the chamber from his supremacy by transferring some at least of his payments to the cofferer, even though no actual trace is to be found in the latter officer's accounts. An entry in the chamber accounts of 1540, in recording a payment to Sir Anthony Browne, gentleman of the

---

[1] E.g. E 405/200.
[2] *L.P.* v, pp. 302, 305, 309 f. Even in 1542, Peckham, the controller, got only £10 from Tuke as his half-year's wage (*L.P.* XVII, p. 483).
[3] *Wriothesley's Chronicle*, I. 112.
[4] *H.O.* 231. The clerks controllers were to see daily 'the Fees which the Officers of the House shall have, or that they shall take out of the House, to view whether they be more largely taken than they ought to be, or not.' No officer was to 'presume to take any Fee away before they have been viewed by one of the Clerkes Comptrollers', on pain of losing that fee for ever.

privy chamber ('which wagis alwayes hath ben heretofore p^d to ye same sir Anthony half yerely by the tresorer of the kinges Chambre'), declares that

at this quarter of the Anunciacion of our lady it was ordred that all gentilmen and other attendant vppon the kinges maieste in his prevy-chambre sholde from xpmas predicto a° xxxj° receyve & take their wagis at the handis of master Edmund Pekham first master & cofferer of the kingis most honorable householde.[1]

The date of the reform was therefore 25 March 1540, but it was to be effective from that Christmas Day 1539 which had inaugurated the 'new ordre' in the household, and the change may safely be taken to have been part of the second stage of Cromwell's household reforms. The people whose wages had been transferred to the cofferer are given in a list of this year as three cup-bearers, three carvers, three sewers, sixteen gentlemen, two gentlemen ushers, and four grooms of the privy chamber, the four squires of the body, the eighty yeomen of the guard, and the twenty-four yeomen of the queen's chamber.[2] Together with a number of increases in salary apparently authorized at about the same time—for the list mentions the elusive spears whose higher wages were appointed on 5 April 1540[3]—the household charges were stated to have increased by £7,327, a sum which goes a long way to explain the steep rise in household expenditure in 1540. As no such increase appears in the cofferer's account except in the item simply described as expenses of the household and entered in his books on a day-by-day basis, the conclusion already arrived at that fees were somehow split up and worked into these 'dieta' appears to be confirmed.

It was, therefore, one of the reforms of 1539 to take away the payment of all important and several lesser regular chamber officers from the treasurer of the chamber and transfer it to the cofferer of

[1] B.M., Arundel MS. 97, fo. 120.

[2] B.M., Royal MS. 7. C. xvi, fo. 129. The list is temp. Henry VIII and datable by the fact that these changes occurred early in 1540. It gives both 'Waiges nowe paid in the houshold which hertofore hath bene paid in the recept and by thandes of the thresourer of the Kinges chamber' and 'Waiges and ffees nowe appoynted to be within the houshold which befor hath not bene paid'. Another, rather less complete, list (summarized in *L.P.* xvi. 394, 3) arrives at a total increase of £6,388; it adds the master of the jewels to the officials now paid in the household. He and the squires of the body had previously drawn their salaries from the exchequer; all the rest from the chamber.

[3] *H.O.* 213.

the household. Oddly enough, some fees due to the controller and cofferer themselves continued to be paid out of chamber money,[1] and the lord great master himself appears to have gone, now or later, on the charge of the chamber,[2] but after 1539 chamber accounts record no payments to members of the privy chamber. This reform seems to have been designed to fulfil the object of welding the privy chamber still more firmly to the household. Not only was the board of greencloth authorized to supervise the attendance of gentlemen of the privy chamber, not only were the clerks controllers made responsible for seeing to their establishment and preventing evasions and abuses, but their very fees were now in the hands of the board. The purpose behind this is clear enough: in all matters to do with the staffing of the household and the financing of its running, the board of greencloth was to have control, even if that involved reducing the lord chamberlain's activity 'above stairs' to the details of the ceremonial life of the court. It will be seen, therefore, that the strict division of the household into lord chamberlain's and lord steward's departments, which is made, for instance, by Chambers, is not quite correct; there was an important element of co-ordination in the supervision exercised by the board. From the time of Cromwell's reforms onwards, the business centre of the whole household lay in the board of greencloth to which even certain details of the chamber were subordinate.

This fact would have been clearer if Cromwell's intentions had been carried out in full. As we saw in discussing the treasurer of the chamber, he had ambitions to withdraw that officer from all household duties and incorporate him as the treasurer of land revenue into his scheme of national financial administration. Such a development would have had to take time, especially as Cromwell rarely worked in the manner of a revolutionary reformer but rather changed things along lines of development already dimly discernible. The further effects of this reform in the payment of household wages were likely to forward his intentions with regard to the chamber. The reform greatly strengthened the independence of the cofferer and therefore of the household as an organization; it increased its departmentalization,

---

[1] *L.P.* XVII, pp. 478 f., 483.
[2] He was certainly paid there in 1547 (E 101/426/5, fos. 23v, 58).

and at the same time it removed one of the chief links—or a major part of one of the chief links—which still bound the treasurer of the chamber to his position as an officer of the household. Perhaps —we have admittedly no means of knowing—Cromwell hoped to continue by taking away, in course of time, the remaining payments of wages from the chamber and thus in the end to free the treasurer for purely national duties in expenditure as well as in the collection of revenue where he had already achieved a high degree of specialization. At any rate, what was done in 1539-40 was a big step in that direction, and it was none of Cromwell's doing or intending when in the reign of Mary the treasurer of the chamber reverted instead into a household treasurer pure and simple, with certain wages in the household as the chief part of his payments. As has already been pointed out, in the treatment of the chamber his successors broke most fully with Cromwell's work, for the simple reason, which he could not foresee, that the squandering of the crown lands enabled them to dispense with the services of the treasurer of the chamber in national finance. Nevertheless, Cromwell's measures bore fruit to this extent that in Elizabeth's reign by far the greater part of household wages was paid by the cofferer of the household.[1]

However, there were no signs of all these coming changes in 1540, and Cromwell's policy was clearly different. As far as the household was concerned—and here his policy was not to be overthrown—he wished to give it that greater bureaucratic and self-contained organization which he required of a genuine department of state. For such the household was on its business side. For this purpose another major reform was very necessary: its finances had to be put on a safe and solid basis. Since the reign of Edward IV, the household had paid its expenses from statutory assignments on the exchequer; an act of parliament of 1482 established the principle that tallies presented for household expenses were to take precedence of all other needs, and the sum involved grew from £11,000 to £19,394 in the reign of Henry VIII.[2] In 1523 it was decided that the cofferer

---

[1] Chambers, *Eliz. Stage*, I. 50.
[2] Newton, *Tudor Studies*, 235. Cf. the acts of 11 Henry VII, c. 62, and 1 Henry VIII, c. 16.

had insufficient means of securing speedy collection, and his income was therefore directed to the treasurer of the chamber, then at the height of his power, who was to dole it out to him.[1] This did not last, and the cofferer's independence was restored in 1531 by an act which reasserted the household's first call on all revenue up to the allocated sum and abolished the office of receiver of these assignments, the holder being compensated with an annuity of £20.[2] By this measure the household was again set on its own feet, a step very much in accordance with the reforms begun in 1526 and completed in 1539.

It was, however, not enough to assign revenue to the household unless the cofferer could actually be sure of obtaining the money and—what mattered as much—of obtaining it in time. The accounts of the years 1530–9 always give the full sum as received from the exchequer,[3] but as these accounts were habitually handed in one or two years after they had been closed, the money may well have trickled in too late to be of use in the year for which it was meant, though not too late for inclusion in the account. That this must have happened at times is plain from the estimate of 1533 which has already been cited: there the assignments received amounted to £7,248 and were expected to reach the total of £7,748 by the end of the year—considerably less than half the sum due.[4] The difference was covered by such 'prests' or advances from reserves as the £8,000 recorded in this estimate, or the £14,000 which Peckham, the cofferer, received 'from the king', that is (as he adds) from Cromwell and Tuke, at various times between 30 November 1529 and 22 February 1534, expressly 'quod maior pars denariorum assignatorum pro huiusmodi expensis non fuerat Solubilis annuatim nisi post clausum Compoti'.[5] What the cofferer in fact received, and what he entered as received in his account, were tallies to be redeemed out of exchequer revenue by local receivers of that revenue, the manner in which the exchequer usually made its advances, and there was no guarantee that the cash for which they were to be exchanged actually existed, the less so as the exchequer made out

---

[1] 14 & 15 Henry VIII, c. 19. [2] 22 Henry VIII, c. 18.
[3] E 361/8, mm. 37–43 d. The figure varied a little above the allocated total because of the varying sums received from the exchequer for the celebration of the feast of St George. [4] E 101/421/11.
[5] Recorded in the account book for 1539–40, E 101/422/17.

tallies appropriated to specific sources of revenue and not usable for others if those sources failed to yield the expected profit. When the cofferer's affairs again became the subject of legislation—in 1540—tallies yet unredeemed but issued before 1531 had to be dealt with.[1] All that the steady record in the cofferer's accounts of £19,394 received from the exchequer really meant was that he had been given tallies to that amount and hoped to get the money for them in due course; in the meantime he lived on the advances granted from reserves which would have to be repaid when his assignments came in.

There was clearly nothing to be said for this practice from a business point of view; it was a thoroughly unsatisfactory system, dating from a past when centralized collection of money was difficult, a system which exchequer conservatism was to prolong in an ever decreasing sphere into the nineteenth century.[2] In the household the pretence that the exchequer supplied all that was necessary, except for an occasional extraordinary deficit to be covered by a special warrant to the treasurer of the chamber, was maintained until Cromwell set about his reforms late in 1539. The readjustment was not completed before his fall, but the preliminary investigations as well as the temporary measures designed to tide things over until the end of the financial year at Michaelmas 1540, were taken in the time of Cromwell's ministry and foreshadowed in his notes.[3]

The cofferer's account for 1538-9 recorded no receipts from the chamber and was therefore left with a marked 'superplusage' or deficit; that for 1539-40 analysed his receipts in a novel manner.[4] Instead of the hitherto usual threefold division—exchequer assignments as authorized by act of parliament, from the treasurer of the chamber by special warrant, and 'foreign' revenue—we now find income from the exchequer (£8,328), the usual 'fforensica', and sums stated to have come from the king, that is by special warrant. These last include, in the first place, the £14,000 already mentioned which were paid to the cofferer in the years 1529-34, and three sums paid in the year 1540: £2,000 from the treasurer of first-fruits (by

---

[1] C 65/148, m. 27. See below, p. 411. As early as 1519 the cofferer held desperate tallies worth £1,499 (*L.P.* III. 456).   [2] Giuseppi, *Guide*, I. 180 f.
[3] *L.P.* xv. 322.   [4] E 101/422/12, 17.

an indenture of 12 March 1540), £4,000 from the treasurer of the chamber (on a warrant of 23 March), and £4,000 from the treasurer of augmentations (on a warrant of 24 July paid on 19 August).[1] What happened was, therefore, this. When the reform of household finances was undertaken, it was first decided to clear the ground by squaring Peckham's account and stopping the fiction which had entered the full exchequer assignments year by year, though they had never been received as cash. Thus the cofferer received no chamber money to cover the deficit for 1538–9, and as far as the current year was concerned he answered for only £8,328, the sum which we may take it he had actually received on his tallies. He was further told to account at last for the special money received six or more years earlier, so as to get it out of the way and give him a chance to start with a clean sheet.[2] For the moment his expenditure was covered by special warrants, two of which were issued in March when the investigation began, and one later in July to tide things over till the next year.

The government thus had a chance to revise the whole system of allocations, and the next step was to discover what was needed. To this end the cofferer was required to draw up an estimate of his full year's expenditure and what revenue he could charge against it; as this was taken in April 1540, part of the estimate had to be a forecast.[3] Peckham's return showed that his expenses from 1 October 1539 to 1 April 1540 had been £14,936; he estimated the remaining half-year's expenditure at £16,000, plus £4,000 for provisions to be laid in for the year after and a sum to cover the previous year's

---

[1] The fact that Gostwick had no warrant is proof that Cromwell was behind the transaction; as usual, he made him pay on his authority only (cf. above, pp. 199 ff.). The indentures covering the last two payments are attached to the account. They show that North (augmentations) paid his £4,000 in one sum on the date given. Tuke's indenture is more complicated. He had advanced Peckham £1,500 on 3 and 5 March for the 'superplusage' of 1537–8, but without a warrant (i.e. presumably on Cromwell's letter); of this Peckham repaid £700, while £500 was deducted from the warrant for £4,000 which was discharged to the cofferer on 12, 21 and 23 March.

[2] This £14,000 is part of the £34,093 which were his receipts for the year (E 361/8, m. 44). As he spent £32,923 in that year (*ibid.* m. 44d) and was allowed a surplus of £1,160, it follows that he actually received the sum stated; the money received in 1529–34 must have been spent long before, and it must be concluded that he received in 1540 an equivalent sum in cash, perhaps from outstanding tallies, to square his account (cf. the terms of the statute 32 Henry VIII, c. 52, below, p. 411).

[3] *L.P.* xv. 599.

deficit of £1,771. Against this total of over £35,000 he had received, by way of loan, £20,000,[1] and expected another £8,000, leaving an estimated deficit of £7,708. He added a note to the effect that of his exchequer assignments he had received only £8,000; the remainder would not come in until the next Candlemas term (in February 1541) and would have to assist with next year's expenses.

With definite details of needs before him, as well as the inescapable proof that the system of exchequer assignments had quite broken down, Cromwell—if it was he, as we make little doubt it was—could turn to the solving of the problem. As, however, the assignments system was sanctioned by an act of parliament, it required another act to do away with it and enable the government to find some better way of providing for the household. This act—32 Henry VIII, c. 52[2]—was not passed during Cromwell's supremacy. It was first introduced in the lords on 15 June 1540, and was returned with the commons' consent on the 19th;[3] it cannot be thought that the whole idea was conceived and the plans made in the five days which had passed since Cromwell's arrest. Cromwell had been personally responsible for the reforms of Christmas 1539; it was under him that the first steps were taken towards a reform of the household finances; it may be taken as assured that the act designed to make the reforms possible and drafted while he was yet in power was devised by him.

The act began by reciting the statute of 1531 and declaring that the sum of £19,394. 16s. 4d. there assigned to the household could no longer be levied because 'diuers and many Mannours Townes and lordeships...whiche were parcell of thesaid assignementis... ben commen to the Kinges handes' and their rents and farms had therefore ceased. For this reason it was enacted that the 1531 act be repealed and the money there scheduled—such as remained— revert to those courts and places where it had belonged before the act; secondly, the king was, 'at his libertie', to assign money for the expenses of his household by the treasurer of the chamber or any

---

[1] This was the £14,000 granted ostensibly between 1529 and 1534, and the money from Gostwick and Tuke.

[2] The act is not printed in *Stat. Realm* but is briefly noted in *L.P.* xv. 498. It is enrolled on the parliament roll, C 65/148, m. 27.

[3] *L.J.* I. 156b, 158b.

other revenue officer. The problem of the unpaid tallies still in Peckham's hands was dealt with: all were to be cancelled and he was to have repayment (presumably in cash) for those up to Michaelmas 1539 from the receipt of the exchequer by virtue of the present act and without further warrant; the remainder were to be 'discharged', that is returned to the exchequer and there cancelled. For all his revenue, however received, from Michaelmas 1539 onwards, and in the future, the cofferer was to account in the exchequer.

This act, which left the government all necessary freedom to work out the details by Michaelmas 1540, established an entirely new principle, unless we prefer to say that the practice which had hitherto been accounted exceptional was now made the rule. Instead of having his expenditure defrayed from tallies on exchequer revenue which it was incumbent upon him to collect, the cofferer would in future receive sums in cash from the king's treasurers on the king's warrants, for which he would account in the exchequer. This completed the organization of the household as a spending depart-ment: it assured the cofferer of his income, freed him from the trouble of chasing his money, and made sure that the king's house-hold should never lack supplies as long as the simple precaution was taken of making out warrants—and as long as the royal coffers were not empty. But there was no way of guarding against the last contingency; as far as a workable and straightforward system could solve the problem, all had been done that could be done or needed doing. The system thus inaugurated lasted as long as did Cromwell's rearrangement of the financial administration. When in 1554 the courts of augmentations and first-fruits were incorporated with the exchequer, the better part of the revenue assigned to the household was no longer obtainable by the same method; it had again to come from the exchequer, and the exchequer naturally rushed to employ its old ways. In 1563 another act of parliament reverted to the earlier system of assignments on tallies.[1] It was a retrograde step, like others of that reign, but at least the queen's government did their best to minimize the proven evil effects of the old method, not only by re-enacting all the old safety devices (fixed dates for payment and penalties for disobedience), but also by including a new clause

---

[1] 5 Elizabeth, c. 32 (*Stat. Realm*, IV, 479 ff.). The sum granted was £40,027. 4s. 2½d.

(sec. iii) authorizing the lord treasurer to make other suitable payments or assignments without warrant if the money provided in the schedule should fail. The act represented an aspect of that triumph of exchequer routine which was marked in the reforms of 1554. There can be no doubt that Cromwell's arrangement was more likely to be efficient, though it also depended more on direct action by the executive and was therefore bound to displease the civil service. It was a fundamental reform which broke with age-old ways of doing things, nor was the example lost entirely: the Elizabethan chamber, at least, was supplied by fixed grants from revenue departments made on the queen's dormant warrant.[1]

There was no point in availing oneself at once of the act of 1540; as has been seen, the cofferer was enabled to carry on till Michaelmas 1540 by dint of a temporary warrant to augmentations. The final step in completing the new scheme was taken on 18 November 1540 when four dormant warrants were issued for a total sum of £30,000 which it was hoped would cover expenses in future; the 'foreign' revenue, being an internal concern in the household, was not affected and would continue to be entered, though in actual fact, of course, it represented not so much income as a book-keeping device. The exchequer and the treasurer of augmentations each contributed £10,000; £6,000 came from the duchy of Lancaster which had previously contributed a slightly smaller sum to the assignments, and £4,000 from first-fruits and tenths.[2] Thus despite the terms of the act the treasurer of the chamber ceased to pay for household expenditure; no doubt it was found that he had hardly enough to pay for his own charges, and the absence of warrants to pay for household 'superplusage' year by year must have been a welcome relief. What mattered was that a fixed income from specified treasurers was now provided, and—all going well—the cofferer would always receive £30,000 to cover his expenses.[3] He would get cash instead of often irredeemable tallies. Admittedly, without a Cromwell in

---

[1] Above, pp. 186 ff.

[2] The warrants are recorded in the accounts from 1540–1 onwards; E 101/423/1, 4, 7, etc.

[3] Indentures attached to the account of 1540–1 (*ibid.* 1) show that in the first year at least the cofferer got the money in good time, though not necessarily at once. Gostwick paid his £4,000 on 4 July 1541; North for augmentations paid £6,000 on 28 November 1540 and the other £4,000 on 16 March 1541.

charge to see that expenditure did not outgrow reason, with Henry's increasing extravagance, and with the debasement of the coinage soon to make nonsense of all planning, the hope that £30,000 would be enough was not fulfilled. There was a deficit in 1541, and a surplus in 1542 proved delusive; even though £500 from the court of wards was added to the cofferer's regular income in 1544–5, the household continued to operate at a loss till the end of the reign.[1] This need not detract from the merits of the new system; it only proves that a system by itself will not ensure solvency—if that fact needs proving. As the addition of £500 shows, everything was very elastic now, and once the country's—and the king's—finances had been brought back to an even keel the new method of providing for the costs of the household would have proved simple and advantageous; however, the conservative trend of later reforms, and the absence of another Cromwell intent on introducing modern business methods into the national finances, led to a return to traditional ways.

This concludes the story of the great household reforms which culminated in 1539–40; it may be well to bring together the outstanding achievements involved. Detailed and effective ordinances were issued respecting both chamber and household proper, the establishment of the court was revised and extravagance hindered by periodic checks, and the financial side of the administration of the household was completely recast. The chamber ordinance of 1532 or 1533 defined the duties of the gentlemen of the privy chamber and organized their attendance. The ordinances of Christmas 1539 laid down in great detail the duties of the governing board of the household (which was itself reorganized at this time), and those precise instructions were to direct its administration for some two hundred

---

[1] E 361/8, mm. 45 ff. The constant increase in expenditure is well brought out by a table drawn up for Sir Julius Caesar in the reign of James I, showing an increase from £16,160 to £40,014 between the first and last years of Henry VIII (LS 13/280, fo. 62). A very interesting table in B.M., Lansd. MS. 3, fo. 124, gives the daily expenditure in the various offices of the household, on a Sunday, in the reigns of Henry VII (£38. 16s.), Henry VIII (£157. 0s. 3¼d.), Edward VI (£149. 19s. 0¾d.), and Mary (£173. 16s. 6¼d.); the most fascinating part of this table is the fact that expenditure decreased in the reign of Edward VI although it increased in nearly every individual department—no doubt because of the rise in prices; the difference lay in wardrobe expenditure which dropped from £82 to £18, a significant sidelight on Henry VIII.

and fifty years. It was really Cromwell who gave to the board of greencloth the constitution and definition which enabled it to discharge its duties for so long and with reasonable efficiency. As for the establishment lists of the household, it need only be said that there were no special signs of determined economy, as there had been in 1526, though a number of supernumeraries were pensioned off; the creation of the gentlemen pensioners in particular worked in the other direction. Economy was less pressing at this time when Cromwell had filled the royal coffers and solvency seemed assured. None the less, Cromwell's instructions explicitly concerned themselves with the most serious source of waste, the crowd of unauthorized hangers-on living on the king's money, and he took practical steps towards keeping them from the court. The financial measures made a big start towards transferring all payment of wages to the cofferer, an officer of the board of greencloth, and away from the treasurer of the chamber whose connexion with the household was at this time uneasy and being deliberately weakened. Finally, the methods used in providing the money necessary to cover household expenditure were completely revised. Altogether, the reforms were designed to increase the bureaucratic organization of the household, to advance its separate existence as a department and concentrate its officers' activities on their specific duties, to keep the household out of national government, to strengthen the hands of the board of greencloth, and to make the household financially secure and independent. Despite the profound importance of the Eltham Ordinance, it was the later reform of 1539, sponsored by Cromwell, which really gave substance to that change from medieval household to modern court which is the story of the royal household in the sixteenth century.

CHAPTER VII

THE ADMINISTRATIVE REVOLUTION

It will be well to review the conclusions already arrived at. It has been shown that between 1530 and 1542 the management of the finances was revolutionized as the chamber declined and became one of a number of parallel revenue courts, and as new courts were set up; that the place of the privy seal as the centre of administration was taken by the office of principal secretary, while both privy seal and signet declined into a formal routine; that the informal council attendant, an inner ring of leading councillors, was organized into a formal government board, the privy council; and that the king's household was given a more perfect departmental organization. To say it once again: in every sphere of the central government, 'household' methods and instruments were replaced by national bureaucratic methods and instruments. The household, driven from the work of administration in which for centuries it had acted as a mainspring and reserve, became a department of state concerned with specialized tasks about the king's person; finance fell to national institutions rather than to the personal servants of the king and those household offices which administered it before 1530; the secretary of state and the privy council stepped out of the household on to the national stage. Every reorganization that took place was in the direction of greater definition, of specialization, of bureaucratic order.

It would, of course, be wrong either to see no signs of such changes before 1530 or to believe that the work was all done by the end of that momentous decade. Yet the rapidity and volume of change, the clearly deliberate application of one principle to all the different sections of the central government, and the pronounced success obtained in applying that principle, justify one in seeing in those years a veritable administrative revolution. Its unity is further demonstrated and indeed caused by the personality which appears in every aspect of it. Thomas Cromwell, whose own career displayed the bureaucrat, was behind this deliberate and profound reforming activity.

So much has been said in praise of Cromwell and his work that it is really necessary to suggest what criticisms may be made of both. Cromwell was an autocrat as well as a bureaucrat in office, concerned with both the development of the weapons of government and his own unrestricted use of them. The former point should not be in doubt after this long account of the reforms he sponsored; the second has already been referred to on occasion. Though he preferred departments of state in the administration of the finances, he also retained a personal treasurer without a proper department for his own immediate needs as a minister of finance. Though he gave ample proof of his desire to see the secretarial offices and the seals more thoroughly organized, he was ready to cut across the organization because his personal control obviated the need for more formal control. Though he preferred a board of government to a loose group of leading councillors, he made no bones about his own outstanding position on that board and apparently saw nothing incongruous in leaving its formal organization incomplete. These are all instances of a common enough thing. Great ministers and administrators habitually use machinery in a personal way, forgetting or ignoring that lesser men may be tempted into disastrous imitation, or into mistaking the personal irregularities for the essence of the system. The consequence often is that the rule of the great man's successors turns out to be particularly ineffective because his hand, so necessary in the smooth running of his system, cannot be replaced. Something of the sort happened when Thomas Cromwell fell, and he must certainly bear some blame for not providing for the rule of lesser men, and therefore some blame for the weaknesses of the twenty years after his death. On the other hand, unlike other autocratic administrators—unlike, for instance, Wolsey—he did many things expressly designed to deal with that danger. All his bureaucratic reforms assisted in creating a government which could dispense with him or his like; such blame as there is attaches only to the incompleteness of the process. And in this connexion it must not be forgotten that Cromwell fell very suddenly.[1] When he was

---

[1] I have shown how sudden it was in *Camb. Hist. Journal*, x. 150 ff.

cut down he had clearly not exhausted his inventiveness and energy; the history of the court of wards and the story of household reform in 1539–40 prove that. It is, to say the least, not inconceivable that further changes were in his mind—that he would have succeeded in creating more and better organization in government if he had lived.

Whether the new administration was more efficient than the old is not the question here, but brief attention must be given to that point. Undoubtedly Cromwell and his assistants and successors believed it to be so, or they would not have laboured to make it. Undoubtedly, too, the theory of a national bureaucracy was more efficient than that of a household administration, since it depended less on the vigour displayed by the sovereign and was less bound up with his life. Continuity and the division of labour are the hallmarks of bureaucracy; they were as marked in the medieval exchequer and chancery as they are in any modern government department. But while the household remained the ultimate source of action, in-dividual qualities and behaviour counted for more than the traditions of a department; to that extent the end of household administration was bound to assure greater reliability and efficiency. However, traditions take their time to grow, and Tudor government continued to depend on personality; indeed, government always depends on personality, as we can see to this day. There are only degrees in such matters: Henry VII's death jeopardized his whole system of government, making necessary statutory and semi-bureaucratic organizations; Cromwell's fall only reduced the thoroughness, honesty, and efficiency of the system he had built up. The failure of medieval government in the Wars of the Roses compelled Edward IV and Henry VII to construct anew the agencies of govern-ment, even though they had example and precedent to guide them. The failure of Tudor government between 1540 and 1558 was redeemed by Elizabeth's council without major administrative reforms and merely by putting fresh energy and drive into the existing institutions. The reforms of the 1530's, the bureaucratiza-tion of government, succeeded in obtaining that continuity which marks modern government and prevents real anarchy even in days of civil war. In this most general aspect of efficiency the reforms did their work.

In more particular aspects there is much diversity. Secretaries of state were more or less able and efficient, but they were at all times better fitted to carry through the work of the remodelled state, both at home and abroad, than were the office of privy seal and the earlier king's secretary with his signet. Revenue courts declined not so much in efficiency as in income after 1540, and the most 'household' of them, general surveyors, declined most; but both they and the reformed exchequer could be used more readily than the old exchequer and more safely than the chamber machinery. The very fact that records were regularly kept transformed the administration in offices where their preservation had at best been spasmodic. As for the privy council, the history of the council under Wolsey shows the undisputable advantages of bureaucratic organization. Ignoring, for the moment, all signs of failure and inefficiency in the hundred years after 1540, we may say that on balance the reforms were a large gain—even pure gain; for nothing, not even the elasticity of household government, was lost altogether in Cromwell's system when worked by the great administrators among his successors. And without the reforms, that classical paternal state, the government of Elizabeth, would not have been possible. In this as in so much else the statesmen of the second half of the century filled in the outlines drawn in the 1530's. The men of the 1530's were revolutionaries and inventors; the Elizabethans employed, developed, and at times altered a little the achievements of that earlier and sterner age.

That further development was necessary goes without saying, and Cromwell's fall brought the need of it home to his successors. In finance, his reforms had to be completed by the reorganization of the exchequer before a truly bureaucratic system existed. The reformed exchequer in its turn posed problems which the Elizabethans had to solve—especially the settling of rivalries in the exchequer of receipt and the development of the lord treasurer's control. Early Tudor failure to attend to the customs left them in the hands of the ancient exchequer machinery; their greater importance after 1560 produced major administrative problems not finally solved until the abandonment of farming after the Restoration. The decline of the lesser seals was more marked in fact than in realization, and the council did without a seal of its own until 1556. It was not until 1584 that the signet office, at last carrying through an essential reform first demanded by Cromwell, began to keep complete records of all that passed through its hands. The new duties and competence of the secretary of state required much testing and experimenting in the hands of great individuals before a departmental routine developed in the seventeenth century. Even the privy council did not at once settle down on the lines prescribed in 1534–6. When Tudor government fell on evil days, under Somerset and Northumberland, the new council looked like going the way of the old, and Mary, hoping to mend matters by tightening up the system of committees set up under Edward VI, nearly perpetuated a great error. By returning to the principle of Cromwell's reform—a small council of equivalent and equally powerful ministers—Elizabeth saved her government from that mixture of divided counsels and undue magnate influence which the creation of a large council split into committees had inevitably produced. The reforms of the 1530's relied on the work of a small council of administrators pledged to do service to the crown and co-ordinating the work of bureaucratic departments of state; an efficient privy council was essential for efficient government on the Tudor model. Therefore the middle period of the sixteenth century and the reign of James I, when the council was weakened by dilution, were periods of bad government, to which Charles I found an answer in the restoration of a strong privy council. Since the privy council, however bureaucratically organized, remained at the sovereign's mercy with regard to size, membership, and even employment, it naturally underwent these vicissitudes. Nevertheless, the sound principles of Cromwell's reforms asserted themselves at intervals, and when the privy council finally fell from power—after 1660—it had to be replaced by a new body which produced within the privy council the same development as that followed by the privy council within the older council. The growth of formal committees never succeeded in creating an efficient government; only the informal 'inner ring' of the eighteenth century inner cabinet (*conciliabulum*) did that.[1]

The administrative history of the seventeenth and eighteenth

---

[1] Cf., for example, Trevor Williams, 'The Cabinet in the Eighteenth Century', *History*, XXII. 240 ff.

centuries is perhaps even less known and studied than that of the sixteenth, and it is not our present task to fill that gap;[1] nevertheless, it will be well to cast off and roam a little about this barely charted ocean, if only because the long-term effects of the administrative changes discussed ought to be suggested. For all three centuries, a precise investigation of such matters might prove a more powerful solvent of accepted ideas on constitutional development than is commonly realized. But in the face of so little certainty and known detail, all we can do here is to trace some lines of development and give hostages to fortune by noting what seem to us the significant points.

Down to 1640 administrative developments were straightforward enough. The reforms of 1530–40 were being worked out, and only details changed. Conciliar government—government through a national bureaucracy under the privy council—was the rule. The experiments of civil war, Commonwealth, and Protectorate are the less important because they were largely abortive and marked by a persistent return to the old ways. But after the Restoration a more fundamental change took place, for the privy council, after a short struggle for survival, virtually vanished. In its heyday it was not only an assembly of executive and advisory ministers, but itself an active organ of administration; the cabinet, on the other hand—whether in its early and obscure days or after it came to full development—has never been more than a directing body. To put it briefly—too briefly perhaps, for exceptions to the rule could no doubt be found—the privy council did things as well as order them to be done, while the cabinet exercised only the second function. The decline of the privy council removed the coping-stone from the earlier administrative structure. Coupled with the new place of parliament and the new independence of great officers of state who were also

---

[1] Apart from W. A. Shaw's prefaces to his *Calendars of Treasury Books and Papers*, and E. Hughes's *Studies in Administration and Finance 1558–1825*, there is nothing of moment in financial administration. F. M. G. Evans's and M. A. Thomson's works on the secretary of state cover that aspect well, though even here there are gaps. The several articles on the privy council are too exclusively concerned with its development into the cabinet. American scholars have dealt with the board of trade. Altogether, there has been practically no co-ordination. S. Pargellis and D. J. Medley, *Bibliography of British History—the Eighteenth Century* (Oxford, 1951), devote three pages to central administration; of the meagre thirty items listed many are really irrelevant to the subject. The fundamental study required is of the civil service.

magnates, this produced a system of government based on ministerial departments individually and directly responsible to the
crown. Not that this was really new, but the existence of the council
had interposed an agency between individuals and the sovereign. To
take two examples: management of finance passed from the council
to the treasury,[1] management of foreign affairs from the council to
the secretaries of state.[2] Furthermore, the making of policy became
the task not of a board of equivalent ministers meeting together to
advise the sovereign, but of a number of ministers relying on the
services of bureaucratic departments and combining in associations
(cabals, cabinets) as their own eminence and the king's will dictated.
The privy council was the king's servant; attempts to make it a
limiting control on the king's freedom of action led to its fall and the
king's reliance on some favourite ministers. Because the seventeenth
century never arrived at a solution which combined the king's
supremacy in execution with parliament's ambitions and the powers
of the great nobility, and because the eighteenth disguised the
problem by its system of 'influence', hiding virtual royal control
behind a veil of apparent parliamentary control, the rigidly bureaucratic methods of the Tudors gave way to a remarkable fluidity. So
fluid was government at the centre that the history of the cabinet
remains in effect unwritten between 1660 and 1784—and will
perhaps never be written because it is easier to feel that something
like a cabinet existed than to say what it amounted to.[3]

The most obvious and important change in the departments of
government after 1660 concerned the armed forces. Their administration has not been touched on here because it was not part of the
regular government of the realm in the sixteenth century. For that
reason, too, when need arose, the management of army and navy
continued to be linked with the household for longer than any other
aspect of government. But even here the sixteenth century moved
towards national institutions.[4] In 1546 Henry VIII set up the navy
board, but it was not until after the Restoration that the demands of

[1] D. M. Gill, 'The Treasury 1660–1714', *E.H.R.* XLVI. 600 ff.
[2] Arlington's career is significant in this context.
[3] I do not feel that E. R. Turner's two volumes on *The Cabinet Council 1622–1784*
(Baltimore, 1930–2) render this point invalid.
[4] Cf. for all this Giuseppi, *Guide*, II. 23, 163.

a new age on naval power and organization led to a rather haphazard growth which by the end of the eighteenth century produced seven separate departments for naval affairs.[1] Army organization took even longer to develop, for only the establishment of a standing army by the Protectorate necessitated far-reaching reforms, culminating in 1660 in the appointment of a secretary at war. The board of ordnance, grown out of a household department (the ordnance office) which showed signs of separating out in the reign of Henry VIII, can be traced back to about 1570. Altogether, however, the administration of naval and military matters remained very incomplete, occasional, and unbureaucratic, until the era of wars and imperial development after 1660 forced government to attend to it. When it did, it still followed the principle of replacing household rule by national departments, the principle which was first employed in 1530–40; the same is true of the establishment of the post office in 1711 which supplanted a household officer, the master of the posts. Ordinary civil administration remained in the hands of the three departments for which the foundations were laid in the years of Cromwell's ministry—in the hands of the treasury and the two secretaries of state.[2] The civil service on which they relied remained of the same kind: small establishments of few but permanent clerks, recruited and promoted by means of the 'clientage' system which in the sixteenth century replaced the medieval reliance on church and household.[3] This bare and rapid outline is quite possibly subject to material objections and qualifications; but the necessary warning, as well as the reason for saying anything about the matter at all, have

---

[1] *Parl. Papers*, 1806 (309), vii: Admiralty, treasurer of the navy, commissioners of the navy, dockyards, sick and hurt office, victualling offices (at home and abroad).

[2] The board of trade proper, established in May 1696, was a non-conciliar commission with advisory, not executive, powers; action continued to be with the secretaries of state. Cf. C. M. Andrews, *The Colonial Period of American History* (Yale, 1938), vol. IV, ch. ix ('The Origins and Work of the Board of Trade').

[3] Eighteenth-century departments of government are admirably described in the report of the commissions which in 1786–8 investigated the 'Fees, Gratuities, Perquisites, and Emoluments in Public Offices': *Parl. Papers*, 1806 (309), vii. The treasury employed about thirty officials, the two secretaries roughly a dozen each. It has been said that the secretaries' clerks were not properly civil servants since they were 'neither employed by the State nor paid by the State' but by the secretaries themselves (M. A. Thomson, *Secretaries of State 1681–1782*, 128); but that ignores the essence of the 'clientage' system. The clerks' permanence (they carried over from one secretary to the next: *ibid.* 130 f.) proves their true status as civil servants—if of a special kind.

already been given. We cannot close without speculating about the distant consequences of the reforms made in the 1530's. Government had grown bigger and more complicated since the days of Thomas Cromwell; there had been further destruction of household influence, and an increase and elaboration of national bureaucratic organizations. But this is only to say that the changes begun in 1530–40 were being worked out in the 250 years which followed, at times slowly, at times—as after 1660—more rapidly.

The collapse of the council did, indeed, alter the efficiency and orientation of government, but it is clear that the important changes in the direction of ministerial departments were not based on any change of principle. Partly they resulted from changed political circumstances: the council declined because it satisfied neither ministers nor king, and because parliament tried to use it as a means of control on both. Partly even these changes after 1660 still involved a working out of the revolution of the 1530's. However profound and far-reaching the changes in detail, however significant as to policy the decline of the paternal council, the principles of administration altered little. The crown remained at the centre of things where Cromwell had firmly established it, but the machinery of government was national and bureaucratic, divorced from service on the king's person and endowed with a lasting independence from the whim of the moment or the influence of individuals. Nothing is more striking than the endurance of eighteenth-century civil servants holding by patent for life, and the change from a civil service recruited from the king's personal servants to one staffed by professional careerists outside the household has already been traced to the reforms of Henry VIII's reign. Equally remarkable is in the eighteenth century the futility of the household sinecurists who provided one of the mainstays of the patronage system; here again the foundations were laid when the household was driven from national government in the 1530's. The great administrative changes after 1660 involved, then, no change of principle; they merely adapted the weapons of the paternal Tudor state to the needs of a rather more parliamentary monarchy. Even as there was no revolutionary change from paternal state to parliamentary monarchy—the Tudor monarchy was essentially parliamentary, too, and there is only a shifting of emphasis—so there was no revolutionary change in the adaptation of the administrative system.[1]

True administrative revolutions are in any case rare. Administration can never really stand still because it has to cope with changing conditions and the desires of new men at the top, but for that reason it usually develops sufficiently by slow degrees not to require rebuilding on new principles. It is only when the state itself is being refashioned fundamentally that revolutions take place in the methods of government. The Anglo-Norman creation of a centralized feudal state governed by the king in his household was one such revolution. It produced a system which endured until a new kind of polity arose. Even though offices of state might leave the household, even though all offices and even the household itself achieved a high degree of bureaucratization, the true driving force of government continued to be with the king in person and the men who immediately surrounded him. The restoration of good government by the Yorkists, Henry VII, and Wolsey, employing as they did the old methods of an elastic household system, proved that point. But the reforms of the 1530's did more than improve details of old practice. They cast off the central principle of centuries and introduced a new one. When an administration relying on the household was replaced by one based exclusively on bureaucratic departments and officers of state, a revolution took place in government. The principle then adopted was not in turn discarded until the much greater administrative revolution of the nineteenth century, which not only destroyed survivals of the medieval system allowed to continue a meaningless existence for some 300 years, but also created an administration based on departments responsible to parliament—an administration in which the crown for the first time ceased to hold the ultimate

[1] I am aware that to stress the revolutionary character of the sixteenth century and to deny that of the seventeenth may have the air of a rather cheap paradox. But let the critic ponder the meaning of the establishment of national sovereignty and parliamentary sovereignty (in law) in the 1530's, and then consider what essential changes—changes of essence and not of forms—he can really trace in 1660 or 1689. So much of what happened under the Stuarts derived in a straight line from the nature of the new polity built under Henry VIII. The Tudors were adepts at disguising revolutions and postponing their effects, while the Stuarts showed superlative skill in provoking revolutionary action in others; but these idiosyncrasies ought not to blind us to the facts. Nor, incidentally, should Tudor efficiency be interpreted as Tudor despotism; the inefficiency of the Stuarts does not prove constitutionalism among the devotees of divine right.

control. Medieval government was government by the king in person and through his immediate entourage. Early modern government was independent of the household, bureaucratically organized in national departments, but responsible to the crown. In present-day government, the bureaucratic departments have ceased to be responsible to the crown and have instead become responsible to the house of commons. It is important to note that these changes are most accurately reflected in what must be the basis of any administrative structure, the civil service itself. The medieval household system was served by men recruited from church and household; the middle period used clients of ministers, trained in their service and promoted by and through them; this second method of supply lasted until it was replaced by the modern civil service with its examinations. Clearer indication of the essential unity of these three periods, the many structural and methodical changes notwithstanding, could hardly be asked for.

There have been, then, only three administrative revolutions, though many more changes and reforms, in English history. As might be expected, they were the work of dynamic governments and of ages when the state itself was being made anew. Indeed, they were only one aspect of profounder revolutions affecting the nature of the society which they served. The Anglo-Norman system was devised to fit the royalist-feudal state, the state ruled by kings who were the heads of the feudal pyramid and the personal source of all government. The reforms of the nineteenth century produced an administration suitable for a parliamentary democracy, and the beginning of real administrative reform coincided significantly with the laying of the foundations for that state—the extension of the franchise and the introduction of the secret ballot. In its time, the Tudor revolution in government also coincided with changes in the structure of society and of politics. It accompanied, resulted from, and in a manner assisted in the creation of the monarchic nation state which prevailed in the sixteenth, seventeenth, and eighteenth centuries. Talk of a 'new monarchy' in the sixteenth century has become a little unfashionable of late,[1] while historians of thought

---

[1] Cf., for example, S. B. Chrimes, *English Constitutional History* (Oxford, 1947). Dr Chrimes's heading for the Tudor period is 'the zenith of the medieval constitution'.

associate the beginning of 'modern times' with the scientific revolution of the seventeenth century.[1] These views are assuredly a healthy and timely reaction against the old-fashioned division which, for instance, ignored the many things in Tudor England that were essentially medieval. But in some ways the reaction has gone too far; as regards political and social structure, the sixteenth century produced something quite new in England—the self-contained sovereign state in which no power on earth could challenge the supremacy of statute made by the crown in parliament. It will not do to dethrone the Reformation.

The fact has perhaps been obscured by the tendency to look upon the age of the Tudors as one homogeneous period to which the Yorkists ought to be added as prototypes and forerunners. Any view which would mark a really significant change in either 1471 or 1485 is indeed bound to fail. But if we admit that 'the Tudors' were not simply a rather static lot established in position by Henry VII and thereafter content to copy his ways, if we endeavour to trace the real lines of change and development in a century whose dynamics have been neglected because it seemed stable in comparison with those that came before and after it—if we do this, we are inexorably forced to see quite astonishingly revolutionary changes in the 1530's. Any attempt to play down the effect of Henry VIII's political Reformation because it was not based on noticeable changes in mental atmosphere (itself a dubious enough thing) puts a very laggard cart before a steeplechaser. In England at least, more often than not, political events precede mental reorientation; events are commonly the result of physical forces and personalities, and many a thinker has limped along after the party to offer his quota of ideas in explanation and justification. It is enough if one man knows what he is about— and Thomas Cromwell, at least, knew that. The establishment of the royal supremacy over the Church, the expulsion of the pope, and the assertion of the unlimited sovereignty of statute destroyed the foundations of medieval polity and society and put something new in their place. Thomas More knew well why he opposed the voice of Christendom to an act of parliament, and Thomas Cromwell knew equally well what his assertion of the omni-competence of parliament

[1] E.g. H. Butterfield, *The Origins of Modern Science* (London, 1949).

meant. They both knew that they were witnessing a revolution. The general intellectual and spiritual effects of the revolution came later —as effects, not causes; but that does not make it any less of a revolution. This is not to deny that symptomatic indications can be traced back even over a hundred years, nor that further changes were necessary later. It is to assert, however, that in the years between the fall of Wolsey and the fall of Cromwell the changes are crowded together so thickly and so deliberately that only the term 'revolution' can describe what happened. In this revolution, in this making of a new kind of state productive of a new kind of society, the administrative reforms which have here been discussed played their part. It is against this background of controlled upheaval that they must be seen and understood.

CROMWELL AND THE MASTERSHIP
OF THE KING'S WARDS

In his life of Cromwell in the *Dictionary of National Biography*, James Gairdner stated that in 1532 Cromwell was made master of the wards, and the assertion was repeated by Merriman.[1] The office was normally granted by patent, but there is no trace of Cromwell having obtained one, so that the evidence must be circumstantial rather than direct. It is true that about the end of 1532 certain indications are found that Cromwell held the office. On 16 September, Sir John Lamplough wrote from Kendal: '...the saying here is, ye shulde be Master off the Wardes', going on to assure Cromwell of his readiness to 'doo the Kynges Henesse suche seruice Concernyng the same as shall pleyss you to Command me'.[2] On 18 October another gentleman wrote from Cumberland: 'Sir, hit his shewyt me y^t z^e ar master off the kynges wardes qwych I wald be glad y^r off, & yff so be ye hade neyd off a substanciall feodore'—and he proceeded to outline the local difficulties of that position.[3] What was rumoured in distant parts of the kingdom is not very good evidence, but twice we find letters addressed to Cromwell as 'Master of the kyng our Souereign lorde wairdes' and 'maister of the kinges wardes',[4] and the second letter is an appeal from a prisoner in the Tower which had not the remotest connexion with wardship. The fact that Cromwell held the office seems therefore to have been sufficiently well known for any letter to be addressed to him by that title.

Nevertheless, there is very much stronger evidence on the other side. The papers of the master of the wards himself do not once show Cromwell active in that capacity; the man who was doing all

[1] *D.N.B.* v. 198b; Merriman, I. 143.
[2] SP 1:71, fo. 38 (*L.P.* v. 1317).
[3] SP 1:71, fo. 138 (*L.P.* v. 1447). *L.P.* here contain a bad misreading, 'y^e' being rendered as 'I' and 'feodore' as 'favour'. The hand is crabbed and the spelling peculiar, but there can be no doubt that the reading given in the text is the correct one.
[4] SP 1:71, fo. 46 (*L.P.* v. 1327), and 76, fo. 137 (*L.P.* VI. 551).

the work was Sir William Paulet.[1] He was appointed sole master on 21 December 1534, on the surrender of the patent of 3 November 1526 which granted the office jointly to him and to Sir Thomas Englefield, then serjeant-at-law and later a judge of common pleas.[2] Englefield and Paulet appear therefore to have been joint masters until December 1534, leaving no room for Cromwell; even after the time when Cromwell was supposed to be master of the wards, Englefield was acting together with Paulet as one party to an indenture,[3] and there survives, filed in one of the miscellaneous books of the court of wards, a royal warrant of 16 April 1533 addressed to Paulet and Englefield as masters of the wards.[4]

The matter might be complicated by a letter which Englefield wrote to Cromwell, 'Thankyng you for your payn taken for me in the Attenyng off my Recompens ffor my office of the Masterschippe of the kynges wardes'. The letter is dated 11 February and the calendar places it into 1532,[5] but this year is wrong. Englefield speaks of 'the new statute' which will enable him to adjudge at Hereford assizes murders committed in Wales, and this can only refer to the act of 26 Henry VIII, c. 6, passed after November 1534. He also mentions the criminals, 'the Vaughans', and their acquittal was reported by Bishop Lee, president of the council in the marches of Wales, on 6 April 1535.[6] Englefield's letter, therefore, also belongs to 1535 and fits perfectly with the date of the surrender of his patent.

Cromwell thus was never master of the wards. There is little difficulty in explaining the contemporary mistake which may have been due to a completely false rumour, or—which we think is more likely—based on some genuine intention of Cromwell's to acquire the office. He had so far secured a footing in two of the financial departments, and the king's wards were certainly an important source of the king's revenue. The idea that the mastership of the wards would appeal to him was reasonable on the face of it. If Englefield, for whom the office was practically a sinecure after his appointment to the common pleas, had thought of giving it up two or three years before he actually did so, Cromwell would certainly

---

[1] Cf., for example, Wards 9/179, an entry book of indentures.
[2] *L.P.* VII. 1601 (29).
[3] Wards 9/179, fo. 209 (26 March 1533).
[4] *Ibid.* 149, fo. 48.
[5] SP 1:69, fo. 122 (*L.P.* V. 799).
[6] *L.P.* VIII. 509.

have been in the running for it. But any such intention, if ever he had it, was never carried out, perhaps because he was becoming too busy on matters of state to take an office which required much detailed work and immediate attention from the master. In Paulet there was an extremely able, experienced, and trustworthy administrator ready to hand who could be relied upon not to go counter to Cromwell's wishes. Altogether, it probably seemed best to give up any idea of holding the wards as well, but not before enough indication had been given for the rumour to start.[1]

---

[1] It may also be suggested, though with some diffidence, that Cromwell's correspondents possibly confused the mastership of the wards with the mastership of the woods. Cromwell was sharing the latter office with Paulet by the beginning of 1533, and the mistake might easily have been made.

DOCUMENTS

A. 'ACCOUNT A', A SPECIMEN OF CROMWELL'S ACCOUNTS (SP 1:72, fos. 156-7)

o. 156 *Hereafter* ensuyth the vew of the Accompt of Thomas Cromwell Esquire, Aswell of all and singuler Sommes of money by hym receyued to the vse of oure most drade Soueraigne lorde the king, *as* of all and singuler paymentes by hym made for oure saide soueraigne lorde and by his commaundement, ffrome the ffeast of saint Michell tharchangell in the xxiiij^{ti} yere of the reigne of oure said soueraigne lorde the king vnto the xvijth day of Decembre then next ensuyng.

that is to say

ffurst, chargid for Arrerages of the last accompt of the said Thomas Cromwell Esquire, endid at the said ffeast of saint Michell tharchangell Anno xxiiij^{to} Regis Henrici viij^{ui}

DCviij li' xvij s' iij d' ob' q' di'

Also, receyued to the kinges vse by the said Thomas Cromwell Esquire sence the Determinacion of the saide Accompte, which was the Secunde day of Aprill inclus', vnto the foresaid xvijth of decembre exclus', *as* by the particuler bookes therof examynid more playnly it may appere

xxv^{M}DClv li' xj s' x d' ob'

Some totall of the Recept with the Arrerages

xxvj^{M}CClxiiij li' ix s' ij d' q' di'

wherof

In sondry paymentes made by the saide Thomas Cromwell Esquire, of and for the Affaires of oure saide soueraigne lord the king and by His commaundement, within the tyme aforesaid, *as* by the bookes therof examyned it may more playnly appere

xxiiij^{M}DCvj li' vj d' q' di'

Ande so remaynith dewe to the king

MDClviij li' vj d' q' di'

for the whiche

fo. 156 v *Ther* is remayning in the Custody and charge of William Body, seruaunte to the said Thomas Cromwell Esquire, the said xvijth day of decembre

MMCCliij li' xij s' di' q'

wherof

Ther is due to oure said soueraigne lord the king the foresaide xvijth day of decembre, as is abouesaide   MDClviij li' vj d' q' di'

And so Remaynith in the Custody of the saide William Body in money of the said Thomas Cromwelles Esquire the saide xvijth day of decembre

Diiij^{xx}xv li' xj s' v d' ob' q'

And more ther is lent by the saide Thomas Cromwell Esquire of his owne moneye to sondry persons, *as* it apperith by the bookes therof examynyd   Diiij^{xx}xiij li' vj s' viij d'

fo. 157 *ffynes* for knyghtes Sessid by the said Thomas Cromwell Esquire to the kinges vse and nat paid, *as* it apperith by the obligacions therof examynyd, the foresaid xvijth day of decembre

MMCiiij^{xx} li' vj s' viij d'

ffynes mad the[1] said Thomas Cromwell Esquire with sondry persons spirituall and temporall to the kinges vse whiche be vnpaide, with CCCC li' for the ffyne of the elect Busschopp of Chester, the said xvijth day of Decembre   xij^MCCl li' v s' j d'

Money lent to sondry personnes by the kinges commaundement and delyuered by the foresaid Thomas Cromwell Esquire, within the tyme aforesaid   MMxx li'

The some of the specialtes forfetted to the kinges vse by sondry persones for conueying of corne, *as* it apperith by obligacions remayning in the custody of the said Thomas Cromwell Esquire the said xvijth day of decembre   MDiiij^{xx} li' xiij s' iiij d'

Summa of the ffynes and the money lent with the forfettes Aforesaid

xviij^Mxxxj li' v s' j d'

fo. 157 v (endorsed) the accompt of M^r C[rom]we[ll]

[1] *Sic.*

432

B. THE FINANCIAL MACHINERY WHEN CROMWELL
CAME TO POWER (SP 1:67, fos. 32–7)

(Passages between ( ) added by Cromwell himself)

fo. 32
(endd.) a Memoriall for the kinges highnes for the regarde of his ffinances

fo. 33 A Memoriall for the Kinges Highnes, declaring the kynde of thingis wherin Risith yerelye aswell his Certain Reuenues as his Casual Reuenues and who be officers to his highnes in that behalf.

The thesaurer of Englonde	ffurst, the yerelie Reuenues and proffites growing of the Kingis Custumes and Subsidies, accompted for in his exchequere by the Custumers of his portis.
The Master of the wardes	Item, the profittes and yerelie Reuenews growing of his Wardes and of theyre Landes and Tenementes, accompted before the generall Surueyours by the Master of the Wardes.
The surueyours of the lyuereys	The Issues proffittes and Summes of Money yerelie groing to the king by the Surueyours of the kingis Lyuereis, accompted before his generall surueyours.
The Butlar of Englonde	The yerelie proffites growing to the king of his Butlerage, Resayued and taken by the Butlar of Englonde and accompted before the generall surueyours.
The Surueyours of vacacions of Busshopriches and Abbasies	The yerelie proffittes and Reuennuewes groing to the king by the surueyours of the vacacions of Bisshopriches Abbasies and priours, accompted before the generall Surueyours.
The surueyours of the Restiticion of the temporalties of Busshopes abbotis and priours	The yerelie proffites and Reuenues growing yerelie to the Kingis highnes for the Restiticion of the Temporalties of Bisshopes Abbotis and priours, accompted before the generall Surueyours.

The Surueyour of the kinges wooddes	The Surueyours of the kingis Woddes for Woodde sales made yerelie on thisside and beyonde Trent, accompted before the general Surueyours.
The Clarke of the Hanaper	The Issues proffites and yerelie Reuenues groing to the King in the office of the Clarke of Hanaper for his gret Seale, for writtes of Enteres, ffines, and other writtes and patentes, accompted for before the generall Surueyours.

The Chanceler of the duchye of Lancastre — The yerelie Issues Reuenues and proffites groing to the king by the Receipuours generall and particular of the Duchie of Lancastre, accompted before the Auditours of his said Duchie.

The Generall Surueyours — The yerelie Issues proffites and Reuenues groing to the king by the handes of his Receipuours generall, particular, and all other his officers being charged with his Landes, being accompted before the kingis Generall Surueyours; that is to saye, Warwike Landes, Spencers Landes, Buckinghams Landes, the Duchie of Cornewall, the Chamberleyn of Chestre, the Chamberleyn of North and South-walles, and the hole Principalite of the same.

The Exchequer — The ffines amerciamentes and Recounsaunce taken fforfeicted and assessid yerelie, groing in the kingis Courtes of his Chauncerie, the Sterred Chambre, the kingis benche, and his Commune place, shold be Streted and accompted for in the exchequere.

434

The Exchequer	The yerelie proffites Which sholde growe to the king by his Exchetours for the proffites coming of Outlaries, Instrucions,[1] and other exchetis of Landes tenementes and Moueable gooddes and catalles, sholde be accompted for in the exchequere.
The Exchequer	The proffittes and Reuenues with the proffers of his Sheriffis which growe vnto his grace of his Counties and ffee ffermes (of his Cytyes & Townes) yerelie accompted for by his said Sheriffes in the Exchequere.
The Exchequer	Recounsaunces ffines and amerciamentes forfeicted and assessid before his Iustice of Assise, Iustices Shewers, Iustices of the peax, Iustices of quorum, and Iustice of Oyer Determyner, sholde be stretid into the Exchequere and there accompted for.
The Exchequer	The yerelie proffittes growing to the king of the Recounsaunces taken and forfeicted before the Thesaurer Chamberlens and Barons of his Exchequour, of Custumers, Receipuours, Alnegeours, gageours, ffermours, Sheriffes, and Exchetours, and other officers, accompted in the Exchequere.
fo. 34 The Generall Surueyours	The yerelie proffittes growing to the king of Recounsaunces taken and forfeicted before the kinges generall Surueyours sholde be Declared and accompted for. (and what they Amownt to at this)
The Chaunceler of the Duchy	The yerelie proffites growing to the king of Recounsaunces and obligacions forfeicted, ffines amerciamentis assessid by the kingis

---

[1] 'Instrucions' crossed out.

Chauncelour of the Duchie of Lancastre Remayning in the said Duchie; and Wolde be knowen What they be.

The Exchequer	Obligations for Imployment of merchaundises brought into the Realme, taken by Custumers of the kingis portes.
The Exchequer	Dettes Remayning vppon the heddes of Dyuers Custumers Alnegerous[1] Gageours Exchetours Sheriffis Receipuours ffermours and other accomptantes in the Exchequere to be sene and Declared. (and what ys dew at this daye)
The Generall surueyours	Dettis Remaynyng vppon the heddis of Dyuers perticuler Receipuours and other accomptauntes accompting before the kinges generall Surueyours to be sene and Declared What they be and what the[2] amounte to at this daye. (dew to the kyng)
The chauncelour of the Duchie of Lancastre	Dettes Remayning vppon the heddes of Dyuers particuler and generall Receipuours Bayliffes and other officers before the Chauncelour of the Duchie of Lancaster to be sene and declared what they be and what the[3] amounte to at this daye. (dew to the Kyng)
The Generall surueyours	Recounsaunces forfeicted before the Chamberlen and other the kingis officers within his Countie Palantine of[4] Chester wolde be demaunded for &[5] sene and What they amounte to at this daye. (dew to the kyng)
fo. 34v The Generall Surueyours	Dettes depending vppon the heddes of dyuers particuler and generall Receipuours of the said Countie Palentine, accompted

---

[1] *Sic.*   [2] *Sic.*   [3] *Sic.*
[4] 'of' corrected from 'and'.   [5] '&' interlined by scribe.

for and yet not paid, Wolde be sene What they amounte to at this daye.

The Generall Surueyours

Recounsaunces ffines Issues and amerciamentes forfeicted within the principalite of Walles, as before the Chamberlens of North and Southwales and also within his Chauncerie of Pembrokeshire, Wolde be sene; And also the dettes due by any of the accomptauntes there to be knowen what they be and what they amounte to at this daye.

The Generall surueyours

The Receipuours and other officers of the kingis Duchie of Cornewall accompting before the generall Surueyours Wolde be examyned, Wherein it ys[1] Supposed the king to be moche dissayued; and What dettes they be and what they amounte to at this daye.

The Generall Surueyours

The yerelie proffites groing to the king of his landes and tenementes within Cales, Guisnes, Hamys, Marke, & Oye, and the Marches of the same, accompted before the generall Receipuours, Wolde also be sene. And what dettis do remayne vppon the heddis of the Accomptauntes accompting for the said landes tenementes and other proffites growing of the said landes in Cales, Guisnes, Hamys, Marke, Oye, and other the kinges landes aforesaid; and what they amounte to at this day. (And who be the dettor, So that leuy might be made therof Spedelye)

(The yerely proffyttes growing to the kyng)
The yerelie proffittes growing[2]

---

[1] 'ys' corrected from 'was'.
[2] These two lines cancelled in the MS.

437

fo. 35[1] The Warden & masters of the kinges mynt	The yerelie proffittes growing to the kinges highnes of his mynt within the towre of London and other places within this Realme Wolde be enquiered for and to knowe what proffittes hath growen to his highnes this Six yeres passed, which I thinke do amount to a greate Summe of money.
The kinges Learned Counsaile	The Reuenues and yerelie proffittes growing to the Kinges highnes of Statutes penall, And also of endes taken with his highnes or Counsaile by obligacion, Indenture, payment, or otherwise, for any maner offence or forfaicture, Wolde be Declared by abooke so that his highnes might be acertayned therof yerelye.
fo. 36[2] The warden and Masters of the kynges mynt	The yerlye proffyttes growing to the kynges highnes of his mynt within the Towre of london And other places with[3] this Realme woolde be [exa][4] inqueryd for and to [Se][4] knowe what proffyttes hathe [C][4] growen to his highnes this [ffy][4] Syx yeres passyd, which I thinke do Amownt to A gret Summa of money.

C. THE EARLIEST SURVIVING WARRANT FOR PAYMENT ADDRESSED TO CROMWELL (E 101/421/1)

Henry R   By the king

Where as we vndrestande that ye haue receyved to our vse certain Somes of money of the Rentes and Revenues of the Landes sumtyme apperteignyng vnto the College within our Vniuersitie of Oxonford, Late called the Cardinall College, We signifye vnto you that we haue appointed our trusty and welbiloued Maister William Tressham and

---

[1] fo. 35 in the hand of a different clerk.   [2] fo. 36 in Cromwell's hand.
[3] *Sic.*   [4] Letters in square brackets crossed out.

Maister William Beattes, Clerkes, to receyve by the waye of prest the Some of Oon hundred poundes sterling of the said Money, for the payment of the Diettes and wages of suche Scolers, studentes, and stipendiaryes as now bee Resident and abidyng within the said College. Wherfore we woll and commaunde you that furthwith vpon the sight herof, Of the said money beyng in your handes, ye not oonly deliuere vnto the said Maister William Tressham and Maister William Beattes or to either of theym the said Some of Oon hundred poundes to thentent abouespecified; But also that you receyve again to our vse at the ffeast of Saint Michell tharchaungell next comyng the said Some of oon hundred poundes of the Rentes and arrerages of suche Landes and Reuenues as hath been by vs Lately assigned to the said College, for the sustentacion and mayntenaunce of the students, Scolers, and stipendiaryes of the same. And these our Letteres shalbe your sufficient warraunt and discharge in this behalf. Yeuen vndre our Signet, at our Monasterye of Chertesey, the xviijth daye of Iuly, the xxiijth yere of our Reigne.

> To our trusty and welbiloued
> seruaunt Thomas Cromwell.

D. CROMWELL'S ORDERS TO THE SIGNET OFFICE
(DL 42/133, fos. 1–1 v)

fo. 1 *A direction* taken by me, Thomas Cromewell, principall secretary to the kinges highnes, aswell concerning the attendance of the clerkes of the Signet, as certeyne other thinges for the ordre of the said office, xx^{mo} die Iulij, Anno Regni Regis Henrici Octaui xxvj^{to}.

First, that monethly twoo of the Clerkes of the Signet, that is to saye, Thomas Derby and William Pachet ioyntly as one person, with Henry Conway for his ayed in consyderacion of his age, one monethe, Thomas Wryothesley and Iohn Godsalue an other monethe, as their courses shall from tyme[1] monethe to monethe com, (the said Thomas Derby and William Pachete begynyng their attendance acording to this direccion the ffyrst of August next en-suyng), shall give their Attendance vppon the kinges highnes and

---

[1] 'tyme' crossed out.

his gracis principall Secretary for the tyme being; aswell endeuoring themselfes to do their duties in thexpedicion of suche the kinges highnes affayres as shalbe appointede vnto them, as to see the haule furnyschede by them selues or by their Clerkes, for the ease, further-aunce, and relif of suche power suteres as shall resorte to the Cowrte for Iustice, Acording to the olde ordre and custume vsede hertofore in the said office.

Item, that non of the saide Clerkes at any tyme receyve receyve[1] or take, ne to his or their handes, the money fee or ffees growing of any Seale or seales; but to remit the receipt of the said ffee belonging to the seale fully and holly to him that shalbe deputed thervnto.

fo. IV *Item*, that noon of the saide Clerkes within the court in tyme of his fellowes moneth intromedle himself with the writing of any war-raunt, bill to be signed, or any other writing to be presented to the kinges Maiestie or to his graces moost honorable counsaill, but to leave the advauntage of all such writinges to the other tow Clerkes that shall then gyve their attendaunce; onles he shall have therunto by the kinges hieghnes or his graces princypall secretary speciall commaundement.

Item, that euery of the Clerkes at the sealing of euery warraunt letter or other thing, what so euer it be, shall entre the same with his oon hande in to a boke to be made for that purpose; And that at euery monethes ende the deuident shalbe made and delyvered to euery of the Clerkes his parte[2] of suche thinges as haue been passed in that moneth.

Item, that noon of[3] the saide Clerkes of the Signet shal not permitt or[4] suffre any personne to write in the king haule, oonles the same be seruaunt to the lorde privie seale, the principall Secretary, or to oon of the clerkes of the Signet, or to oon of the clerkes of the privie Seale.

Item, that no lettere passe the Signet but that the same be first examined by oon of the clerkes of the same, and the saide clerk, so

---

[1] *Sic.*
[2] Corrected from 'pakte'.
[3] 'that noon of' crossed out.
[4] 'or? corrected from 'of'.

hauing examined it, do write in the neyther parte of the saide lettere for a testimonye of his said examination his name.

Finally, it is appointed that the last daye of euery moneth the two clerkes whose cours shalbe to waite the moneth folowing shall repaire to the place wher the principall Secretary shalbe, or in his absence to suche other as shall haue the Keping of the seale, and so receving their deuydentes as is appointed bifore; and they to entre euer their attendaunce the first daye of the moneth folowing.

E. THOMAS DERBY'S APPOINTMENT AS CLERK OF THE COUNCIL (C 82/664, no. 25)

Henry the eight by the grace of god King of England and of ffraunce, Defensour of the feith and lord of Irland, To our trusty and right welbiloued Counsaillour Sir Thomas Audeley, knight, our Chauncellour, greting. We woll and commaunde you that vnder our greate Seale, being in your keping, ye make forth our letteres patentes in maner and fourme folowing: Henry the eight &c, To our trusty and right welbiloued Counsaillour sir Bryan Tuke, knight, Treasourer of our Chamber, and to the Treasourer of our Chamber That herafter shalbe, greting. We late you witt that of our grace especiall and mere mocion and in consideracion of the acceptable seruice to vs hertofore doon by our trusty and welbiloued seruaunt Thomas Derbye, oon of the clerkes of your[1] signet, we haue geuen and graunted vnto him the rowme or office of Clarke of our Counsaill attending vppon our person which Richard Eden lately had; To haue and to holde the same office to our said seruaunt and his sufficient Deputie or his assignes, During his lif; together with the ffee and wages of twenty poundes by yere, And with all other profittes, commodities, prehemynences, aduantages, and emolumentes therunto belonging or in any wise apperteynyng, in as large and ample maner and fourme as the said Richard Eden or oon   [2] Belous or any other hertofore hath enioyed and perceived in and for thexercising of the said office; his said wages and ffee to be paied from tyme to tyme by the handes of you, our Treasourer, frome the feast of Mydsomer last

---

[1] *Sic.*   [2] Blank in MS.

passed, and so quarterly During the lif of our said seruaunt as afore. That express mencion &c. And a transumpt of thies our letteres to be entrid in your boke of warrauntes shalbe your sufficient warraunt and discharge in this behalf. Yeuen vnder our priue Seale, at our Manor of Grenewich, The xxviijth day of Ianuary The xxiiijth yere of our Reigne.

T. Iefferey

(endd.) Derby

(Delivered into chancery on 29 January 1533).

INDEX

Sadler, Ralph (*cont.*)
118; keeper of the great wardrobe, 106; principal secretary, 106, 125, 267, 279, 312–14, 355

St Asaph, bishop of, *v.* Henry Standish; diocese of, 206

St David, diocese of, 206

St James's Palace, 327

St John, Lord, *v.* Sir William Paulet

St John of Jerusalem, lands of, 229; prior of, 128

St Mary's Abbey, York, *v.* York

St Paul's (London), cross of, 361; dean of, 61, 196

Salisbury, 89; bishop of, *v.* Nicholas Shaxton; dean of, 61; earldom of, 26

Sampson, Richard (bishop of Chichester), acts as secretary, 57; councillor, 336–9, 347–8, 365; dean of the chapel, 61, 135, 337, 347 n. 5, 348; master of requests, 136 and n. 5

Sandes, William, Lord (lord chamberlain), 85–6, 324, 328, 333, 338–9, 347–8, 378

Saucery, *v.* Household, officers of

Saxilby, Edward (baron of the Exchequer), 249 n. 2, 254 n. 3

Schmalkaldic League, *v.* Germany

Scotland, ambassadors from, 326; ambassadors to, 149 n. 4, 153 and n. 10, 193; marches against, 148–9, 305; spies sent to, 362, 365

Secretariats of the crown, 5, 52, 123, 131–3, 158, 416; *v. also* Chancery, Privy seal, Secretary, Signet

Secretary, French, 126 n. 2, 169, 306

—, Latin, 126 n. 2, 283, 336

—, principal, 37, 418; under Lancastrians, 15; under Edward IV and Henry VII, 31–2, 36; under Wolsey, 54, 56–9, 68; under Elizabeth, 189, 304–5, 315; Cromwell becomes, 123–5; made chief minister by Cromwell, 299–303, 315, 415; office divided (1540), 312–15; at court but out of the household, 303, 375; controls expenditure, 282; king's correspondence, 284; privy council, 352–4, 359, 367–8; signet office, 210, 259, 268, 270–2, 274–5, 280, 293, 440–1; a councillor, 48 n. 1, 61, 341, 348; his

emoluments, 125–6, functions, 126–7, 134, staff, 304–12.—Cromwell as, 70, 98–9, 110, 113–14, 120–2, 134, 139, 146, 157 n. 1, 158, 266, 269, 277, 288; Gardiner as, 84, 95–6, 298–9, 348; Pace as, 56–9, 298–9; Sadler as, 106, 312–14; Wriothesley as, 308, 312–14

— of state (post-Tudor), 303, 372, 419, 421–2; his department, 304–5

Serjeants-at-law, *v.* Council, learned

Sewers of the chamber, *v.* Household, officers of

Seymour, Sir Edward (Viscount Beauchamp 1536, earl of Hertford 1537, duke of Somerset 1547), 319, 323–4, 338–9, 340 n. 2, 348–9, 419

—, Jane (queen of Henry VIII), 338, 349, 401

Shakespeare, William, 353 n. 2

Shaxton, Nicholas (bishop of Salisbury), 195, 357–8

Sheriff, at the exchequer, 20–1, 116, 161, 163, 246 n. 3, 435–6; swearing in of, 60; parliamentary return, 79; attachment against, 117; and land revenue, 236, 243–5, 249; rewards to, 271, 291; also mentioned, 146, 295, 356

Ships, king's, *v.* Navy

Shrewsbury, earl of, *v.* George Talbot

Shropshire, 206

Shyrlande, William (Cromwell's servant), 154 and n. 2

Signed bills, 46 n. 5, 49, 54, 265, 276–9, 285–90, 309, 310 n. 4

Signet, 11, 70, 287, 345; rivalry with privy seal, 15, 17–18; instrument of strong monarchy, 31, 36, 52, 57, 259; under Wolsey, 53, 55; Cromwell's orders for, 261–8, 275, 380, 439–41; Cromwell's personal activity for, 268–70, 300; proposal to substitute it for privy seal, 273–4; sealing of royal letters with, 282–4; decline under Cromwell, 284–6, 293–4, 415, 418; signet letter, 298; and secretary's private office, 305–7; two signets (1540), 313; not used by council, 352

—, clerks of, 54 n. 1, 98, 123, 210, 351; under Richard II, 15; under Wolsey, 58–9, 61; Cromwell's